MW01672831

Get the ebook FREE!

To get a free PDF copy of this book (sold separately for $27.50) purchase the print book and register it at the Manning website following the instructions inside this insert.

That's it!

Thanks from Manning!

To register this book and download your free ebook:

1. Go to http://www.manning.com/ebookoffer
2. Enter the codes from this table when prompted
3. Download ebook using link emailed to you

	A	B	C	D	E	F	G	H	I
1	**IM 482 8332**	AO 754 2697	QN 865 0487	MP 276 6181	**XA 830 3624**	EU 409 9396	XC 367 5814	EW 160 0886	IX 268 8941
2	CC 960 5051	UM 973 8585	**CO 528 3954**	**CL 252 0038**	UN 734 9344	TT 833 7454	**ET 730 5221**	XJ 599 4617	**BS 154 8526**
3	**CK 207 8607**	**ZL 574 5833**	MB 811 7609	DU 519 5242	CU 649 8943	**HV 397 7950**	ML 458 1663	**WQ 176 5296**	PU 904 6190
4	BX 324 7582	**CI 742 5396**	FA 588 0815	KY 395 6058	**EG 833 0190**	GX 633 1084	**ZY 186 5060**	MB 425 3733	IY 200 0629
5	BU 925 8071	MF 419 9129	**SI 466 4539**	ZB 450 9908	UQ 310 9318	IE 120 1199	VG 118 4054	SP 542 0869	**SA 963 9052**
6	YF 756 5252	**LL 239 5061**	TV 887 5862	**FH 929 4485**	BT 106 6472	VN 185 4852	**CH 592 8659**	ZE 277 8967	**ZY 883 9856**

	A	B	C	D	E	F	G	H	I
7	**IL 446 3278**	DU 182 7381	ZI 342 1351	GY 331 1949	**UT 245 3460**	**TM 286 6624**	**OP 267 2767**	**FF 655 2848**	FY 120 4196
8	HI 315 5033	**MY 362 3261**	**AJ 661 8255**	KR 396 0906	XJ 807 5356	CZ 906 0896	OP 629 2411	GY 556 5153	RN 155 0873
9	BO 996 5619	GH 560 0848	GC 424 5010	CH 250 0667	**QV 137 7182**	DN 229 1127	HP 843 6232	UE 706 5383	HE 144 3488
10	**GG 745 0209**	OM 657 3692	FM 219 0775	IH 948 8737	EY 803 2850	OF 281 7143	NV 782 6893	EB 895 3000	**EK 598 9679**
11	**LZ 286 0025**	ZQ 913 5450	**HO 411 9493**	PL 969 8821	LW 725 8622	**DG 490 9750**	**DO 531 4103**	AH 166 2848	PI 201 3447
12	NL 757 7381	**CH 149 6051**	OZ 307 4363	RQ 741 3118	**II 691 6117**	**HQ 648 0608**	HT 403 3529	EA 495 5274	**XN 285 6030**
13	**TV 369 1013**	**CH 176 2735**	**AP 297 6288**	EI 310 0449	TV 865 2923	SG 430 2936	BL 670 4087	TP 441 6642	**BB 915 7857**
14	MD 966 2171	KY 951 7015	EM 239 0890	**WB 884 8743**	TY 748 8319	PC 199 9903	**RL 810 1611**	GR 440 1621	LM 722 3077
15	**AU 129 3602**	MS 830 4094	WU 130 8160	**SV 179 0008**	**KE 486 3606**	PG 841 4817	**SQ 557 4170**	VR 959 9844	CH 944 2431
16	EX 226 5135	**NH 594 0631**	**XX 878 6416**	RW 862 6106	EB 994 7737	CH 343 0474	AV 432 8982	**YH 362 3928**	**GY 226 3894**
17	**KZ 883 7178**	OD 903 9296	RY 389 0078	UT 119 1803	ES 716 4633	**AN 330 4835**	EW 115 7809	OP 946 3622	**ZA 157 6749**
18	ZE 616 0328	**JB 285 6787**	CD 791 5738	RU 101 4083	**AB 547 9791**	QG 599 5105	AS 913 6628	**XZ 676 3773**	KR 256 9330
19	**BL 106 9612**	**UQ 441 6667**	HA 870 2617	LK 699 7768	IE 114 6843	RZ 717 8275	GF 430 9744	PS 204 1104	LZ 804 5568
20	RP 400 1564	ZB 102 1806	BK 578 6537	**OJ 515 3163**	**RA 490 6857**	AJ 575 9519	RX 463 1570	**MC 432 6014**	OR 772 7159

JavaFX in Action

JavaFX in Action

SIMON MORRIS

MANNING
Greenwich
(74° w. long.)

For online information and ordering of this and other Manning books, please visit www.manning.com. The publisher offers discounts on this book when ordered in quantity. For more information, please contact

Special Sales Department
Manning Publications Co.
Sound View Court 3B
Greenwich, CT 06830
email: orders@manning.com

∞ Recognizing the importance of preserving what has been written, it is Manning's policy to have the books we publish printed on acid-free paper, and we exert our best efforts to that end. Recognizing also our responsibility to conserve the resources of our planet, Manning books are printed on paper that is at least 15% recycled and processed without the use of elemental chlorine.

Manning Publications Co.
Sound View Court 3B
Greenwich, CT 06830

Development Editor: Tom Cirtin
Copyeditor: Linda Recktenwald
Proofreader: Elizabeth Martin
Typesetter: Gordan Salinovic
Cover designer: Leslie Haimes

ISBN 978-1-933988-99-3
Printed in the United States of America
1 2 3 4 5 6 7 8 9 10 – MAL – 14 13 12 11 10 09

To my father, the coolest folk singer this side of the Mersey.
(Be honest, Dad, if you'd known how obsessed I was going to get, would you have agreed to buy my first computer?)

contents

2 *JavaFX Script data and variables 15*

3 *JavaFX Script code and structure 46*

preface

I suppose for many it was just another unremarkable mid-May Wednesday; certainly I don't recall the weather making any effort to surprise. What might have made the day slightly memorable for some, perhaps, was that Manchester United was playing Chelsea in the final of the ultra-prestigious soccer European Champions League. A couple of days earlier I'd returned from a few weeks' sampling of random pubs and music clubs in North America, starting in Los Angeles (actually, starting in Dublin, Ireland, but I'll not complicate the story) and ending in Vancouver. Now I sat in front of my TV, hoping, somewhat optimistically, for a 3–0 destruction of United, to round off the perfect holiday.

And that's when the phone rang.

Mike Stephens, associate publisher at Manning Publications, was on the other end. Earlier that day he'd emailed me to request a one-to-one, and, bang!, on the agreed time, there he was! Over the next 60 minutes or so I hardly noticed any of the game. We talked about Java and the way the industry was going, and inevitably the topic drifted toward JavaFX. At that time JavaFX was still in an embryonic state: features were being added, evaluated, and then modified or dropped. Anything and everything could change with each prototype release. Yet, to me at least, the ideas behind JFX showed great promise. If enough backing was put behind the project, and with a fair wind to guide it, I thought JavaFX had the potential to really shake up the whole front-end (user-facing) rich internet application market. With those sentiments in mind, some weeks earlier, I'd blogged about my early experiences—good and bad—with the platform on java.net.

I've always had an interest in computer graphics. I consider myself fortunate to have been born at just the right time to catch the wave of 8-bit computers that swamped the market in the early 1980s. The Commodore 64 was the first computer I owned, a machine with truly overwhelming potential and decidedly underwhelming documentation. Thankfully the version of BASIC that shipped with the C64 was only half finished—I say *thankfully*, because it meant wannabe programmers like me had no alternative but to learn the mystic black arts of machine code hacking and metal bashing (programming the graphics and sound chips directly).

As the 8-bit era gave way to the 16-bit era and then the 32-bit era, graphics programming became ever more removed from physical hardware. Bashing the metal was discouraged in favor of multiple layers of software abstraction. Not that I objected; I understood why these changes were necessary, but they *did* take all the fun out of programming. Compared to the instant gratification of the *poke'n'peek* 8-bit days, modern graphics programming was more like a huge exercise in complex logistics.

Scene graph-based graphics systems put the immediacy back into UI programming: the coder no longer worries about how or when the screen will update, just what goes where and how it should all animate. Yet I considered that only part of the solution. None of the popular programming languages was specifically designed to tackle the unique circumstances in graphics programming. When the likes of Java or C# *did* introduce new language features, they tended to be for the benefit of web frameworks or database programming, not pixel pushing.

But JavaFX was different. It was a clear—and unashamed—attempt to build a product optimized for slick graphics and media. Not only did it use a scene graph, but it had a programming language tailor-made for creating modern UIs and animation. The perfect marriage of these ideas, for me, was what really set JavaFX apart. Someone, somewhere, cared about coding beautiful UIs as much as I did and wanted to make it fun again!

Suffice to say, by the time the phone call ended, Mike had talked me into writing a book about JavaFX—although, to be honest, I didn't really need much persuasion. Oh, and Manchester United beat Chelsea, 6–5, on sudden death penalties. I guess you can't have everything!

acknowledgments

Let me start with a big thank you to the people at Manning, for their professional and ever-courteous guidance as this book evolved. They include Marjan Bace, Tom Cirtin, Steven Hong, Elizabeth Martin, Nermina Miller, Mary Piergies, Linda Recktenwald, Gordan Salinovic, Maureen Spencer, Mike Stephens, and Karen Tegtmeyer. No doubt there were many others, through whose hands the manuscript passed during its journey from pixels to paper—I am grateful to you all for your support, your trust in me as a writer, and your patience.

Thanks also to Jasper Potts and Brian Goetz, of the JavaFX team at Sun Microsystems, whose invaluable corrections and clarifications helped improve the text. Guys, I'm even prepared to forgive the breaking changes the team introduced with each revision, requiring me to rewrite parts of existing chapters several times!

Special thanks, and possibly a medal of valor, must go to Jonathan Giles, who managed a technical proofreading of the manuscript, despite my best efforts to undo him by shuffling bits of the chapters around. Congrats, Jonathan, on joining Sun's JFX team!

Thanks also to the following reviewers who read the manuscript at different stages of its development for their feedback and comments: Jeremy Anderson, Horaci Macias Viel, Peter Johnson, Valentin Crettaz, Carol McDonald, Kevin Munc, Kenneth McDonald, Tijs Rademakers, Timothy Binkley-Jones, Edmon Begoli, Riccardo Audano, Sean Hogg, Reza Rahman, and Carl Dea.

And finally, a quick mention to Sally Lupton, whose photos grace some of the figures in chapter 8, and the MEAP readers who suggested ideas and corrections on the book's forum. They include Pradeep Bashyal, Dirk Detering, user EdZilla, Raul Guerrero, Joshua Logan, Jerry Lowery, Mike Mormando, Thomas Schütt, Pete Siemsen, user swvswvswv, and Kendrick Wilson. Hope you enjoy the finished product, guys.

Anyone I've forgotten, consider yourself thanked, and feel free to pencil your name in here: ___________.

about this book

Perhaps it's best to start by explaining one thing this book categorically is not: *JavaFX in Action* is *not* a retread of readily available online documentation. If you want that kind of thing, no doubt other books will suffice. In the age of search engines and IDEs with context-sensitive help, a complete list of functions for a given class is never more than a few keystrokes away. API documentation is plentiful—what's usually lacking is an explanation of how the various classes fit together, and interact, to solve particular problems.

This book seeks to teach JavaFX from first principles through practical examples instead of merely repackaging API documentation. The opening third (chapters 1 to 3) introduces the platform and the JavaFX Script language, while the remaining two-thirds (chapters 4 to 11) use a project-driven approach to study the JavaFX APIs.

The overriding theme of the book is *cool ways to learn a cool technology*. The projects are fun, the text permits itself occasional flashes of humor (without being overly flippant), and the problem/solution format brightens up even the most mundane parts of the API. But the text doesn't shy away from hard-nosed technical detail when necessary: if you want to understand *why*, and not just *how*, this is the book for you.

JavaFX is a brash, new, energetic, and entertaining technology—this book attempts to capture that spirit: an invaluable desktop companion, alongside the official API documentation.

Project structure

Each project chapter begins by outlining an application with specific needs and challenges and then shows how to develop the code to meet those needs. At the end of the chapter the reader has a working program that doubles as a framework for further experimentation on the topics covered in the chapter. The project types range from puzzle games to data-driven forms. Some chapters also contain mini-bonus projects, extending the techniques of the main project into a business-oriented context when appropriate or covering ad hoc related topics.

Although each chapter stands as a tutorial in its own right, the book as a whole is designed to slowly build competence with core JavaFX tools, classes, and techniques. Early chapters use only simple scene graph structures (the data determining what's drawn on screen), but slowly the complexity builds, chapter on chapter, as the reader acquires more familiarity with scene graph code.

Who should read this book?

JavaFX in Action requires prior knowledge of software development. A familiarity with Java would be very useful, although not absolutely necessary. The book does not cover IDEs or other development tools (except if they are specifically part of the JavaFX SDK or associated packages), but it *does* contain the URLs of tutorials and other resources that may be of interest to users of specific IDEs or tools.

Prior experience with graphics and animation is not required, although a familiarity with programs such as Adobe Photoshop, Adobe Illustrator, or Inkscape would be handy if you want to adapt some of the code demonstrated in later chapters to your own projects.

Roadmap

Chapter 1 acts as an introduction to the world of rich internet applications and explains JavaFX's place within it. This chapter briefly compares JavaFX to its main commercial rivals and shows a couple of code examples as a taster.

Chapters 2 and 3 introduce the JavaFX Script language, using short and to-the-point examples to demonstrate each syntax variant and language feature.

Chapter 4 is the first project chapter, focusing on practicing newfound JavaFX Script skills (like binds and triggers) to build a Model/View/Controller–based application. The project shows how to use Swing from within JavaFX. The bonus project looks at using binds to validate a form.

Chapters 5 and 6 introduce scene graph coding: animation, layouts, effects, mouse events, and node manipulation. Chapter 6 also covers video playback, while its bonus project explains how to embed custom fonts into a JFX application.

Chapter 7 looks specifically at building business-centric applications, using JavaFX's standard chart and UI control libraries. This chapter also covers device-agnostic persistent storage, and the bonus project deals with writing your own controls.

Chapters 8 considers web services, parsing data formats, and off-the-shelf animation classes.

Chapters 9 and 10 deal with writing cross-platform applications for web applets and cell phones. Chapter 9 also looks at the designer/programmer workflow and considers how to import designer artwork into JavaFX applications and manipulate it.

Chapter 11 is a short chapter on using JavaFX from within a Java program.

Appendix A tackles what to download and install to develop JavaFX code, including IDE plug-ins. It also provides URLs of useful resources.

Appendix B is a JavaFX Script reference, with fragments of code demonstrating all the syntax patterns and conventions.

Appendixes C and D provide background material for readers unfamiliar with the Java platform or whose programming experience may be limited (for example, someone whose primary skills lie in graphic design, not full-time programming).

When appropriate, the text may briefly mention other topics or techniques as they relate to the problems being solved in a given section. Consult the table of contents or the index for an indication of whether specific topics are covered.

Typographical conventions

- `Courier` is used for listings, language keywords, class names, variable names, function names, and any other identifiers (elements the JavaFX Script compiler would recognize) relating directly to the source code.
- `Faint courier` in listings represents code unchanged from a previous revision. Because some projects develop their code over more than one revision, this allows the reader to quickly see the differences between a new version of a listing and its previous incarnation.
- **`Bold courier`** in listings is used to annotate source code edits made for the benefit of the manuscript. For example, large blocks of repeating code might be replaced by a comment, in bold, explaining that the listing has been summarized for the sake of readability.

Source code

The source code for each project chapter and the language introduction chapters are available for download as an archive from the book's website, at http://www.manning.com/JavaFXinAction.

Some projects are developed in stages, over successive versions, throughout the course of a chapter. When this is the case, the code for each individual version is presented separately and complete, in a version subdirectory within the chapter's main directory. Required resource files for each version are also bundled correctly inside each version's subdirectory

The source code archive does not contain IDE-specific project files but is laid out in such a way as to make it easy to import into an IDE.

Source code updates

JavaFX is a fast moving technology, each release not necessarily backward compatible with existing releases. This book covers JavaFX 1.2, the first version featuring a full complement of standard UI libraries, which should limit breaking changes in later releases.

In order for readers not to be caught out by updates, for a reasonable period after publication, the author will post revised source code for new JavaFX releases, along with brief notes updating each chapter, to his site at http://www.jfxia.com/. The updates will also be available from the publisher's website at http://www.manning.com/JavaFXinAction.

Author Online

Purchase of *JavaFX in Action* includes free access to a private web forum run by Manning Publications where you can make comments about the book, ask technical questions, and receive help from the author and from other users. To access the forum and subscribe to it, point your web browser to http://www.manning.com/JavaFXinAction. This page provides information on how to get on the forum once you are registered, what kind of help is available, and the rules of conduct on the forum. It also provides links to the source code for the examples in the book, errata, and other downloads.

Manning's commitment to our readers is to provide a venue where a meaningful dialog between individual readers and between readers and the authors can take place. It is not a commitment to any specific amount of participation on the part of the author, whose contribution to the Author Online remains voluntary (and unpaid). We suggest you try asking the author some challenging questions lest his interest stray!

The Author Online forum and the archives of previous discussions will be accessible from the publisher's website as long as the book is in print.

about the title

By combining introductions, overviews, and how-to examples, the *In Action* books are designed to help learning and remembering. According to research in cognitive science, the things people remember are things they discover during self-motivated exploration.

Although no one at Manning is a cognitive scientist, we are convinced that for learning to become permanent it must pass through stages of exploration, play, and, interestingly, retelling of what is being learned. People understand and remember new things, which is to say they master them, only after actively exploring them. Humans learn in action. An essential part of an *In Action* guide is that it is example-driven. It encourages the reader to try things out, to play with new code, and explore new ideas.

There is another, more mundane, reason for the title of this book: our readers are busy. They use books to do a job or to solve a problem. They need books that allow them to jump in and jump out easily and learn just what they want just when they want it. They need books that aid them in action. The books in this series are designed for such readers.

about the cover illustration

The figure on the cover of *JavaFX in Action* is a "carny" which is a slang term for a carnival or fun fair employee. The word carnival means a time of merrymaking, and fairs with animals, magicians, jugglers, rides, and booths selling trinkets as well as food and drink have been popular in Europe and America for centuries.

The illustration is taken from a 19th century edition of Sylvain Maréchal's four-volume compendium of regional dress customs published in France. Each illustration is finely drawn and colored by hand. The rich variety of Maréchal's collection reminds us vividly of how culturally apart the world's towns and regions were just 200 years ago. Isolated from each other, people spoke different dialects and languages. In the streets or in the countryside, it was easy to identify where they lived and what their trade or station in life was just by what they were wearing.

Dress codes have changed since then and the diversity by region, so rich at the time, has faded away. It is now hard to tell apart the inhabitants of different continents, let alone different towns or regions. Perhaps we have traded cultural diversity for a more varied personal life—certainly for a more varied and fast-paced technological life.

At a time when it is hard to tell one computer book from another, Manning celebrates the inventiveness and initiative of the computer business with book covers based on the rich diversity of regional life of two centuries ago, brought back to life by Maréchal's pictures.

1 Welcome to the future: introducing JavaFX

This chapter covers

- Reviewing the history of the internet-based application
- Asking what promise DSLs hold for UIs
- Looking at JavaFX Script examples
- Comparing JavaFX to its main rivals

"If the only tool you have is a hammer, you tend to see every problem as a nail," American psychologist Abraham Maslow once observed.

Language advocacy is a popular pastime with many programmers, but what many fail to realize is that programming languages are like tools: each is good at some things and next to useless at others. Java, inspired as it was by prior art like C and Smalltalk, sports a solid general purpose syntax that gets the job done with the minimum of fuss in the majority of cases. Unfortunately, there will always be those areas that, by their very nature, demand something a little more specialized. Graphics programming has typically been one such area.

Graphics programming used to be fun! Early personal computer software sported predominantly character-based UIs. Bitmap displays were too expensive, although some computers offered the luxury of hardware sprites. For the programmer, the simple act of poking values into RAM gave instant visual gratification.

These days things are a lot more complicated; we have layers of abstraction separating us from the hardware. Sure, they give us the wonders of scrollbars, rich text editors, and tabbed panes, but they also constrain us. The World Wide Web raised the bar; users now expect glossier visuals, yet the graphical toolkits used to create desktop software are little evolved from the days of the first Macintosh or Amiga.

But it's not just the look of software that has been changed by the web. Increasingly data is moving away from the hard disk and onto the internet. Our tools are also starting to move that way, yet the fledgling attempts to build online applications using HTML and Ajax have resulted in nothing more than pale imitations of their desktop cousins. At the same time, consumer devices like phones and TV set top boxes are getting increasingly sophisticated in terms of their UI, and faster wireless networks are reaching out to these devices, allowing applications to run in places previously unheard of.

If only there were a purpose-built tool for writing the next generation of internet software, one that could serve up the same rich functionality of a desktop application, yet with drop-dead-gorgeous visuals and rich media content within easy reach, delivered to whatever device (PC, television, or smart phone) we wanted to work from today.

Sound too good to be true? Let me introduce you to JavaFX!

1.1 Introducing JavaFX

JavaFX is the name of a family of technologies for developing visually rich applications across a variety of devices. Version 1.0 was launched in December 2008, focusing on the desktop and web applets. Version 1.1 arrived a couple of months later, adding phone support to the mix, and by summer 2009 version 1.2 was available, sporting a modern UI toolkit. Later editions promise to expand the platform's reach even further, onto TV devices, Blu-ray disc players, and possibly even personal video recorders, plus further enhance its desktop support with more next-gen UI controls.

The JavaFX APIs have a radically different way of handling graphics, known as *retained mode*, shifting focus away from the pixel-pushing *immediate mode* (à la the Java2D library used by Swing), toward a more structured approach that makes animation cleaner and easier. At JavaFX's center is a major new programming language, *JavaFX Script*, built from the ground up for modeling and animating multimedia applications. JavaFX Script is compiled and object oriented, with a syntax independent of Java but capable of working with Java class files. Together JavaFX Script (the language) and JavaFX (the APIs and tools) create a modern, powerful, and convenient way to create software.

1.1.1 Why do we need JavaFX Script? The power of a DSL

A very good question: why *do* we need yet another language? The world is full of programming languages—wouldn't one of the existing languages do? Perhaps JavaScript, or Python, or Scala? Indeed, what's wrong with Java? Certainly JavaFX Script makes writing slick graphical applications easier, but is there more to it than that?

What makes graphics programming such an ill fit for modern programming languages? There are many problems; ask a dozen experts and you'll get thirteen answers, but let me (your humble author) risk suggesting a couple of prime suspects:

- UIs generally require quite large nested data structures: trees of elements, each providing a baffling array of configurable options and behaviors. Figure 1.1 demonstrates the hierarchy within a typical desktop application: controls laid out within panels, panels nested within other panels (tabbed panes, for example), ultimately held within windows. Procedural languages like to work in clearly delineated steps, but this linear pattern conflicts with the tree pattern inherent in most GUIs.
- Graphics code tends to rely heavily on concurrency—processes running in parallel. Modern UI fashions have amplified this requirement, with several transition effects often running within a single interface simultaneously. The boilerplate code demanded by many languages to create and manage these animations is verbose and cumbersome.

Perhaps you can think of other problems, but the above two I mentioned (at least in my experience) seem to create more than enough trouble between them. It's deep, fundamental problems like these that a *domain-specific language* can best address.

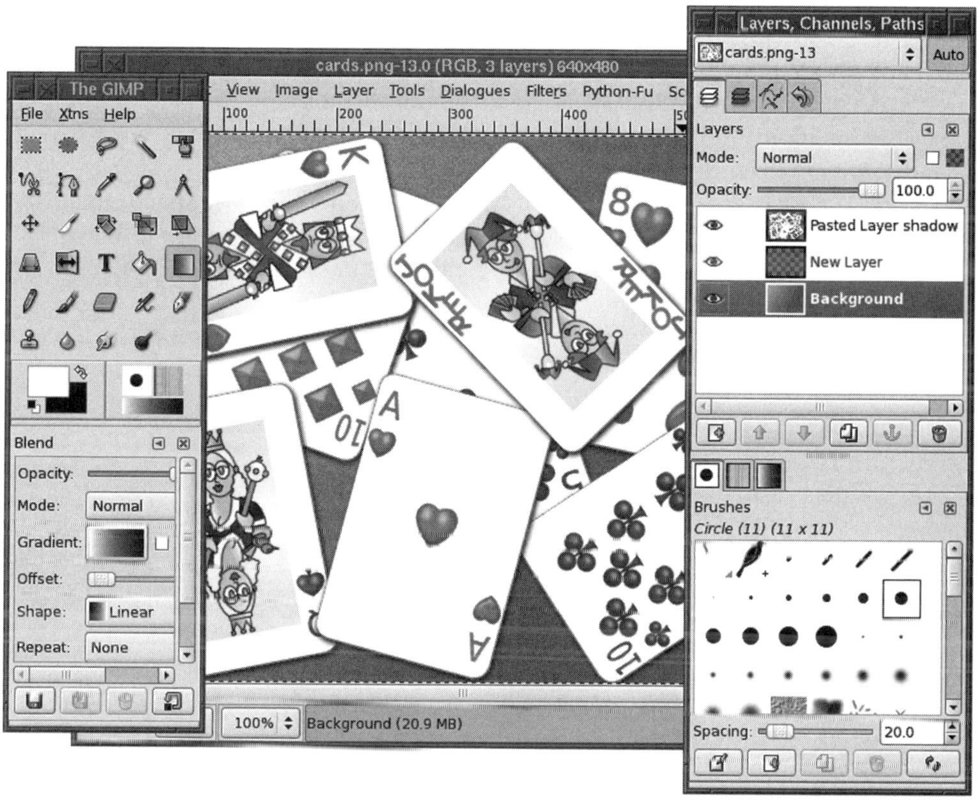

Figure 1.1 A complex GUI typical of modern desktop applications. Two windows host scrolling control palettes, while another holds an editable image and rulers.

A domain-specific language (DSL) is a programming language designed from the ground up to meet a particular set of challenges and solve a specific type of problem. The language at the heart of JavaFX, JavaFX Script, is an innovative DSL for creating visually rich UIs. It boasts a declarative syntax, meaning the code structure mirrors the structure of the interface. Associated UI components are kept in one place, not strewn across multiple locations. Simple language constructs soothe the pain of updating and animating the interface, reducing code complexity while increasing productivity. The language syntax is also heavily expression-based, allowing tight integration between *object models* and the code that controls them.

In layperson's terms, JavaFX Script is a tool custom made for UI programming.

But JavaFX isn't just about slick visuals; it's also an important weapon in the arms race for the emerging Rich Internet Application (RIA) market. But what is an RIA?

1.1.2 Back to the future: the rise of the cloud

Douglas Adams wrote, "I suppose the best way to find out where you come from is to find out where you're going, and then work backwards."

Sometimes we become so engrossed in the here and now, we forget to stop and consider how we arrived at where we are. We know where we want to go, but can our past better help us get there?

In the pre-internet age, software was installed straight onto the hard drive. If suddenly overcome by an urge to share with friends your latest poetic masterpiece, you needed at your disposal both the document file and the software to open it. Chances are neither would be available. Your friends might be grateful, but clearly this was a problem needing a solution.

The World Wide Web was a small step toward that solution. Initially, *applications* were nothing more than query/response database lookups, but web mail changed all that (figure 1.2). Web mail marked a fundamental shift in the relationship between

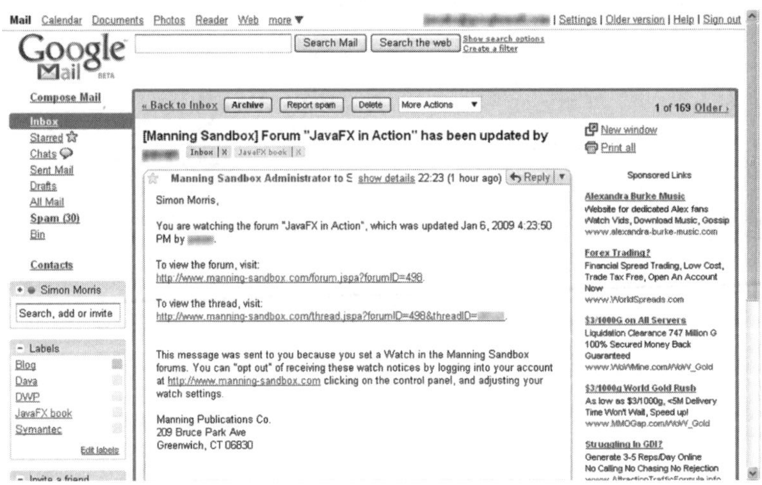

Figure 1.2 Google's Gmail is an example of a website application that attempts to mimic the look and function of a desktop application.

site and visitor. Previously the site held content that the visitor browsed or queried, but web mail sites supplied no content themselves, relying instead on content from (or for) the user. The role of the site had moved from information source to storage depot, and the role of the visitor from passive consumer to active producer.

A new generation of websites attempted to ape the look and feel of traditional desktop software, earning the moniker "Rich Internet Application" after Macromedia (subsequently purchased by Adobe) coined the term in a 2002 white paper noting the transition of applications from the desktop onto the web. By late 2007 the term *cloud computing* was in common use to describe the anticipated move from the hard disk to the network for storing personal data such as word processor documents, music files, or photos.

Despite the enthusiasm, progress was slow and frustrating. Ajax helped paper over some of the cracks, but at its heart the web was designed to show page-based content, not run software. Web content is *poured* into the window, left to right down the page, echoing the technology's publishing origins, while input is predominantly restricted to basic form components. Mimicking the layout and functionality of a desktop application inside a document-centric environment was not easy, as numerous web developers soon discovered (figure 1.3).

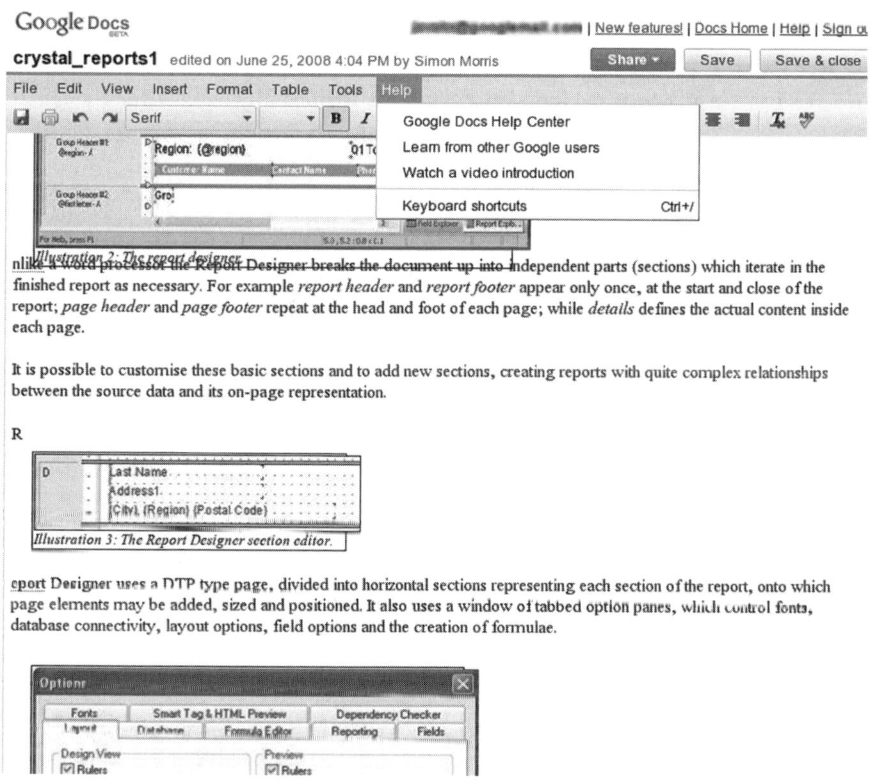

Figure 1.3 Google Docs runs inside a browser and has a much simpler GUI than Microsoft Office or OpenOffice.org. (Google Docs shown.)

At the bleeding edges of the software development world some programmers dared to commit heresy; they asked whether the web browser was really the best platform for creating RIAs. Looking back they saw a wealth of old desktop software with high-fidelity UIs and sophisticated interactivity. But this software used old desktop toolkits, bound firmly to one hardware and OS platform. Web pages could be loaded dynamically from the internet on any type of computer; web RIAs were nimble, yet they lacked any capacity for sophistication.

1.1.3 Form follows function: the fall and rebirth of desktop Java

From its first release in 1995 Java had featured a powerful technology for deploying rich applications within a web page. So called *Java applets* could be placed on any page, just like an image, and ran inside a secure environment that prevented unauthorized tampering with the underlying operating system (figure 1.4). While applets boosted the visibility of the Java brand, the idea initially met with mixed success. The applet was a hard-core programming technology in a world dominated by artists and designers, and while many page authors drooled over Java's power, few understood how to install an applet onto their own site, let alone how to create one from scratch.

Java applet's main rival was Macromedia Flash, an animation and presentation tool boasting a more designer-friendly development experience. Once Macromedia's plug-in began to gain ground, the writing was on the wall for the humble Java applet. Already Sun was starting to ignore user-facing Java in favor of big back-end systems running enterprise web applications. The Java applet vanished almost as quickly as it arrived.

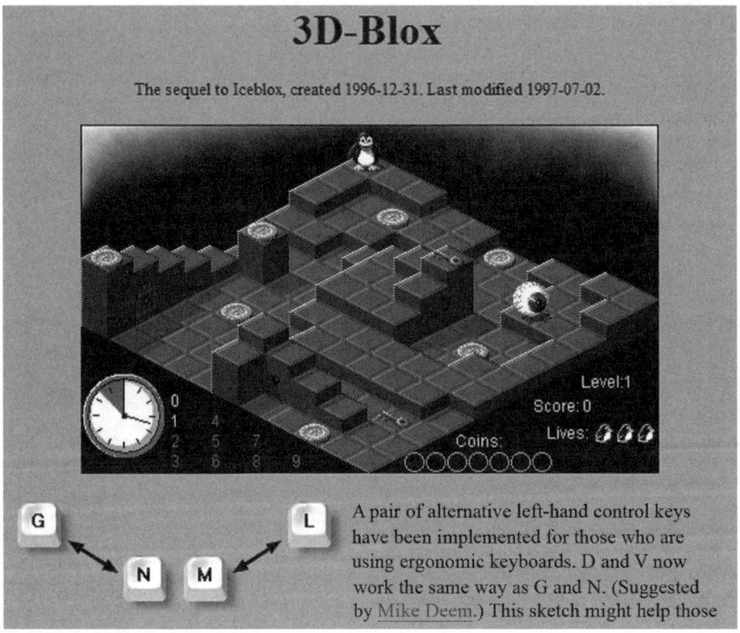

Figure 1.4 An applet (the game 3D-Blox) runs inside a web page, living alongside other web content like text and images.

Fast forward 10 years and the buzz was once again about online applications: RIAs and cloud computing. Yet Ajax and HTML were struggling to provide the kind of refined UI many now wanted, and Flash's strengths lay more in animation than solid *functional* GUIs and data manipulation.

Could Java be given a second chance?

Java had proved itself in the enterprise space, amassing many followers in the software community and a vast archive of third-party libraries. Yet Java still had one major handicap—on the desktop it remained a tool for cola-swigging, black-T-shirt-wearing code junkies, not trendy cappuccino-sipping, goatee-stroking artists. If Java was to be the answer to the RIA dilemma, it needed to be more Leonardo da Vinci and less Bill Gates (figure 1.5).

In 2005 Sun Microsystems acquired SeeBeyond Technology Corporation, and in the process it picked up a talented software engineer by the name of Chris Oliver. Oliver's experimental F3 (Form Follows Function) programming language sought to make GUI programming easier by designing the syntax around the specific needs of UI programming. As they pondered how best to exploit the emerging RIA market, the folks at Sun could surely not have failed to note the potential of combining the existing Java platform with Oliver's new graphics power tool. So in 2007, at the JavaOne Conference (the community's most important annual gathering), F3 was given center stage as Java's beachhead into the new RIA market.

And as if to demonstrate its importance, F3 was blessed with a sexy new name: *JavaFX*!

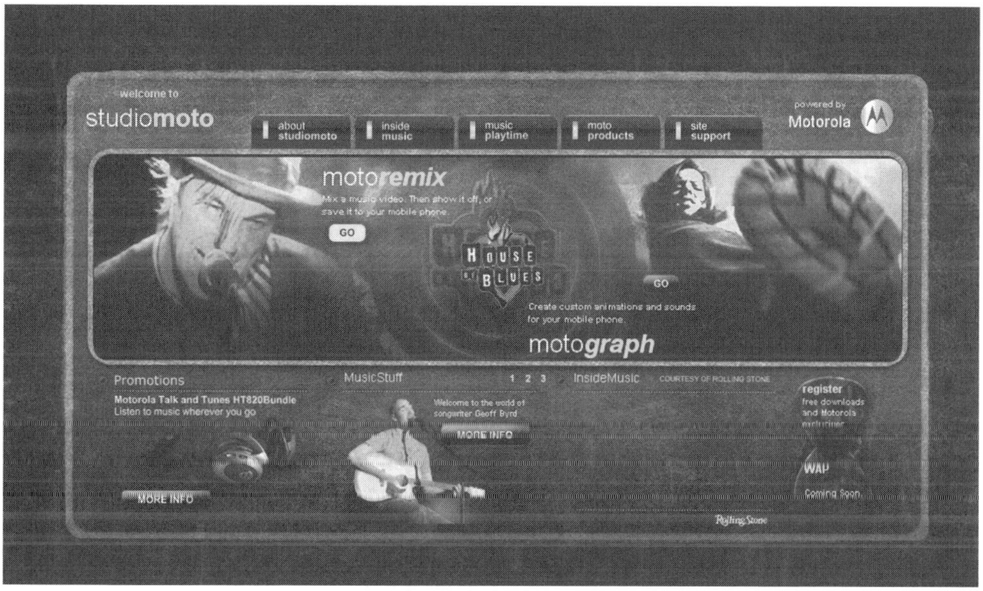

Figure 1.5 The StudioMOTO demo, one of the original JavaFX examples, shows off a glossy UI with animation, movement, and rotating elements all responding to the user's interaction.

1.2 Minimum effort, maximum impact: a quick shot of JavaFX

It's hard to visualize the difference a new technology will make to your working life from a description alone. What's often needed is a short but powerful example of what's possible. A picture is worth a thousand words, and so in lieu of a few pages of text, I give you figure 1.6.

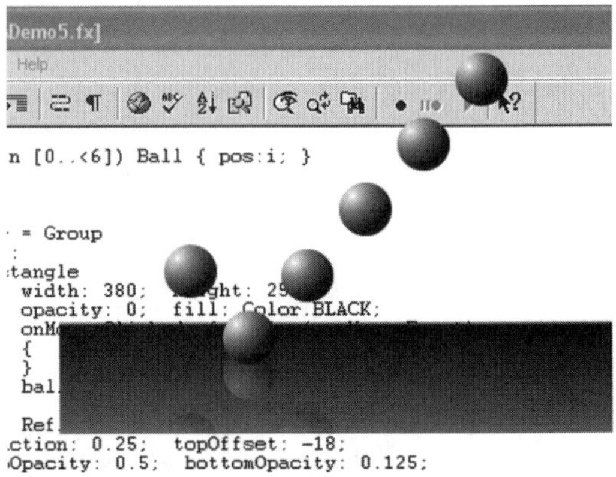

Figure 1.6 The bouncing balls demo, with color shading, reflection effect, and a shaped window (that's a text editor behind, with source code loaded, demonstrating the app's transparency).

Six shaded balls bounce smoothly up and down onto a reflective shaded surface, as the desktop is exposed behind the balls. The window has no title bar (the title bar you see belongs to the text editor behind), but clicking inside its boundary will close the window and exit the bouncing ball application.

Now, the sixty-four-thousand-dollar question: how many lines of code does it take to construct an application like this? Consider what's involved: multiple objects moving independently, circular shading on each ball, linear shading on the ground, a reflection effect, transparency against the desktop, and a click event handler. If you said "less than 70," then you'd be right! Indeed, the whole source file is only 1.4k in size and weighs in at a mere 69 lines. Don't believe me? Take a look at listing 1.1.

Listing 1.1 The bouncing ball demo

```
import javafx.animation.*;
import javafx.stage.*;
import javafx.scene.*;
import javafx.scene.effect.*;
import javafx.scene.shape.*;
import javafx.scene.input.*;
import javafx.scene.paint.*;

var balls = for(i in [0..<6]) {
    var c = Circle {
        translateX: (i*40)+90;  translateY: 30;
        radius: 18;
        fill: RadialGradient {
            focusX: 0.25;  focusY:0.25;
            proportional: true;
            stops: [
                Stop { offset: 0; color: Color.WHITE; } ,
                Stop { offset: 1; color: Color.BLACK; }
            ]
        };
    }
}
```

```
Stage {
    scene: Scene {
        content: Group {
            content: [
                Rectangle {
                    width: 380;  height: 250;
                    opacity: 0.01;
                    onMouseClicked:
                        function(ev:MouseEvent) { FX.exit(); }
                } , balls
            ]
            effect: Reflection {
                fraction: 0.25;  topOffset: -18;
                topOpacity: 0.5;  bottomOpacity: 0.125;
            }
        }
        fill: LinearGradient {
            endX: 0;  endY: 1;  proportional: true;
            stops: [
                Stop { offset: 0.74;  color: Color.TRANSPARENT; } ,
                Stop { offset: 0.75;  color: Color.BLACK } ,
                Stop { offset: 1;  color: Color.GRAY }
            ]
        }
    };
    style: StageStyle.TRANSPARENT
};

Timeline {
    keyFrames: for(i in [0..<sizeof balls]) {
        KeyFrame {
            time: i*200ms;
            action: function() {
                Timeline {
                    repeatCount: Timeline.INDEFINITE;
                    autoReverse: true;
                    keyFrames: [
                        at (0s) { balls[i].translateY => 30 } ,
                        at (1s) { balls[i].translateY => 230
                            tween Interpolator.EASEIN }
                    ]
                }.play();
            }
        }
    }
}.play();
```

Since this is an introductory chapter, I'm not going to go into detail about how each part of the code works. Besides, by the time you've finished this book you won't need an explanation of its mysteries, because you'll already be writing cool demos of your own. Suffice to say although the code may look cryptic now, it's all pretty straightforward once you know the few simple rules that govern the language syntax. Make a mental note, if you want, to check back with listing 1.1 as you read the first half of this book; you'll be surprised at how quickly its secrets are revealed.

1.3 Comparing Java and JavaFX Script: "Hello JavaFX!"

So far we've discussed what JavaFX is and why it's needed. We've looked at an example of JavaFX Script and seen that it's very different from Java, but just how different? For a true side-by-side comparison to demonstrate the benefits of JavaFX Script over Java, we need to code the same program in both languages. Listings 1.2 and 1.3 do just that, and figure 1.7 compares them visually.

Listing 1.2 Hello World as JavaFX Script

```
import javafx.scene.Scene;
import javafx.scene.text.*;
import javafx.stage.Stage;
Stage {
    title: "Hello World JavaFX"
    scene: Scene {
        content: Text {
            content: "Hello World!"
            font: Font { size: 30 }
            layoutX: 114
            layoutY: 45
        }
    }
    width:400  height:100
}
```

Listing 1.2 is a simple JavaFX Script program. Don't panic if you don't understand it yet–this isn't a tutorial; we're merely contrasting the two languages. The program opens a new frame on the desktop with "Hello World JavaFX" in the title bar and the legend "Hello World!" as the window contents. Perhaps you can already decipher a few clues as to how it works.

Listing 1.3 Hello World as Java

```
import javax.swing.*;
class HelloWorldJava {
    public static void main(String[] args) {
        Runnable r = new Runnable() {
            public void run() {
                JLabel l = new JLabel("Hello World!",JLabel.CENTER);
                l.setFont(l.getFont().deriveFont(30f));
                JFrame f = new JFrame("Hello World Java");
                f.getContentPane().add(l);
                f.setSize(400,100);
                f.setVisible(true);
            }
        };
        SwingUtilities.invokeLater(r);
    }
}
```

The Java equivalent is presented in listing 1.3. It certainly looks busier, although actually it has been stripped back, almost to the point of becoming crude. The Java code is typical of GUIs programmed under popular languages like Java, C++, or BASIC. The frame and the label holding the "Hello World" legend are constructed and combined in separate discrete steps. The order of these steps does not necessarily tally with the structure of the UI they build; the label is created before its parent frame is created but added after.

Figure 1.7 Separated at birth: "Hello World!" as a JavaFX application and as a Java application

As the scale of the GUI increases, Java's verbose syntax and disjointed structure (compared to the GUI structure) quickly become a handful, while JavaFX Script, a bit like the famous Energizer Bunny, can keep on going for far longer, thanks to its declarative syntax.

For readers unfamiliar with the Java platform, appendix D provides an overview, including how the "write once, run anywhere" promise is achieved, the different editions of Java, and the versions and revision names over the years. Although JavaFX Script is independent of Java as a language, it's reliance on the Java runtime platform means background knowledge of Java is useful.

1.4 Comparing JavaFX with Adobe AIR, GWT, and Silverlight

JavaFX is not the only technology competing to become king of the RIA space: Adobe, Google, and Microsoft are all chasing the prize too. But how do their offerings compare to JavaFX? Now that we've explored some of the concepts behind JavaFX, we're in a better position to contrast the platform against its alleged rivals.

Comparing technologies is always fraught with danger. Each technology is a multifaceted beast, and it's impossible to sum up all the nuanced arguments in just a few paragraphs. Readers are encouraged to seek second opinions in deciding which technology to adopt.

1.4.1 Adobe AIR and Flex

Flex is a toolkit adding application-centric features to Flash movies, making it easier to write serious web apps alongside games and animations. AIR (Adobe Integrated Runtime, originally codenamed Apollo) is an attempt to allow Flex web applications to become first-class citizens on the desktop. AIR programs can be installed just like regular desktop programs on a PC, Mac, or Linux computer, assuming the appropriate AIR runtime has been installed beforehand. Using WebKit (the open source HTML/JavaScript component), AIR provides a web-page-like shell in which HTML, JavaScript, Flex, Flash, and PDF content can interact. AIR has made it possible to transfer web programming skills directly onto the desktop, and Adobe plans to extend this concept to allow AIR programmers to target mobile devices as well.

1.4.2 Google Web Toolkit

Google Web Toolkit (GWT) is an open source attempt to smooth over the bumps in HTML/Ajax application development with a consistent cross-browser JavaScript library of desktop-inspired widgets and functions. It's said that GWT started as an internal

Google project to help write sites like Gmail and Google Calendar (although which Google sites actually use GWT is unknown). GWT applications are coded in Java, compiled to JavaScript, and run entirely within the web browser. They can make use of optionally installed plug-ins, such as Gears, to provide offline support.

1.4.3 Microsoft Silverlight

With Silverlight, Microsoft is seeking to shift its desktop software prowess inside the browser. Silverlight is a proprietary browser plug-in for recent editions of Windows and Mac OS X. Linux is also covered via an open source project and a deal with Novell (licensing difficulties may exist for non-Novell Linux customers). Silverlight supports rich vector-based UIs, coded in .NET languages (like C#) and a UI markup language called XAML (Extensible Application Markup Language). Microsoft worked hard to create a fluid video/multimedia environment, with solid support for all the formats supported by its Windows Media framework.

1.4.4 And by comparison, JavaFX

While other RIA technologies blur the line between desktop and browser, JavaFX removes the distinction entirely. A single JavaFX application can move seamlessly (quite literally, by being dragged from the browser window) from one environment to the other. Desktop, applets, and smart phones can already be targeted, while Blu-ray and other TV devices are expected to join this list at a later date. With a common core across all environments, complemented by device-specific extensions, JavaFX lets us target every device or exploit the full power of a particular device.

While other RIA technologies recycle existing languages, JavaFX Script is built from the ground up specifically for creating sophisticated UIs and animation. Studying common working methods found in UI software, the JavaFX team created a language around those patterns. The declarative syntax permits code and structure to be interwoven with a degree of ease not found in the bilingual approach of its rivals. Direct relationships can be defined between an object and the data or functions it depends on; the heavy lifting of model/view/controller is done for you. And because JavaFX Script is compatible with Java classes, it has access to over a decade of libraries and open source projects.

It's true that the need to learn a new language may discourage some, but the reward is a much more powerful tool, shaped specifically for the job at hand. Picking the best tool can often mean the difference between success and failure, while holding onto our familiar tools for too long can sometimes put us at a disadvantage. The skill is in knowing when to embrace a new technology, and hopefully this section has helped clarify whether JavaFX is the right technology for you!

1.5 But why should I buy this book?

Good question—indeed, why buy a book at all? The APIs are documented online, and there are blogs aplenty guiding coders through that tricky first application.

This book specifically seeks not to regurgitate existing documentation, like so many programming tomes tend to do. You won't find laborious enumerations of every variation of every shade of every nuance of every class. This book assumes you're intelligent enough to read the documentation for yourself, once pointed in the right direction; you don't need it reprinted here. So what *is* in this book?

The early chapters give a quick and entertaining (yet comprehensive) guide to the JavaFX Script language; then it's straight into the projects! Each project chapter houses a self-contained miniapplication requiring specific skills and works from initial goals toward a solution in JavaFX. Successive projects reinforce acquired skills and add new ones. Concepts are demonstrated and explained in real-world scenarios; it's an approach centered on common practices, solutions, and patterns, rather than merely ticking off every variation of, for example, a scene graph node or animated transition included in the API.

The code in each chapter seeks to be ideas-rich but compact and fresh. What's the point of page upon page of stuff the reader already saw in previous chapters? Although functional, each completed project leaves room for readers to experiment further, practicing newfound skills by adding features or polishing the UI with extra color blends and animations.

For better or worse, the text attempts to remain agnostic of any particular IDE or tool, other than those shipped with the standard JavaFX SDK. Illustrated click-by-click guides for each IDE would be page hungry and offer little over the online tutorials already provided with (or for) each plug-in. Again, it's about complementing available documentation, not reproducing it, leaving more room for JavaFX examples and advice, not IDE-specific tutorials. (This is, after all, *JavaFX in Action* not *NetBeans in Action*!) Relevant plug-in/IDE links are provided in the appendices.

So, is this book for you? If you're merely looking for a hard copy of the API documentation, perhaps not. But if you want something that goes deeper, exploring JavaFX through *real-world* code, solving *real-world* problems, I hope you'll find what you're looking for in the pages to come.

1.6 Summary

This chapter has been an introduction to the world of JavaFX and JavaFX Script. We started by considering the power of domain-specific languages, designed specifically to meet the needs of particular tasks. Then we considered the rise of the RIA and the challenges in developing such applications using current browser-based technologies. We revisited Java's disappointing track record on the desktop, particularly with lightweight internet applications like applets, but saw how this could change with the introduction of JavaFX to address a new generation of internet applications. We saw an example of JavaFX Script doing modestly impressive things in only a few dozen lines of code, and we reviewed side-by-side the differences in styles and size of Java and JavaFX Script source code. Finally, we considered how JavaFX stacks up against the apparent opposition.

I hope this has been enough to grab your attention and fire your imagination, because in the next chapter we leave the theory behind and dive straight into the detail.

Over the next couple of chapters we'll tour the JavaFX Script language, with, I hope, plenty of nice surprises along the way. This will get us ready to tackle subsequent chapters, where we use practical miniprojects to demonstrate different aspects of JavaFX. (For those expert Java programmers who would prefer more of a whistle-stop tour of the new language, appendix B acts as both a flash-card tutorial and an aide-mémoire).

Before we move on, you will almost certainly want to take a detour to appendix A, which acts as a setup guide for downloading and installing JavaFX, plus getting your code to build. It also features some very useful JavaFX links for help and further reading. Also, if you're not a Java programmer, let me draw your attention to the crash course in object-oriented programming in appendix C and the introduction to the Java platform (and how JavaFX fits into it) in appendix D.

So that's the introduction out of the way. Are you excited? Well, I certainly hope so! Let the fun begin.

2 JavaFX Script DATA AND VARIABLES

This chapter covers

- Introducing JavaFX Script variables
- Doing interesting things to strings
- Getting linear, with ranges and sequences
- Automating variable updates using binds

If chapter 1 has had the desired effect, you should be eager to get your hands dirty with code. But before we can start dazzling unsuspecting bystanders with our stunning JavaFX visuals, we'll need to become acquainted with Java FX Script, JavaFX's own programming language. In this chapter, and the one that follows, we'll start to do just that.

In this chapter we will look at how variables are created and manipulated. JavaFX Script has a lot of interesting features in this area, beyond those offered by languages like Java or JavaScript, such as sophisticated array manipulation and the ability to bind variables into automatic update relationships. By the end of this chapter you'll understand how these features work, so in the next chapter we can explore how they integrate into standard programming constructs like loops, conditions, and classes.

In writing this tutorial I've attempted to create a smooth progression through the language, with later sections building on the knowledge gleaned from previous reading. This logical progression wasn't always possible, and occasionally later detail bleeds into earlier sections.

QUICK START If you don't fancy a full-on tutorial right now, and you consider yourself a good enough Java programmer, you might try picking up the basics of JavaFX Script from the quick reference guide in appendix B.

Each of the code snippets in this tutorial should be runnable as is. Many output to *standard out*, and when this is the case the console output is presented following the code snippet, in bold text.

One final note: from now on I'll occasionally resort to the familiar term *JavaFX* or *JFX* in lieu of the more formal language title. Strictly speaking, this is wrong (JavaFX is the platform and not the language), but you'll forgive me if I err on the side of making the prose more digestible, at the risk of annoying a few pedants. (You know who you are!)

2.1 Annotating code with comments

Before we begin in earnest, let's look at JavaFX Script's method for code commenting. That way you'll be able to comment your own code as you play along at home during the sections to come. There's not a lot to cover, because JavaFX Script uses the same C++-like syntax as many other popular languages (see listing 2.1).

Listing 2.1 JavaFX Script comments

```
// A single line comment.

/* A multi line comment.
   Continuing on this line.
   And this one too! */

/* Another multi line comment
 * in a style much preferred by
 * many programmers...
 */
```

That was short and sweet. Unlike listing 2.1, the source code in this book is devoid of inline comments, to keep the examples tight on the printed page (reducing the need to flip to and from multiple pages when studying a listing), but as you experiment with your own code, I strongly recommend you use comments to annotate it. Not only is this good practice, but it helps your little gray cells reinforce your newly acquired knowledge.

JavaFX Script also supports the familiar Javadoc comment format. These are specially formatted comments, written directly above class, variable, or function definitions, that can be turned into program documentation via a tool called javafxdoc. JavaFXDoc comments are multiline and begin with `/**`, the extra asterisk signaling the special JavaFXDoc format. All manner of documentation details can be specified inside one of

> **Give reasons for your answer**
>
> There's undoubtedly a certain resistance to source code commenting among programmers. It was ever thus! Comments acquired a bad name during the 1970s and 1980s, when the prevailing mood was for vast quantities of documentation about every variable and parameter. Pure overkill. I'd suggest the ideal use for comments is in explaining the reasoning behind an algorithm. "Give reasons for your answer," as countless high school examination papers would demand. To the oft-heard complaint "my code is self-documenting," I'd counter, "only to the compiler!" Justifying your ideas in a line or two before each code "paragraph" is a useful discipline for double-checking your own thinking, with a bonus that it helps fellow coders spot when your code doesn't live up to the promise of your comments.

these comments; the available fields are listed on the OpenJFX project site (details of which can be found in appendix A).

Now that you know how to write code the compiler ignores, let's move on to write something that has an effect. We'll begin with basic data types.

2.2 Data types

At the heart of any language is data and data manipulation. Numbers, conditions, and text are all typical candidates for data types, and indeed JavaFX Script has types to represent all of these. But being a language centered on animation, it also features a type to represent time.

JavaFX Script's approach to variables is slightly different than that of Java. Java employs a dual strategy, respecting both the *high-level* objects of object-orientation and the *low-level* primitives of bytecode, JavaFX Script has only objects. But that's not to say it doesn't have any of the syntactic conveniences of Java's primitive types, as we'll see in the following sections.

2.2.1 Static, not dynamic, types

Variables in JavaFX Script are statically typed, meaning each variable holds a given type of information, which allows only a compatible range of operations to be performed on it. Strings will not, for example, magically turn themselves into numbers so we can perform arithmetic on them, even if these strings contain only valid number characters. In that regard they work the same way as the Java language.

Java novices, or other curious souls, can consult appendix C for more on static versus dynamic variable types in programming languages.

2.2.2 Value type declaration

Value types are the core building blocks for data in JavaFX Script, designed to hold commonplace data like numbers and text. Unlike Java primitives, JavaFX Script's value types are fully fledged objects, with all the added goodness that stems from using classes.

Table 2.1 JavaFX Script value types

Type	Details	Java equivalent
`Boolean`	True or false flag	`java.lang.Boolean`
`Byte`	Signed 8-bit integer. JFX 1.1+	`java.lang.Byte`
`Character`	Unsigned 16-bit Unicode. JFX 1.1+	`java.lang.Character`
`Double`	Signed 64-bit fraction. JFX 1.1+	`java.lang.Double`
`Duration`	Time interval	None
`Float`	Signed 32-bit fraction. JFX 1.1+	`java.lang.Float`
`Integer`	Signed 32-bit integer	`java.lang.Integer`
`Long`	Signed 64-bit integer. JFX 1.1+	`java.lang.Long`
`Number`	Signed 32-bit fraction.	`java.lang.Float`
`Short`	Signed 16-bit integer. JFX 1.1+	`java.lang.Short`
`String`	Unicode text string	`java.lang.String`

One thing making value types stand out from their object brethren is that special provision is made for them in the JavaFX Script syntax. Not sure what this means? Consider the humble `String` class (`java.lang.String`) in Java: although just another class, `String` is blessed with its own syntax variants for creation and concatenation, without need of constructors and methods. This is just syntactic sugar; behind the scenes the source is implemented by familiar constructors and methods, but the string syntax keeps source code readable.

Another difference between value types and other objects is that uninitialized (unassigned) value types assume a default value rather than `null`. Indeed value types cannot be assigned a null value. We'll look at default values shortly.

JavaFX Script offers several basic types, detailed in table 2.1.

Many of the types in table 2.1 are recognizable as variations on the basic primitive types you often find in other programming languages. The `Duration` type stands out as being unusual. It reflects JavaFX Script's focus on animation and demands more than just a basic explanation, so we'll put it aside until later in this chapter.

Changes for JavaFX Script 1.1

In JavaFX Script 1.0 the only fractional (floating point) type was `Number`, which had double precision, making it equivalent to Java's `Double`. In JavaFX Script 1.1 six new types were introduced: `Byte`, `Character`, `Double`, `Float`, `Long`, and `Short`. This resulted in `Number` being downsized to 32-bit precision, effectively becoming an alternative name for the new `Float` type.

Let's look at example code defining the types we're looking at in this section.

Listing 2.2 Defining value types

```
var valBool:Boolean = true;
var valByte:Byte = -123;
var valChar:Character = 65;
var valDouble:Double = 1.23456789;
var valFloat:Float = 1.23456789;
var valInt:Integer = 8;
var valLong:Long = 123456789;
var valNum:Number = 1.245;
var valShort:Short = 1234;
var valStr:String = "Example text";
println("Assigned: B: {valBool}, By: {valByte}, "
    "C: {valChar}, D: {valDouble}, F: {valFloat}, ");
println("  I: {valInt}, L: {valLong}, N: {valNum}, "
    "Sh: {valShort}, S: {valStr}");

var hexInt:Integer = 0x20;
var octInt:Integer = 040;
var eNum:Double = 1.234E-56;
println("hexInt: {hexInt}, octInt: {octInt}, "
    "eNum: {eNum}");
```

```
Assigned: B: true, By: -123, C: A, D: 1.23456789, F: 1.2345679,
  I: 8, L: 123456789, N: 1.245, Sh: 1234, S: Example text
hexInt: 32, octInt: 32, eNum: 1.234E-56
```

The keyword var begins variable declarations, followed by the variable name itself. Next comes a colon and the variable's type, and after this an equals symbol and the variable's initial value. A semicolon is used to close the declaration.

Keen-eyed readers will have spotted the use of the keyword `true` in the boolean declaration; just as in Java, `true` and `false` are reserved words in JavaFX Script. You may also have noted the differing results for the `Float` and `Double` types, born out of their differences in precision.

It's also possible to express integers using hexadecimal or octal, and floating point values using scientific E notation, as per other programming languages. The final output line shows this in effect.

println() and strange-looking strings

The listings in this section, and other sections in this chapter, make reference to a certain `println()` function. Common to all JavaFX objects, thanks to its inclusion in the `javafx.lang.FX` base class, `println()` is the JavaFX way of writing to the application's default output stream. Java programmers will be familiar with `println()` through Java's `System.out` object but may not recognize the bizarre curly braced strings being used to create the formatted output. For now accept them—we'll deal with the details in a few pages.

As in many languages, the initializer is optional. We could have ended each declaration after its type, with just closing semicolons, resulting in each variable being initialized to a sensible default value. Listing 2.3 shows a handful of examples.

Listing 2.3 Defining value types using defaults

```
var defBool:Boolean;
var defInt:Integer;
var defNum:Number;
var defStr:String;
println("Default: B: {defBool}, "
    "I: {defInt}, N: {defNum}, S: {defStr}");

Default: B: false, I: 0, N: 0.0, S:
```

You'll note in listing 2.3 the absence of any initial values. Despite being objects, value types cannot be `null`, so defaults of `false`, zero, or empty are used. But the initial value is not the only thing we can leave off, as listing 2.4 shows:

Listing 2.4 Defining value types using type inference

```
var infBool = true;
var infFlt = 1.0;              <-- Be careful declaring non-ints
var infInt = 1;
var infStr = "Some text";
println("Infered: B: {infBool}, "
    "F: {infFlt}, I: {infInt}, S: {infStr}");
println("{infFlt.getClass()}");

Infered: B: true, F: 1.0, I: 1, S: Some text
class java.lang.Float
```

JavaFX Script supports type inference when declaring variables. In plain English, this means if an initializer is used and the compiler can unambiguously deduce the variable's type from it, you can omit the explicit type declaration. In listing 2.4, if we'd initialized `infFlt` with just the value 1, it would have become an `Integer` instead of a `Float`; quoting the fractional part drops a hint as to our intended type.

2.2.3 Initialize-only and reassignable variables (var, def)

So far we've seen variables declared using the `var` keyword. But there's a second way of declaring variables, as listing 2.5 is about to reveal.

Listing 2.5 Declaring variables with def

```
var canAssign:Integer = 5;
def cannotAssign:Integer = 5;
canAssign = 55;
//cannotAssign = 55;           <-- Compiler error if uncommented
```

Using `def` instead of `var` results in variables that cannot be reassigned once created.

It's tempting to think of `def` variables only as constants; indeed that's how they're often used, but it's not always the case. A `def` variable cannot be reassigned, but the object it references can mutate (change its contents). Some types of objects are immutable (they provide no way to change their content once created, examples being `String` and `Integer`), so we might assume a `def` variable of an immutable type *must* be a constant. But again, this is not always the case. In a later section we'll investigate bound variables, revisiting `def` to see how a variable (even of an immutable type) can change its value without actually changing its content.

So, ignoring bound variables for the moment, a valid question is "when should we use `var` and when should we use `def`?" First, `def` is useful if we want to drop hints to fellow programmers as to how a given variable should be used. Second, the compiler can detect misuse of a variable if it knows how we intend to use it, but crucially, JFX can better optimize our software if given extra information about the data it's working with.

For simple assignments like those in listing 2.5, it's largely a matter of choice or style. Using `def` helps make our intentions clear and means our code might run a shade faster.

2.2.4 Arithmetic on value types (+, -, etc.)

Waxing lyrical about JavaFX Script's arithmetic capabilities is pointless: they're basically the same as those of most programming languages. Unlike Java, JavaFX Script's value types are *objects*, so they respond to both conventional operator syntax (like Java primitives) and method calls (like Java objects). Let's see how that works in practice, in listing 2.6.

Listing 2.6 Arithmetic on value types

```
def n1:Number = 1.5;
def n2:Number = 2.0;
var nAdd = n1 + n2;
var nSub = n1 - n2;
var nMul = n1 * n2;
var nDiv = n1 / n2;
var iNum = n1.intValue();                    <-- Converting nl to an integer
println("nAdd = {nAdd}, nSub = {nSub}, "
    "nMul = {nMul}, nDiv = {nDiv}");
println("iNum = {iNum}");
```

```
nAdd = 3.5, nSub = -0.5, nMul = 3.0, nDiv = 0.75
iNum = 1
```

The variables `n1` and `n2` (listing 2.6) are initialized, and a handful of basic mathematical operations are performed. Note the conversion of `n1` to an integer via `intValue()`, made possible by value types actually being objects. We'll look at objects later—for now be aware that value types are more than just primitives.

Table 2.2 List of arithmetic operators

Operator	Function
`+`	Addition
`-`	Subtraction; unary negation
`*`	Multiplication
`/`	Division
`mod`	Remainder (Java's equivalent is `%`)
`+=`	Addition and assign
`-=`	Subtract and assign
`*=`	Multiply and assign
`/=`	Divide and assign
`++`	Prefix (pre-increment assign) / suffix (post-increment assign)
`--`	Prefix (pre-decrement assign) / suffix (post-decrement assign)

In table 2.2 is a list of the common arithmetic operators; let's see some of them in action (see listing 2.7).

Listing 2.7 Further examples of arithmetic operations

```
var int1 = 10;
var int2 = 10;
int1 *= 2;
int2 *= 5;
var int3 = 9 mod (4+2*2);
var num:Number = 1.0/(2.5).intValue();      <-- Number literals are objects too
println("int1 = {int1}, "
    "int2 = {int2}, int3 = {int3}, num = {num}");
```

```
int1 = 20, int2 = 50, int3 = 1, num = 0.5
```

It's all very familiar. The only oddity in listing 2.7 is the value 2.5 having a method called on it (surrounding brackets avoid ambiguity over the *point* character). This is yet another example of the lack of true primitives, including literals too! The numeric literal 2.5 became a JavaFX `Float` type, allowing function calls on it.

2.2.5 Logic operators (and, or, not, <, >, =, >=, <=, !=)

In the next chapter we'll look at code constructs, such as conditions. But, as we're currently exploring the topic of data, we might as well take a quick gander (courtesy of listing 2.8) at the logic operations that form the backbone of condition code.

For most programmers, apart from a few differences in keywords (`and` and `or` instead of `&&` and `||`), there's no great surprise lurking in listing 2.8. As in Java, the instanceof operator is used for testing the type of an object, in this case a Java Date. It's all rather predictable—but then, isn't that a good thing?

Listing 2.8 Logic operators

```
def testVal = 99;
var flag1 = (testVal == 99);
var flag2 = (testVal != 99);
var flag3 = (testVal <= 100);
var flag4 = (flag1 or flag2);
var flag5 = (flag1 and flag2);
var today:java.util.Date = new java.util.Date();
var flag6 = (today instanceof java.util.Date);
println("flag1 = {flag1}, flag2 = {flag2}, "
"flag3 = {flag3}");
println("flag4 = {flag4}, flag5 = {flag5}, "
"flag6 = {flag6}");
```

Creating a Java Date object

```
flag1 = true, flag2 = false, flag3 = true
flag4 = true, flag5 = false, flag6 = true
```

2.2.6 Translating and checking types (as, instanceof)

Because JavaFX Script is a statically typed language, casts may be required to convert one data type into another. If the conversion is guaranteed to be safe, JavaFX Script allows it without a fuss, but where there's potential for error or ambiguity, JavaFX Script insists on a *cast*.

Casts are performed by appending the keyword as, followed by the desired type, after the variable or term that needs converting. Listing 2.9 shows an example.

Listing 2.9 Casting types

```
import java.lang.System;
var pseudoRnd:Integer =
    (System.currentTimeMillis() as Integer) mod 1000;

var str:java.lang.Object = "A string";
var inst1 = (str instanceof String);
var inst2 = (str instanceof java.lang.Boolean);
println("String={inst1} Boolean={inst2}");
```

```
String=true Boolean=false
```

Usually casting is required when a larger object is downsized to a smaller one, as in the example, where a 64-bit value is being truncated to a 32-bit value. Another example is when an object type is being changed *down* the hierarchy of classes, to a more specific subclass. For non-Java programmers there's more detail on the purpose of casts in appendix C—look under section C2.

Checking the type of a variable can be done with instanceof, which returns true if the variable matches the supplied type and false if it doesn't.

This concludes our look at basic data types. If it's been all rather tame for you, don't worry; the next section will start to introduce some JFX power tools.

2.3 Working with text, via strings

Where would we be without strings? This book wouldn't be getting written, that's for sure (pounding the whole manuscript out on a manual typewriter somehow doesn't endear itself). We looked at defining basic string variables previously; now let's delve deeper to unlock the power of string manipulation in JavaFX.

2.3.1 String literals and embedded expressions

String literals allow us to write strings directly into the source code of our programs. JavaFX Script string literals can be defined using single or double quotes, as listing 2.10 demonstrates.

Listing 2.10 Basic string definitions

```
def str1 = 'Single quotes';
def str2 = "Double quotes";
println("str1 = {str1}");
println("str2 = {str2}");
```

```
str1 = Single quotes
str2 = Double quotes
```

Is there a difference between these two styles? No. Either double or single quotes can be used to enclose a string, and providing both ends of the string match it doesn't matter which you use. Listing 2.11 shows even more string syntax variations.

Listing 2.11 Multiline strings, double- and single-quoted strings

```
def multiline = "This string starts here, "
'and ends here!';
println("multiline = {multiline}");

println("UK authors prefer 'single quotes'");
println('US authors prefer "double quotes"');
println('I use "US" and \'UK\' quotes');
```

```
multiline = This string starts here, and ends here!
UK authors prefer 'single quotes'
US authors prefer "double quotes"
I use "US" and 'UK' quotes
```

String literals next to each other in the source code, with nothing in between (except whitespace), are concatenated together, even when on separate source code lines. Single-quoted strings can contain double-quote characters, and double-quoted strings can contain single-quote characters, but to use the same quote as delimits the string you need to escape it with a backslash. This ability to switch quote styles is particularly useful when working with other languages from within JavaFX Script, like SQL. (By the way, yes, I know many *modern* British novelists prefer double quotes!)

In the listings shown previously some of the strings have contained a strange curly brace format for incorporating variables. Now it's time to find out what that's all about.

Listing 2.12 Strings with embedded expressions

```
def rating = "cool";
def eval1 = "JavaFX is {rating}!";
def eval2 = "JavaFX is \{rating\}!";
println("eval1 = {eval1}");
println("eval2 = {eval2}");

def flag = true;
def eval3 =
    "JavaFX is {if(flag) "cool" else "uncool"}!";
println("eval3 = {eval3}");
```

```
eval1 = JavaFX is cool!
eval2 = JavaFX is {rating}!
eval3 = JavaFX is cool!
```

Strings can contain expressions enclosed in curly braces. When encountered, the expression body is executed, and the result is substituted for the expression itself. In listing 2.12 we see the value of the variable `rating` is inserted into the string content of `eval1` by enclosing a reference to `rating` in braces. Escaping the opening and closing braces with a backslash prevents any attempted expression evaluation, as has happened with `eval2`.

We can get more adventurous than just simple variable references. The condition embedded inside the curly braces of `eval3` displays either "JavaFX is cool!" or "JavaFX is uncool!" depending on the contents of the boolean variable `flag`. We'll be looking at the `if/else` syntax later, of course, but for now let's continue our exploration of strings, because JavaFX Script offers even more devious ways to manipulate their contents.

2.3.2 *String formatting*

We've seen how to expand a variable into a string using the curly brace syntax, but this is only the tip of the iceberg. Java has a handy class called `java.util.Formatter`, which permits string control similar to C's infamous `printf()` function. The `Formatter` class allows commonly displayed data types, specifically strings, numbers, and dates, to be translated into text form based on a pattern. Listing 2.13 shows the JFX equivalent.

Listing 2.13 String formatting

```
import java.util.Calendar;
import java.util.Date;

def magic = -889275714;
println("{magic} in hex is {%08x magic}");          <- Eight-digit hexadecimal

def cal:Calendar = Calendar.getInstance();
cal.set(1991,2,4);
def joesBirthday:Date = cal.getTime();
println("Joe was born on a {%tA joesBirthday}");    <- Display date's weekday
```

```
-889275714 in hex is cafebabe
Joe was born on a Monday
```

In the two `println()` calls of listing 2.13 we see the string formatter in action. The first uses a format of `%08x` to display an eight-digit hexadecimal representation of the value of `magic`. The second example creates a date for 4 March 1991 using Java's `Calendar` and `Date` classes (months are indexed from 0, while days are indexed from 1). The format pattern `%tA` displays the day name (Monday, Tuesday, ...) from any date it is applied to.

For more details on the various formatting options, consult the Java documentation for the `java.util.Formatter` class.

> **Being negative**
>
> Perhaps you're wondering how the hexadecimal value CAFEBABE could be represented in decimal as -889275714, not 3405691582. Like Java, JavaFX Script uses a 32-bit signed `Integer` type, meaning the lower 31 binary digits of each integer represent its value and the most significant digit stores whether the value is positive or negative. Because the hex value CAFEBABE uses all 32 bits, its 32nd bit causes JFX to see it as negative in many circumstances. If we tried to store the number 3405691582 in an integer, the compiler would inform us it's too big. However -889275714 results in exactly the same 32-bit pattern.
>
> In case you didn't know, CAFEBABE is the 4-byte *magic* identifier starting every valid Java bytecode class file. You learn something new every day! (Or maybe not.)

As well as in built string formatting, JavaFX Script has a specific syntax for string localization, which is what we'll look at next.

2.3.3 String localization

The internet is a global phenomenon, and while it might save programmers a whole load of pain if everyone would agree on a single language, calendar, and daylight saving time, the fact is people cherish their local culture and customs, and our software should respect that. An application might use dozens, hundreds, or even thousands of bits of text to communicate to its user. For true internationalization these need to be changeable at runtime to reflect the native language of the user (or, at least, the language settings of the computer the user is using). To do this we use individual property files, each detailing the strings to be used for a given language.

Listing 2.14 is a simple two-line localization property file for UK English. Its filename and location are important.

Listing 2.14 String localization: the <classname>_en_UK.fxproperties file

```
"Trash" = "Rubbish"
"STR_KEY" = "UK version"
```

The filename must begin with the name of the script it is used in, followed by an underscore character, then a valid ISO Language Code as specified in the standard,

ISO-639.2. These codes comprise two lowercase characters, signifying which language the localization file should be used for. If a specific variant of a language is required (for example, UK English instead of US English) a further underscore and an ISO Country Code may be added, as specified by ISO-3166. These codes are two uppercase characters, documenting a specific country. Finally, the extension .fxproperties must be added.

In the book's source code the script for testing listing 2.14 is called Examples3.fx, so the properties file for UK English would be Examples3_en_UK.fxproperties. If we created a companion property file for all Japanese regions, it would be called Examples3_ja.fxproperties (ja being the language code for Japanese).

All properties files must be placed somewhere on the classpath so JavaFX can find them at runtime. Listing 2.15 shows the code to test our localization strings.

Listing 2.15 String localization

```
println(##"Trash");
println(##[STR_KEY]"Default version");
```

```
Trash
Default version
```

```
Rubbish
UK version
```

The listing demonstrates two examples of localized strings in JavaFX Script and the output for two runs of the program, one non-UK and the other UK.

The ## prefix means JFX will look for an appropriate localization file and use its contents to replace the following string. In the first line of code the string `"Trash"` is replaced by `"Rubbish"` using the en_UK file we created earlier. The `"Trash"` string is used as a key to look up the replacement in the properties file. If we're not running the program in the United Kingdom, or the property file cannot be loaded, the `"Trash"` string is used as a default.

The second line does the same, except the key and the default are separate. So `"STR_KEY"` is used as a key to look up the localization property, and `"Default version"` is used if no suitable localization can be found.

You might be wondering how you can test the code without bloating your carbon footprint with a round-the-world trip. Fortunately, the JVM has a couple of system properties to control its region and language settings, namely `user.region` and `user.language`. They should be settable within the testing environment of your IDE (look under "System properties") or from the command line using the `-D` switch. Here are a couple of examples:

```
-Duser.region=UK -Duser.language=en
-Duser.region=US
```

And that's strings. Thus far we've looked at very familiar data types, but next we'll look at a value type you won't find in any other popular programming language: the `Duration`.

2.4 Durations, using time literals

You *really* know a language is specialized to cope with animation when you see it has a literal syntax for time durations. What are *time literals*? Well, just as the quoted syntax makes creating strings easy, the time literal syntax provides a simple, specialized notation for expressing intervals of time. Listing 2.16 shows it in action.

Listing 2.16 Declaring `Duration` types

```
def mil = 25ms;
def sec = 30s;
def min = 15m;
def hrs = 2h;
println("mil = {mil}, sec = {sec}, "
    "min = {min}, hrs = {hrs}");
```

Milliseconds, seconds, minutes, and hours

Output is milliseconds

```
mil = 25ms, sec = 30000ms, min = 900000ms, hrs = 7200000ms
```

Appending `ms`, `s`, `m`, or `h` to a value creates an object of type `Duration` (not unlike wrapping characters with quotes turns them into a `String`). Listing 2.16 demonstrates times expressed using the literal notation: 25 milliseconds, 30 seconds, 15 minutes, and 2 hours. No matter how they were defined, `Duration` objects default to milliseconds when `toString()` is called on them. This handy notation is pretty versatile and can be used in a variety of ways, including with arithmetic and boolean logic. Listing 2.17 shows a few examples of what can be done, using Java's `System.printf()` method to add platform-specific line separators into the output string.

Listing 2.17 Arithmetic on duration types

```
import java.lang.System;
def dur1 = 15m * 4;
def dur2 = 0.5h * 2;
def flag1 = (dur1 == dur2);
def flag2 = (dur1 > 55m);
def flag3 = (dur2 < 123ms);
System.out.printf(
    "dur1 = {dur1.toMinutes()}m , "
    "dur2 = {dur2.toMinutes()}m%n"
    "(dur1 == dur2) is {flag1}%n"
    "(dur1 > 55m) is {flag2}%n"
    "(dur1 < 123ms) is {flag3}%n");
```

15 minutes times 4

Half an hour times 2

Converted to minutes

```
dur1 = 60.0m , dur2 = 60.0m
(dur1 == dur2) is true
(dur1 > 55m) is true
(dur1 < 123ms) is false
```

Both `dur1` and `dur2` are created as `Duration` objects, set to one hour. The first is created by multiplying 15 minutes by 4, and the second is created by multiplying half an hour by 2. These `Duration` objects are then compared against each other and against other literal `Duration` objects. To make the console output more readable, we convert the usual millisecond representation to minutes.

When we start playing with animation we'll see how time literals help create compact, readable, source code for all manner of visual effects. But we still have a lot to explore before we get there, for example "sequences".

2.5 Sequences: not quite arrays

Sequences are collections of objects or values with a logical ordered relationship. As the saying goes, they do "exactly what it says on the tin"; in other words, a sequence is a sequence of *things*!

It's tempting to think of sequences as arrays by another name—indeed they can be used for array-like functionality—but sequences hide some pretty clever extra functionality, making them more useful for the type of work JavaFX is designed to do. In the following sections we'll look at how to define, extend, retract, slice, and filter JavaFX sequences. Sequences have quite a rich syntax associated with them, so let's jump straight in.

2.5.1 Basic sequence declaration and access (sizeof)

We won't get very far if we cannot define new sequences. Listing 2.18 shows us how to do just that.

Listing 2.18 Sequence declaration

```
import java.lang.System;
def seq1:String[] = [ "A" , "B" , "C" ];
def seq2:String[] = [ seq1 , "D" , "E" ];
def flag1 = (seq2 == ["A","B","C","D","E"]);
def size = sizeof seq1;
System.out.printf("seq1 = {seq1.toString()}%n"
    "seq2 = {seq2.toString()}%n"
    "flag1 = {flag1}%n"
    "size = {size}%n");
```

```
seq1 = [ A, B, C ]
seq2 = [ A, B, C, D, E ]
flag1 = true
size = 3
```

Listing 2.18 exposes a few important sequence concepts:

- A new sequence is declared using square-brackets syntax.
- When one sequence is used inside another, it is expanded in place. Sequences are always linear; multidimensional sequences are not supported.
- Sequences are equal if they are the same size and each corresponding element is equal; in other words, the same values in the same order. The notation for referring to the type of a sequence uses square brackets after the plain object type. For example, `String[]` refers to a sequence of `String` objects.
- Sequence type notation is the plain object type followed by square brackets. For example, `String[]` refers to a sequence of `String` objects.
- The `sizeof` operator can be used to determine the length of a sequence.

To reference a value in a sequence we use the same square-bracket syntax as many other programming languages. The first element is at index zero, as listing 2.19 proves.

Listing 2.19 Referencing a sequence element

```
import java.lang.System;
def faceCards = [ "Jack" , "Queen" , "King" ];
var king = faceCards[2];
def ints = [10,11,12,13,14,15,16,17,18,19,20];
var oneInt = ints[3];
var outside = ints[-1];
System.out.printf("faceCards[2] = {king}\n"
    "ints[3] = {oneInt}\n"
    "ints[-1] = {outside}\n");
```

```
faceCards[2] = King
ints[3] = 13
ints[-1] = 0
```

You'll note how referring to an element outside of the sequence bounds returns a default value, rather than an error or an exception. Apart from this oddity, the code looks remarkably close to arrays in other programming languages—so, what about those clever features I promised? Let's experience our first bit of sequence cleverness by looking at ranges and slices.

2.5.2 *Sequence creation using ranges ([..], step)*

The examples thus far have seen sequences created explicitly, with content as comma separated lists inside square brackets. This may not always be convenient, so JFX supports a handy range syntax. Check out listing 2.20.

Listing 2.20 Sequence creation using a range

```
def seq3 = [ 1 .. 100 ];                                  // Two dots create a range
println("seq3[0] = {seq3[0]},"
    "seq3[11] = {seq3[11]}, seq3[89] = {seq3[89]}");
```

```
seq3[0] = 1,seq3[11] = 12, seq3[89] = 90
```

The sequence is populated with the values 1 to 100, inclusive. Two dots separate the start and end delimiters of the range, enclosed in the familiar square brackets. Is that all there is to it? No, not by a long stretch! Take a look at listing 2.21.

Listing 2.21 Sequence creation using a stepped range

```
def range1 = [0..100 step 5];
def range2 = [100..0 step -5];
def range3 = [0..100 step -5];       // Compiler warning under JavaFX 1.2
def range4 = [0.0 .. 1.0 step 0.25];
println("range1 = {range1.toString()}");
println("range2 = {range2.toString()}");
println("range3 = {range3.toString()}");
println("range4 = {range4.toString()}");
```

```
range1 = [ 0, 5, 10, 15, 20, 25, 30, 35, 40, 45,
```

```
➥  50, 55, 60, 65, 70, 75, 80, 85, 90, 95, 100 ]
range2 = [ 100, 95, 90, 85, 80, 75, 70, 65, 60, 55,
➥  50, 45, 40, 35, 30, 25, 20, 15, 10, 5, 0 ]
range3 = [ ]
range4 = [ 0.0, 0.25, 0.5, 0.75, 1.0 ]
```

Listing 2.21 shows ranges created using an extra `step` parameter. The first runs from 0 to 100 in steps of 5 (0, 5, 10, ...), and the second does the same in reverse (100, 95, 90, ...) The third goes from 0 to 100 backwards, resulting (quite rightly!) in an empty sequence. Finally, just to prove ranges aren't all about integers, we have a range from 0 to 1 in steps of a quarter.

Ranges can nest inside larger declarations, expanding in place to create a single sequence. We can exploit this fact for more readable source code, as listing 2.22 shows.

Listing 2.22 Expanding one sequence inside another

```
def blackjackValues = [ [1..10] , 10,10,10 ];
println("blackjackValues = "
    "{blackjackValues.toString()}");
```

Expanding a range inside another declaration

```
blackjackValues = [ 1, 2, 3, 4, 5, 6, 7, 8, 9, 10, 10, 10, 10 ]
```

Listing 2.22 creates a sequence representing the card values in the game Blackjack: aces to tens use their face value, while picture cards (jack, queen, king) are valued at 10. (Yes, *I am* aware aces are also 11—what do you want, blood?)

2.5.3 Sequence creation using slices ([..<])

The range syntax can be useful in many circumstances, but it's not the only trick JavaFX Script has up its sleeve. For situations that demand more control, we can also take a slice from an existing sequence to create a new one, as listing 2.23 shows.

Listing 2.23 Sequence declaration using a slice

```
import java.lang.System;
def source = [0 .. 100];
var slice1 = source[0 .. 10];
var slice2 = source[0 ..< 10];
var slice3 = source[95..];
var slice4 = source[95..<];
var format = "%s = %d to %d%n";
System.out.printf(format, "slice1",
    slice1[0], slice1[(sizeof slice1)-1] );
System.out.printf(format, "slice2",
    slice2[0], slice2[(sizeof slice2)-1] );
System.out.printf(format, "slice3",
    slice3[0], slice3[(sizeof slice3)-1] );
System.out.printf(format, "slice4",
    slice4[0], slice4[(sizeof slice4)-1] );
```

```
slice1 = 0 to 10
slice2 = 0 to 9
slice3 = 95 to 100
slice4 = 95 to 99
```

Just the start/end values

Here the double-dot syntax creates a slice of an existing sequence, `source`. The numbers defining the slice are element indexes, so in the case of `slice1` the range `[0..10]` refers to the first 11 elements in `source`, resulting in the values 0 to 10.

The `..` syntax describes an inclusive range, while the `..<` syntax can be used to define an exclusive range (0 to 10, not including 10 itself). If you leave the trailing delimiter off a `..` range, the slice will be taken to the end of the sequence, effectively making the end delimiter the sequence size minus 1. If you leave the trailing delimiter off a `..<` range, the slice will be taken to the end of the sequence minus one element, effectively dropping the last index.

2.5.4 Sequence creation using a predicate

The next weapon in the sequence arsenal we'll look at (and perhaps the most powerful) is the predicate syntax, which allows us to take a conditional slice from inside another sequence. The predicate syntax takes the form of a variable and a condition separated by a bar character. The destination (output) sequence is constructed by loading each element in the source sequences into the variable and applying the condition to determine whether it should be included in the destination or not. Listing 2.24 shows this in action.

Listing 2.24 Sequence declaration using a predicate

```
def source2 = [0 .. 9];
var lowVals = source2[n|n<5];
println("lowVals = {lowVals.toString()}");

def people =
    ["Alan","Andy","Bob","Colin","Dave","Eddie"];
var peopleSubset =
    people[s | s.startsWith("A")].toString();
println("predicate = {peopleSubset}");
```

```
lowVals = [ 0, 1, 2, 3, 4 ]
predicate = [ Alan, Andy ]
```

Take a look at how `lowVals` is created in listing 2.24. Each of the numbers in `source2` is assigned to `n`, and the condition `n<5` is tested to determine whether the value will be added to `lowVals`. The second example applies a test to see if the sequence element begins with the character *A*, meaning in our example only "Alan" and "Andy" will make it into the destination sequence.

Predicates are pretty useful, particularly because their syntax is nice and compact. But even this isn't the end of what we can do with sequences.

2.5.5 Sequence manipulation (insert, delete, reverse)

Sequences can be manipulated by inserting and removing elements dynamically. We can do this either to the end of the sequence, before an existing element, or after an existing element. The three variations are demonstrated with listing 2.25.

Listing 2.25 Sequence manipulation: insert

```
var seq1 = [1..5];
insert 6 into seq1;
println("Insert1: {seq1.toString()}");
insert 0 before seq1[0];
println("Insert2: {seq1.toString()}");
insert 99 after seq1[2];
println("Insert3: {seq1.toString()}");
```

```
Insert1: [ 1, 2, 3, 4, 5, 6 ]
Insert2: [ 0, 1, 2, 3, 4, 5, 6 ]
Insert3: [ 0, 1, 2, 99, 3, 4, 5, 6 ]
```

This example shows a basic range sequence created with the values 1 through 5. The first insert appends a new value, 6, to the end of the sequence, the next inserts a new value, 0, before the current first value, and the final insert shoehorns a value, 99, after the third element in the sequence.

That's covers insert, but what about deleting from sequences? Here's how.

Listing 2.26 Sequence manipulation: delete

```
var seq2 = [[1..10],10];
delete seq2[0];
println("Delete1: {seq2.toString()}");
delete seq2[0..2];
println("Delete2: {seq2.toString()}");
delete 10 from seq2;
println("Delete3: {seq2.toString()}");
delete seq2;
println("Delete4: {seq2.toString()}");
```

```
Delete1: [ 2, 3, 4, 5, 6, 7, 8, 9, 10, 10 ]
Delete2: [ 5, 6, 7, 8, 9, 10, 10 ]
Delete3: [ 5, 6, 7, 8, 9 ]
Delete4: [ ]
```

It should be obvious what listing 2.26 does. Starting with a sequence of 1 through 10, plus another 10, the first delete operation removes the first index, the second deletes a range from index positions 0 to 2 (inclusive), the third removes any tens from the sequence, and the final delete removes the entire sequence.

One final trick is the ability to reverse the order of a sequence, as shown here.

Listing 2.27 Sequence manipulation: reverse

```
var seq3 = [1..10];
seq3 = reverse seq3;
println("Reverse: {seq3.toString()}");
```

```
Reverse: [ 10, 9, 8, 7, 6, 5, 4, 3, 2, 1 ]
```

The code in listing 2.27 merely flips the order of `seq3`, from 1 through 10 to 10 through 1.

All this inserting, deleting, and reversing may seem pretty useful, but perhaps some of you are worried about how much processing power it takes to chop and change large runs of data during the course of a program's execution. Because sequences aren't merely simple arrays, the answer is "surprisingly little."

2.5.6 Sequences, behind the scenes

I hinted briefly in the introduction to sequences of how they're not really arrays. Indeed, I am indebted to Sun engineer Jasper Potts, who pointed out the folly of drawing too close an analogy between JFX sequences and Java arrays and collections.

Behind the scenes, sequences use a host of different strategies to form the data you and I actually work with. Sequences are immutable (they cannot be changed; modifications result in new sequence objects), but this does not make them slow or inefficient. When we create a number range, like `[0..100]` for example, only the bounds of the range are stored, and the *n*th value is calculated whenever it is accessed. By supporting different composite techniques, a sequence can hold a collection of different types of data represented with different strategies and can add/remove elements within the body of the sequence without wholesale copying.

Suffice to say, when we reversed the sequence in listing 2.27 no data was actually rearranged!

> **More details**
>
> Michael Heinrichs has an interesting blog entry covering, in some detail, the types of representations and strategies sequences use beneath the surface to give the maximum flexibility, with minimum drudgery:
>
> http://blogs.sun.com/michaelheinrichs/entry/internal_design_of_javafx_sequences1

And that's it for sequences, at least until we consider the `for` loop later on. In the next section we'll start to look at binding, perhaps JavaFX Script's most powerful syntax feature.

2.6 Autoupdating related data, with binds

Binding is a way of defining an automatic update relationship between data in one part of your program and data elsewhere it depends on. Although binding has many applications, it's particularly useful in UI programming.

Writing code to ensure a GUI always betrays the true state of the data it is representing can be a thankless task. Not only is the code that links model and UI usually verbose, but quite often it lives miles away from either. Binding connects the interface directly to the source data or (more accurately) to a nugget of code that interprets the data. The code that controls the interface's state is defined in the interface declaration itself!

Because binding is such a useful part of JavaFX, in the coming sections we'll cover not only its various applications but also the mechanics of how it works, for those occasions when it's important to know.

2.6.1 Binding to variables (bind)

Let's start with the basics. Listing 2.28 is a straightforward example:

Listing 2.28 Binding into a string

```
var percentage:Integer;
def progress = bind "Progress: {percentage}% finished";
for(v in [0..100 step 20]) {
    percentage = v;
    println(progress);
}
```

This is a for loop

```
Progress: 0% finished
Progress: 20% finished
Progress: 40% finished
Progress: 60% finished
Progress: 80% finished
Progress: 100% finished
```

This simple example updates the variable `percentage` from 0 to 100 in steps of 20 using a `for` loop (which we'll study next chapter), with the variable `progress` automatically tracking the updates.

You'll note the use of the `bind` keyword, which tells the JavaFX Script compiler that the code that follows is a bound *expression*. Expressions are bits of code that return values, so what `bind` is saying is "the value of this variable is controlled by this piece of code." In listing 2.28 the bound `progress` string reevaluates its contents each time the variable it depends on changes. So, whenever `percentage` changes, its new value is automatically reflected in the `progress` string.

But hold on—how can `progress` change when it's declared using `def`, not `var`? Technically it doesn't ever change. Its value changes, true, but its *real* content (the expression) never actually gets reassigned. This is why, back when we covered `var` and `def`, I warned against thinking of `def` variables as simple constants, even if their type is immutable. Because a one-way bound variable should not be *directly* assigned to, using `def` is more correct than using `var`.

Bind works not only with strings but other data types too, as we'll see in listing 2.29.

Listing 2.29 Binding between variables

```
var thisYear = 2008;
def lastYear = bind thisYear-1;
def nextYear = bind thisYear+1;
println("2008: {lastYear}, {thisYear}, {nextYear}");
thisYear = 1996;
println("1996: {lastYear}, {thisYear}, {nextYear}");
```

```
2008: 2007, 2008, 2009
1996: 1995, 1996, 1997
```

In listing 2.29 the values of `lastYear` and `nextYear` are dependent on the current contents of `thisYear`. A change to `thisYear` causes its siblings to recalculate the expression associated with their binding, meaning they will always be one year behind or ahead of whatever `thisYear` is set to.

2.6.2 *Binding to bound variables*

What about bound variables themselves—can they be the target of other bound variables, creating a chain of bindings? The answer, it seems, is yes! Check out listing 2.30.

Listing 2.30 Binding to bound variables

```
var flagA = true;
def flagB = bind not flagA;
def flagC = bind not flagB;
println("flagA = {flagA}, "
    "flagB = {flagB}, flagC = {flagC}");
flagA = false;
println("flagA = {flagA}, "
    "flagB = {flagB}, flagC = {flagC}");
```

```
flagA = true, flagB = false, flagC = true
flagA = false, flagB = true, flagC = false
```

The first two variables in listing 2.30, `flagA` and `flagB`, will always hold opposite values. Whenever `flagA` is set, its companion is set to the inverse automatically. The third value, `flagC`, is the inverse of `flagB`, creating a chain of updates from A to B to C, such that C is always the opposite of B and the same as A.

2.6.3 *Binding to a sequence element*

How do you use the `bind` syntax with a sequence? As luck would have it, that's the next bit of example code (listing 2.31).

Listing 2.31 Binding against a sequence element

```
var range = [1..5];                       <-- 'range' is [1,2,3,4,5]
def reference = bind range[2];
println("range[2] = {reference}");
delete range[0];                          <-- 'range' is [2,3,4,5]
println("range[2] = {reference}");
delete range;                             <-- 'range' is empty
println("range[2] = {reference}");
```

```
range[2] = 3
range[2] = 4
range[2] = 0
```

When we bind against a sequence element, we do so by way of its index—when the sequence is extended or truncated, the bind does not track the change by adjusting its index to match. In listing 2.31, even though the first element of `range` is deleted, causing the other elements to *move down* the sequence, the bind still points to the third index. Also, as we'd expect, accessing the third index after all elements have been deleted returns a default value.

2.6.4 Binding to an entire sequence (for)

In the previous section we witnessed what happens when we bind against an individual sequence element, but what happens when we bind against an entire sequence? Listing 2.32 has the answer.

Listing 2.32 Binding to a sequence itself

```
var multiplier:Integer = 2;
var seqSrc = [ 1..3 ];
def seqDst = bind for(seqVal in seqSrc) { seqVal*multiplier; }
println("seqSrc = {seqSrc.toString()},"
    " seqDst = {seqDst.toString()}");
insert 10 into seqSrc;                          <— Change source sequence
println("seqSrc = {seqSrc.toString()},"
    " seqDst = {seqDst.toString()}");
multiplier = 3;                                 <— Change multiplier
println("seqSrc = {seqSrc.toString()},"
    " seqDst = {seqDst.toString()}");
```

```
seqSrc = [ 1, 2, 3 ], seqDst = [ 2, 4, 6 ]
seqSrc = [ 1, 2, 3, 10 ], seqDst = [ 2, 4, 6, 20 ]
seqSrc = [ 1, 2, 3, 10 ], seqDst = [ 3, 6, 9, 30 ]
```

The code shows one sequence, `seqDst`, bound against another, `seqSrc`. The bind expression takes the form of a loop, which doubles the value in each element of the source sequence. (In JavaFX Script, `for` loops create sequences; we'll look at the syntax in detail next chapter.) When the source sequence changes, for example, a new element is added, the bind ensures the destination sequence is kept in step, using the expression.

When the `multiplier` changes, the destination sequence is again kept in step. So, both `seqSrc` and `multiplier` affect `seqDst`. Binds are sensitive to change from every variable within their expression, something to keep in mind when writing your own bind code.

2.6.5 Binding to code

In truth, all the examples thus far have demonstrated binding to code—a simple variable read is, after all, code. The `bind` keyword merely attaches an *expression* (any unit of code that produces a result) to a read-only variable. This section looks a little deeper into how to exploit this functionality. For example, what if we need some logic to control how a bound variable gets updated? That's the first question we'll answer, using listing 2.33.

Listing 2.33 Binding to a ternary expression

```
var mode = false;
def modeStatus = bind if(mode) "On" else "Off";
println("Mode: {modeStatus}");
mode = true;
println("Mode: {modeStatus}");
```

```
Mode: Off
Mode: On
```

Listing 2.33 contains a binding that uses an `if/else` block to control the update of the string `modeStatus`, resulting in the contents being either "on" or "off." The `if/else` block is reevaluated each time `mode` changes.

Listing 2.34 shows an even more ambitious example.

Listing 2.34 A more complex binding example

```
var userID = "";
def realName = bind getName(userID);
def status = bind getStatus(userID);
def display = bind "Status: {realName} is {status}";
println(display);
userID = "adam";
println(display);
userID = "dan";
println(display);

function getName(id:String) : String {
    if(id.equals("adam")) { return "Adam Booth"; }
    else if(id.equals("dan")) { return "Dan Jones"; }
    else { return "Unknown"; }
}

function getStatus(id:String) : String {
    if(id.equals("adam")) { return "Online"; }
    else if(id.equals("dan")) { return "Offline"; }
    else { return "Unknown"; }
}
```

Functions, accept and return a string

```
Status: Unknown is Unknown
Status: Adam Booth is Online
Status: Dan Jones is Offline
```

We haven't covered functions yet, but it shouldn't be hard to figure out what the example code is doing. Working forward, down the chain, we start with `userID`, bound by two further variables called `realName` and `status`. These two variables call functions with `userID` as a parameter, both of which return a string whose contents depend on the `userID` passed in. A string called `display` adds an extra layer of binding by using the two bound variables to form a status string. Merely changing `userID` causes `realName`, `status`, and `display` to automatically update.

2.6.6 Bidirectional binds (with inverse)

We've seen some pretty complex binding examples thus far, but suppose we wanted only a simple bind that directly mirrored another variable. Would it be possible to have the bind work in both directions, so a change to either variable would result in a change to its *twin*? Listing 2.35 shows how this can be achieved.

Listing 2.35 Bidirectional binding

```
var dictionary = "US";
var thesaurus = bind dictionary with inverse;
println("Dict:{dictionary} Thes:{thesaurus}");
```

```
thesaurus = "UK";
println("Dict:{dictionary} Thes:{thesaurus}");

dictionary = "FR";
println("Dict:{dictionary} Thes:{thesaurus}");
Dict:US Thes:US
Dict:UK Thes:UK
Dict:FR Thes:FR
```

The code uses the `with inverse` keywords to create a two-way link between the variables `dictionary` and `thesaurus`. A change to one is automatically pushed across to the other. We can do this only because the bound expression is a simple, one-to-one reflection of another variable.

This may not seem like the most exciting functionality in the world; admittedly listing 2.35 doesn't do the idea justice. Imagine a data structure whose members are displayed on screen in editable text fields. When the data structure changes, the text fields should change. When the text fields change, the data structure should change. You can imagine the fun we'd have implementing that with a unidirectional bind: whichever end we put the bind on would become beholden to the bind expression, incapable of being altered. Bidirectional binds neatly solve that problem—both ends are editable.

By the way, did you spot anything unusual about the `dictionary` and `thesaurus` variables? (Well done, if you did!) Yes, we're using `var` instead of `def`. Unidirectional binds could not, by their very nature, be changed once declared. But bidirectional binds, by their very nature, are intended to allow change. Thus we use `var` instead of `def`.

2.6.7 The mechanics behind bindings

The OpenJFX project's own language documentation goes into some detail on how binding works and possible side effects that may occur if a particular set of circumstances conspire. You need to know two things when working with binds.

First, you aren't free to put just any old code inside a bind's body; it has to be an expression (a single unit of code that returns a value). This means, for example, you can't update the value of an outside variable (that is, one defined outside the bind) from within the body of code associated with a bind. This makes sense—the idea is to define relationships between data sources and their interfaces; bindings are not general-purpose triggers for running code when variables are accessed.

> **Expression mystery**
>
> Eagle-eyed readers may be saying at this point, "Hold on, in previous sections we saw binds working against conditions and loops, yet they aren't in themselves expressions!" Well, you'd be wrong if you thought that. In JavaFX Script *they are* expressions! But a full exploration of this will have to wait until next chapter.

The only exception to the expression rule is variable declarations. You are allowed, it seems, to declare new variable definitions within a bound body. You cannot update the variable once declared, so you must use the `def` keyword. (The JavaFX Script 1.0 compiler allows both `var` and `def` keywords to be used, but the documentation appears to suggest only `def` will be supported in the future.)

Moving on to our second topic: when it comes to bound expressions, JavaFX Script attempts to perform something called a *minimal recalculation*, which sounds rather cryptic but means only it's as lazy as possible. An example (listing 2.36) will explain all.

Listing 2.36 Minimal recalculation

```
var x = 0;
def y = bind getVal() + x;
for(loop in [1..5]) {
    x = loop;
    println("x = {x}, y = {y}");
}
function getVal() : Integer {
    println("getVal() called");
    return 100;
}
```

```
getVal() called
x = 1, y = 101
x = 2, y = 102
x = 3, y = 103
x = 4, y = 104
x = 5, y = 105
```

The bind in listing 2.36 has two parts: a call to a function, `getVal()`, and a variable, x. As `x` gets updated in the `for` loop, you might expect the `println()` call in `getVal()` to be triggered repeatedly, but it's called only once. The result from the first half of the expression (the function call) was reused, because JavaFX knows it's not dependent on the value that caused the update. This speeds things along, keeping the execution tight, but it could have unexpected side effects if your code assumes every part of a bound expression will always run. Best practice, therefore, dictates avoiding such assumptions.

2.6.8 Bound functions (bound)

In the previous section we saw how bindings try to perform the minimal amount of recalculation necessary for each update. This is fine when the expression we're binding against is transparent, but what if the bind is against some *black box* piece of code with outside dependencies?

Functions provide such a black box. When a bind involves a function, it only *watches* the parameters passed into the function to determine when recalculation is needed. The mechanism inside the function (the code it contains) is not considered, and thus any dependencies it may have are not factored into the bind recalculations. Listing 2.37 shows both the problem and the solution.

Listing 2.37 Bound functions

```
var ratio = 5;
var posX = 5;
var posY = 10;
def coords1 = bind "{scale1(posX)},{scale1(posY)}";
def coords2 = bind "{scale2(posX)},{scale2(posY)}";

function scale1(v:Integer) : Integer {
    return v*ratio;
}
bound function scale2(v:Integer) : Integer {
    return v*ratio;
}

println("1={coords1}  2={coords2}");
posX = 6;
println("1={coords1}  2={coords2}");
posY = 9;
println("1={coords1}  2={coords2}");
ratio = 3;
println("1={coords1}  2={coords2}");
```

```
1=25,50  2=25,50
1=30,50  2=30,50
1=30,45  2=30,45
1=30,45  2=18,27
```

Listing 2.37 shows two binds, `coords1` and `coords2`, which both call a function. We'll look at `coords1` first, since this is the one presenting the problem.

The variable `coords1` is updated via two calls to a function called `scale1()`. The function is used to scale two coordinates, `posX` and `posY`, by a given factor, `ratio`. The `scale1()` function accepts each coordinate and scales it by the appropriate factor using a reference to the external `ratio` variable. Watch what happens as we change the three variables involved in the bind: `posX`, `posY`, and `ratio`.

We change `posX`, and the value of `coords1` is automatically updated. This is because the bind knows that `posX` is integral to the bind. Likewise for `posY`. But a change to `ratio` does not force a recalculation of `coord1`. Why? The fact that this external variable is key to the integrity of the `coords1` bind is lost—the function body is a black box and was not scanned for dependencies.

And now the solution: `coords2` uses *exactly* the same code, except the function it binds against, named `scale2()`, carries the `bound` keyword prefix. This keyword is a warning to the compiler, flagging potential external dependencies. When JavaFX Script binds against a function marked `bound`, it looks inside for variables to include in the binding. Therefore `coord2` gets correctly recalculated when `ratio` is changed, even though the reference to `ratio` is hidden inside a function.

We call functions like `scale1()` *unbound functions*—their body is never included in the list of dependencies for a bind. We call functions like `scale2()` *bound functions*—their body is scanned for external variables they rely on, and these are included as triggers to cause a recalculation of the bind.

When writing your own API libraries, you need to be aware of whether the return value of each function is entirely self-contained or dependent on some external data (perhaps a class instance variable?). If data other than the function parameters could influence the return value, you should consider marking the function as bound.

2.6.9 Bound object literals

Now that we've explored how binding works, and the difference between bound and unbound functions, we can look at how they respond to object literals.

Object *what*? Sorry, but this is one of those occasions when I have to skip ahead and introduce something we won't cover fully until chapter 3. Object literals are JavaFX Script's way of declaratively creating complex objects. You should still be able to follow the basics of what follows, in listing 2.38, although you may want to bookmark this section and revisit it once you've read chapter 3.

Listing 2.38 Binding and object literals

```
class TextContainer {          <-- Create a class
    var label:String;
    var content:String;
    init {
        println("Object created: {label}");
    }
}
var someContent:String = "Pew, Pew, Barney, Magreu";     <-- Some text to bind to

def obj1 = bind TextContainer {     <-- Causes output line 1
    label: "obj1";
    content: someContent;
};
def obj2 = bind TextContainer {     <-- Causes output line 2
    label: "obj2";
    content: bind someContent;
};

someContent = "Cuthbert, Dibble and Grub";     <-- Causes output line 3

Object created: obj1
Object created: obj2
Object created: obj1
```

In the example we start by creating a new class with two variables. The first, `label`, merely tags each object so we can tell them apart in the output. The other, `content`, is the variable we're interested in. You'll note there's also a block of `init` code in our class; this will run whenever an object is created from the class, printing the `label` variable so we can see when objects are created.

We then define a `String` called `someContent`, to use in our object literals. The next two blocks of code are object literals. We create two of them, named `obj1` and `obj2`, applying a bind to both. We use the variable `someContent` to populate the `content` variable of the objects, although there is a subtle difference between the two declarations that will alter the way binding works.

Creating the two objects causes the init code to run, resulting in the first two lines of our output; no great surprises there. But look what happens when we change the someContent variable, which was used by the objects. The first object (obj1) is re-created, while the second (obj2) is not. Why is that?

Think back to the way binds worked with functions. When one of the function parameters changes, the bind reruns the function with the new data. Object literals work the same way: the bind applies not only to the object but to the variables used when declaring it. When one of those variables changes, the object literal is *rerun* with the new data, causing a new object to be created. So that explains why a new obj1 was created when someContent was changed, but why didn't obj2 suffer the same fate?

If you look at where someContent is used in the declaration of obj2, you'll see a second bind. This inner bind effectively shields the outer bind from changes affecting the object's content variable, creating a kind of nested context that prevents the recalculation from bubbling up to the object level. Remember this trick whenever you need to bind against an object literal but don't want the object creation *rerun* whenever one of the variables the declaration relied on changes.

If you don't yet appreciate how useful JavaFX bindings are, you'll get plenty of examples in our first project in chapter 4. In the next section we'll examine some bits of syntax that, although not as powerful as binds, can be just as useful.

2.7 Working nicely with Java

JavaFX Script is designed to work well with Java. As you'll see in the next chapter, Java classes can be brought directly into JavaFX programs and used with the same ease as JavaFX Script classes themselves. But inevitably there will be a few areas where the two languages don't mesh quite so easily. In the following sections we'll look at a couple of useful language features that help keep the interoperability cogs well oiled.

2.7.1 Avoiding naming conflicts, with quoted identifiers

Quoted identifiers are the bizarre double angle brackets wrapping some terms in JFX source code, for example, <<java.lang.System>>. Strange as these symbols look, they actually perform a very simple yet vital function. Because JavaFX sits atop the Java platform and has access to Java libraries, it's possible names originating in Java may clash with keywords or syntax patterns in JavaFX Script. Those peculiar angle brackets resolve this discord, ensuring a blissful harmony of Java and JavaFX at all times.

The double angle brackets wrap identifiers (*identifiers* are the names referring to variables, functions, classes, and so on) to exclude them from presumptions the compiler might otherwise make. Listing 2.39 shows an example.

Listing 2.39 Quoted identifiers

```
var <<var>> = "A string variable called var";
println("{<<var>>}");
```

```
A string variable called var
```

Please (please, please!) don't do something as stupid as listing 2.39 in real production code. By using (abusing?) quoted identifiers, we've created a variable with the name of a JavaFX Script keyword. Normally we'd only do this if "var" were something in Java we needed to reference.

2.7.2 Handling Java native arrays (nativearray of)

Alongside its array classes (like `Vector` and `ArrayList`) Java also has in built native arrays. Java native arrays are a fixed size and feature a square-bracket syntax similar to JavaFX Script's sequences. But native arrays and sequences are not quite the same thing, as you may have guessed if you've read section 2.5.6. When working with Java classes we may encounter native arrays, and we need some easy way of bringing them into our JavaFX programs. Listing 2.40 shows how it can be done.

Listing 2.40 Native arrays

```
def commaSep:java.lang.String = "one,two,three,four";
def numbers:nativearray of java.lang.String =
    commaSep.split(",");
println("1st: {numbers[0]}");
for(i in numbers) { println("{i}"); }
```

```
1st: one
one
two
three
four
```

Here we create a Java `String` object containing a comma-separated list and then use a `String.split()` call to break the list up into its constituent parts, resulting in an array of `String` objects. To bring this array into JavaFX Script as an actual array (rather than a sequence), we declare `numbers` as being of type `nativearray of String`. The `numbers` object can then be read and written to use the familiar square-bracket syntax and even feature as part of a `for` loop.

While this eases the process of working with Java native arrays, it's important to remember that a variable declared using `nativearray` is not a sequence; for example, it may contain `null` objects, and the `insert/delete` syntax from section 2.5.5 will not work.

> **Java strings versus JavaFX strings**
>
> There's no significance in declaring `commaSep` as a Java `String`. Under-the-hood JavaFX Script strings use Java strings, so either would have worked. However, because `split()` is a Java method, returning a Java native array, I thought the code would be more readable if I spelled out explicitly the Java connection.

WARNING *Experimental feature* The `nativearray` functionality was added to JavaFX 1.2 as an experiment. It may be modified, or even removed, in later revisions of the JavaFX Script language.

2.8 Summary

As you've now seen, JavaFX Script value types and sequences house some pretty powerful features. Chief among them is the ability to bind data into automatically updating chains, slashing the amount of code we have to write to keep our UI up to date. String formatting and sequence manipulation also offer great potential when used in a graphics and animation-rich environment.

And speaking of animation, there was one small piece of the JavaFX Script's data syntax we missed in this chapter. JFX provides a literal syntax for quick and easy creation of points on an animation time line, using the keywords `at` and `tween`. This is quite a specialist part of the language, without application beyond of the remit of animation. Because it's impossible to demonstrate how this syntax works without reference to the graphics classes and packages it supports, I've held over discussion of this one small part of the language for a later chapter.

In the next chapter we'll complete our tour of the JavaFX Script language by looking at the meat of the language, the stuff that actually gets our data moving.

JavaFX Script CODE AND STRUCTURE

This chapter covers

- Writing, inheriting, and using classes
- Mixing code with conditions and loops
- Running code when a variable changes
- Dealing with accidents and the unexpected

In chapter 2 we looked at JavaFX Script's data types and manipulations; this chapter looks at its code constructs. Separating the two is somewhat arbitrary—we saw plenty of code hiding in the previous chapter's examples because code and data are flip sides of the same coin. Ahead we'll see how the concepts we discovered last chapter integrate into the syntax as a whole. Our grounding in *data* will hopefully engender a more immediate understanding as we encounter conditions, loops, functions, classes, and the like.

As mentioned in chapters 1 and 2, JavaFX Script is what's referred to as an *expression language,* meaning most executable bits of code return either zero or one or more values (aka: void, a value, or a sequence). Even loops and conditions will work on the right-hand side of an assignment. It's important to fix this idea in your mind as we progress through this chapter, particularly if you're not used to languages working this way. I'll point out the ramifications as the chapter unfolds.

We'll start with higher-level language features like classes and objects and work our way down into the trenches to examine loops and conditions. It goes without saying that you'll require an understanding of the material in the previous chapter, so if you skipped ahead to the juicy code stuff, please consider backtracking to at least read up on *binds* and *sequences*.

I've maintained a couple of conventions from the last chapter. First, source code is presented in small chunks that (unless otherwise stated) compile and run independently, with the console output presented in bold. Second, to avoid too much repetition I'm continuing to incur the wrath of pedants by occasionally referring to the language variously as JavaFX Script (its proper name) or by the shorthand JavaFX or JFX.

We have quite an exciting journey ahead, with a few twists and turns, so let's get going. We'll start by looking at the highest level of structure we can apply to our code: the package.

3.1 Imposing order and control with packages (package, import)

The outermost construct for imposing order on our code is the package. Packages allow us to relate portions of our code together for convenience, to control access to variables and functions (see *access modifiers*, later), and to permit classes to have identical names but different purposes. Listing 3.1 shows an example.

Listing 3.1 Using the `package` statement to shorten class names

```
import java.util.Date;

var date1:Date = Date {};
var date2:java.util.Date = java.util.Date {};
```

Date lives in the package java.util

Here we see two different ways of creating a `Date` object. The first makes use of the `import` statement at the start of the code (and would fail to compile without it), while the second does not. As in Java, an asterisk can be used at the end of an `import` statement instead of a class name to include all the classes from the stated package without having to list them individually. Listing 3.2 shows how we can create our own packages.

Listing 3.2 Including a class inside a package

```
package jfxia.chapter3;

public class Date {
    override function toString() : String {
        "This is our date class";
    }
};
```

Should go in the file Date.fx

The `package` statement, which must appear at the start of the source, places the code from this example into a package called `jfxia.chapter3`, from where `import` may be used to pull it into other class files.

In terms of how packages are physically stored, JavaFX Script uses the same combination of directories and class files as Java. For non-Java programmers there's a more in-depth discussion of packages in appendix C, section C3. Next we turn our attention to the class content itself.

3.2 Developing classes

Classes are an integral part of object orientation (OO), encapsulating state and behavior for components in a larger system, allowing us to express software through the relationships linking its autonomous component parts. Object orientation has become an incredibly popular way of constructing software in recent years; both Java and its underlying JVM environment are heavily object-centric. No surprise, then, that JavaFX Script is also object-oriented.

JavaFX's implementation of OO is close, but not identical, to Java's. The key difference is that JavaFX Script permits something called *mixin* inheritance, which offers more power than Java's interfaces but stops short of full-blown multiple-class inheritance. In the coming subsections we'll explore the ins and outs of JFX classes and how to define, create, inherit, control, and manipulate them.

> **Changes to object orientation**
>
> Starting with JavaFX 1.2, full-blown multiple inheritance was dropped from the JavaFX Script language in favor of *mixins*. The former proved to have too many *edge case* issues, while the latter is apparently much cleaner. We'll look at how mixins work later in this chapter.

3.2.1 Scripts

In some languages source code files are just arbitrary containers for code. In other languages the compiler attaches significance to where the code is placed, as with the Java compiler's linking of class names with source files. In JavaFX Script the source file has a role in the language itself.

In JFX a single source file is known as a *script*, and scripts can have their own code, functions, and variables, distinct from a class. They can also be used to create an application's top-level code (see listing 3.3), the stuff that runs when your program starts. The code, in listing 3.3, lives in a file called "Examples2.fx".

Listing 3.3 Scripts and classes

```
package jfxia.chapter3;

def scriptVar:Integer = 99;      <-- Script variable
```

```
function scriptFunc() : Integer {
    def localVar:Integer = -1;
    return localVar;
}
```

Script function

```
println (
    "Examples2.scriptVar = {Examples2.scriptVar}\n"
    "Examples2.scriptFunc() = {Examples2.scriptFunc()}\n"
    "scriptVar = {scriptVar}\n"
    "scriptFunc() = {scriptFunc()}\n"
);
```

Bootstrap code

```
Examples2.scriptVar = 99
Examples2.scriptFunc() = -1
scriptVar = 99
scriptFunc() = -1
```

Listing 3.3 shows variables and functions in the script context. We saw plenty of examples of this type of code in chapter 2, where almost every listing used the script context for its code.

Script functions and variables live outside of any class. In many ways they behave like static methods and variables in Java. They can be accessed by using the script name as a prefix, like `Examples2.scriptVar` or `Examples2.scriptFunc()`, although when accessed from inside their own script (as listing 3.3 shows) the prefix can be omitted. They are visible to all code inside the current script, including classes. External visibility (outside the script) is controlled by *access modifiers*, which we'll study later in this chapter.

When the JavaFX compiler runs, it turns each script into a bytecode class (plus an interface, but we won't worry about implementation details here!). The script context functions and variables effectively become what Java would term static methods and variables in the class, but the script context can also contain loose code that isn't inside a function. What happens to this code?

It gets bundled up and executed if we run the script. In effect, it becomes Java's `public static main()` method. In listing 3.3 the `println()` will run if we launch the class `jfxia.chapter3.Examples2` using the JavaFX runtime. There is one restriction on loose expressions: they can only be used in scripts with no externally visible variables, functions, or classes. This is another *access modifiers* issue that will be explained later in this chapter.

Now that you've seen scripts in action, it's about time we looked at some class examples.

3.2.2 Class definition (class, def, var, function, this)

Creating new classes is an important part of object orientation, and true to form the JavaFX Script syntax boasts its trademark brevity. In this section we'll forgo mention of inheritance for now, concentrating instead on the basic format of a class, its data, and its behavior.

We've seen script context variables and functions in the last section (and last chapter too), and their class equivalents are no different. The official JFX language documentation refers to them as *instance variables* and *instance functions*, because they are accessed via a class instance (an object of the class type), so we'll stick to that terminology. To make the following prose flow more readily I'll sometimes refer to functions and variables using the combining term *members*, as in "script members" or "instance members."

Listing 3.4 defines a music track with three variables and two functions.

Listing 3.4 Class definition, with variables and functions

```
class Track {              <-- Track class
    var title:String;
    var artist:String;
    var time:Duration;                                 Instance variables

    function sameTrack(t:Track) : Boolean {
        return (t.title.equals(this.title) and
            t.artist.equals(this.artist));                Instance function
    }

    override function toString() : String {
        return '"{title}" by "{artist}" : '
            '{time.toMinutes() as Integer}m '
            '{time.toSeconds() mod 60 as Integer}s';      Another instance function
    }
}

var song:Track = Track {
    title: "Special"
    artist: "Garbage"                                  Declaring a new object from Track
    time: 220s
};
println(song);
```

```
"Special" by "Garbage" : 3m 40s
```

Note that JavaFX Script uses the same naming conventions as Java: class names begin with a capital letter, function and variable names do not. Both use camel case to form names from multiple words. You don't have to stick to these rules, but it helps make your code readable to other programmers.

The `title`, `artist`, and `time` are the variables that objects of type `Track` will have, the instance variables. Just like script variables, they can be assigned initial values, although the three examples in listing 3.4 all use defaults.

Functions in JFX classes are defined using the keyword `function`, followed by the function's name, a list of parameters, and their type in parentheses, followed by a colon and the return type (where `Void` means no return). There are two functions in listing 3.4: the first accepts another `Track` and checks whether it references the same song as the current object; the second constructs a `String` to represent this song.

The `toString()` function has the keyword `override` prefixing its definition. This is a requirement of JavaFX Script's inheritance mechanism, which we'll look at later this chapter. As with Java, all objects in JavaFX Script have a `toString()` function. Just

> **Properties: what's in a name?**
>
> Although the JavaFX Script documentation prefers the formal term *instance variables*, sometimes public class variables are referred to as *properties*. In programming, a property is a class element whose read/write syntax superficially resembles a variable, but with code that runs on each access. The result is much cleaner code than, for example, Java's verbose getter/setter method calls (although the function is the same).
>
> JavaFX Script variables can be bound to functions controlling their value, and triggers may run when their value changes. Yet binds and triggers are not intended as a property syntax. The real reason JavaFX Script's instance variables are sometimes called properties likely has more to do with JFX's declarative syntax giving the same clean code feel as the *real* properties found in languages like C#.

like Java, this function is called automatically whenever the compiler encounters an object in circumstances that require a `String`. So `println(song)` is silently translated by the compiler into `println(song.toString())`.

The keyword `this` can be used inside the class to refer to the current object, although its use can usually be inferred, as the `toString()` function demonstrates. A class's instance members are accessible to all code inside the class, and the enclosing script via objects of the class. External access (outside the script) is controlled by access modifiers (discussed later).

Once we've defined our class, we can create objects from it. We'll look at different ways of doing that in the next section, but just to complete our example I've included a sneak preview at the tail of listing 3.4. In the code, `song` is created as an object of type `Track`. We didn't strictly need to specify the type after `song` (*type inference* would work), but since this is your first proper class example, I thought it wouldn't hurt to go that extra mile.

Before we move on, some bits and pieces need extra attention. Take a look at the source code in listing 3.5.

Listing 3.5 A closer look at functions

```
function doesReturn() : String {
    "Return this";
}
function doesNotReturn() {
    var discarded = doesReturn();
}
```

There are a couple of things to note in listing 3.5. First, the `doesNotReturn()` function fails to declare its return type. It seems that explicitly declaring the return type is unnecessary when the function doesn't return anything—`Void` is assumed.

Second, and far more important, shouldn't `doesReturn()` have a `return` keyword in there somewhere? Recall that JavaFX Script is an expression language, and most of its code constructs *give out* a result. Thus, the last expression of a function can be used for the return value, even if the `return` keyword itself is missing.

3.2.3 Object declaration (init, postinit, isInitialized(), new)

We saw an example of creating an object from a class in the previous section. Many other object-oriented languages call a constructor, often via a keyword such as `new`, but JavaFX Script objects have no constructors, preferring its distinctive declarative syntax.

By invoking what the JFX documentation snappily calls the *object literal* syntax, we can declaratively create new objects. Listing 3.6 shows how. Simply state the class name, open curly braces, list each instance variable you want to give an initial value to (using its name and value separated by a colon), and don't forget the closing curly braces. (The source file for listing 3.6 is SpaceShip.fx.)

Listing 3.6 Object declaration, using declarative syntax or the `new` keyword

```
package jfxia.chapter3;

def UNKNOWN_DRIVE:Integer = 0;          | Script
def WARP_DRIVE:Integer = 1;             | variables

class SpaceShip {
    var name:String;
    var crew:Integer;
    var canTimeTravel:Boolean;
    var drive:Integer = SpaceShip.UNKNOWN_DRIVE;

    init {
        println("Building: {name}");
        if(not isInitialized(crew))
            println("  Warning: no crew!");
    }
    postinit {
        if(drive==WARP_DRIVE)
            println("  Engaging warp drive");
    }
}

def ship1 = SpaceShip {
    name:"Starship Enterprise"
    crew:400
    drive:SpaceShip.WARP_DRIVE
    canTimeTravel:false
};

def ship2 = SpaceShip {
    name:"The TARDIS" ; crew:1 ; canTimeTravel:true
};

def ship3 = SpaceShip{ name:"Thunderbird 5" };

def ship4 = new SpaceShip();
ship4.name="The Liberator";
ship4.crew=7;
ship4.canTimeTravel=false;
```

Annotations: class SpaceShip block — Our class, including init / postinit blocks; ship1 — Declarative syntax; ship2 — Again, declarative syntax; ship3 — Only name set; ship4 — Java-style syntax

```
Building: Starship Enterprise
  Engaging warp drive
Building: The TARDIS
Building: Thunderbird 5
  Warning: no crew!
Building:
  Warning: no crew!
```

We create four objects: the first three using the JavaFX Script syntax and the final one using a Java-style syntax.

From the first three examples you'll note how JFX uses the colon notation, allowing us to set any available variable on the object as part of its creation. This way of explicitly writing out objects is what's referred to as an *object literal*. The second example uses a more compact layout: multiple assignments per line, separated by semicolons.

Before looking at the third example, we need to consider the `init` and `postinit` blocks inside the class. As you may have guessed, these run when an object is created. The sequence of events is as follows:

1. The virgin object is created.
2. The Java superclass default constructor is called.
3. The object literal's instance variable values are computed *but not set*.
4. The instance variables of the JavaFX superclass are set.
5. The instance variables of this class are now set, in lexical order.
6. The `init` block of each class in the object's class hierarchy is called, if present, starting from the top of the hierarchy. The object is now considered initialized.
7. The `postinit` block of each class in the object's hierarchy is called, if present, starting from the top of the hierarchy.

The `isInitialized()` built-in function allows us to test whether a given variable has been explicitly set. In our third example only the `name` variable is set in the object literal, so the warning message tells us that Thunderbird 5 has no crew (which, in itself, might demand the attention of International Rescue!). Conveniently, `isInitialized()` isn't fooled by the fact that `crew`, as a value type, will have a default (unassigned) value of 0.

The `isInitalized()` function is handy for knowing whether an object literal bothered to set an instance variable, so we can assign appropriate initial values to those variables it missed. Alternatively you could provide multiple means of configuring an object, like separate `lengthCm` and `lengthInches` variables, and detect which was used.

Moving on to the fourth example, you'll note that it looks like the way we create new object instances in Java. Indeed, that's intentional. There may be times when we are forced to instantiate a Java object using a specific constructor; the `new` syntax allows us to do just that. But `new` can be used on any class, including JavaFX Script classes; however, we should resist that temptation. The `new` syntax should be used only when JavaFX Script's declarative syntax will not work (the example is *bad practice*!)

Because the fourth object's instance variables don't get set until after the object is created, the `Building` message has an empty `name` and the `crew` warning is triggered.

> **JavaFX Script and semicolons**
>
> We touched on the issue of semicolons in the previous text. As in Java, semicolons are used to terminate expressions, but the JavaFX Script compiler seems particularly liberal about when a semicolon is necessary. When we meet ternary expressions in section 3.3.3, we'll see an example of where they cannot be used, but other than that there's apparently little enforcement of where they *must* be used. It seems when the compiler can infer the end of a construct using a closing brace or whitespace alone, it is happy to do so.
>
> For the purposes of this book's source code, I'm adopting a general style of adding in semicolons at appropriate places, even if they can be omitted. You can drop them from your own code if you want, but I'm keeping them in the sample code to provide both clarity and familiarity.

3.2.4 Object declaration and sequences

There's nothing special about listing 3.7. It simply pulls together the object-creation syntax we saw previously with the sequence syntax we witnessed last chapter. It's worth an example on its own, as this mixing of objects and sequences crops up frequently in JavaFX programming.

Listing 3.7 creates two `Track` objects inside a sequence (note the `Track[]` type). To run this code you need the `Track` class we saw in listing 3.4.

Listing 3.7 Sequence declaration

```
var playlist:Track[] = [
    Track {
        title: "Special"
        artist: "Garbage"
        time: 220s
    } ,
    Track {
        title: "End of the World..."
        artist: "REM"
        time: 245s
    }
];
println(playlist.toString());
```

toString() could be omitted

```
[ "Special" by "Garbage" : 3m 40s, "End of the World..."
➥ by "REM" : 4m 5s ]
```

Instead of a boring list of comma-separated numbers or strings, the sequence contains object literal declarations between its square brackets. For readability I've used only two tracks in `playlist`, but the sequence could hold as many as you want—although be careful, the JavaFX compiler may issue warnings if you attempt to add anything by Rick Astley.

3.2.5 Class inheritance (abstract, extends, override)

One of the most important tenets of object orientation is *subclassing*, the ability of a class to inherit fields and behavior from another. By defining classes in terms of one another, we make our objects amenable to *polymorphism*, allowing them to be referenced as more than one type. (For readers unfamiliar with terms like *polymorphism*, there's a beginners' guide to object orientation in appendix C, section C5).

Java programmers may be surprised to learn that JavaFX Script deviates from the Java model for object orientation. As well as supporting Java's single inheritance, JavaFX Script supports *mixin inheritance*. We'll look at mixins a little later; first we need to get familiar with the basics of single inheritance from a JavaFX point of view. The following example (listings 3.8, 3.9, and 3.10) has been broken up into parts, which we'll explore piece by piece.

Listing 3.8 Class inheritance, part 1

```
import java.util.Date;

abstract class Animal {
    var life:Integer = 0;                   Instance
    var birthDate:Date;                     variables

    function born() : Void {
        this.birthDate = Date{};
    }                                            Instance
                                                 functions, new
    function getName() : String {                for this class
        "Animal"
    }

    override function toString() : String {
        "{this.getName()}  Life: {life}  "                   Instance function,
            "Bday: {%te birthDate} {%tb birthDate}";         inherited
    }
}
```

Listing 3.8 shows a simple Animal class. It's home to just a life gauge and a date of birth, plus three functions: born() for when the object is just created, getName() to get the animal type as a String, and toString() for getting a printable description of the object. This is the base class onto which we'll build in the following parts of the code.

The abstract keyword prefixing the class definition tells the compiler that objects of this class cannot be created directly. Sometimes we need a class to be only a base (parent) class to other classes. We can't create Animal objects directly, but we can subclass Animal and create objects of the subclass. Thanks to polymorphism, we can even assign these subclass objects to a variable of type Animal, although handling objects as type Animal is not the same as actually creating an Animal object itself. We'll see an example of this shortly.

Our second chunk of code (listing 3.9) inherits the first by using the extends keyword after its name followed by the parent class name, in this case Animal. As you may expect, this makes Mammal a type of Animal.

Listing 3.9 Class inheritance, part 2

```
class Mammal extends Animal {                         <-- Subclass of Animal
    override function getName() : String {           Overrides the
        "Mammal"                                      one in Animal
    }

    function giveBirth() : Mammal {
        var m  = Mammal { life:100 };               Brand-new
        m.born();                                   instance
        return m;                                   method
    }
}
```

The class overrides the getName() method to provide its own answer, which explains the override keyword prefixing the function. The extra keyword is required at the start of any function that overrides another; it doesn't do anything other than help document the code and make it harder for bugs to creep into our programs. If you leave it off, you'll get a compiler warning. If you include it when you shouldn't, you'll get a compiler error.

You should use the override keyword even when subclassing Java classes, which is why you may have spotted it on the toString() function of Animal, in listing 3.8. All objects in the JVM are descendants of java.lang.Object, which means all JavaFX objects are too, even if they don't explicitly extend any class. Thus toString(), which originates in Object, needs the override keyword.

The Animal class adds an extra function for giving birth to a new Mammal. The new function creates a fresh Mammal, sets its initial life value, and then calls born(). The born() function is inherited from Animal, along with the toString() function.

So far, so good; how about another Animal subclass? Take a look at listing 3.10.

Listing 3.10 Class inheritance, part 3

```
class Reptile extends Animal {
    override var life =  200;                    <-- Override inherited initial value

    override function getName() : String {       Overrides the
        "Reptile"                                 function in Animal
    }

    function layEgg() : Egg {
        var e = Egg {
            baby: Reptile {}              Create a Reptile
        };                                inside an Egg
        e;
    }
}
```

```
class Egg {
    var baby:Reptile;
    function toString() : String {
         return "Egg => Baby:{baby}";
    }
}
```

The Egg class itself

Again we have a subclass of Animal, this time called Reptile, with its own overridden implementation of getName() and its own new function. The new function in question creates and returns a fourth type of object, Egg, housing a new Reptile.

At the head of the Reptile class is an overridden instance variable. Why do we need to override an instance variable? Think about it: overriding an instance function redefines it, replacing its (code) contents. Likewise, overriding an instance variable redefines its contents, giving it a new initial value. This means any Reptile object literal failing to set life will get a value of 200, not the 0 value inherited from Animal.

Before we move on, check out the use of JFX's declarative syntax in layEgg(). The Reptile object is literally constructed inside the Egg. We could have done it longhand (the Java way), first creating a Reptile, then creating the Egg, then plugging one into the other, but the JavaFX Script syntax allows us far more elegance.

Now finally we need code to test our new objects. Listing 3.11 does just that.

Listing 3.11 Virtual functions demonstrated

```
def mammal = Mammal { life:150  ; birthDate: Date{} };
def animal:Animal = mammal.giveBirth();
println(mammal);                          // First output line
println(animal);                          // Second output line
println(animal.getName());                // Third output line
def reptile = Reptile { life:175  ; birthDate: Date{} };
def egg = reptile.layEgg();
println(reptile);                         // Fourth output line
println(egg);                             // Final output line
```

```
Mammal  Life: 150  Bday: 3 Aug
Mammal  Life: 100  Bday: 3 Aug
Mammal
Reptile  Life: 175  Bday: 3 Aug
Egg => Baby:Reptile  Life: 200  Bday: null null
```

In listing 3.11 we create two Mammal objects, but here's the clever part: we store one of them as an Animal. Even though Animal is abstract and we can't create Animal objects themselves, we can still reference its subclasses, such as Mammal, as Animal objects. That's the power of polymorphism.

Here's a quiz question: after printing both Mammal objects, we call getName() on the object typed as an Animal. The getName() function exists in both Mammal and its parent *super*class, Animal. So what will it return: "Mammal," which is the type it truly is, or "Animal," the type it's being stored as?

The answer is "Mammal." Because JavaFX functions are *virtual*, the subclass redefinition of getName() replaces the original in the parent class, even when the object is referenced by way of its parent type.

The last output line shows the `Reptile` inside the `Egg`. But why is its output different from that of the other `Reptile` object? Well, `layEgg()` never calls `born()`, so `birthDate` is null. This is what causes the null values when we print out the day and month. And because `life` is not set either, the overridden initial value of 200 is used.

By the way, before we move on I do want to acknowledge to any women reading this that I fully acknowledge childbirth is not as painless as creating a new object and calling a function on it! Likewise, similar sentiments to any reptiles that happen to be reading this.

3.2.6 Mixin inheritance (mixin)

Mixin, a portmanteau of *mix* and *in*, is the name of a *lightweight* inheritance model that complements the class inheritance we've already seen. In JavaFX Script each class can be subclassed from one parent at a time; this neatly sidesteps potential conflicts and ambiguities between multiple parents but creates a bit of a straitjacket. Mixins allow a class to acquire the characteristics of another type (a mixin class) without full-blown multiple inheritance.

Changes to JavaFX Script inheritance

Early JavaFX Script compilers supported full-blown multiple inheritance; however, JavaFX 1.2 heralded a shift toward mixins and introduced the `mixin` keyword to the language. The intent was to remove some of the edge-case complications and performance costs caused by multiple inheritance, while keeping much of its benefit.

Each JavaFX Script class can inherit at most one Java or JavaFX class but any number of Java interfaces and/or JavaFX mixins. In turn, each JavaFX mixin can inherit from any number of Java interfaces and/or JavaFX mixins. A mixin provides a list of functions and variables any inheriting class must have, plus optional default content. A class that inherits a mixin is called a *mixee* (because it's the recipient of a mixin).

The process works like this: if the mixee extends another regular class, the variables and functions (the class *members*) in this superclass are inherited as per usual, before the *mixing* process begins. Then each mixin class is considered in turn, as they appear on the `extends` list (we'll look at the syntax in a moment). If the *mixee* omits a function or a variable, rather than flag a compiler error, the missing content is automatically copied in ("mixed in") to the mixee, almost as if it had been cut and pasted. Mixin variables and functions can also carry default content—initial values and function bodies—and that too will be mixed in if absent from the mixee.

This is a lot to take in at once, so let's work through the process by way of an example. Listing 3.12 shows code that might be used in a role-playing game.

Listing 3.12 Mixins

```
mixin class Motor {
    public var distance:Integer = 0;

    public function move(dir:Integer,dist:Integer) : Void {
        distance+=dist;
    }
}

mixin class Weapon {
    public var bullets:Integer
        on replace { println("Bullets: {bullets}"); }
    }

    init {
        reload();
    }

    public function fire(dir:Integer) : Void {
        if(bullets>0)  bullets--;
    }

    public abstract function reload() : Void;
}

class Robot extends Motor,Weapon {
    override var bullets = 1000
        on replace { println("Bang"); }

    override function reload() : Void {
        bullets=100;
    }
}

class Android extends Robot , Weapon,Motor {
}
```

Mixin for movement

Mixin for weapons

Inherits both mixins

Weapon/Motor are redundant

Here we have two mixin classes and two *regular* classes. The `Robot` and `Android` classes might be character types, while the `Motor` and `Weapon` mixins might represent traits characters can have. As you can see, the `mixin` keyword prefixes a class definition to flag it as a mixin. Mixins are then inherited by listing them after the `extends` keyword, separated by commas. To implement mixin content in a mixee, we use the same syntax as for overriding class members in regular inheritance, including the `override` keyword.

Using the code in listing 3.12 for reference, the process of mixing would be as follows:

1 The `Robot` class does not inherit from any superclass, so we start from a clean slate, so to speak.
2 Because `Motor` appears first on the `extends` list, it's first to be considered. Our `Robot` class implements neither a `distance` variable nor a `move()` function, so

the default implementations are inherited, including their value/body. (If you can't be bothered to provide your own, you get one for free!)

3 The `Weapon` mixin is considered next. It specifies one variable and two functions: default content is provided for `bullets` and `fire()`, but `reload()` is abstract, forcing any potential mixee to provide its own body implementation. The `Robot` class provides implementations of `bullet` and `reload()`, but `fire()` is absent, so `Weapon`'s default is inherited.

4 `Robot` is complete, with the content of `Robot`, `Motor`, and `Weapon` mixed to create one class. The result can be successfully cast to any of these three types.

5 The `Android` class extends `Robot`, and as such its inheritance of `Weapon` and `Motor` has no effect—all the necessary members are already present. Even changing the order on the `extends` line cannot alter anything. `Android` should probably be amended to remove `Motor` and `Weapon` from its `extends` list—although they don't do any harm, their presence is potentially confusing.

You'll note from the code that mixins can contain `init` (and `postinit`) blocks, and their variables also support `on replace` triggers (we haven't looked at triggers yet, so you might want to bookmark this page and come back to it). How do these work when the mixee is used?

In the case of `init` blocks, when any object is created its class's superclass is initialized first (which in turn initializes its own superclass, creating a chain reaction up the class hierarchy), and then the class itself is initialized. Initialization involves the `init` blocks of each mixin being run in the order in which they appeared on the `extends` list, and then the class's own `init` block being run. The `postinit` blocks are then run, using the same order (mixins first, class last).

The effect for `on replace` blocks is similar, with triggers farther up the inheritance tree running before those in the class itself. In our example both `Weapon.bullets` and `Robot.bullets` have a trigger block (the latter complements, rather than overrides, the former). When `bullets` is assigned, the `on replace` block for `Weapon.bullets` runs first, followed by the one in `Robot.bullets`.

We can quickly mop up some of the remaining mixin questions with a mini-FAQ:

- *Q*: Can I declare an object using a mixin class?
  A: Not directly—mixins are effectively abstract. But you can create the object using its regular class type and then cast to one of its mixin types.
- *Q*: What's the relationship between mixins and Java interfaces?
  A: Java's interfaces are effectively viewed as mixins with only abstract functions.
- *Q*: Do I have to fully implement all the members of every mixin I inherit?
  A: No, but if any of the functions still have no bodies after the inheritance process (they are still abstract), the resulting class must be declared abstract. (Mixin classes themselves are, effectively, abstract.)
- *Q*: Can I use the `super` and `this` keywords in a mixin function body?
  A: Yes. They work much like they do with regular classes.

- *Q*: Can I use `super` in a mixee, in reference to a mixin's default function body?
  A: Yes. If you provide your own function body, you can still reference the default one you overrode from the mixin using `super`.
- *Q*: What if mixin member names clash with existing mixee member names?
  A: If they are compatible with the existing members, then nothing happens—they're considered to already be inherited. But if they are incompatible (like a variable having a different type than its namesake), a compiler error results.
- *Q*: What if two mixins have identical members, with different defaults?
  A: Mixin inheritance follows the order of the extends list—the earliest mixin wins!
- Q: If two mixins have identical functions, which does `super` reference?
  A: When a mixee provides its own implementation of a function that appears in more than one of its mixins, using `super` *to reference the original isn't sufficient. To specify precisely which mixin we're referring to, we can use its class name instead, thus,* `Eggs.scramble()` *and* `SecretMessage.scramble()`.

That concludes our look at class inheritance; you may wish to revisit it (particularly the stuff on mixins) once you've read through the remainder of this chapter, but for now let's push on with our exploration of the JavaFX Script language.

3.2.7 Function types

Function types in JavaFX are incredibly useful. Not only do they provide a neat way of creating event handlers (see *anonymous functions*, later in this chapter) but they allow us to plug bits of bespoke code into existing software algorithms. Functions in JavaFX Script are *first-class objects*, meaning we can have variables of function type and can pass functions into other functions as parameters. Listing 3.13 shows a simple example.

Listing 3.13 Function types

```
var func : function(:String):Boolean;
func = testFunc;
println( func("True") );
println( func("False") );

function testFunc(s:String):Boolean {
    return (s.equalsIgnoreCase("true"));
}
```

```
true
false
```

Listing 3.13 centers on the function at its tail, `testFunc()`, which accepts a `String` and returns a `Boolean`.

First we define a new variable, `func`, with a strange-looking type. The variable will hold a reference to our function, so its type reflects the function signature. The keyword `function` is followed by the parameter list in parenthesis (variable names are optional) and then a colon and the return type. In listing 3.13 the type is `function(:String):Boolean`, a function that accepts a single `String` and returns a

Boolean. We can assign to this variable any function that matches that signature, and indeed in the very next line we do just that when we assign testFunc to func, using what looks like a standard variable assignment. We can now call testFunc() by way of our variable reference to it, which the code does twice just to prove it works.

Passing functions to other functions works along similar lines (see listing 3.14). The receiving function uses a function signature for its parameters, just like the variable in listing 3.13.

Listing 3.14 Passing functions as parameters to other functions

```
function manip(s:String ,
    f:function(:String):String) : Void {      Function with
    println("{s} = {f(a)}");                   parameter function
}

function m1(s:String) : String {
    s.toLowerCase();
}                                              Functions we pass
                                               into manip()
function m2(s:String) : String {
    s.substring(0,4);
}

manip("JavaFX" , m1);
manip("JavaFX" , m2);

JavaFX = javafx
JavaFX = Java
```

The first function in listing 3.14, manip(), accepts two parameters and returns Void. The first parameter is of type String, and the second is of type function(:String):String, which in plain English translates as a function that accepts a String and returns a String. Fortunately we happen to have two such functions, m1() and m2(), on hand. Both accept and return a String, with basic manipulation in between. We call manip() twice, passing in a String and one of our functions each time. The manip() function invokes the parameter function with the String and prints the result. A simple example, perhaps, yet one that adequately demonstrates the effect.

Being able to reference functions like this is quite a powerful feature. Imagine a list class capable of being sorted or filtered by a plug-in-able function, for example. But this isn't the end of our discussion. In the next section we continue to look at functions, this time with a twist.

3.2.8 Anonymous functions

We've just seen how we can pass functions into other functions and assign them to variables, but what application does this have? The most obvious one is callbacks, or *event handlers* as they're more commonly known in the Java world.

In a GUI environment we frequently need to respond to events originating from the user: when they click a button or slide a scrollbar we need to know. Typically we register a piece of code with the class generating the event, to be called when that event happens. JavaFX Script's function types, with their ability to point at code, fit the bill perfectly. But having to create script or class functions for each event handler is a pain, especially because in most cases they're used in only one place. If only there were a shortcut syntax for one-time function creation. Well, unsurprisingly, there is. And listing 3.15 shows us how.

Listing 3.15 Anonymous functions

```
import java.io.File;

class FileSystemWalker {
    var root:String;
    var extension:String;
    var action:function(:File):Void;

    function go() { walk(new File(root)); }

    function walk(dir:File) : Void {
        var files:File[] = dir.listFiles();
        for(f:File in files) {
            if(f.isDirectory()) {
                walk(f);
            }
            else if(f.getName().endsWith(extension)) {
                action(f);
            }
        }
    }
}

var walker = FileSystemWalker {
    root: FX.getArguments()[0];
    extension: ".png";
    action: function(f:File) {
        println("Found {f.getName()}");        Anonymous function
    }
};
walker.go();
```

The class `FileSystemWalker` has three variables and two functions. One of the variables is a function type, called `action`, which can point to functions of type `function(:File):Void`—or, in plain English, any function that accepts a `java.io.File` object and returns nothing.

The most important function is `walk()`, which recursively walks a directory tree looking for files that end with the desired `extension`, calling whichever function has been assigned to `action` for each match, passing the file in as a parameter. The other function, `go()`, merely acts as a convenience to kick-start the recursive process from a given `root` directory. So far, nothing new! But it starts to get interesting when we see how `walker`, an object of type `FileSystemWalker`, is created.

In its declaration `walker` assigns the `root` directory to the first parameter passed in on the command line—so when you run the code, make sure you nominate a directory!

(The `FX.getArguments()` function is how we get at the command-line arguments, by the way.) The `extension` is set to PNG files, so `walk()` will act only on filenames with that ending. But look at the way `action` is assigned.

Rather than pointing to a function elsewhere, the `action` code merely defines a nameless (anonymous) function of the required type right there as part of the assignment. This is an *anonymous function*, a define-and-forget piece of code assigned to a variable of function type. It allows us to plug short snippets of code into existing classes without the inconvenience of having to fill up our scripts with fully fleshed-out functions, making it ideal for quick and easy event handling.

3.2.9 Access modifiers (package, protected, public, public-read, public-init)

We round off our look at classes by examining how to keep secrets. Classes encapsulate related variables and functions into self-contained objects, but an object becomes truly self-contained when it can lock out third parties from its implementation detail.

JavaFX's access modifiers are tailored to suit the JavaFX Script language and its declarative syntax. Access modifiers can be applied to script members (functions and variables at script level), instance members (functions and variables inside a class), and classes themselves. They cannot be used with, indeed make no sense for, local variables inside functions. (See listing 3.3 for an example of different types of variables.)

There are four basic modes of visibility in JavaFX Script, outlined in table 3.1.

Table 3.1 Basic access modifiers

Modifier keyword	Visibility effect
(default)	Visible only within the enclosing script. This default mode (with no associated keyword) is the least visible of all access modes.
`package`	Visible within the enclosing script and any script or class within the same package.
`protected`	Visible within the enclosing script, any script or class within the same package, and subclasses from other packages.
`public`	Visible to anyone, anywhere.

There are two additive access modifiers, which may be combined with the four modes in table 3.1—modifiers to the modifiers, if you like. They are designed to complement JavaFX Script's declarative (object literal) syntax. As such, they apply only to `var` variables (capable of being modified) and cannot be used with functions, classes, or any `def` variables. Table 3.2 details them.

Table 3.2 Additive access modifiers

Modifier keyword	Visibility effect
`public-read`	Adds public read access to the basic mode.
`public-init`	Adds public read access and object literal write access to the basic mode.

The `public-read` modifier grants readability to a variable, while writing is still controlled by its basic mode. The `public-init` modifier also grants public writing, but only during object declaration. Writing at other times is still controlled by the basic mode.

Each modifier solves a particular problem, so the clearest way to explain their use is with a task-centric mini-FAQ, like the one up next:

- *Q*: I've written a script/class and don't want other scripts messing with my functions or variables, as I might change them at a later date. Can I do this?
  A: Stick with the default access mode. It gives you complete freedom with your variables and functions because no other script can interact with them.
- *Q*: I'm writing a package. Some functions and variables need to be accessible across scripts and classes of the package, but I don't want other programmers getting access to them. Is this possible?
  A: Sure, the `package` *access modifier will do that for you.*
- *Q*: Some of my class's functions and variables would be useful to authors of subclasses, but I don't want to open them up to the world. How is this done?
  A: Check out the `protected` *access modifier; it grants package visibility, plus any subclasses from outside the package.*
- *Q*: I have a class with some variables I'd like to make readable by everyone, but I still want to control write access to them. Can JavaFX Script do this?
  A: Indeed! Just combine `public-read` *with one of the four basic modes.*
- *Q*: I'd like to control writing to my instance variables, except when the instance is first created. Is this possible?
  A: Funny you should ask. Just add `public-init` *to one of the four basic modes, and your variables will become public writable when used from an object literal.*
- *Q*: So, why can't I use these additive modifiers with `def` variables?
  A: Common sense. A `public-read def` *would be the same as a* `public def`*, and a* `public-init def` *would be rather pointless.*

Enough questions, let's consider some actual source code (listing 3.16).

Listing 3.16 Access modifiers on a class

```
package jfxia.chapter3.access;

public class AccessTest {
    var sDefault:String;
    package var sPackage:String;
    protected var sProtected:String;
    public var sPublic:String;

    public-read var sPublicReadDefault:String;
    public-read package var sPublicReadPackage:String;
    public-init protected var sPublicInitProtected:String;

    init {
        println("sDefault = {this.sDefault}");
        println("sPackage = {this.sPackage}");
        println("sProtected = {this.sProtected}");
```

Basic modes (annotation for the four basic-mode variables)

Additive modes (annotation for the three public-read/public-init variables)

```
        println("sPublic = {this.sPublic}");
        println("sPublicReadDefault = "
            "{this.sPublicReadDefault}");
        println("sPublicReadPackage = "
            "{this.sPublicReadPackage}");
        println("sPublicInitProtected = "
            "{this.sPublicInitProtected}");
    }
}
```

Listing 3.16 shows a class with instance variables displaying various types of access visibility. Note that the class is in package `jfxia.chapter3.access`. To test it we need some further sample code such as in listing 3.17.

Listing 3.17 Testing access modifiers

```
package jfxia.chapter3;
import jfxia.chapter3.access.AccessTest;

def a:AccessTest = AccessTest {
    // ** sDefault has script only (default) access
    //sDefault: "set";

    // ** sPackage is not public; cannot be accessed
➥  from outside package
    //sPackage: "set";

    // ** sProtected has protected access
    //sProtected: "set";

    sPublic: "set";                                  <-- Always works

    // ** sPublicReadDefault has script only (default)
➥  initialization access
    //sPublicReadDefault: "set";

    // ** sPublicReadPackage has package initialization
➥  access
    //sPublicReadPackage: "set";

    sPublicInitProtected: "set";                     <-- Works during declaration
};

// ** sPublicInitProtected has protected write access
//a.sPublicInitProtected = "set2";                   <-- Fails outside declaration

def str:String = a.sPublicReadDefault;               <-- Read is okay

sDefault =
sPackage =
sProtected =
sPublic = set
sPublicReadDefault =
sPublicReadPackage =
sPublicInitProtected = set
```

Listing 3.17 tests the `AccessTest` class we saw in listing 3.16. It lives in a different package than `AccessTest`, so we can expect all manner of access problems. The script builds an instance of `AccessTest`, attempting to set each of its instance members. The lines that fail have been commented out, with the compilation error shown in a comment on the preceding line.

Of the seven variables, only two are successfully accessible during the object's declaration, one of which is the `public` variable allowing total unhindered access.

Keen eyes will have spotted that the `protected` variable cannot be assigned, but its `public-init protected` cousin can. The `public-init` modifier grants write access only during initialization—which is why a second assignment, outside the object literal, fails.

Also, note how the `public-read 'default'` variable has become read-only outside of its class.

So that's it for access modifiers. By sensibly choosing access modes we can create effective components, allowing other programmers to interact with them through clearly defined means, while protecting their inner implementation detail.

And so ends our discussion of classes. In the next section we begin studying familiar code constructs like conditions and loops, but with an expression language twist.

3.3 Flow control, using conditions

Conditions are a standard part of all programming languages. Without them we'd have straight line code, doing the same thing every time with zero regard for user input or other runtime stimuli. This would cut dramatically the number of bugs in our code but would ever so slightly render all software completely useless.

JavaFX Script's conditions behave in a not-too-dissimilar fashion to other languages, but the expression syntax permits one or two interesting tricks.

> **Use your imagination**
>
> The demonstration conditions in the following sections are somewhat contrived. Hard-coded values mean the same path is always followed each time the code is run. I *could* have written each example to accept some runtime *variable* (an external factor, not determinable at compile time) such that each path could be exercised. While this would add an element of *real-world-ness*, it would also make the code much longer, without adding any demonstration value. It goes without saying that I consider readers of this book to be intelligent enough to study each example and dry run in their heads how different data would activate the various paths through the code.

First let's look at some basic conditions.

3.3.1 Basic conditions (if, else)

We'll kick things off with a basic example (listing 3.18).

Listing 3.18 Conditions

```
var someValue = 99;

if(someValue==99) {
    println("Equals 99");
}
```

```
if(someValue >= 100) {
    println("100 or over");
}
else {
    println("Less than 100");
}

if(someValue < 0) {
    println("Negative");
}
else if(someValue > 0) {
    println("Positive");
}
else {
    println("Zero");
}
```

```
Equals 99
Less than 100
Positive
```

There are three condition examples in this code, all depending on the variable `someValue`. The first is a straight `if` block; its code is either run or it is not. The second adds an `else` block, which will run if its associated condition is false. The third adds another condition block, which is tested only if the first condition is false.

3.3.2 Conditions as expressions

So JavaFX's `if/elseif/else` construct is the same as that of countless other programming languages, but you'll recall mention of "interesting tricks"—let's look at listing 3.19.

Listing 3.19 Conditions as expressions

```
var negValue = -1;
var sign = if(negValue < 0) { "Negative"; }
    else if(negValue > 0) { "Positive"; }
    else { "Zero"; }
println("sign = {sign}");
```

```
sign = Negative
```

Your eyes do not deceive, we are indeed assigning from a condition!

The variable `sign` takes its value directly from the result of the condition that follows. It will acquire the value `"Positive"`, `"Negative"`, or `"Zero"`, depending on the outcome of the condition. How is this happening? Let's chant the mantra together, shall we? "JavaFX Script is an expression language! JavaFX Script is an expression language!"

JavaFX's conditions give out a result and thus can be used on the right-hand side of an assignment, or as part of a bind, or in any other situation in which a result is expected. Now perhaps you understand why we were able to use conditions directly inside formatted strings or to update bound variables.

3.3.3 Ternary expressions and beyond

Let's expand on this notion. In other languages there's a concept of a *ternary expression*, which consists of a condition followed by two results; the first is returned if the condition is true, the second if it is false. We can achieve the same thing via JavaFX Script's if/else, as shown in listing 3.20.

Listing 3.20 Ternary expressions

```
import java.lang.System;

var asHex = true;
System.out.printf (
    if(asHex) "Hex:%04x%n" else "Dec:%d%n" ,
    12345
);
```

```
Hex:3039
```

Depending on the value of isHex either the first or the second formatting string will be applied to the number 12345. Note the lack of curly braces and the absence of a closing semicolon in each block of the if/else. When used in a ternary sense, each part of the if construct should house just a single expression; semicolons and braces would be needed only for multiple expressions, which would not fit the ternary format. Any semicolon should therefore come at the end of the entire if/else construct.

Listing 3.21 shows something a little more ambitious.

Listing 3.21 Beyond ternary expressions

```
var mode = 2;
println (
    if(mode==0) "Yellow alert"
    else if(mode==1) "Orange alert"
    else if(mode==2) "Mauve alert"
    else "Red alert"
);
```

```
Mauve alert
```

Here we see the true power of conditions being expressions. What amounts to a *switch* construct is actually directly providing the parameter for a function call, without setting a variable first or wrapping itself in a function. Naturally because of our hard-coded mode, the alert will always be set to mauve. (Besides, as every Red Dwarf fan knows, red alert requires changing the light bulb!)

This idea of conditions having results is a powerful one, so let's push it to its logical (or should that be illogical?) conclusion, with listing 3.22.

Listing 3.22 Condition expressions taken to an extreme

```
import java.lang.System;

var rand = (System.currentTimeMillis() as Integer) mod 2;
var flag:Boolean = (rand == 0);
```

```
var ambiguous = if(flag) 99 else "Hello";

println("{rand}: flag={flag}, ambiguous={ambiguous} "
    "({ambiguous.getClass()})");
```

```
0: flag=true, ambiguous=99 (class java.lang.Integer )
1: flag=false, ambiguous=Hello (class java.lang.String)
```

Two different executions

Admittedly, when I first wrote this code, I expected a compiler error. None was forthcoming. This time we use not hard-coded values but a weak pseudorandom event to feed the decision logic. First we use a Java API method to get the POSIX time in milliseconds (the number of milliseconds elapsed since midnight, 1 January 1970), setting a variable called `flag` such that sometimes when we run the code the result will be true and other times false. Another variable, `ambiguous`, is then set depending on `flag`—if true it will be assigned an `Integer` and if false a `String`.

So the type of `ambiguous` is dependent on the path the code takes—I'm not sure I like this (and would strongly urge you not to make use of such ambiguous typing in your own code), but JFX seems to handle it without complaint.

Anyway, with that rather dangerous example, we'll leave conditions behind and move on to something else—loops.

3.4 Sequence-based loops

Loops are another staple of programming, allowing us to repeatedly execute a given section of code until a condition is met. In JavaFX Script loops are strongly associated with sequences, and like conditions they hold a trick or two when it comes to being treated as expressions.

3.4.1 Basic sequence loops (for)

Let's begin with listing 3.23; a basic example that introduces the `for` syntax.

Listing 3.23 Basic `for` loops

```
for(a in [1..3]) {
    for(b in [1..3]) {
        println("{a} x {b} = {a*b}");
    }
}
```

```
1 x 1 = 1
1 x 2 = 2
1 x 3 = 3
2 x 1 = 2
2 x 2 = 4
2 x 3 = 6
3 x 1 = 3
3 x 2 = 6
3 x 3 = 9
```

If you ever forget your three times table, now you have a convenient JavaFX program to print it for you—two loops, one inside the other, with a `println()` at the center of it all. Note how we tie the loop to a sequence, defined by a range, and then pull each element out into the loop variable.

3.4.2 For loops as expressions (indexof)

Now for something that exploits the expression language facilities; check out listing 3.24.

Listing 3.24 Sequence creation using `for` expressions

```
var cards =
    for(str in ["A",[2..10],"J","Q","K"]) {
        str.toString();
}
println(cards.toString());

cards =
    for(str in ["A",[2..10],"J","Q","K"])
        if(indexof str < 10) null else str.toString();
println(cards.toString());
```

```
[ A, 2, 3, 4, 5, 6, 7, 8, 9, 10, J, Q, K ]
[ J, Q, K ]
```

A `for` loop returns a sequence, and listing 3.24 shows us exploiting that fact by using a loop to construct a sequence of strings using `toString()` over a mixture of strings and integers. Each pass through the loop an element is plucked from the source sequence, converted into a string, and added to the destination sequence, `cards`. The loop variable becomes a `String` or an `Integer` depending on the element in the source sequence. Fortunately all variables in JavaFX Script inherit `toString()`.

If you ever need to know the index of an element during a `for` expression, `indexof` is your friend. The first element is 0, the second is 1, and so on. Null values are ignored when building sequences, so not every iteration through the loop need extend the sequence contents. The second part of listing 3.24 shows both these features in action.

3.4.3 Rolling nested loops into one expression

The loop syntax gives us an easy way to create loops within loops, allowing us, for example, to drill down to access sequences inside objects within sequences. In listing 3.25 we use a sequence of `SoccerTeam` objects, each containing a sequence of player names.

Listing 3.25 Nested loops within one `for` expression

```
class SoccerTeam {
    public-init var name: String;            // A soccer
    public-init var players: String[];       // team class
}

var fiveAsideLeague:SoccerTeam[] = [
    SoccerTeam {                               // First soccer
        name: "Java United"                    // team object
```

```
        players: [ "Smith","Jones","Brown",
            "Johnson","Schwartz" ]
    } ,
    SoccerTeam {
        name: ".Net Rovers"
        players: [ "Davis","Taylor","Booth",
            "May","Ballmer" ]
    }
];

for(t in fiveAsideLeague, p in t.players) {
    println("{t.name}: {p}");
}
```

First soccer team object

Second soccer team object

Print players within teams

```
Java United: Smith
Java United: Jones
Java United: Brown
Java United: Johnson
Java United: Schwartz
.Net Rovers: Davis
.Net Rovers: Taylor
.Net Rovers: Booth
.Net Rovers: May
.Net Rovers: Ballmer
```

First we define our team class; then we create a sequence of two five-on-a-side teams, each team with a name and five players. The meat of the example comes at the end, when we use a single `for` statement to print each player from each team. Each level of the loop is separated by a comma. We have the outer part that walks over the teams, and we have the inner part that walks over each player within each team. It means we can unroll the whole structure with just one `for` expression instead of multiple nested expressions.

3.4.4 Controlling flow within for loops (break, continue)

JavaFX Script supports both the `continue` and `break` functionality of other languages in its `for` loops. Continues skip on to the next iteration of the loop without executing the remainder of any code in the body. Breaks terminate the loop immediately. Unlike with other languages, JavaFX Script breaks do not support a label to point to a specific `for` loop to break out of. Listing 3.26 provides an example.

Listing 3.26 Flow control within `for`, with `break` and `continue`

```
var total=0;
for(i in [0..50]) {
    if(i<5) { continue; }
    else if (i>10) { break; }
    total+=i;
}
println(total);
```

```
45
```

The loop runs, supposedly, from 0 to 50. However, we ignore the first five passes by using a `continue`, and we force the loop to terminate with a `break` when it gets beyond 10. In effect `total` is updated only for 5 to 10, which explains the result (5 + 6 + 7 + 8 + 9 + 10 = 45).

3.4.5 Filtering for expressions (where)

There's one final trick we should cover when it comes to loops (see listing 3.27): applying a filter to selectively pull out only the elements of the source sequence we want.

Listing 3.27 Filtered `for` expression

```
var divisibleBy7 =
    for(i in [0..50] where (i mod 7)==0) i;
println(divisibleBy7.toString());
```

```
[ 0, 7, 14, 21, 28, 35, 42, 49 ]
```

The loop in the example code runs over each element in a sequence from 0 to 50, but the added `where` clause filters out any loop value that isn't evenly divisible by 7. The result is the sequence `divisibleBy7`, whose contents we print. (Incidentally, in this particular example, since all we wanted to do was add the filtered elements into a new sequence, we could have used the predicate syntax we saw last chapter.)

That's it for sequence-based loops, at least for now. We'll again touch briefly on sequences when we visit triggers. In the next section we'll consider a more conventional type of loop.

3.5 Repeating code with while loops (while, break, continue)

As well as sequence-centric `for` loops, JavaFX Script supports `while` loops, in a similar fashion to other languages. The syntax is fairly simple, so we begin, as ever, with an example. Cast an eye over listing 3.28.

Listing 3.28 Basic `while` loops

```
var i=0;
var total=0;
while(i<10) {
    total+=i;
    i++;
}
println(total);

i=0;
total=0;
while(i<50) {
    if(i<5) { i++; continue; }
    else if (i>10) { break; }
    total+=i;
    i++;
}
println(total);
```

```
45
45
```

Two while loops are shown in listing 3.28, the first a simple loop, the second involving break and continue logic. To create a while loop we use the keyword while, followed by a terminating condition in parentheses and the body of the loop in curly braces. The first loop walks over the numbers 0 to 9, by way of the variable i, totaling each loop value as it goes. The result of totaling all the values 0 to 9 is 45.

The second loop performs a similar feat, walking over the values 0 to 50—or does it? The continue keyword is triggered for all values under 5, and the break statement is triggered when the loop exceeds 10. The former will cause the body of the loop to be skipped, jumping straight to the next iteration, while the latter causes the loop to be aborted. The result is that only the values 5 to 10 are totaled, also giving the answer 45.

As with for loops, break statements do not support a label pointing to which loop (of several nested) to break out of.

3.6 Act on variable and sequence changes, using triggers

Triggers allow us to assign some code to run when a given variable is modified. It's a simple yet powerful feature that can greatly aid us in creating sophisticated code that reacts to data change.

3.6.1 Single-value triggers (on replace)

Listing 3.29 demonstrates a simple trigger in action.

Listing 3.29 Trigger on variable change

```
class TestTrigger {
    var current = 99
        on replace oldVal = newVal {
            previous = oldVal;
        };
    var previous = 0;

    override function toString() : String {
        "current={current} previous={previous}";
    }
}

var trig1 = TestTrigger {};
println(trig1);
trig1.current = 7;
println(trig1);
trig1.current = -8;
println(trig1);
```

Runs when current is changed

```
current=99 previous=0
current=7 previous=99
current=-8 previous=7
```

The TestTrigger class has two variables, the first of which has a trigger attached to it. Triggers are added to the end of a variable declaration, using the keyword phrase on replace, followed by a variable to hold the current value, an equals sign, and a variable to hold the replacement value. In the example oldVal will contain the existing value of current when the trigger is activated, and newVal will contain the updated value. We use the old value to populate a second variable, previous, ensuring it is always one step behind current.

Note: the equals sign used as part of the on replace construct is just a separator, not an assignment. I suppose oldVal and newVal could have been separated by a comma, but the language designers presumably thought the equals sign was more intuitive.

The code block is called *after* the variable is updated, so newVal is already in place when our code starts. Actually, we could have just read current instead of newVal.

For convenience, the trigger syntax can be abbreviated, as shown in listing 3.30.

Listing 3.30 Shorter trigger syntax

```
var onRep1:Integer = 0 on replace {        <-- No old or new value
    println("onRep1: {onRep1}");
}
var onRep2:Integer = 5 on replace oldVal {     <-- Old value only
    println("onRep2: {oldVal} => {onRep2}");
}
onRep1 = 99;
onRep2++;
onRep2--;
```

```
onRep1: 0            | Initialization
onRep2: 0 => 5       |
onRep1: 99
onRep2: 5 => 6
onRep2: 6 => 5
```

This shows two shorter syntax variants. The first doesn't bother with either the newVal or the oldVal, while the second bothers only with the oldVal.

3.6.2 Sequence triggers (on replace [..])

As you'd expect, we can also assign a trigger to a sequence. To do this we need to also tap into not only the previous and replacement values but also the range of the sequence that's being affected. Fortunately we can use a trigger itself to demonstrate how it works, as listing 3.31 proves.

Listing 3.31 Triggers on a sequence

```
var seq1 = [1..3]
    on replace oldVal[firstIdx..lastIdx] = newVal {
        println (
            "Changing [{firstIdx}..{lastIdx}] from "
            "{oldVal.toString()} to "
            "{newVal.toString()}"
        );
    };
println("Inserts");
insert 4 into seq1;
insert 0 before seq1[0];
insert [98,99] after seq1[2];
```

```
println("Deletes");
delete seq1[0];
delete seq1[0..2];
delete seq1;
println("Assign then reverse");
seq1 = [1..3];
seq1 = reverse seq1;
```

```
Changing [0..-1] from [ ] to [ 1, 2, 3 ]
Inserts
Changing [3..2] from [ 1, 2, 3 ] to [ 4 ]
Changing [0..-1] from [ 1, 2, 3, 4 ] to [ 0 ]
Changing [3..2] from [ 0, 1, 2, 3, 4 ] to [ 98, 99 ]
Deletes
Changing [0..0] from [ 0, 1, 2, 98, 99, 3, 4 ] to [ ]
Changing [0..2] from [ 1, 2, 98, 99, 3, 4 ] to [ ]
Changing [0..2] from [ 99, 3, 4 ] to [ ]
Assign then reverse
Changing [0..-1] from [ ] to [ 1, 2, 3 ]
Changing [0..2] from [ 1, 2, 3 ] to [ 3, 2, 1 ]
```

The output tells the story of how the trigger was used. The `on replace` syntax has been complemented by a couple of new variables boxed in square brackets. Don't be confused: this extension to `on replace` isn't actually a sequence itself; the language designers just borrowed the familiar syntax to make it look more intuitive.

Watch carefully how the two values change as we perform various sequence operations.

When the sequence is first created, a trigger call is made adding the initial values at index 0. Then we see three further insert operations. Each time `oldVal` is set to the preinsert contents, `newVal` is set to the contents being added; `firstIdx` is the index to which the new values will be added, and `lastIdx` is one behind `firstIdx` (it has little meaning during an insert, so it just gets an arbitrary value).

We next see three delete operations. Again `oldVal` is the current content of the sequence before the operation, `newVal` is an empty sequence (there are no new values in a delete, obviously), and `firstIdx` and `lastIdx` describe the index range of the elements being removed.

Finally we repopulate the sequence with fresh data, causing an insert trigger, and then reverse the sequence to cause a mass replacement. Note how during the reverse the `firstIdx` and `lastIdx` values actually express the elements being modified, unlike with an insert where only the lower index is used.

Triggers can be really useful in certain circumstances, but we should avoid temptation to abuse them; the last thing we want is code that's hard to understand and a nightmare to debug. And speaking of code that doesn't do what we think it should, in the next section we look at exceptions (talk about a slick segue!)

3.7 Trap problems using exceptions (try, catch, any, finally)

To misquote the famous cliché, "Stuff happens!" And when it happens, we need some way of knowing about it. Exceptions give us a way to assign a block of code to be run when a problem occurs or to signal a problem within our own code to outside code that may be using our API. As always, we begin with an example. Take a look at listing 3.32.

Listing 3.32 Exception handling

```
import java.lang.NullPointerException;
import java.io.IOException;

var key = 0;
try {
    println(doSomething());
}
catch(ex:IOException) {
    println("ERROR reading data {ex}")
}
catch(any) {
    println("ERROR unknown fault");
}
finally {
    println("This always runs");
}

function doSomething() : String {
    if(key==1) {
        throw new IOException("Data corrupt");
    }
    else if(key==2) {
        throw new NullPointerException();
    }
    "No problems!";
}
```

```
No problems!
This always runs
```
key = 0

```
ERROR reading data java.io.IOException: Data corrupt
This always runs
```
key = 1

```
ERROR unknown fault
This always runs
```
key = 2

The code hinges on the value of `key`, determining which exceptions may be thrown. The example is a little contrived, but it's compact and demonstrates the mechanics of exceptions perfectly well. The `try` block is the code we want to trap exceptions on, and the `catch` blocks are executed if the `doSomething()` function actually throws an exception. The first block will be activated if the function throws an `IOException`. The second uses the `any` keyword to trap other exceptions that might be thrown. And last, the `finally` block will always be executed, regardless of whether or not an exception occurred.

The results, in bold, show the code being run with different values for `key`. First we have a clean run with no exceptions; the function returns normally, the results are printed, and the `finally` block is run. Second we have a (simulated) IO failure, causing the function to abort by throwing an `IOException`, which is trapped by our first `catch` block, and again the `finally` block runs at the close. In the third run we cause the function to abort with a `NullPointerException`, triggering the catchall exception handler, and once again the `finally` block runs at the close.

The `finally` block is a useful device for cleaning up after a piece of code, such as closing a file properly before leaving a function. To avoid identical code in multiple places the `finally` block should be used. Its contents will run no matter how the `try` block exits. We can even use `finally` blocks without `catch` blocks, keeping code clean by putting must-run terminating code in a single place.

3.8 Summary

JavaFX Script may seem a little quirky in places to someone coming to it fresh, but its quirks all generally seem to make sense. Its expression language syntax might seem a little bizarre at first—assigning from `if` and `for` blocks takes some getting used to—but it permits code and data structures to be interwoven seamlessly. Binding and triggers allow us to define relationships between variables, and code to run when those variables change. But more important, they permit us to put such code right next to the variables they relate to, rather than in some disparate block or source file miles away from where the variable is actually defined.

We've covered so much over the last few dozen pages, I wouldn't be at all surprised if you feel your head is spinning. What we need is a nice, gentle project to get us started. Something fun, yet with enough challenge to allow us to practice some of the unique JavaFX Script features you've just learned about.

In the next chapter we're not going to jump straight in with animations and swish UIs; instead we're keeping it nice and simple by developing a Swing-like application—a number puzzle game like the ones found in many newspapers. So, brew yourself a fresh cup of coffee, and I'll see you in the next chapter.

4 Swing by numbers

This chapter covers

- Practicing core JavaFX Script skills
- Using model/view/controller, without reams of boilerplate
- Building a user interface that swings
- Validating a simple form

You've had to take in a lot in the last couple of chapters—an entirely new language, no less! I know many of you will be eager to dive straight into creating media-rich applications, but you need to learn to walk before you can run. JavaFX Script gives us a lot of powerful tools for writing great software, but all you've seen thus far is a few abstract examples.

So for this, our first project, we won't be developing any flashy visuals or clever animations. Be patient. Instead we need to start putting all the stuff you learned over the last few dozen pages to good use. A common paradigm in UI software is Model/View/Controller, where data and UI are separate, interacting by posting updates to each other. The *model* is the data, while the *view/controller* is the display and its input. We're going to develop a data class and a corresponding UI to see how the language features of JavaFX Script allow us to bind them together (pun only partially intended). But first we need to decide on a simple project to practice on, something fun yet informative.

We're going to develop a version of the simple, yet addictive, number puzzle game found in countless newspapers and magazines around the world. If you've never encountered such puzzles before, take a look at figure 4.1.

The general idea is to fill in the missing cells in a grid with unique numbers (in a standard puzzle, 1 to 9) in each *row*, each *column*, and each *box*. A successful solution is a grid completely filled in, without duplicates in any row, column, or box.

> **The number puzzle**
>
> Number puzzles like the one we're developing have been published in magazines and newspapers since the late nineteenth century. By the time of WWI, their popularity had waned, and they fell into obscurity. In the late 1970s the puzzle was reinvented, legend has it, by Howard Garns, an American puzzle author, and it eventually found its way to Japan where it gained the title "Sudoku." It took another 25 years for the puzzle to become popular in the West. Its inclusion in the UK's *Sunday Times* newspaper was an overnight success, and from there it has gone on to create addicts around the world.
>
> By far the most common puzzle format is a basic 9 x 9 grid, giving us nine rows of nine cells each, nine columns of nine cells each, and nine 3 x 3 boxes of nine cells each. At the start of the puzzle a grid is presented with some of the numbers already in place. The player must fill in the missing cells using only the numbers 1 to 9, such that all 27 *groups* (nine rows, nine columns, nine boxes) contain only one occurrence of each number.

We'll be using JavaFX's `javafx.ext.swing` package to develop our UI. These classes wrap Swing components, allowing us to use Java's UI toolkit in a JavaFX desktop application. For those of you who have developed with Swing in the past, this will be a real eye opener. You'll see firsthand how the same UIs you previously created with reams and reams of Java code can be constructed with relatively terse declarative JavaFX code. For those who haven't encountered the delights of Swing, this will be a gentle introduction to creating traditional UIs with the power tools JFX provides. Either way, we'll have fun.

This project is not a comprehensive Swing tutorial. Swing is a huge and very complex beast, with books the size of telephone directories published about it. JavaFX

5	3			7				
6			1	9	5			
	9	8					6	
8				6				3
4			8		3			1
7				2				6
	6					2	8	
			4	1	9			5
				8			7	9

5	3	4	6	7	8	9	1	2
6	7	2	1	9	5	3	4	8
1	9	8	3	4	2	5	6	7
8	5	9	7	6	1	4	2	3
4	2	6	8	5	3	7	9	1
7	1	3	9	2	4	8	5	6
9	6	1	5	3	7	2	8	4
2	8	7	4	1	9	6	3	5
3	4	5	2	8	6	1	7	9

Figure 4.1 A number puzzle grid, shown both empty and recently completed

itself provides direct support (JFX wrappers) for only a handful of core Swing components, although the whole of Swing can be used directly as Java objects, of course. The project is primarily about showing how a Swing-like UI can be constructed quickly and cleanly, using JavaFX Script.

> **JavaFX and Swing**
>
> JavaFX has two UI toolkits: its own `javafx.scene.control` library and the `javafx.ext.swing` wrappers around Java's Swing. What's the difference? The Swing wrappers will allow desktop apps to have native look 'n' feel, but Swing can't easily be ported to phones and TVs. So JavaFX's own library will allow greater portability between devices and better harmony with JavaFX's *scene graph*.
>
> The new controls are really where the engineers at Sun want JavaFX to go; the Swing wrappers were initially a stop-gap until the controls library was ready. But the Swing wrappers are unlikely to vanish for a while—some developers of existing Swing applications have expressed interest in moving over to JavaFX Script for their GUI coding. The Swing library may, eventually, become an optional extension, rather than a standard JavaFX API.

Enough about Swing—what about our number puzzle? I don't know if you've ever noticed, but often the simpler the idea, the harder it is to capture in words alone. Sometimes it's far quicker to learn by seeing something in action. Our number puzzle uses blissfully simple rules, yet it's hard to describe in the abstract. So to avoid confusion we need to agree on a few basic terms before we proceed:

- The *grid* is the playing area on which the puzzle is played.
- A *row* is horizontal line of cells in the grid.
- A *column* is a vertical line of cells in the grid.
- A *box* is a subgrid within the grid.
- A *group* is any segment of the grid that must contain unique numbers (all rows, columns, and boxes).
- A *position* is a single cell within a group.

The elements are demonstrated in figure 4.2.

Rather than throw everything at you at once, we're going to develop the application piece by piece, building it as we go. With each stage we'll add in a more functionality, using the language features we learned in the previous two chapters, and you'll see how they can be employed to make our application work.

Right then, compiler to the ready, let's begin.

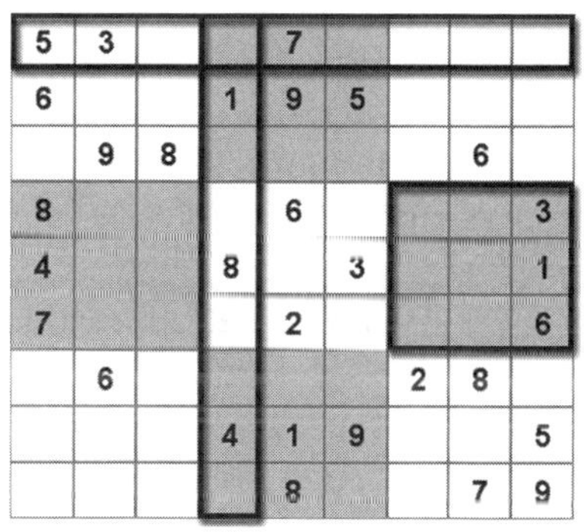

Figure 4.2 Groups are rows, columns, or boxes within the grid, which must hold unique values.

4.1 Swing time: Puzzle, version 1

What is Swing? When Java first entered the market, its official UI API was known as AWT (Abstract Window Toolkit), a library that sought to smooth over the differences between the various *native* GUI toolkits on Windows, the Mac, Linux, and any other desktop environment it was ported to. AWT wrapped the operating system's own native GUI widgets (buttons, scrollbars, text areas, etc.) to create a consistent environment across all platforms. Yet because of this it came under fire as being a lowest-common-denominator solution, a subset of only the features available on all platforms. So in answer to this criticism a more powerful alternative was developed: Swing!

Swing sits atop AWT but uses only its lowest level features—pixel pushing and keyboard/mouse input mainly—to deliver an entirely Java-based library of UI widgets. Swing is a large and very powerful creature, quite possibly one of the most powerful (certainly one of the most complex) UI toolkits ever created. In this project, we'll be looking at only a small part of it.

Because we're developing our puzzle bit by bit, in version 1 we won't expect to have a working game. We're laying the foundations for what's to come.

> **What's in a name?**
>
> The generic name for a UI control differs from system to system and from toolkit to toolkit. In the old Motif (X/X-Windows) toolkit they were called *widgets*; Windows uses the boring term *controls*, Java AWT/Swing calls them by the rather bland name *components*, and I seem to recall the Amiga even referred to them by rather bizarre name *gadgets*. Looks like nobody can agree!
>
> With so many terms in use for the same thing, the conversation could quickly become confusing. Therefore, when referring to GUI elements in the abstract, I'll use the term *widgets*; when referring specifically to Swing or AWT elements, I'll use the term *components*; and when referring specifically to JavaFX elements, I'll use the term *controls*.

4.1.1 Our initial puzzle data class

We need to start somewhere, so here's some basic code that will get the ball rolling, defining the data we need to represent our puzzle. Listing 4.1 is our initial shot at a main puzzle grid class, but as you'll see it's far from finished.

Listing 4.1 PuzzleGrid.fx (version 1)

```
package jfxia.chapter4;

package class PuzzleGrid {
    public-init var boxDim:Integer = 3;
    public-read def gridDim:Integer = bind boxDim*boxDim;
    public-read def gridSize:Integer = bind gridDim*gridDim;

    package var grid:Integer[] =
        for(a in [0..<gridSize]) { 0 }
}
```

So far all we have is four variables, which do the following:

- The `boxDim` variable is the dimension of each box inside the main grid. Boxes are square, so we don't need separate width and height dimensions.
- The `gridDim` variable holds the width and height of the game grid. The grid is square, so we don't need to hold separate values for both dimensions. This value is always the square of the `boxDim` variable—a 3 x 3 box results in a 9 x 9 grid, a 4 x 4 box results in a 16 x 16 grid, and so on—so we utilize a bind to ensure they remain consistent.
- The `gridSize` variable is a convenience for when we need to know the total number of cells in the grid. You'll note that we're using a bind here too; when `gridDim` is changed, `gridSize` will automatically be updated.
- The `grid` itself, represented as a sequence of `Integer` values. We'll create an initial, default, grid with all zeros for now using a `for` loop.

So far, so good. We've defined our basic data class and used some JavaFX Script cleverness to ensure `gridSize` and `gridDim` are always up to date whenever the data they depend on changes. When `boxDim` is set, it begins a chain reaction that sees `gridDim` and then `gridSize` recalculated. Strictly speaking, it might have made more sense to bind `boxDim` to the square root of `gridDim` rather than the other way around, but I don't fancy writing a square root function for a project like this.

Note that although the puzzle requires the numbers 1 to 9, we also use the number 0 (zero) to represent an empty cell. Thus the permissible values for each cell range from 0 to 9.

Our initial data class is missing a lot of important functionality, but it should be sufficient to get a UI on the screen. We can then further refine and develop both the puzzle class and the interface as the chapter progresses.

4.1.2 Our initial GUI class

So much for the puzzle grid class; what about a GUI?

Recall that JavaFX encourages software to be built in a declarative fashion, especially UIs. Until now this has been a rather cute idea floating around in the ether, but right now you're finally about to see a concrete example of how this works in the real world and why it's so powerful.

Listing 4.2 is the entry point to our application, building a basic UI for our application using the previously touted declarative syntax.

Listing 4.2 Game.fx (version 1)

```
package jfxia.chapter4;

import javafx.ext.swing.SwingButton;
import javafx.scene.Scene;
import javafx.scene.text.Font;
import javafx.stage.Stage;

def cellSize:Number = 40;                  <—— Cell dimensions
```

```
def puz = PuzzleGrid { boxDim:3 };          <- Our puzzle class

def gridFont = Font {                       A font we
    name: "Arial Bold"                      wish to reuse
    size: 15
};

Stage {
    title: "Game"
    visible: true
    scene: Scene {
        content: for(idx in [0..<puz.gridSize]) {
            var x:Integer = (idx mod puz.gridDim);      Index to grid x/y
            var y:Integer = (idx / puz.gridDim);
            SwingButton {
                layoutX: x * cellSize;
                layoutY: y * cellSize;
                width: cellSize;
                height: cellSize;

                text: bind notZero(puz.grid[idx]);      Each grid cell is
                font: gridFont;                         a Swing button
                action: function():Void {
                    var v = puz.grid[idx];
                    v = (v+1) mod (puz.gridDim+1);
                    puz.grid[idx] = v;
                }
            }
        }
        width: puz.gridDim * cellSize;
        height: puz.gridDim * cellSize;
    }
}                                                                    Hide
function notZero(i:Integer):String { if(i==0) " " else "{i}"; }  <- zero
```

You can see from the import statements at the head of the source file that it's pulling in several GUI-based classes from the standard JavaFX APIs. The Swing wrapper classes live in a JavaFX package named, conveniently, `javafx.ext.swing`. We could use the classes in the original Swing packages directly (like other Java API classes, they *are* available), but the JFX wrappers make it easier to use common Swing components declaratively.

The `cellSize` variable defines how big, in pixels, each square in the grid will be. Our game needs a `PuzzleGrid` object, and we create one with the variable `puz`, setting `boxDim` to declaratively describe its size. After `puz` we create a font for our GUI. Since we're using the same font for each grid cell, we may as well create one font object and reuse it. Again, this is done declaratively using an object literal. The final chunk of the listing—and quite a hefty chunk it is too—consists of the actual user interface code itself.

We've using Swing buttons to represent each cell in the grid, so we can easily display a label and respond to a mouse click, but let's strip away the button detail for the moment and concentrate on the outer detail of the window.

```
Stage {
    title: "Game"
    visible: true
    scene: Scene {
        content: /*** STRIPPED, FOR NOW ***/
        width: puz.gridDim * cellSize
        height: puz.gridDim * cellSize
    }
};
```

Here's an abridged reproduction of the code we saw in listing 4.2. We see two objects being created, one nested inside the other. At the outermost level we have a `Stage`, and inside that a `Scene`. There are further objects inside the `Scene`, but the previous snippet doesn't show them.

The `Stage` represents the link to the outside world. Because this is a desktop application, the `Stage` will take the form of a window. In a web browser applet, the `Stage` would be an applet container. Using a common top-level object like this aids portability between desktop, web, mobile, TV, and the like.

Three variables are set on `Stage`: the window's title as shown in its drag bar, the window's visibility to determine whether it's shown (we didn't *need* to set this because it's `true` by default), and the window's content. The content is a `Scene` object, used to describe the root of a scene graph. We'll look at the scene graph in far more detail in the next chapter; for now all you need to know is that it's where our UI will live.

The `Scene` object has its own variables, aside from `content`. They are `width` and `height`, and they determine the size of the inner window area (the part inside the borders and title bar). The window will be sized around these dimensions, with the total window size being the `Scene` dimensions plus any borders and title (drag) bars the operating system adds to decorate the window.

There's a chunk of code missing from the middle of the previous snippet, and now it's time to see what it does.

4.1.3 Building the buttons

Here's a reminder of the mysterious piece of code we left out of our discussion in the last section:

```
content: for(idx in [0..<puz.gridSize]) {
    var x:Integer = (idx mod puz.gridDim);
    var y:Integer = (idx / puz.gridDim);
    SwingButton {
        layoutX: x * cellSize;
        layoutY: y * cellSize;
        width: cellSize;
        height: cellSize;

        text: bind notZero(puz.grid[idx]);
        font: gridFont;
        action: function():Void {
            var v = puz.grid[idx];
            v = (v+1) mod (puz.gridDim+1);
```

```
                puz.grid[idx] = v;
            }
        }
}
```

The code goes inside a Scene, which in turn provides the contents for our Stage, you'll recall—but what does it do? Put simply, it creates a square grid of SwingButton objects, tied to data inside the puz object. You can see the effect in figure 4.3.

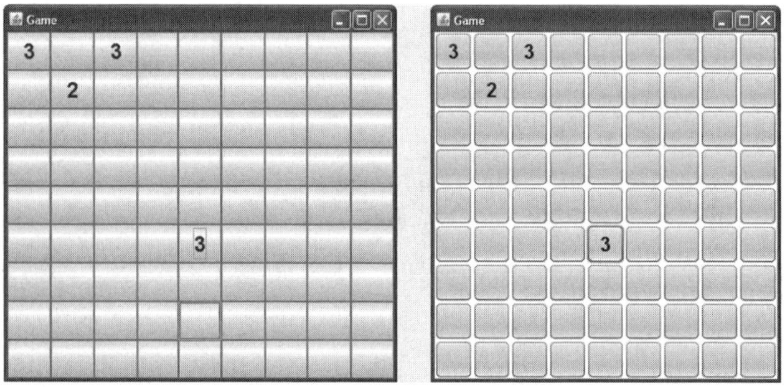

Figure 4.3 The game as it appears after clicking on a few cells (note the highlight on the lower 3). Depending on your JRE version, you'll get Ocean- (left) or Nimbus- (right) themed buttons.

The for loop runs for as many times as the puzzle's grid size, creating a fresh button for each cell. Before the button is created we convert the loop index, stored in idx, into an actual grid x and y position. Dividing by the grid width gives us the y position (ignoring any fractional part), while the remainder of the same division gives us the x position.

Each button has seven variables declaratively set. The first four are the button's position and size inside the scene, in pixels. They lay the buttons out as a grid, relying on the cellSize variable we created at the head of the file. The three other variables are the button's text, its font, and an event handler that fires when the button is clicked.

The button's text is bound to the corresponding element in the puzzle's grid sequence. Thus the first button will be bound to the first sequence element, the second to the second, and so on, as shown in figure 4.4. We do not want the value 0 to be shown to the user, so we've created a convenience function called notZero(), which you can see at the foot of the script. This function returns any Integer passed into it as a String, except for 0, which results in a space.

You may recognize the action as an anonymous function. The function reads its corresponding element in the puzzle grid sequence, increments it, ensuring that the

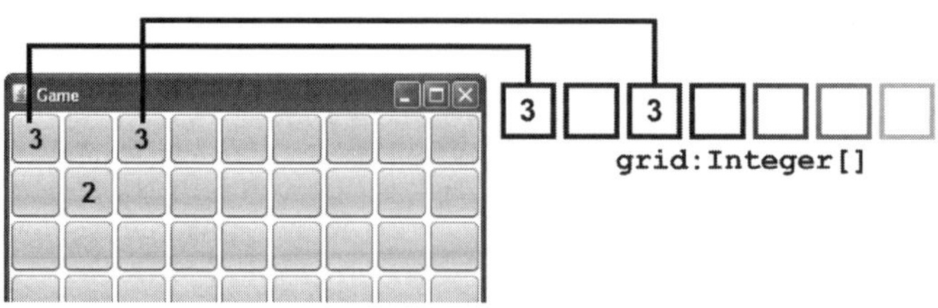

Figure 4.4 The text of each button is bound to the corresponding value in the puzzle's grid sequence.

> **Sometimes binds can be too clever!**
>
> Some of you may be wondering why it was necessary to wrap the button text's `if/else` code in the `notZero()` function. What's wrong with the following?
>
> ```
> text: bind if(puz.grid[idx]==0) " " else "{puz.grid[idx]}"
> ```
>
> The answer lies with the way binds work and how they strive to be as efficient as possible. When `puz.grid[idx]` goes from 0 to 1, the result of the condition changes from `true` to `false`, but when it goes from 1 to 2, the result remains `false`. The bind tries to be clever; it thinks to itself, "Well, the result of the condition hasn't changed, so I'm not going to reevaluate its body," and so the `SwingButton` displays 1 for every value except 0. Fortunately, by hiding the `if` condition inside a black-box function (see chapter 2, section 2.6.8), we can neatly sidestep bind's cleverness.

value wraps around to 0 if it exceeds the maximum number allowed, and then stores it back in the sequence. Here's the clever part: because the `text` variable is bound to the sequence element, whenever `action`'s function changes the element value, the button's text is automatically updated.

4.1.4 Model/View/Controller, JavaFX Script style

We touched on the Model/View/Controller paradigm briefly in the introduction, and hopefully those readers familiar with the MVC concept will already have seen how this is playing out under JavaFX Script.

In languages like Java, MVC is implemented by way of interfaces and event classes. In JavaFX Script this is swept away in favor of a much cleaner approach built deep into the language syntax. The relationships between our game UI and its data are formed using binds and triggers. The *model* (game data) uses triggers to respond to input from the *view/controller* (UI display). In turn, the *view* binds against variables in the *model*, establishing its relationship with them as expressions. The relationship is shown in figure 4.5.

This is how MVC works in JavaFX Script. Any code that is dependent on a model expresses that dependency using a bind, and JavaFX Script automatically honors that relationship without the programmer having to manually maintain it. The beauty of

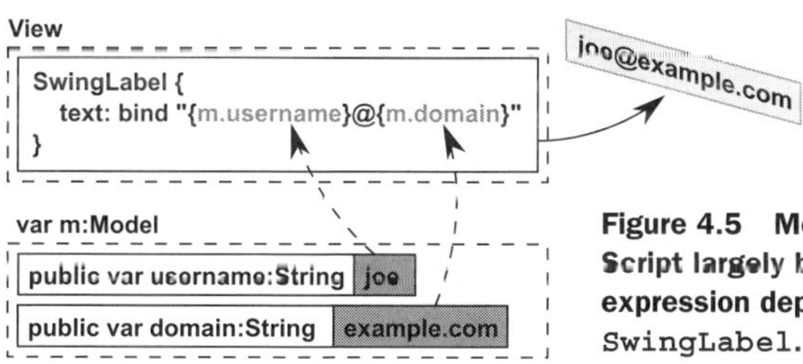

Figure 4.5 Model/View/Controller is achieved in JavaFX Script largely by way of bound expressions. Here one such expression depends on two strings for the contents of its `SwingLabel`.

this approach is it strips away the boilerplate classes and interfaces of other languages, like Java, distilling everything down to its purest form. If a given part of our UI is dependent on some external data, that dependency is expressed immediately (meaning inline) as part of its definition. It is not scattered throughout our code in disparate event handlers, interfaces, and event objects, as in Java.

If there is a two-way relationship between the UI and its data, a bidirectional bind (the `with inverse` syntax) can be used. For example, a text field may display the contents of a given variable in a model. If the variable changes, the text field should update automatically; if the text field is edited, the variable should update automatically. Providing the relationship is elemental in nature, in other words a direct one-to-one relationship, a bidirectional bind will achieve this.

When I told you binds were really useful things, I wasn't kidding!

4.1.5 Running version 1

It may not be the most impressive game so far, but it gives us a solid foundation to work from. When version 1 of the puzzle is run, it displays the puzzle grid (see figure 4.3) and responds to mouse clicks by cycling through the available numbers.

This is just a start, but already we've seen some of the power tools we learned about in the previous two chapters making a big contribution: the declarative syntax, bound variables, and anonymous functions are all in full effect.

So let's continue to build up the functionality of our game by making it more useful.

4.2 Better informed and better looking: Puzzle, version 2

So far we have a basic UI up and running, but it lacks the functionality to make it a playable game. There are two problems we need to tackle next:

- The buttons don't look particularly appealing, and it's hard to see where the boxes are on the puzzle grid.
- The game doesn't warn us when we duplicate numbers in a given group. If I, as the player, put two 3s on the same row, for example, the game does not flag this as an error.

In this section we'll remedy these faults. The first is entirely the domain of the UI class, `Game`, while the second is predominantly the domain of the data class, `PuzzleGrid`.

4.2.1 Making the puzzle class clever, using triggers and function types

The data class was tiny in version 1, with only a handful of variables to its name. To make the class more aware of the rules of the puzzle, we need to add a whole host of code. Let's start with PuzzleGrid.fx, shown in listing 4.3, and see what changes need to be made. Following the listing I'll explain the key changes, one by one. (In listing 4.3, and in other listings throughout this book, code unchanged from the previous revision is shown as slightly fainter, allowing the reader to immediately see where the additions/alterations are.)

Listing 4.3 PuzzleGrid.fx (version 2)

```
package jfxia.chapter4;

package class PuzzleGrid {
    public-init var boxDim:Integer = 3;
    public-read def gridDim:Integer = bind boxDim*boxDim;
    public-read def gridSize:Integer = bind gridDim*gridDim;

    package var grid:Integer[] =
        for(a in [0..<gridSize]) { 0 }
        on replace current[lo..hi] = replacement {
            update();
        }

    package var clashes:Boolean[] =
        for(a in [0..<gridSize]) false;

    function update() : Void {
        clashes = for(a in [0..<gridSize]) false;
        for(grp in [0..<gridDim]) {
            checkGroup(grp,row2Idx);
            checkGroup(grp,column2Idx);
            checkGroup(grp,box2Idx);
        }
    }

    function checkGroup (
        group:Integer ,
        func:function(:Integer,:Integer):Integer
    ) : Void {
        var freq = for(a in [0..gridDim]) 0;
        for(pos in [0..<gridDim]) {
            var val = grid[ func(group,pos) ];
            if(val > 0) { freq[val]++; }
        }
        for(pos in [0..<gridDim]) {
            var idx = func(group,pos);
            var val = grid[idx];
            clashes[idx] = clashes[idx] or (freq[val]>1);
        }
    }

    function row2Idx(group:Integer,pos:Integer) : Integer {
        return group*gridDim + pos;
    }

    function column2Idx(group:Integer,pos:Integer) : Integer {
        return group + pos*gridDim;
    }

    function box2Idx(group:Integer,pos:Integer) : Integer {
        var xOff = (group mod boxDim) * boxDim;
        var yOff = ((group/boxDim) as Integer) * boxDim;
        var x = pos mod boxDim;
        var y = (pos/boxDim) as Integer;
        return (xOff+x) + (yOff+y)*gridDim;
    }
}
```

Trigger an update to clashes

Does this cell clash with another?

Update clashes sequence

Check a given group for clashes

Whew! That's quite bit of code to be added in one go, but don't panic; it's all rather straightforward when you know what it's meant to do.

The purpose of listing 4.3 is to update a new sequence, called `clashes`, which holds a flag set to `true` if a given cell currently conflicts with others and `false` if it does not. The UI can then bind to this sequence, changing the way a grid cell is displayed to warn the player of any duplicates.

The function `update()` clears the `clashes` sequence and then checks each group in turn. In our basic 9 x 9 puzzle there are 27 groups: nine rows, nine columns, and nine boxes. Each group has nine positions it needs to check for duplicates. However, most of the work is deferred to the function `checkGroup()`, which handles the checking of an individual group. Let's take a closer look at this function, so we can understand how it fits into `update()`.

4.2.2 Group checking up close: function types

Here's the `checkGroup()` function we're looking at, reproduced on its own to refresh your memory and save ambiguity:

```
function checkGroup (
    group:Integer ,
    func:function(:Integer,:Integer):Integer
) : Void {
    var freq = for(a in [0..gridDim]) 0;
    for(pos in [0..<gridDim]) {
        var val = grid[ func(group,pos) ];
        if(val > 0) { freq[val]++; }
    }
    for(pos in [0..<gridDim]) {
        var idx = func(group,pos);
        var val = grid[idx];
        clashes[idx] = clashes[idx] or (freq[val]>1);
    }
}
```

The first four lines are the function's signature; unfortunately it's quite long, so I split it over four separate lines in an attempt to make it more readable. You can see the function is called `checkGroup`, and it accepts two parameters: an `Integer` and a function type. The function type accepts two `Integer` variables and gives a single `Integer` in return. The `Void` on the end signifies `checkGroup()` has no return value.

So, why do we need to pass a function to `checkGroup()`? Think about it: when we're checking each position in a row group we're working horizontally across the grid, when we're checking each position in a column group we're working vertically down the grid, and for a box group we're working line by line within a portion of the grid. Figure 4.6 demonstrates this.

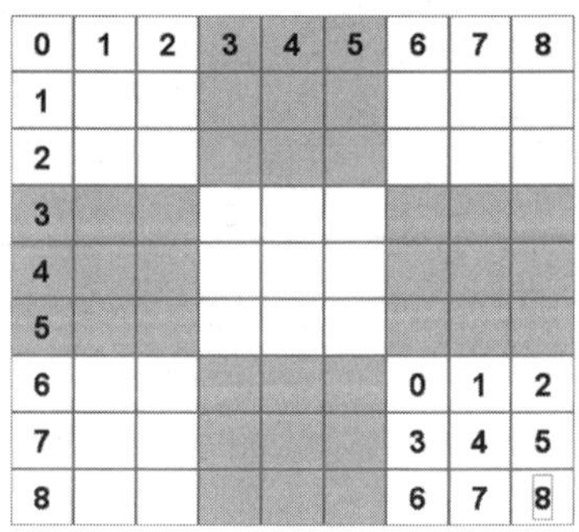

Figure 4.6 Coordinate translations for column, row, and box groups

We have three different ways of translating group and position to grid coordinates:

- For rows the group is the y coordinate in the grid and the position is the x coordinate. So position 0 of group 0 will be (0,0) on the grid, and position 2 of group 1 will be (2,1) on the grid.
- For columns the group is the x coordinate in the grid and the position is the y coordinate. So position 2 of group 1 will be (1,2) when translated into grid coordinates.
- For boxes we need to do some clever math to translate the group to a subsection of the grid, so group 8 (in the southeast corner) will have its first cell at coordinates (6,6). We then need to do some more clever math to turn the position into an offset within this subgrid. Position 1, for example, would be offset (1,0), giving us an absolute position of (7,6) on the grid when combined with group 8.

The code that actually checks for duplicates within a given group is identical, as we've just seen—all that differs is the way the group type translates its group number and position into grid coordinates. So the function passed in to `checkGroup()` abstracts away this translation. The two values it accepts are the group and the position. The value it returns is the grid coordinate, or rather the index in the grid sequence that corresponds with the group and position. (One of the benefits of storing the grid as a single-dimension sequence is that we don't need to figure out a way to return two values, an x and a y, from these three translation functions.)

Now that you understand what the passed-in function does, let's examine the code inside `checkGroup()` to see what it does. It's broken into two stages:

```
var freq = for(a in [0..gridDim]) 0;
for(pos in [0..<gridDim]) {
    var val = grid[ func(group,pos) ];
    if(val > 0) { freq[val]++; }
}
```

Here's the first stage reproduced on its own. We kick off by defining a new sequence called `freq`, with enough space for each unique number in our puzzle. This will hold the frequency of the numbers in our group. Recall that we're using 0 to represent an empty cell, so to make the code easier we've allowed space in the sequence for 0 plus the 1 to 9. Then we extract each position in the group, using the parameter function to translate group/position to a `grid` index. We increment the frequency corresponding to the value at the grid index—so if the value was 1, `freq[1]` would get incremented.

This builds us a table of how often each value occurs in the group. Now we want to act on that data.

```
for(pos in [0..<gridDim]) {
    var idx = func(group,pos);
    var val = grid[idx];
    clashes[idx] = clashes[idx] or (freq[val]>1);
}
```

The second stage of the `checkGroup()` function is reproduced here. It should be quite obvious what needs doing; we take a second pass over each position in the group, pulling out its value once again with help from our translation function. Then we set the flag in `clashes` if the value appears in the group more than once (signifying a clash!)

Note: a given cell in the puzzle grid may cause a clash in some groups but not others. It is important, therefore, that we preserve the clashes already discovered with other groups. This is why the clash check is `or`'d with the current value in the `clashes` sequence, rather than simply overwriting it.

4.2.3 Firing the update: triggers

Now we know how each group is checked, and we've seen the power of using function types to allow us to reuse code with *plug-in-able* variations, but we still need to complete the picture. The function `update()` will call `checkGroup()` 27 times (assuming a standard 9 x 9 grid), but what makes `update()` run?

Perhaps a better question might be, "When should `update()` run?" To which the answer should surely be, "Whenever the `grid` sequence is changed!"

We *could* wire something into our button event handler to always call `update()`, but this would be exposing the `PuzzleGrid` class's inner mechanics to another class, something we should avoid if we can. So why not wire something into the actual `grid` sequence itself?

```
package var grid:Integer[] =
    for(a in [0..<gridSize]) { 0 }
        on replace current[lo..hi] = replacement {
            update();
        }
```

Using a trigger we can ensure `update()` runs whenever the `grid` sequence is modified. It's a simple, effective, and clean solution that means the `clashes` sequence will never get out of step with `grid`.

4.2.4 Better-looking GUI: playing with the underlying Swing component

We've managed to soup up the puzzle class itself by making it responsive to duplicates under the rules of the puzzle. We can now exploit that functionality in our GUI, but we also need to make the game look more appealing.

Listing 4.4 gives us version 2 of the `Game` class.

Listing 4.4 Game.fx (version 2)

```
package jfxia.chapter4;

import javax.swing.JButton;
import javax.swing.border.LineBorder;
import javafx.ext.swing.SwingButton;
import javafx.scene.Scene;
import javafx.scene.paint.Color;
import javafx.scene.text.Font;
```

```
import javafx.stage.Stage;

def gridCol1 = java.awt.Color.WHITE;
def gridCol2 = new java.awt.Color(0xCCCCCC);
def border = new LineBorder(java.awt.Color.GRAY);

def cellSize:Number = 40;

def puz = PuzzleGrid { boxDim:3 };

def gridFont = Font {
    name: "Arial Bold"
    size: 20
};

Stage {
    title: "Game"
    visible: true
    scene: Scene {
        content: for(idx in [0..<puz.gridSize]) {
            var x:Integer = (idx mod puz.gridDim);
            var y:Integer = (idx / puz.gridDim);
            var b = SwingButton {
                layoutX: x * cellSize;
                layoutY: y * cellSize;
                width: cellSize;
                height: cellSize;

                text: bind notZero(puz.grid[idx]);
                font: gridFont;
                foreground: bind
                    if(puz.clashes[idx]) Color.RED
                    else Color.GRAY;
                action: function():Void {
                    var v = puz.grid[idx];
                    v = (v+1) mod (puz.gridDim+1);
                    puz.grid[idx] = v;
                }
            };

            x/=puz.boxDim;  y/=puz.boxDim;
            var bg = if((x mod 2)==(y mod 2)) gridCol1
                else gridCol2;

            var jb = b.getJComponent() as JButton;
            jb.setContentAreaFilled(false);
            jb.setBackground(bg);
            jb.setOpaque(true);
            jb.setBorder(border);
            jb.setBorderPainted(true);
            b;
        }
        width: puz.gridDim * cellSize;
        height:puz.gridDim * cellSize;
    }
}

function notZero(i:Integer):String { if(i==0) " " else "{i}"; }
```

Two-tone background (gridCol1, gridCol2)

Lines between grid cells (border)

A Button reference (var b)

Bind the foreground color to clashes

Background color from index

Manipulate the button via Swing

Listing 4.4 adds a couple of new imports at the head of the file and two new variables: `gridCol1` and `gridCol2`. These will help us to change the background color of the buttons to represent the boxes on the grid. We'll use the `border` variable to give us a gray pin line around each box, as shown in figure 4.7.

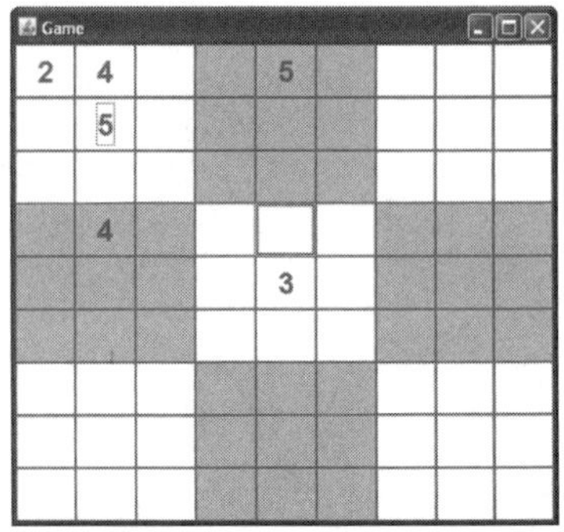

Figure 4.7 The restyled user interface, with differentiated boxes using background color and duplicate warnings using foreground (text) color

All the changes center on the button sequence being created and added into the `Scene`. You'll note from figure 4.7 that the button's `foreground` color is now bound to the `clashes` sequence we developed previously. You'll recall that when the contents of `puz.grid` change, `puz.clashes` is automatically updated via the trigger we added to the `PuzzleGrid` class. With this bind in place, the UI's buttons are immediately recolored to reflect any change in the clash status.

But those aren't the only changes we've made. In version 1 (listing 4.2) we added a new `SwingButton` straight into the scene graph, but now we capture it in a variable reference to manipulate it further before it gets added. After the button is created, we extract the underlying Swing component using the function `getJComponent()`, giving us full access to all its methods. First we remove the shaded fill effect. Next we set our own flat color background, creating a checkerboard effect for the boxes, and ensure the background is painted by making the button opaque. Finally we assign the `border` we created earlier, to create a gray pin line around each button.

Note that the background color is calculated by translating the cell's raw grid coordinate into a box coordinate (just scale them by the box size) and using this to assign colors based on a checkerboard pattern.

At the end of the loop we restate the variable used to hold the button reference. Because JavaFX Script is an expression language, this becomes our returned value to the loop's sequence.

With our new version of the game class in place, we're ready to try running the code again and seeing how the changes play out on the desktop.

4.2.5 Running version 2

Thanks to some clever trigger action, and a little bit of Swing coding, we've managed to get a puzzle game that now looks more the part and can warn players when they enter duplicate numbers within a group. See figure 4.7 for how the game currently looks.

It may seem like we're still a million miles away from a completed game, but actually we're in the home stretch, and the finishing line is within sight. So let's push on to the next, and final, version of the game.

Boxing clever: how to create a checkerboard pattern

In the `box2Idx()` function we witnessed in `PuzzleGrid`, and now with the checkerboard background pattern, we've had to do some clever math to figure out where the boxes are. Perhaps you're not interested in how this was done—but for those who are curious, here's an explanation.

We need to convert a sequence index (from 0 to 80, assuming a standard 9 x 9 grid) to a box coordinate (0,0) through (2,2) assuming nine boxes. The pattern itself is quite easy to produce once you have these coordinates: if x and y are both odd or both even, we use one color; if x and y are odd/even or even/odd, we use the other color. We can figure out whether a number is odd or even by dividing the remainder (the `mod`) of a division by 2: odd numbers result in 1; even numbers result in 0. Try it for yourself on a piece of paper if you don't believe me.

Let's assume we're given a `grid` sequence index, like 29; should this cell be shaded with a white or a gray background? First we convert the number 29 into a coordinate on the grid. The y coordinate is the number of times the grid dimension will divide into the number: 29 divided by 9 is 3. The x coordinate is the remainder of this division: 29 mod 9 is 2. Therefore index 29 is grid coordinate (x = 2,y = 3), assuming the coordinates start at 0. But we need to translate this into a box coordinate, which is easily done by scaling it by the box size: 2 divided by 3 is 0, and 3 divided by 3 is 1. So grid index 29 becomes grid coordinate (2,3) and becomes box coordinate (0,1). We then compare the oddness/evenness of these coordinates to determine which background shade to use.

What about the `box2Idx()` function? It's similar in principle, except we're almost working backwards: we're given a group and a position, and we need to work out the `grid` sequence index. To do this we first need to find the origin (northwest) coordinate of the box representing the group in the grid, which we can do by dividing and `mod`-ing the group by the box size to get x and y coordinates. We do the same thing to the position to get the coordinate offset within the box. Then we add the offset to the origin to get the absolute x and y within the grid. Finally, to convert the grid x,y to an index, we multiple y by the grid dimension and add on x.

4.3 Game on: Puzzle, version 3

We're almost there; the puzzle is nearly complete. But what work do we have left to do on our game? Let's make a list:

1. We need to add actual numbers for the start point of the puzzle; otherwise, the grid is just empty, and the puzzle wouldn't be very...well...puzzling.
2. We need to lock these starting numbers, so the player can't accidentally change them.
3. We need to notify the player when they've solved the puzzle. It would also be nice to inform them how many empty grid cells, and how many clashes, they currently have.

This is really just a mopping-up exercise, dealing with all the outstanding issues necessary to make the puzzle work. Yet there's still opportunity for learning, and for practicing our JavaFX skills, as you'll shortly see.

4.3.1 Adding stats to the puzzle class

In order to inform the player of how many clashes and empty cells we have, the puzzle class needs added functionality. We also need the class to provide some way of fixing the starting cells, so the GUI knows not to change them.

Listing 4.5 is the final version of the class, with all the new code added.

Listing 4.5 PuzzleGrid.fx (version 3)

```
package jfxia.chapter4;

package class PuzzleGrid {
    public-init var boxDim:Integer = 3;
    public-read def gridDim:Integer = bind boxDim*boxDim;
    public-read def gridSize:Integer = bind gridDim*gridDim;

    package var grid:Integer[] =
        for(a in [0..<gridSize]) { 0 }
        on replace current[lo..hi] = replacement {
            update();
        }

    package var clashes:Boolean[] =
        for(a in [0..<gridSize]) false;

    package var fixed:Boolean[] =
        for(a in [0..<gridSize]) false;

    package var numEmpty = 0;                          The new
    package var numClashes = 0;                        variables
    package def completed:Boolean = bind
        ((numEmpty==0) and (numClashes==0));

    public function fixGrid() : Void {
        for(idx in [0..<gridSize]) {                  Fix the static
            fixed[idx] = (grid[idx]>0);               starting cells
        }
    }

    function update() : Void {
        clashes = for(a in [0..<gridSize]) false;
        for(grp in [0..<gridDim]) {
            checkGroup(grp,row2Idx);
            checkGroup(grp,column2Idx);
            checkGroup(grp,box2Idx);
        }
        checkStats();                        <-- Call the stats updater
    }

    function checkGroup (
        group:Integer ,
        func:function(:Integer,:Integer):Integer
```

```
    ) : Void {
        var freq = for(a in [0..gridDim]) 0;
        for(pos in [0..<gridDim]) {
            var val = grid[ func(group,pos) ];
            if(val > 0) { freq[val]++; }
        }
        for(pos in [0..<gridDim]) {
            var idx = func(group,pos);
            var val = grid[idx];
            clashes[idx] = clashes[idx] or (freq[val]>1);
        }
    }

    function checkStats() : Void {
        numEmpty = 0;
        numClashes = 0;
        for(idx in [0..<gridSize]) {
            if(grid[idx]==0)  numEmpty++;
            if(clashes[idx])  numClashes++;
        }
    }

    function row2Idx(group:Integer,pos:Integer) : Integer {
        return group*gridDim + pos;
    }

    function column2Idx(group:Integer,pos:Integer) : Integer {
        return group + pos*gridDim;
    }

    function box2Idx(group:Integer,pos:Integer) : Integer {
        var xOff = (group mod boxDim) * boxDim;
        var yOff = ((group/boxDim) as Integer) * boxDim;
        var x = pos mod boxDim;
        var y = (pos/boxDim) as Integer;
        return (xOff+x) + (yOff+y)*gridDim;
    }
}
```

Count empty and clashing cells

Four new variables have been added in listing 4.5: the first, `fixed`, is a sequence that denotes which cells in the grid should not be changeable. The next three provide basic stats about the puzzle: `numEmpty`, `numClashes`, and `completed`.

We've also added a new function, `fixGrid()`, which walks over the puzzle grid and marks any cells that are non-zero in the `fixed` sequence. The GUI class can call this function to lock all existing cells in the puzzle, but why didn't we use some clever device like a bind or a trigger to automatically update the `fixed` sequence?

The `grid` sequence gets updated frequently, indeed, each time the player changes the value of a cell in the puzzle. We need the `fixed` sequence to update only when the `grid` is initially loaded with the starting values of the puzzle. We could rather cleverly rewrite the trigger to spot when the entire `grid` is being written, rather than a single cell (it can see how many cells are being changed at once, after all), but this might cause confusion later on. For example, suppose we added a load/save feature to our game. Restoring the grid after a load operation would cause the trigger to mistakenly fix all the existing non-zero cells, including those added by the player. Some may be wrong; indeed some may be clashes! How would the player feel if she were unable to change them?

For all the power JavaFX Script gives us, it must be acknowledged that sometimes the simplest solution is the best, even if it doesn't give us a chance to show fellow programmers just how clever-clever we are.

We have one final new function in our class: `checkStats()` populates the `numEmpty` and `numClashes` variables. It's called from the `update()` function, so it will run whenever the `grid` sequence is changed. The `completed` variable is bound to these variables and will become `true` when both are 0.

Let's now turn to the final piece of the puzzle (groan!), the GUI.

4.3.2 *Finishing off the puzzle grid GUI*

If you survived the horrendous pun at the end of the last section, you'll know this is the part where we pull everything together in one final burst of activity on the GUI class, to complete our puzzle game.

We have two aims with these modifications:

- Provide an actual starting grid, to act as a puzzle. The game is pointless without one.
- Plug in a status line at the bottom of the grid display, to inform the player of empty cells, clashing cells, and a successfully completed puzzle.

We'll look at the former in this section and the latter in the next section.

You might think these changes would be pretty mundane, but I've thrown in a layout class to keep you on your toes. Check out listing 4.6.

Listing 4.6 Game.fx (version 3)

```
package jfxia.chapter4;

import javax.swing.JButton;
import javax.swing.border.LineBorder;
import javafx.ext.swing.SwingButton;
import javafx.ext.swing.SwingLabel;
import javafx.scene.Scene;
import javafx.scene.layout.Flow;
import javafx.scene.paint.Color;
import javafx.scene.text.Font;
import javafx.stage.Stage;

def gridCol1 = java.awt.Color.WHITE;
def gridCol2 = new java.awt.Color(0xCCCCCC);
def border = new LineBorder(java.awt.Color.GRAY);

def cellSize:Number = 40;

var puz = PuzzleGrid {
    boxDim: 3
```

```
    grid: [
        5,3,0 , 0,7,0 , 0,0,0 ,
        6,0,0 , 1,9,5 , 0,0,0 ,
        0,9,8 , 0,0,0 , 0,6,0 ,
        8,0,0 , 0,6,0 , 0,0,3 ,
        4,0,0 , 8,0,3 , 0,0,1 ,
        7,0,0 , 0,2,0 , 0,0,6 ,
        0,6,0 , 0,0,0 , 2,8,0 ,
        0,0,0 , 4,1,9 , 0,0,5 ,
        0,0,0 , 0,8,0 , 0,7,9
    ]
};
puz.fixGrid();

var gridFont = Font {
    name: "Arial Bold"
    size: 20
};

Stage {
    title: "Game"
    visible: true
    scene: Scene {
        content: [
            for(idx in [0..<puz.gridSize]) {
                var x:Integer = (idx mod puz.gridDim);
                var y:Integer = (idx / puz.gridDim);
                var b = SwingButton {
                    layoutX: x * cellSize;
                    layoutY: y * cellSize;
                    width: cellSize;
                    height: cellSize;
                    text: bind notZero(puz.grid[idx]);
                    font: gridFont;
                    foreground: bind
                        if(puz.clashes[idx]) Color.RED
                        else if(puz.fixed[idx])  Color.BLACK
                        else Color.GRAY;
                    action: function():Void {
                        if(puz.fixed[idx]) { return; }
                        var v = puz.grid[idx];
                        v = (v+1) mod (puz.gridDim+1);
                        puz.grid[idx] = v;
                    }
                };

                x/=puz.boxDim;  y/=puz.boxDim;
                var bg = if((x mod 2)==(y mod 2)) gridCol1
                    else gridCol2;

                var jb = b.getJComponent() as JButton;
                jb.setContentAreaFilled(false);
                jb.setBackground(bg);
                jb.setOpaque(true);
                jb.setBorder(border);
                jb.setBorderPainted(true);
                b;
```

Some puzzle data, at last!

Fix the initial puzzle cells

Grid loop now inside larger sequence

```
            } ,                          ⊲— End of grid loop
            Flow {
                layoutX: 10;
                layoutY: bind puz.gridDim * cellSize;
                hgap: 50;
                content: [
                    SwingLabel {
                        text: bind "Empty: {puz.numEmpty}"
                            "   Clashes: {puz.numClashes}";
                    } ,
                    SwingLabel {
                        text: "Complete!";
                        visible: bind puz.completed;
                        foreground: Color.GREEN
                    }
                ]
            }
        ]
        width: puz.gridDim * cellSize;
        height:puz.gridDim * cellSize + 20;    ⊲— Allow for status line
    }
}
function notZero(i:Integer):String { if(i==0) " " else "{i}"; }
```

The status panel

You can see a couple of new imports at the head of the file—one is a Swing label class, and the other is the promised JFX layout class.

You'll note the `grid` variable of the `PuzzleGrid` class is now being set, and `fixGrid()` is being called to lock the initial puzzle numbers in place. You could provide your own puzzle data here if you want; I used the data that illustrates the Wikipedia Sudoku article as an example.

In this version of the game we'll be adding more elements to the scene graph beyond those created by the `for` loop. For this reason the loop (which creates a sequence of Swing buttons) has been moved inside a set of square brackets, effectively wrapping it inside a larger sequence. Embedded sequences like this are expanded in place, you'll recall, so the buttons yielded from the loop are expanded into the outer sequence, and our new elements (discussed later) are added after them.

Taking a closer look at the `SwingButton` definition you see a couple of minor but important additions. Here's the snippet of code we're talking about, extracted out of the main body of the button creation:

```
foreground: bind
    if(puz.clashes[idx]) Color.RED
    else if(puz.fixed[idx])  Color.BLACK
    else Color.GRAY
action: function():Void {
    if(puz.fixed[idx]) { return; }
    var v = puz.grid[idx];
    v = (v+1) mod (puz.gridDim+1);
    puz.grid[idx] = v;
}
```

In the foreground code we now look for and colorize fixed cells as solid black. And to complement this, in the event handler we now check for unchangeable cells, exiting if one is clicked without modifying its contents. These two minor changes, coupled with the work we did with the PuzzleGrid class, ensure the starting numbers of a puzzle will not be editable.

4.3.3 Adding a status line to our GUI with a label

The bulk of the changes come with the introduction of a status line to the foot of the GUI declaration. Here, for your convenience, is the code once more, devoid of its surrounding clutter:

```
Flow {
    layoutX: 10;
    layoutY: bind puz.gridDim * cellSize;
    hgap: 50;
    content: [
        SwingLabel {
            text: bind "Empty: {puz.numEmpty}"
                "   Clashes: {puz.numClashes}";
        } ,
        SwingLabel {
            text: "Complete!";
            visible: bind puz.completed;
            foreground: Color.GREEN
        }
    ]
}
```

This code is placed inside a larger sequence, used to populate the Scene. The UI elements it defines appear after all the grid buttons, which were created using a for loop, as you saw earlier.

You'll immediately notice a Flow, which is one of JavaFX's layout nodes, otherwise known as a *container*. It controls how its children are positioned on screen. Look at figure 4.8 and you'll see another example of Flow in action. The gray shapes are arranged, from left to right, in the order in which they appear inside the content sequence.

Like the Scene class, Flow accepts a sequence for its contents but doesn't add any new graphics itself. Instead it positions its children on the display by placing them one after another, either horizontally or vertically (depending upon how it has been configured), wrapping onto a new row or column when necessary. It has several options, including hgap, which determines the number of pixels to place between consecutive nodes in a row. The javafx.scene.layout package has several different container nodes, each specializing in a different geometry, and no doubt new ones will be added with each JavaFX release. Using these layout nodes we can place screen

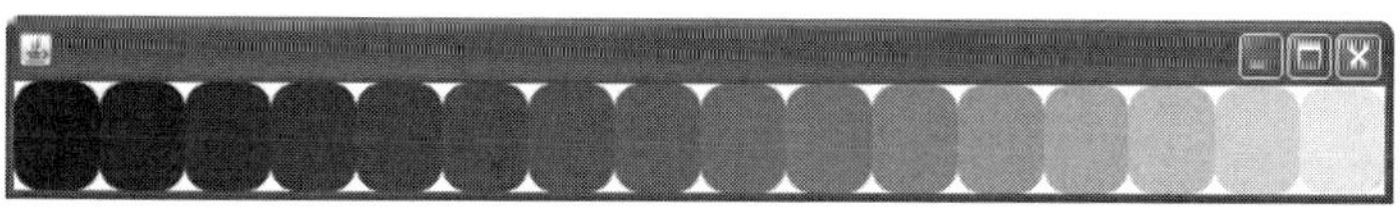

Figure 4.8 Elements inside a Flow are lined up in rows or columns, wrapping when necessary.

objects in relation to one another without resorting to absolute x/y positioning as we did with the button grid.

To ensure the status line is at the foot of the display, we use its `layoutY` variable to lower it below the button grid. It you check out the `Scene`, you'll note it has had its `height` amended to accommodate the new content. You can see how it looks in figure 4.9.

To implement the status bar we need to arrange five pieces of text, so we'll use `SwingLabel` classes. These are the equivalent of the Swing `JLabel` class, designed to show small quantities of text (typically used for labeling, hence the name) on our UI. We can group the "Empty" and "Clashes" text into one label, but the "Completed!" text needs to be a different color. So we need two labels.

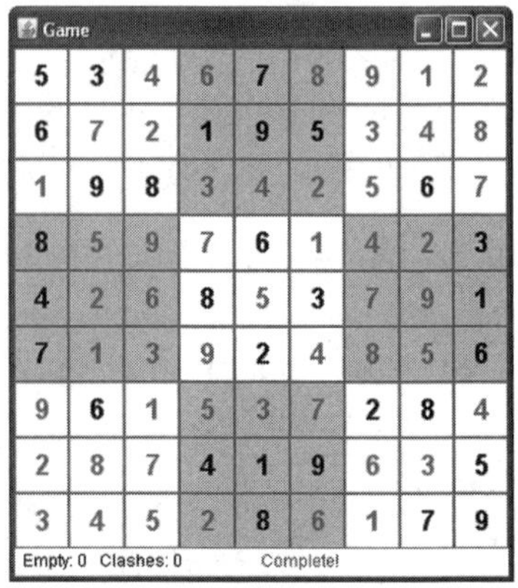

Figure 4.9 The puzzle game with its status panel, implemented using `Flow`

```
SwingLabel {
    text: bind "Empty: {puz.numEmpty}"
        "   Clashes: {puz.numClashes}";
} ,
SwingLabel {
    text: "Complete!";
    visible: bind puz.completed;
    foreground: Color.GREEN
}
```

Here's the declarative code for the two labels again, and you can immediately see how they are both bound to variables in the `puz` object. The first label binds its text to a string expression containing the number of empty and clashing cells; the second shows the "Complete!" message, its visibility dependent on the `puz.completed` variable.

So there we go—our GUI!

4.3.4 Running version 3

We now have a functioning number puzzle game, as depicted in figure 4.9. Clicking on a changeable cell causes its numbers to cycle through all the possibilities. Duplicate numbers (clashes) are shown in red, while the fixed numbers of the initial puzzle are shown in black. The status bar keeps track of our progress and informs us when we have a winning solution.

Almost all of this was done by developing an intelligent puzzle class, `PuzzleGrid`, which automatically responds to changes in the grid with updates to its other data. The GUI in turn is bound to this data, using it to colorize cells in the grid and show status information.

A single click on a button sets off a chain reaction, updating the grid, which updates the other status variables, which updates the GUI. Once the bind and trigger relationships are defined, the code runs automatically, without us having to prompt it each time the grid is altered. In our example the grid gets altered from only one place (the anonymous function event handler on each button), so this might not seem like much of a saving, but imagine how much easier life would be if we expanded our game to include a load/save feature or a hint feature—both of which alter the grid contents. Indeed, it becomes no extra work at all, so long as the relationships between the variables are well defined through binds.

4.4 Other Swing components

In our lightning tour of JavaFX's Swing support we looked at a couple of common widgets, namely `SwingButton` and `SwingLabel`. We also looked at some core scene graph containers like `Stage`, `Scene`, and `Flow`. Obviously it's hard to create an example project that would include every different type of widget, so here's a quick rundown of a few key UI classes we didn't look at:

- `SwingCheckBox`—A button that is either checked or unchecked.
- `SwingComboBox`—Displays a drop-down list of items, optionally with a free text box.
- `SwingList` and `SwingListItem`—Displays a list of items from which the user can select.
- `SwingRadioButton`, `SwingToggleGroup`—Together these classes allow for groups of buttons, in which only one button is selectable at any given time.
- `SwingScrollPane`—Allows large UI content to be displayed through a restricted *viewport*, with scrollbars for navigation. Useful if you have a big panel of widgets, for example, which you want to display inside a scrollable area.
- `SwingSlider`—A thumb and track widget, for selecting a value from a range of possibilities using a mouse.
- `SwingTextField`—Provides text entry facilities, unsurprisingly.

These are just a few of the classes in the `javafx.ext.swing` package, and Swing itself provides many more. You could get some practice with them by expanding our puzzle application; for example, how about a toggle that switches the highlighting of clashing cells on or off? This could be done by way of a `SwingCheckBox`, perhaps.

4.5 Bonus: using bind to validate forms

This chapter has been a fun way to introduce key JavaFX Script language constructs, like binds and triggers. These tools are very useful, particularly for things like form validation. Before we move on, let's detour to look at a bonus example, by way of listing 4.7.

Listing 4.7 Using bind for form validation

```
import javafx.ext.swing.*;
import javafx.geometry.VPos;
import javafx.scene.Scene;
import javafx.scene.shape.Circle;
```

```
import javafx.scene.input.KeyEvent;
import javafx.scene.layout.*;
import javafx.scene.paint.Color;
import javafx.stage.Stage;

var ageTF:SwingTextField;
def ageValid:Boolean = bind checkRange(ageTF.text,18,65);

Stage {
    scene: Scene {
        content: VBox {
            layoutX: 5;  layoutY: 5;
            content: [
                Flow {
                    nodeVPos: VPos.CENTER;
                    hgap: 10;  vgap: 10;
                    width: 190;
                    content: [
                        SwingLabel {
                            text: "Age: ";
                        },
                        ageTF = SwingTextField {
                            columns: 10
                        },
                        Circle {
                            radius: bind
                                ageTF.layoutBounds.height/4;
                            fill: bind if(ageValid)
                                Color.LIGHTGREEN else Color.RED;
                        },

                        SwingButton {
                            text: "Send";
                            disable: bind not ageValid;
                        }
                    ]
                }

            ]
        }
        width: 190;  height: 65;
    }
}

function checkRange(s:String,lo:Integer,hi:Integer) :Boolean {
    try {
        def i:Integer = Integer.parseInt(ageTF.text);
        return (i>=lo and i<=hi);
    }
    catch(any) { return false; }
}
```

This self-contained demo uses a function, `checkRange()`, to validate the contents of a text field. Depending on the validity state, an indicator circle changes and the Send button switches between disabled and enabled. We'll be dealing with raw shapes like circles in the next chapter, so don't worry too much about the unfamiliar code right now; the important part is in the binds involving `ageValid`.

The circle starts out red, and the button is disabled. As we type, these elements update, as shown in figure 4.10. An age between 18 and 65 changes the circle's color and enables the button, all thanks to the power of binds (you may need to squint to see the Swing button's subtle appearance change). The `ageValid` variable is bound to a function for checking whether the text field content is an integer within the specified range. This variable is in turn bound by the circle and the Send button.

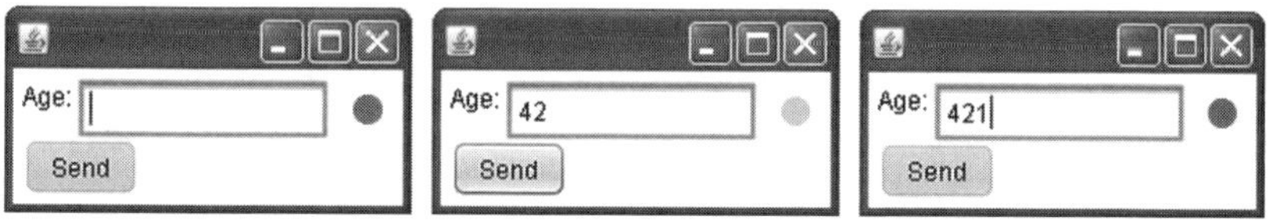

Figure 4.10 Age must be between 18 and 65 inclusive. Incorrect content shows a red circle and disables Send (left and right); correct content shows a light-green circle and enables Send (middle).

In a real application we would have numerous form fields, each with its own validity boolean. We would use all these values to control the Send button's behavior. We might also develop a convenience class using the circle, pointing it at a UI component (for sizing) and binding it to the corresponding validity boolean. In the next chapter we'll touch on creating custom graphic classes like this, but for now just study the way bind is used to create automatic relationships between parts of our UI.

4.6 Summary

In this chapter we developed a working number-puzzle game, complete with a fully responsive desktop GUI. And in less than 200 lines of code—not bad!

Assuming you haven't fallen foul to our fiendish number puzzle game (may I remind you, the screen shots give the solution away, so there's really no excuse!), you've—I hope—learned a lot about writing JavaFX code during the course of this chapter. Although the number puzzle wasn't the most glamorous of applications in terms of visuals, it was still fun, I think, and afforded us much-needed practice with the JFX language. And that's all we need right now.

The game could be improved; for example, it would be nice for the cells to respond to keyboard input so the player didn't have to cycle through each number in turn, but I'll leave that as an exercise to the reader. You've seen enough of JavaFX by now that you can extract the required answers from the API documentation and implement them yourself.

In the next chapter we're getting up close and personal with the scene graph, JavaFX's backbone for presenting and animating flashy visuals. So make sure you pack your ultratrendy shades.

5 Behind the scene graph

This chapter covers

- Defining a scene graph
- Animating stuff on screen, with ease
- Transforming graphics and playing with color
- Responding to mouse events

In chapter 4 we looked at building a rather traditional UI with Swing. Although Swing is an important Java toolkit for interface development, it isn't central to JavaFX's way of working with graphics. JavaFX comes at graphics programming from a very different angle, with a focus more on free-form animation, movement, and effects, contrasting to Swing's rather rigid widget controls. In this chapter we'll be taking our first look at how JFX does things, constructing a solid foundation onto which we can build in future chapters with evermore sophisticated and elaborate graphical effects.

The project we'll be working on is more fun than practical. The idea is to create something visually interesting with comparatively few lines of source code—certainly far fewer than we'd expect if we were forced to build the same application using a language like Java or C++. One of the driving factors behind JFX is to allow rapid prototyping and construction of computer visuals and effects, and it's this speed and ease of development I hope to demonstrate as we progress through the chapter.

We'll be exploring what's known as the *scene graph*, the very heart of JavaFX's graphics functionality. We touched on the scene graph briefly in the last chapter; now it's time to get better acquainted with it. The scene graph is a remarkably different beast than the Java2D library typically used to write Java graphics, but it's important to remember that one is not a replacement for the other. Both JavaFX's scene graph and Java2D provide different means of getting pixels on the screen, and each has its strengths and weaknesses. For slick, colorful visuals the scene graph model has many advantages over the Java2D model—we'll be seeing exactly why that is in the next section.

5.1 What is a scene graph?

There are two ways of looking at graphics: a blunt, low-level "throw the pixels on the screen" approach and a higher-level abstraction that sees the display as constructed from recognizable primitives, like lines, rectangles, and bitmap images.

The first is what's called an *immediate mode* approach, and the second a *retained mode* approach. In immediate mode each element on the display is instructed to draw itself into a designated part of the display immediately—no record is kept of what is being drawn (other than the destination bitmap itself, of course). By comparison, in retained mode a tree structure is created detailing the type of graphic elements resident on the display—the upkeep of this (rendering it to screen) is no longer the responsibility of each element.

Figure 5.1 is a representation of how the two systems work.

We can characterize the immediate mode approach like so: "When it's time to redraw the screen I'll point you toward your part of it, and you take charge of drawing what's necessary." Meanwhile the retained mode approach could be characterized as follows: "Tell me what you look like and how you fit in with the other elements on the display, and I'll make sure you're always drawn properly, at the correct position, and updated when necessary."

This offloading of responsibility allows any code using the retained mode model to concentrate on other things, like animating and otherwise manipulating its elements, safe in the knowledge that all changes will be correctly reflected on screen.

So, what is a scene graph? It is, quite simply, the structure of display elements to be maintained onscreen in a retained mode system.

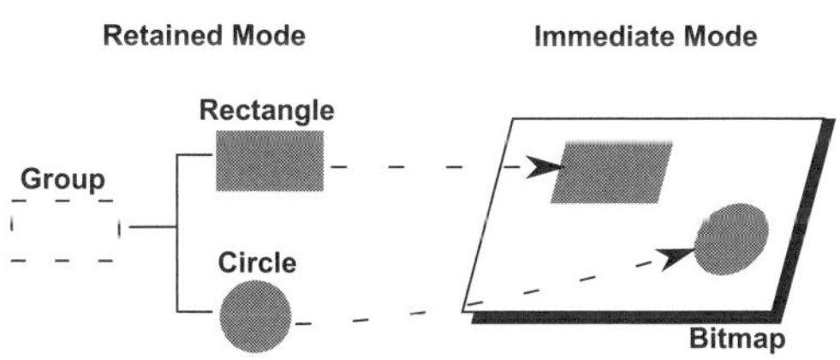

Figure 5.1 A symbolic representation of retained mode and immediate mode. The former sees the world as a hierarchy of graphical elements, the latter as just pixels.

5.1.1 Nodes: the building blocks of the scene graph

The elements of the scene graph are known as *nodes*. Some nodes describe drawing primitives, such as a rectangle, a circle, a bitmap image, or a video clip. Other nodes act as grouping devices; like directories in a filesystem, they enable other nodes to be collected together and a treelike structure to be created. This treelike structure is important for deciding how the nodes appear when they overlap, specifically which nodes appear in front of other nodes and how they are related to one another when manipulated. We can best demonstrate this functionality using figure 5.2.

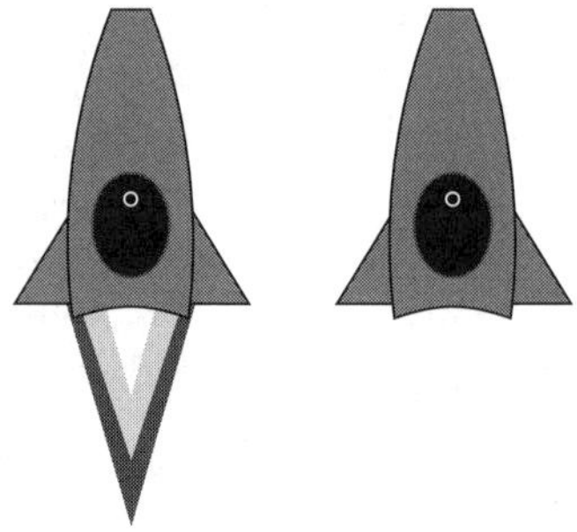

Figure 5.2 Elements in a scene graph can be manipulated without concern for how the actual pixels will be repainted. For example, hiding elements will trigger an automatic update onscreen.

A rocket ship might be constructed from several shapes: a distorted rectangle for its body, two triangular fins, and a black, circular cockpit window. It may also have a little rocket jet pointing out of its tail, likewise constructed from shapes. Each shape would be one primitive on the scene graph, one node in a tree-like structure of elements that can be rendered to screen. When nodes are manipulated, such as toggling the rocket jet to simulate a flickering flame, the display is automatically updated.

5.1.2 Groups: graph manipulation made easy

Once shapes have been added to a scene graph, we can manipulate them using such transformations as a rotation. But the last thing we want is for the constituent parts to stay in the same location when rotated. The effect might be a tad unsettling if the fins on our rocket ship appeared to fly off on an adventure all their own (figure 5.3). We want the whole ship to rotate consistently, as one, around a single universal origin.

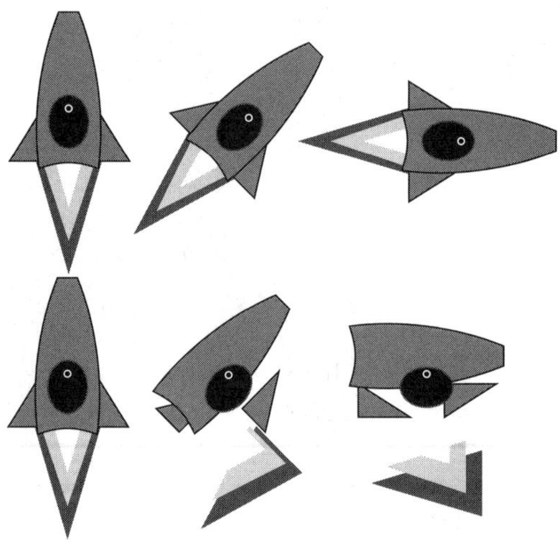

Figure 5.3 Grouping nodes in a scene graph allows them to be manipulated as one. The upper rocket has been rotated as a group; the lower rocket has been rotated as separate constituent nodes.

Groups are the answer! They allow us to combine several scene graph elements so they can be manipulated as one. Groups can be used within groups to form a hierarchy; the rocket's body and flame could be grouped separately within a main group, allowing the latter to be toggled on or off by flipping its visibility, as shown in figure 5.2.

This introductory text has only brushed the surface of the power scene graphs offer us. The retained mode approach allows sophisticated scaling, rotation, opacity (transparency), filter, and other video effects to be applied to entire swathes of objects all at once, without having to worry about the mechanics of rendering the changes to screen.

So that's all there really is to the scene graph. Hopefully your interest has been piqued by the prospect of all this pixel-pushing goodness; all we need now is a suitable project to have some fun with.

5.2 Getting animated: LightShow, version 1

The eighties were a time of massive change in the computer industry. As the decade began, exciting new machines, such as Space Invaders and Pac-Man, were already draining loose change from the pockets of unsuspecting teenage boys, and before long video games entered the home thanks to early consoles and microcomputers. An explosion in new types of software occurred, some serious, others just bizarre.

Pioneered by the legendary llama-obsessed games programmer Jeff Minter, Psychedelia (later, Colourspace and Trip-a-Tron) provided strange real-time explosions of color on computer monitors, ideal for accompanying music. The concept would later find its way into software like Winamp and Windows Media Player, under the banner of *visualizations.*

In this chapter we're going to develop our own, very simple *light synthesizer.* It won't respond to sound, as a real light synth should, but we'll have a lot of fun throwing patterns onscreen and getting them to animate—a colorful introduction (in every sense) to the mysterious world of JavaFX's scene graph.

At the end of the project you should have a loose framework into which you can plug your own scene graph experiments. So let's plunge in at the deep end by seeing how to plug nodes together.

5.2.1 Raindrop animations

The JavaFX scene graph API is split into many packages, specializing in various aspects of video graphics and effects. You'll be glad to know we'll be looking at only a handful of them in this chapter. At its heart, the scene graph centers on a single element known as a *node.* There are numerous nodes provided in the standard API; some draw shapes, some act as groups, while others are concerned with layout. All the nodes are linked, at the top level, into a *stage*, which provides a bridge to the outside world, be that a desktop window or a browser applet.

For our light synthesizer we're going to start by creating a raindrop effect, like tiny droplets of water falling onto the still surface of a pond. For those wondering (or perhaps *pondering*) how this might look, the effect is caught in action in figure 5.4.

Figure 5.4 Raindrops are constructed from several ripples. Each ripple expands outward, fading as it goes.

Before we begin, it's essential to pin down exactly how a raindrop works from a computer graphics point of view:

- Each raindrop is constructed from multiple ripple circles.
- Each ripple circle animates, starting at zero width and growing to a given radius, over a set duration. As each ripple grows, it also fades.
- Ripples are staggered to begin their individual animation at regular beats throughout the lifetime of the overall raindrop animation.

Keen-eyed readers will have spotted two different types of timing going on here: at the outermost level we have the raindrop activating ripples at regular beats, and at the lowest level we have the smooth animation of an individual ripple running its course, expanding and fading. These are two very different types of animation, one digital in nature (jumping between states, with no midway transitions) and the other analog in nature (a smooth transition between states), combining to form the overall raindrop effect.

5.2.2 The RainDrop class: creating graphics from geometric shapes

Now that you know what we're trying to achieve, let's look at a piece of code that defines the scene graph. See listing 5.1.

Listing 5.1 RainDrop.fx

```
package jfxia.chapter5;

import javafx.animation.Interpolator;
import javafx.animation.KeyFrame;
import javafx.animation.Timeline;
import javafx.lang.Duration;
import javafx.scene.Group;
import javafx.scene.paint.Color;
import javafx.scene.shape.Circle;

package class RainDrop extends Group {            <- Subclasses Group
    public-init var radius:Number = 150.0;
    public-init var numRipples:Integer = 3;
    public-init var rippleGap:Duration = 250ms;
    package var color:Color = Color.LIGHTBLUE;     | External interface variables

    var ripples:Ripple[];
    var masterTimeline:Timeline;

    init {
        ripples = for(i in [0..<numRipples]) Ripple {
            stroke: bind color;
            animRadius: radius;
        };                                         | Multiple Ripple instances
        content = ripples;
        masterTimeline = Timeline {
            keyFrames:
                for(i in [0..<numRipples]) KeyFrame {
                    time: i*rippleGap;
                    action: function() {           | Timeline to activate ripples
```

```
                    ripples[i].rippleTimeline
                        .playFromStart();
                }
            };
        };
    }

    package function start(x:Integer,y:Integer) : Void {
        this.layoutX = x;
        this.layoutY = y;
        masterTimeline.playFromStart();
    }
}

class Ripple extends Circle {
    var animRadius:Number;
    override var fill = null;

    def rippleTimeline = Timeline {
        keyFrames: [
            at (0ms) {
                radius => 0;
                opacity => 1.0;
                strokeWidth => 10.0;
                visible => true;
            } ,
            at (1.5s) {
                radius => animRadius
                    tween Interpolator.EASEOUT;
                opacity => 0.0
                    tween Interpolator.EASEOUT;
                strokeWidth => 5.0
                    tween Interpolator.LINEAR;
                visible => false;
            }
        ]
    };
}
```

Timeline to activate ripples

Starts animating ripples

Subclasses Circle

Start animation state

Finish animation state

Listing 5.1 creates two classes, `Raindrop` and `Ripple`. Together they form our desired raindrop effect onscreen, with multiple circles fanning out from a central point, fading as they go. The code will not run on its own—we need another bootstrap class, which we'll look at in a moment. For now let's consider how the raindrop effect works and how the example code implements it.

The second class, `Ripple`, implements a single animating ripple, which is why it subclasses the `javafx.scene.shape.Circle` class. Each circle is a node in the scene graph, a geometric shape that can be rendered onscreen. A raindrop with just one ripple would look rather lame. That's why the first class, `RainDrop`, is a container for several `Ripple` objects, subclassing `javafx.scene.Group`, which is the standard JavaFX scene graph group node.

The `Group` class works like the `Flow` class we encountered last chapter, except it does not impose any layout on its children. The `content` attribute is a sequence of

Node objects, which it will draw, from first to last, such that earlier nodes are drawn below later ones.

Child nodes are positioned within their parent Group using the layoutX and layoutY variables inherited from Node, which is the aptly named parent class of all scene graph node objects. Circle objects use their center as a coordinate origin, while other shapes (like Rectangle) might use their top-left corner. Coordinates are local to their parent, as figure 5.5 explains. The actual *onscreen* coordinates of a given node are the sum of its own layout translation plus all layout translations of its parent groups, both direct and indirect.

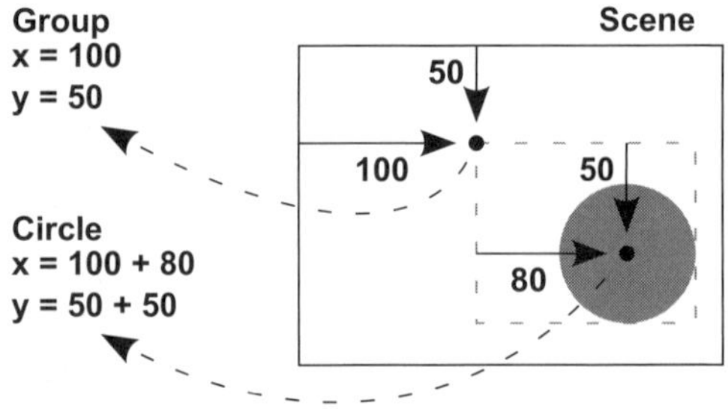

Figure 5.5 Groups provide a local coordinate space for their children. The Group is laid out to (100,50) and the Circle (positioned around its center) to (80,50), giving an absolute position of (180,100).

Enough of groups—what about our code? We'll study the animation inside Ripple shortly, but first we need to understand the container class, RainDrop, where the raindrop's external interface lies.

First we define public-init variables, allowing other classes to manipulate our raindrop declaratively. The radius is the width each ripple will grow to, while numRipples defines the number of ripples in the overall raindrop animation, and rippleGap is the timing between each ripple being instigated. Finally color is, unsurprisingly, the color of the ripple circles. Later in the project we're going to manipulate the raindrop hue, so we've made color externally writable.

The private variable ripples holds our Ripple objects. You can see it being set up in the init block and then plugged into the scene graph via content in (parent class) Group.

Another private variable being set up in init is masterTimeline, which fires off each individual ripple circle animation at regular beats, controlled by rippleGap. The remainder of the class is a function that activates this animation. The function moves RainDrop to a given point, around which the ripples will be drawn, and kicks off the animation.

Now all we need to know is how the animation works.

5.2.3 Timelines and animation (Timeline, KeyFrame)

Animation in JavaFX is achieved through *timelines*, as represented by the appropriately named Timeline class. A timeline is a duration into which points of change can be defined. In JavaFX those points are known as *key frames* (note the KeyFrame class reference in listing 5.1), and they can take a couple of different forms.

The first form uses a function type to assign a piece of code to run at a given point on the timeline, while the second changes the state of one or more variables across the duration between key frames, as represented in figure 5.6 (think back to the end of section 5.2.1 when we discussed digital- and analog-style animations).

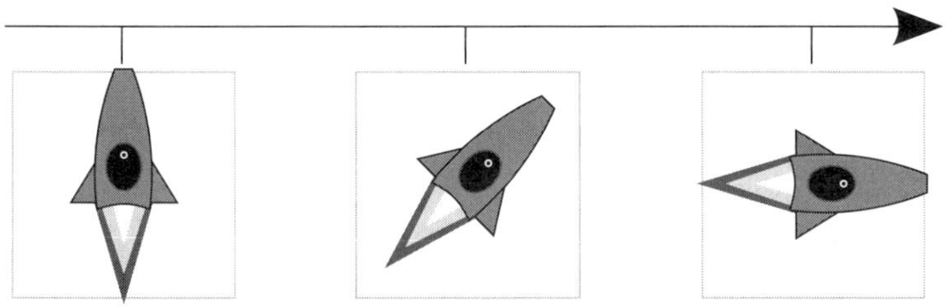

Figure 5.6 One use of key frames is to define milestones throughout an animation, recording the state scene graph objects should be in at that point.

The code for the masterTimeline variable of the RainDrop class is conveniently reproduced next. It deals with the outermost part of the raindrop animation, firing off the ripples at regular beats.

```
masterTimeline = Timeline {
    keyFrames:
        for(i in [0..<numRipples]) KeyFrame {
            time: i*rippleGap;
            action: function() {
                ripples[i].rippleTimeline
                    .playFromStart();
            }
        }
};
```

In the example snippet we see only the first form of timeline in play. The masterTimeline is a Timeline object containing several KeyFrame objects, one for each ripple in the animation. Each key frame consists of two parts: the action to be performed (the action) and the point on the timeline when it should start (the time). The result is a timeline that works through the ripples sequence one by one, with a delay of rippleGap milliseconds between each, calling playFromStart() on the timeline inside each Ripple object and thereby starting its animation. In a nutshell, masterTimeline controls the triggering of each ripple in the raindrop; figure 5.7 shows how this works in diagrammatic form.

As the master timeline runs (shown vertically in figure 5.7), it triggers the individual ripple's animation (shown horizontally), which uses the second form of timeline to manipulate a circle over time. In the next section we'll take a look at this second, transitional timeline form.

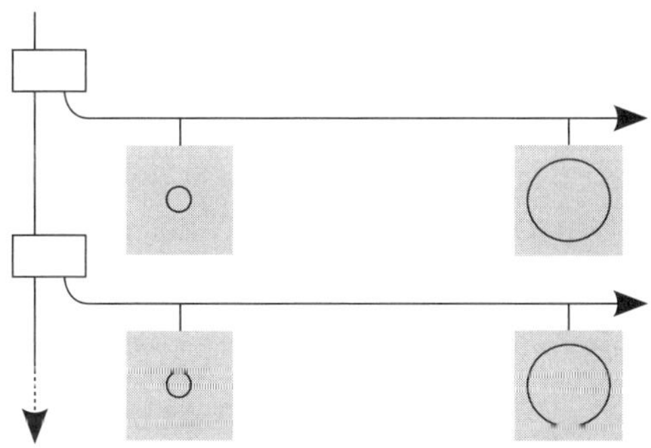

Figure 5.7 The master timeline awakes at regular intervals and fires off the next ripple's timeline. The effect is a raindrop of several ripples with staggered start times.

5.2.4 *Interpolating variables across a timeline (at, tween, =>)*

We've seen how Timeline and KeyFrame objects can be combined to call a piece of code at given points through the duration of an animation. This is like constructing a timeline digitally, with actions triggered at set points along the course of the animation. But what happens if we wish to smoothly progress from one state to another?

The ripples in our animation demonstrate two forms of smooth animation: they grow outward toward their maximum radius, and they become progressively fainter as the animation runs. To do this we need a different type of key frame, one that marks waypoints along a journey of transition.

```
def rippleTimeline = Timeline {
    keyFrames: [
        at (0ms) {
            radius => 0;
            opacity => 1.0;
            strokeWidth => 10.0;
            visible => true;
        } ,
        at (1.5s) {
            radius => animRadius
                tween Interpolator.EASEOUT;
            opacity => 0.0
                tween Interpolator.EASEOUT;
            strokeWidth => 5.0
                tween Interpolator.LINEAR;
            visible => false;
        }
    ]
};
```

I've reproduced the `Timeline` constructed for the `Ripple` class—it uses a very unusual syntax compared to the one we saw previously in the `RainDrop` class. You may recall that earlier in this book I noted that one small part of the JavaFX Script syntax was to be explained later. Now it's time to learn all about that missing bit of syntax.

The `at/tween` syntax is a shortcut to make writing `Timeline` objects easier. In effect, it's a literal syntax for `KeyFrame` objects. Each `at` block contains the state of variables at a given point in the timeline, using a `=>` symbol to match value with variable. The duration literal following the `at` keyword is the point on the timeline to which those values will apply. Remember, those assignments will be made at some point in the future, when the timeline is executed—they do not take immediate effect.

Taking the previous example, we can see that at 0 milliseconds the `Ripple`'s `visible` attribute is set to `true`, while at 1.5 seconds (1500 milliseconds) it's set to `false`. Because invisible nodes are ignored when redrawing the scene graph, this shows the ripple at the start of the animation and hides it at the end. We also see changes to the ripple's `radius` (from 0 to `animRadius`, making the ripple grow to its desired size), its opacity (from fully opaque to totally transparent), and its line thickness (from 10 pixels to 5). But what about that `tween` syntax at the end of those lines?

The `tween` syntax tells JavaFX to perform a progressive *analog* change, rather than a sudden *digital* change. If not for `tween`, the ripple circle would jump immediately from 0 to maximum radius, fully opaque to totally transparent, and thick line to thin line, once the 1.5 second mark was reached. Tweening makes the animation run through all the stages in between.

But you'll note we do more than just move in a linear fashion from one key frame to another; we actually define how the progression happens. The constants that follow the `tween` keyword (like `Interpolator.EASEOUT` and `Interpolator.LINEAR` in the example code) define the pace of transition across that part of the animation. In our example the ease-out interpolator starts slowly and builds up speed (a kind of soft acceleration), while a linear one maintains a constant speed across the transition (no wind up or wind down).

Limitations with the literal syntax, pre-1.2

It would seem that while the `at` syntax is happy to accept literal durations for times, the JavaFX Script 1.1 compiler had problems with variables. This made it difficult to vary the time of a key frame using a variable. The problem seems to have been addressed in the 1.2 compiler, but if you find yourself maintaining any old code, you need to be aware of this issue. In version 2 of this project you'll see a slightly more verbose syntax for key frames that has the same effect as `at/tween` but without this issue.

5.2.5 How the RainDrop class works

Before we move on to consider the bootstrap that will display our lovely new `RainDrop` class, I want to recap, step by step, exactly how the `RainDrop` works. We've covered quite a bit of new material in the last few pages, and it's important that you understand how it all fits together.

The `RainDrop` class is a `Node` that can be rendered in a JavaFX scene graph. It's constructed from other nodes, specifically several instances of the `Ripple` class, each of which draws and animates one circle (a ripple) in the drop animation. When the `RainDrop.start(x:Integer,y:Integer)` function is called, it fires up a `Timeline`, which periodically starts the timeline inside each `Ripple`, transitioning the radius, opacity, and stroke width of the circle to make it animate.

Now that we have something to animate, we need to plug it into a framework to show it onscreen. In the next section we'll see how that looks.

5.2.6 The LightShow class, version 1: a stage for our scene graph

To get our raindrops onscreen we need to create a scene graph window and hook the `RainDrop` class into its stage. A single raindrop wouldn't look very good, so how about we create multiple drops, which fire repeatedly as we move the mouse around? Listing 5.2 does just that!

Listing 5.2 LightShow.fx (version 1)

```
package jfxia.chapter5;

import javafx.scene.Scene;
import javafx.scene.input.MouseEvent;
```

```
import javafx.scene.paint.Color;
import javafx.scene.shape.Rectangle;
import javafx.stage.Stage;

import java.lang.System;

Stage {
    scene: Scene {
        def numDrops = 10;
        var currentDrop = 0;
        var lastDropTime:Long=0;
        var drops:RainDrop[];

        content: [
            Rectangle {
                width:400;  height:400;
                fill: Color.LIGHTCYAN;
                onMouseMoved: function(ev:MouseEvent) {
                    def t:Long =
                        System.currentTimeMillis();
                    if((t-lastDropTime) > 200) {
                        drops[currentDrop]
                            .start(ev.x,ev.y);
                        currentDrop =
                            (currentDrop+1) mod numDrops;
                        lastDropTime=t;
                    }
                }
            } ,
            drops = for(i in [0..<numDrops]) {
                RainDrop {};
            }
        ]
        width: 400;
        height: 400;
    }
    title: "LightShow v1";
    resizable: false;
}
```

Local variables, including RainDrop sequence

The background rectangle

Mouse event handler

Stage dimensions

Window configuration

We first encountered the `javafx.stage.Stage` class in the previous chapter. Its `scene` variable is the socket into which our scene graph should be plugged, which we do using the `javafx.scene.Scene` class.

The animation works by creating several instances of the `RainDrop` class, cycling through them over and over as the mouse moves. What happens if we run out of raindrops? Well, if we time things right, a `RainDrop` will have finished its animation by the time it is called into service again. By knowing how long each `RainDrop` animation takes and how frequently it is triggered, we can work out how many `RainDrop` nodes we need to continually run the animation.

Inside our `Scene` we first define some variables, local to that node:

- The `numDrops` variable defines the size of the `RainDrop` sequence—how many will be included in the scene graph, while `currentDrop` remembers which drop in the sequence is next to be animated.

- The lastDropTime variable records the time of the last drop animation, to ensure a reasonable gap between raindrops.
- drops is the RainDrop sequence itself.

We will manipulate these variables in an event handler. The first node in the Scene is a Rectangle, which is another kind of geometric shape similar to the Circle class. It will give our raindrop animation a colorful backdrop. We set the dimensions of the Rectangle within its parent and define a fill color. Then we assign an event handler to it.

```
onMouseMoved: function(ev:MouseEvent) {
    def t:Long = System.currentTimeMillis();
    if((t-lastDropTime) > 200) {
        drops[currentDrop].start(ev.x,ev.y);
        currentDrop = (currentDrop+1) mod numDrops;
        lastDropTime=t;
    }
}
```

The onMouseMoved variable is a function type, allowing us to attach event handling code to the Rectangle that responds to mouse movements across its surface. The example code has fewer line breaks, for extra readability. It works the same way as the button event handlers we saw in the Swing project in the last chapter, except it responds to mouse movement rather than button clicks. This event-handling code is the hub of the LightShow class; it's here that we initiate the raindrop animation. The code is assigned to the Rectangle because it covers the whole of the window interior, and thus it will receive movement events wherever the mouse travels.

But how does the event handler code work?

The first thing we do is get the current time from the computer's internal clock, using the Java method inside java.lang.System. We don't want to fire off new raindrops too quickly, so the next line is a check to see when we last started a fresh raindrop animation; if it's within the last 200 milliseconds, we exit without further action.

Assuming we're outside the time limit, we proceed by creating a fresh raindrop animation. This requires three steps: first we call start(x:Integer,y:Integer) on the next available raindrop, passing in the mouse event's x and y position, causing the class to begin animating around those coordinates. Then we move the currentDrop variable on to the next RainDrop in the sequence, wrapping around to the start if necessary, cycling through RainDrop objects as the mouse events are acted upon. Finally we store the current time, ready for the next handler invocation.

The Rectangle needs to access the RainDrop sequence from its onMouseMoved event handler, which is why we created a reference to the sequence as a local variable called drops before we declaratively created the Rectangle. Having added the Rectangle to the Group we can then add drops, so they'll be drawn above the Rectangle. Because JavaFX Script is an expression language, the assignment to the drops variable also acts as an assignment into the enclosing scene graph sequence.

5.2.7 Running version 1

Running the code is as simple as compiling both classes and starting up `jfxia.chapter5.LightShow` and waving your mouse over the window that appears. The effect is of circular patterns tracing the flow of your mouse, expanding and fading as they go. While they may serve no useful purpose, the application's visuals are (I hope) interesting and fun to play with. They demonstrate how rich animation can be created quite quickly from within JavaFX, with reasonably little code.

So far we've thrown a few shapes on screen and looked at how the scene graph groups things together. But the `RainDrop` is perhaps not the most efficient example of writing custom scene graph nodes. For a start, what happens if our custom node isn't a convenient subclass of an existing node? In the next section we'll see how using JavaFX's purpose-made `CustomNode` class helps us create unique custom nodes. We'll also be spinning a few psychedelic shapes on screen, so if you have a lava lamp around, now would be a good time to switch it on.

5.3 Total transformation: LightShow, version 2

Subclassing `CustomNode` is the recommended way of creating custom-made nodes in JavaFX. Although we managed perfectly well by subclassing `Group` for the `RainDrop`, a `CustomNode` subclass allows us a bit more control. For a start it includes a `create()` function that gets called when the node is created, acting as a lightweight constructor.

In our second version of the `LightShow` project we're going to write a `CustomNode` that will slot into the main bootstrap class, just like the `RainDrop`. We're also going to explore exotic uses of animation timelines, to bring a splash of Technicolor to our software.

5.3.1 The swirling lines animation

We'll start with a new class to create animated swirling lines, radiating out from a center point. The lines are like spokes on a wheel, spaced evenly around all 360 degrees of a ring, as in figure 5.8.

The `SwirlingLines` class uses transformations on `Rectangle` shapes to rotate and position each line within the scene graph. All the shapes in a given ring are contained within (and controlled via) a parent group, which is in turn linked to a custom node.

As with the `RainDrop`, we'll use the class multiple times in the `LightShow`, the end effect being several nested rings of colored lines rotating in different directions, while transitioning through several hues.

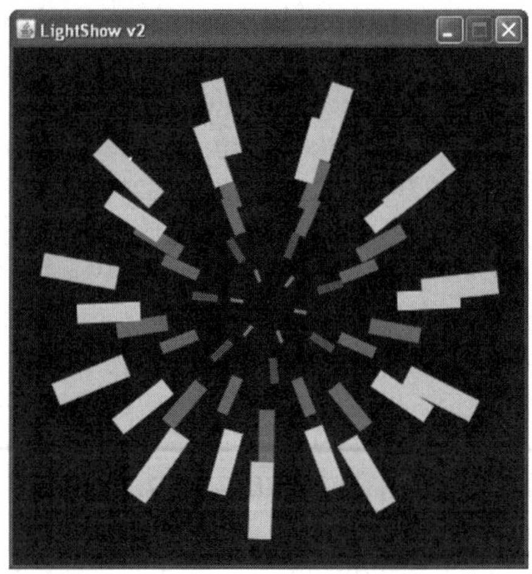

Figure 5.8 The `SwirlingLines` class creates a single ring of spokes, rotating around a central origin. Instances demonstrating different attribute settings are displayed.

Figure 5.8 shows the result. The animation will run continuously and will not interact with the user.

We have a lot of interesting new ideas to cover; all we need now is source code.

5.3.2 The SwirlingLines class: rectangles, rotations, and transformations

The `SwirlingLines` source code is presented in listing 5.3. It contains quite a host of instance variables for configuring its operation, from line length and thickness to the speed and direction of rotation. This will give us plenty of stuff to play with when we incorporate it into our project application a little later on.

Previously I mentioned that the lines in the finished application will continually change color. This class does not concern itself with the color changes, but it *does* bind a handy-dandy color variable, which some other class (the `LightShow` being a prime suspect) might want to manipulate. Listing 5.3 is the code.

Listing 5.3 SwirlingLines.fx

```
package jfxia.chapter5;

import javafx.animation.Interpolator;
import javafx.animation.KeyFrame;
import javafx.animation.Timeline;
import javafx.lang.Duration;
import javafx.scene.CustomNode;
import javafx.scene.Group;
import javafx.scene.Node;
import javafx.scene.paint.Color;
import javafx.scene.shape.Rectangle;
import javafx.scene.transform.Transform;

package class SwirlingLines extends CustomNode {
    public-init var antiClockwise:Boolean = false;
    public-init var baseAngle:Number = 0.0;
    public-init var numLines:Integer = 12;
    public-init var rotateDuration:Duration = 1s;
    public-init var lineLength:Number = 100.0;
    public-init var lineThickness:Number = 20.0;
    public-init var centerRadius:Number = 20.0;
    package var color:Color;

    var rotateSlice:Number =
        (if(antiClockwise) -360.0 else 360.0) / numLines;
    var animRotateInc:Number;

    override function create():Node {
        def node = Group {
            content: for(i in [0..<numLines]) {
                Rectangle {
                    width: lineLength;
                    height: lineThickness;
                    fill: bind color;
                    transforms: [
                        Transform.rotate (
                            baseAngle + rotateSlice*i ,
```

External attributes

Internal attributes, mainly animation

Bound to external attributes

Transformation ops array

```
                        0,0
                    ) ,
                    Transform.translate (
                        centerRadius ,
                        0-lineThickness/2
                    )
                ];
            };
        };
        rotate: bind baseAngle + animRotateInc;
    };

    Timeline {
        repeatCount: Timeline.INDEFINITE;
        keyFrames: [
            KeyFrame {
                time: 0s;
                values: [
                    animRotateInc => 0.0
                ];
            } ,
            KeyFrame {
                time: rotateDuration;
                values: [
                    animRotateInc => rotateSlice
                        tween Interpolator.LINEAR
                ];
            }
        ];
    }.play();

    return node;
  }
}
```

Annotations: Transformation ops array; Rotate Group; Run forever; Start of rotation; End of rotation; Start animation

The SwirlingLines class in listing 5.3 is a custom node, as denoted by its subclassing of the javafx.scene.CustomNode class. While subclassing Group was fine for our simple ripples, we need something more powerful for the effect we're building. CustomNode subclasses permit the building of complex multishape graphs inside their create() function, beyond just extending an existing predefined shape.

What's interesting about create() is that it gets called once, *before* the init or postinit blocks are run. Yes, you read that correctly: create() is run after the declared variables are set but before the class is fully initialized! Be sure to keep this in mind when designing your own CustomNode subclasses. Figure 5.9 is a diagrammatic rendering of what the SwirlingLines code produces.

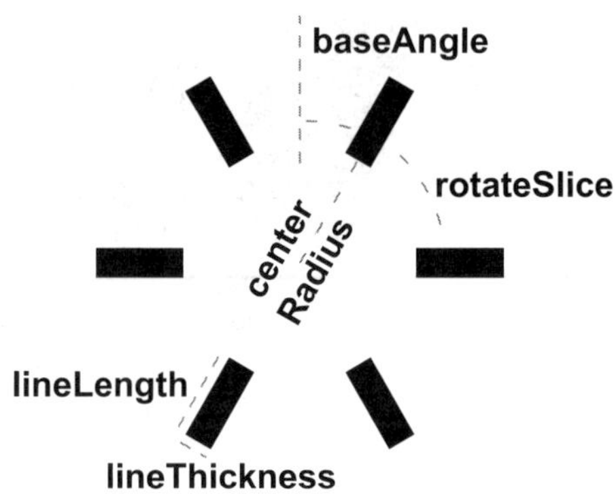

Figure 5.9 SwirlingLines **creates a ring of rectangles, fully customizable from its instance variables.**

Taking a look at the class we can clearly see several instance variables available for tailoring the class declaratively. Figure 5.9 shows the main initialization variables in diagram form, but here's a description of what they do:

- The `color` variable controls the line color (obviously!), while `lineLength` and `lineThickness` control the size of the lines. Since we'll be manipulating `color` throughout the run of the application, it has been made package visible, and its reference in the scene graph is bound.
- The `antiClockwise` flag determines the direction of animation, while `baseAngle` controls how the lines are initially oriented (the first line doesn't have to start at 0 degrees).
- The `numLines` determines how many lines form the ring; they will be evenly spaced around the total 360 degrees.
- The `rotateDuration` attribute controls how long it takes for the ring to perform one animation cycle. If there are 16 lines, this will be the time it takes to animate through one-sixteenth of a total 360-degree revolution.
- `centerRadius` details the empty space between the rotation center and the inner end of each line—in other words, how far away from the hub the lines are positioned.

There are some private variables, used to control the internal mechanics of the class.

- The `rotateSlice` value is the angle between each line in the ring. This is 360 divided by the number of lines. The value is used to constrain the animation (which we'll look at in a moment) and is either positive or negative, depending on in which direction the ring will spin.
- The `animRotateInc` object is the value we change during the timeline animation.

The rotation is performed at the group level, thanks to the group node's `rotate` variable being bound to `animRotateInc`. Although the ring will appear to rotate freely through a full 360 degrees, this is an optical illusion. The animation moves only between lines, so if there are four lines, our animation will continually run between just 0 and 90 degrees. (There's no great advantage in not making the ring spin a full 360 degrees; it just wasn't necessary to create the desired effect.)

The next part of the class is a function called `create()`, which returns a `Node`. The `CustomNode` class provides this function specifically for us to override with code to build our own scene graph structure (note the `override` keyword). The node we return from this function will be added to the scene graph, which is what we'll look at next.

5.3.3 Manipulating node rendering with transformations

The `create()` function is rather unusual, in that it gets called *before* the class's `init` block. This means if you're going to use `init` to set up any of your variables, they need to be bound in the scene graph to ensure the changes are reflected on screen.

Our `create()` function, in listing 5.3, does all the work of setting up the nodes in the swirling lines scene graph and defining the animation timeline. The first of these

> **Custom node initialization and older JavaFX versions**
>
> Be warned, JavaFX 1.2 was the first version of JavaFX in which `create()` was called before `init`. In previous versions `init` was called first, then `create()`, and finally `postinit`.

two responsibilities involves creating a sequence of `Rectangle` objects, the inner code for which is reproduced here with fewer line breaks:

```
Rectangle {
    width: lineLength;
    height: lineThickness;
    fill: bind color;
    transform: [
        Transform.rotate(baseAngle + rotateSlice*i, 0,0) ,
        Transform.translate(centerRadius , 0-lineThickness/2)
    ];
};
```

The function uses a `for` loop to populate a `Group` with `Rectangle` objects. Width, height, and fill color all reference the class variables, with `fill` being bound so it responds to changes. So far nothing new, but take a look at the `transform` assignment; what's going on there?

Transformations are discrete operations applied to a node (and thereby its children) during the process of rendering it to the screen. The `javafx.scene.transform.Transform` class contains a host of handy transformation functions that can be applied to our nodes. Transformations are executed in order, from first to last, and the order in which they are applied is often crucial to the result.

Let's consider the two operations in our example code: first we perform a rotation of a given angle around a given point, and then we move (translate) the node a given distance in the x and y directions. The first operation ensures the line is drawn at the correct angle, rotated around the origin (which is the center of the ring, recall). The second operation moves the line away from the origin but also centers it along its radial by moving *up* half its height. I realize it might be a little hard to visualize why this centering is necessary; figure 5.10 should clarify what's happening.

Without the negative y axis translation the rectangle would hang off the radial line like a flag on a flagpole. We want the rectangle to straddle the radial, and that's what the translation achieves.

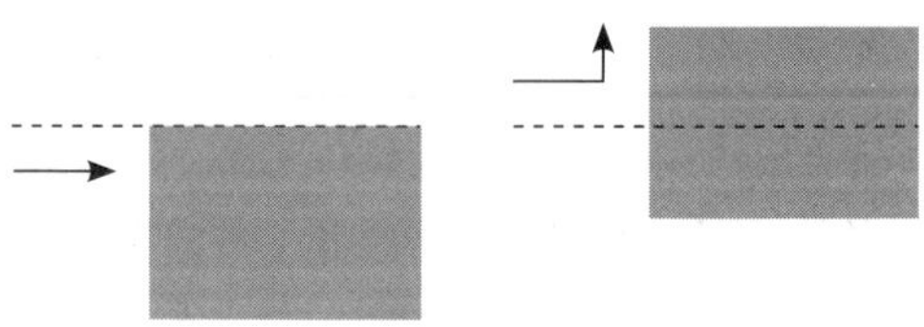

Figure 5.10 With and without centering: moving the `Rectangle` negatively in the y axis, by half its height, has the effect of centering it on its origin—in this case the radial spoke of a ring.

As previously noted, it's important to consider the order in which transforming operations are performed. Turning 45 degrees and then walking forward five paces is not the same as walking forward

When *up* sometimes means *down*

When I say the second transformation moves the `Rectangle` "up," it's a relative term—up in relation to the rotation we previously applied. If thinking about this hurts your head, picture it this way: the screen is a giant wall, and tacked onto that wall are separate pieces of paper with drawings on them (like you'd find in an elementary school classroom, where students have their crayon masterpieces on display).

We can take any one of these pieces of paper and rotate in on the wall; for example, we could display a given picture upside-down. If we take one of the drawings down from the wall and erase an object, redrawing it higher up (like moving the sun farther up in the sky), then we tack the drawing back onto the wall upside-down, did we move the object up or down? In terms of the paper, we moved it up. But after we applied the rotation, we moved it down in terms of the overall wall. We have two coordinate spaces in operation here, the global one (the wall) and the local one (the paper).

To return to our project source code, when we said we moved the `Rectangle` "up," we meant in terms of its local coordinate space. That space (like the paper on the wall) is rotated, but it doesn't matter, because from a local point of view *up* still means *up* (*left* still means *left*, etc.), even if the rotation actually changes the effect in terms of the global space.

five paces and then turning 45 degrees; check out figure 5.11 if you don't believe me. Always remember the golden rule: each time a node is drawn, its transformations are applied in order, from first to last.

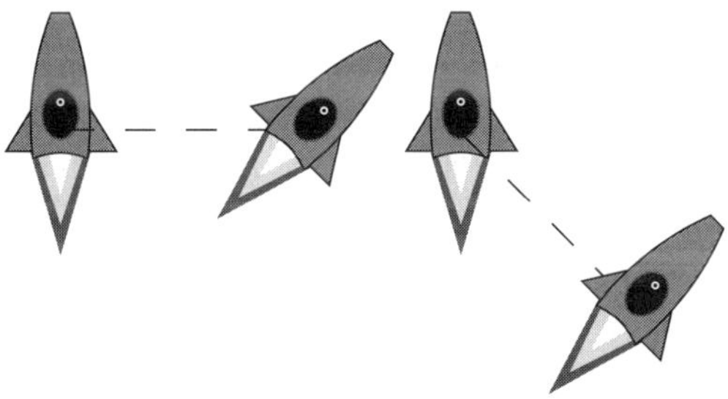

Figure 5.11 Two examples of transformations: translate and then rotate (left), and rotate and then translate (right). The order of the operations results in markedly different results.

Now that you understand transformations, let's look at the remainder of the code:

```
Timeline {
    repeatCount: Timeline.INDEFINITE,
    keyFrames: [
        KeyFrame {
            time: 0s;
            values: [
                animRotateInc => 0.0
            ];
        } ,
        KeyFrame {
            time: rotateDuration;
```

```
                values: [
                    animRotateInc => rotateSlice
                        tween Interpolator.LINEAR
                ];
            }
        ];
    }.play();
```

The example creates a timeline that runs continually once started, thanks to `Timeline.INDEFINITE`, with two `KeyFrame` objects, one marking its start and the other its end. All the timeline does is tween the variable `animRotateInc`, which the `Group` binds to. These changes cause the `Group`, and its `Rectangle` contents, to rotate.

The timeline looks a little different from the `at` syntax we saw in action in the `Ripple` class. There's no difference in terms of functionality; we're just writing out the `KeyFrame` objects longhand instead of using the briefer syntax. The `KeyFrame` code is quite easy to define declaratively; `time` is obviously the point at which the key frame should be active, while `values` is a comma-separated list (a sequence) of *attribute* => *value* definitions.

> **Limitations with the literal syntax, pre-1.2, part 2**
>
> As previously mentioned, the `at` syntax for describing key frames worked fine with time literals, but not variables, when used with JavaFX 1.1 compiler. However, the verbose syntax in our example doesn't seem to suffer from this problem. (As already noted, the issue seems to have been addressed in the 1.2 compiler.)

Once we've created the timeline, we kick it off immediately by calling its `play()` function. The `Timeline` class has a number of functions for controlling playback. The two we've seen in this project are `playFromStart()` and `play()`. The former restarts a timeline from the beginning, while the latter picks up where it left off. Because our timeline will run indefinitely, we can use either.

5.3.4 *The LightShow class, version 2: color animations*

Now that we have a swirling lines class, let's add it into our application class, `LightShow`. We also want to create some kind of psychedelic color effect as well. Listing 5.4 shows how the updates change the code.

Listing 5.4 LightShow.fx (version 2)

```
package jfxia.chapter5;

import javafx.animation.Interpolator;
import javafx.animation.KeyFrame;
import javafx.animation.Timeline;
import javafx.lang.Duration;
import javafx.scene.Scene;
import javafx.scene.input.MouseEvent;
```

```
import javafx.scene.paint.Color;
import javafx.scene.shape.Rectangle;
import javafx.stage.Stage;

import java.lang.System;

def sourceCols = [
     "#ff3333","#ffff33","#33ff33",
     "#33ffff","#3333ff","#ff33ff"
];
def colorShifts = for(i in [0..<6]) {
    ColorShifter {
        sourceColors: sourceCols;
        duration: 3s;
        offset: i;
    };
}

def sceneWidth:Number = 400;
def sceneHeight:Number = 400;
Stage {
    scene: Scene {
        def numDrops = 10;
        var currentDrop = 0;
        var lastDropTime:Long=0;
        def drop = for(i in [0..<numDrops]) {
            RainDrop {};
        }

        def lines = for(i in [0..<6]) {
            SwirlingLines {
                def ii = i+1;
                layoutX: sceneWidth/2;
                layoutY: sceneHeight/2;
                numLines: 6+i;
                color: bind colorShifts[i].color;
                centerRadius: (ii)*20;
                lineLength: (ii)*10;
                lineThickness: (ii)*3;
                antiClockwise: ((i mod 2)==0);
                rotateDuration: 1s/(ii);
            }
        };

        def rect = Rectangle {
            width: sceneWidth;
            height: sceneHeight;
            fill: Color.BLACK;
            onMouseMoved: function(ev:MouseEvent) {
                def t:Long =
                    System.currentTimeMillis();
                if((t-lastDropTime) > 200) {
                    drop[currentDrop].color =
                        colorShifts[0].color;
                    drop[currentDrop]
                        .start(ev.x,ev.y);
                    currentDrop =
```

Create six color animations (annotation for the `colorShifts` definition)

Swirling lines sequences, declaratively defined (annotation for the `lines` definition)

Color shift our raindrops (annotation for `drop[currentDrop].color = colorShifts[0].color;`)

```
                        (currentDrop+1) mod numDrops;
                    lastDropTime=t;
                }
            }
        };
        content: [
            rect ,
            lines ,
            drop
        ]
        width: sceneWidth;
        height: sceneHeight;
    }
    title: "LightShow v2";
    resizable: false;
    onClose: function() { FX.exit(); }
}

class ColorShifter {
    public-init var duration:Duration = 3s;
    public-init var sourceColors:String[];
    public-init var offset:Integer=0;

    var color:Color;
    var tLine:Timeline;

    init {
        def gap = duration / ((sizeof sourceColors)-1);
        Timeline {
            def arrSz = sizeof sourceColors;
            repeatCount: Timeline.INDEFINITE;
            keyFrames: for(i in [0..<arrSz+1]) {
                KeyFrame {
                    def pos = (offset+i) mod arrSz;
                    time: gap * i;
                    values: color =>
                        Color.web(sourceColors[pos])
                        tween Interpolator.LINEAR;
                }
            }
        }.play();
    }
}
```

Lines added to scene graph

Explicitly close window

Declaration variables

Output color

A KeyFrame for each color, wrapped around

We'll have a look at the color shifter first. At the start of listing 5.4 there's a sequence of colors called `sourceCols`, using web-style definitions (#rrggbb, as hex). Following that, a `for` loop creates seven `ColorShifter` objects.

The `ColorShifter` provides us with ever-shifting color, cycling through a collection of shades over a period of time. You can find its code at the bottom of listing 5.4. The external interface is as follows:

- The `duration` attribute is the time it will take to do one *full circle* of the colors.
- The sequence `sourceColors` provides the hues to cycle through, and `offset` is the index to use as the first color.
- `color` is the output—the current hue.

The class creates a timeline with a `KeyFrame` for each color, using tweening to ensure a smooth transition between each. The first color is used twice, at both ends of the animation, to ensure a smooth transition when wrapping around from last to first color. That's why the loop runs for one greater than the actual size of the source sequence and the `mod` operator is applied to the loop index to keep it within range. Once created, the `ColorShifter` timeline is started and runs continually.

That's it for the color animations. Returning to the scene graph, let's have a look at how the `SwirlingLines` are added to our `Group` node:

```
def lines = for(i in [0..<6]) {
    SwirlingLines {
        def ii = i+1;
        layoutX: fWidth/2;
        layoutY: fHeight/2;
        numLines: 6+i;
        color: bind colorShifts[i].color;
        centerRadius: (ii)*20;
        lineLength: (ii)*10;
        lineThickness: (ii)*3;
        antiClockwise: ((i mod 2)==0);
        rotateDuration: 1s/(ii);
    }
};
```

Nothing particularly unusual here. We create seven rings of lines, and each is bound to a different ever-changing `ColorShifter`. Because the `ColorShifter` objects were all declared with different source colors (we used a different `offset` each time), each ring pulses with a different part of the `sourceCols` input sequence. Each successive ring has more lines, longer and thicker, with a larger gap at the center. The rings alternate clockwise and counterclockwise, with outer rings rotating faster than inner ones.

Now that we have the code, let's see what happens when we run it.

5.3.5 Running version 2

Version 2 adds rotating patterns of lines and ever-changing colors, all animating merrily away without our having to get involved in any ugly code to draw them on screen as we'd need to if this was a Swing application using immediate mode rendering. Figure 5.12 shows the application running.

When you run the code, you'll see I added a few extra changes to version 1: the background is now black, and the raindrops are bound to a `ColorShifter` too. The effect is an explosion of color patterns across the window as the mouse is moved.

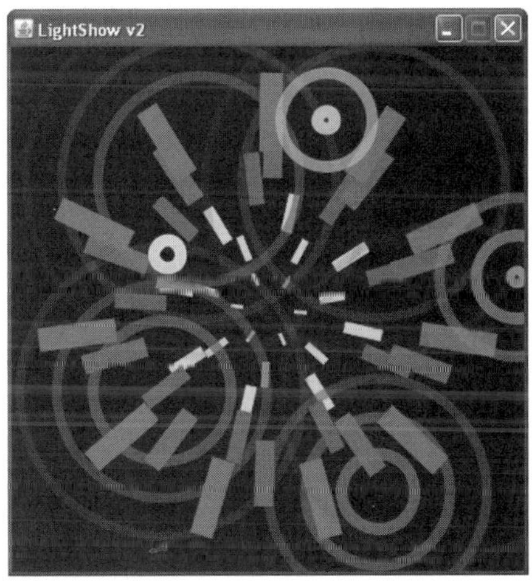

Figure 5.12 Version 2 of the project application, featuring both swirling lines and raindrops

5.4 Lost in translation? Positioning nodes in the scene graph

Before we round out this chapter, there's one topic we really *should* review: the relationship between a scene graph node's layout (`layoutX` and `layoutY`), its translation (`translateX` and `translateY`), and its coordinates. It's vital that you understand how these three work with one another.

Each scene graph node has a way of specifying its location within its own local space; for example, `Rectangle` has `x` and `y`, `Circle` has `centerX` and `centerY`, and so on. These define points within the node's own local coordinate space, quite separate to (although ultimately combined with) its location as a whole (see figure 5.13).

To borrow section 5.3.3's paper/wall analogy, if each shape is a drawing on a piece of paper tacked onto a wall, we might say `Rectangle.x` and `Rectangle.y` represent the rectangle's position within the paper, while `Rectangle.layoutX` and `Rectangle.layoutY` represent the paper's position within the wall. The former is the shape's location within its own space; the latter is its location within its parent's space. The important point to remember is this: the node's local space is unchanged no matter how it is rotated, bent, folded, or otherwise manipulated in the scene graph outside.

Actually, that isn't the whole story, because a shape's location isn't just determined by `layoutX` and `layoutY`. If you check the documentation for `Node`, you'll see there's a second set of coordinates, called `translateX` and `translateY`.

In versions of JavaFX prior to 1.2 the layout variables didn't exist, and the translate variables were used to position nodes. But 1.2 introduced the *controls* API, and with it more sophisticated layout management. The designers of JavaFX realized they needed to separate a node's layout position from any movement it might subsequently make as part of an animation; thus the concept of separate *layout* and *translation* coordinates was born. So, the location of a node is determined by its layout coordinates (its home within its parent), combined with its translation coordinates (where an animation has since moved it), combined with its own local coordinates after transformations have been applied.

Whew! Hopefully that clears everything up.

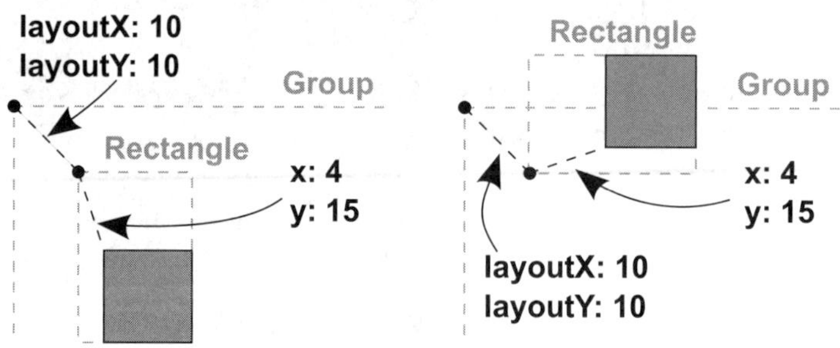

Figure 5.13 A `Rectangle` with its own local coordinates, translated within a `Group`. The local coordinates are not affected when the node is transformed in its parent's space, like a rotation by 270 degrees.

5.5 Bonus: creating hypertext-style links

We ended the last chapter with a bonus example listing, to frame the skills learned in more of a business/e-commerce context. This chapter's light synthesizer served as a fun way to introduce the scene graph, but it has little practical value beyond simply being entertaining. So before I sum up, let's indulge in another little detour, by way of listing 5.5.

Listing 5.5 Link.fx

```
import javafx.scene.*;
import javafx.scene.input.MouseEvent;
import javafx.scene.paint.Color;
import javafx.scene.shape.Rectangle;
import javafx.scene.text.*;
import javafx.stage.Stage;

var border:Number = 20;
var hyperLink:Group = Group {
    var t:Text;
    var r:Rectangle;
    layoutX: border;  layoutY: border;
    content: [
        r = Rectangle {
            width: bind t.layoutBounds.width;
            height: bind t.layoutBounds.height;
            opacity: 0;
            onMouseClicked: function(ev:MouseEvent) {
                println("Ouch!");
            }
        } ,
        t = Text {
            content: "Link text";
            font: Font.font("Helvetica",56);
            textOrigin: TextOrigin.TOP;
            underline: bind r.hover;
            fill: bind if(r.pressed) Color.RED
                else Color.BLACK;
        }
    ]
}

Stage {
    scene: Scene {
        content: hyperLink;
        width: hyperLink.layoutBounds.width + border*2;
        height: hyperLink.layoutBounds.height + border*2;
    }
    resizable: false;
}
```

What the listing does is to create a hypertext-like button from some text. Actually, JavaFX 1.2 came with a link control as standard, but that doesn't mean we can't learn something from crafting our own. Figure 5.14 shows how it looks when running. The

Figure 5.14 The link text depicted in three states: idle (left), underlined when hovered over (center), and red upon a mouse button press (right)

text is normally displayed black and undecorated, but it becomes underlined when the mouse is over it. When the mouse button is pressed, the color changes to red, before returning to black upon release.

The core of the code is in the `Rectangle` and `Text` objects used to populate the scene (via a `Group`). The `Text` object is akin to Swing's `JLabel`; it's used to include text within a scene graph. We'll cover `Text` in far more details next chapter, so for now please forgive me if I gloss over some of its details. The important point to note is that `Text`, like other scene graph nodes we encountered this chapter, behaves like a shape, meaning its concept of *area* is not limited to merely being rectangular. As the mouse travels over the text, it constantly enters and leaves the shape, the pointer passing inside and outside each letter.

Clearly we need the link to behave like a rectangle when it comes to its interaction with the mouse. To do this we employ an invisible `Rectangle` behind the `Text`, taking responsibility for mouse events. Note how the size of the `Rectangle` node is bound tightly to its companion `Text` node, while the `underline` decoration and `fill` color of the `Text` node are bound to the `Rectangle`'s `hover` state. Also note how the event function (which runs when the link is clicked) is attached to `onMouseClicked()` on the `Rectangle`, not the `Text` node.

Now that we have our own handmade hypertext link, we can customize it to our heart's content—perhaps make the underline fade in and out, or apply a drop shadow on mouse over. This was just an example to show how the scene graph sometimes requires a jot of lateral thinking when it comes to getting the effect you want. In the next chapter you'll see further examples of using nodes in clever ways, not just as proxies for event handling but to add padding around parts of the UI during layout and to define clipping areas to shape the visibility of a scene graph.

5.6 Summary

In this chapter we took our first look at the scene graph and played around with throwing shapes on screen. We saw multiple examples of timeline–based animation and explored how to define timelines to suit different purposes: triggering events at given moments and progressively transitioning variables between different states. We also witnessed how timelines could be used to animate more than just shapes onscreen. And to cap it all, we dabbled with mouse events.

The `LightShow` example isn't the most useful application in the world, and we didn't even wire it up to a sound source like true visualizations, but I hope you found it suitably entertaining. You can use the LightShow application as a framework for plugging in and trying your own CustomNode experiments, if you wish. There are plenty of different transformations we didn't have space to cover in this chapter—you might want to try playing with some of them, distorting the Rectangle lines or even adding different shapes of your own and seeing what effects they create.

The bonus listing, I hope, got you thinking about how to adapt the techniques we used in this chapter for more practical purposes. Indeed in some ways it was a taste of what's to come, because in the very next chapter we'll be staying with the scene graph but looking at building a slightly more useful application (using video, no less!). We'll also be creating our own custom UI components and looking at some of the effects we can create using the scene graph.

For now, have fun extending and adapting the LightShow, and when you're ready I'll see you in the next chapter!

6 Moving pictures

This chapter covers

- Interacting with complex custom nodes
- Laying stuff out on screen, using containers
- Playing video
- Embedding fonts into an application

In previous chapters we developed an application using JavaFX's Swing wrappers and played around with the scene graph. Now it's time to turn our hands toward creating a UI that combines the functionality of a traditional desktop application with the visual pizzazz of the new scene graph library. And when it comes to desktop software, you don't often get showier than media players.

Some applications demand unique interfaces, games and media players being prime candidates. They don't just stick to the conventional form controls but create a less-rigid *experience*, with sophisticated use of imagery, sound, movement, and animation. In the chapter 5 we started to explore the JavaFX scene graph, and in the next chapter we'll be looking at JavaFX's standard form controls. So, by way of a bridge between the two, in this chapter we'll be getting far more interactive with the scene graph, by making it respond and animate to a range of mouse events. The nodes we'll develop will be far showier (and specialized to the UI experience of this project) than the standard controls shipped with JavaFX or Swing. For this reason, we will be developing them as `CustomNode` classes, rather than formal `Control` classes. (There's no reason why they couldn't be written as full-blown controls, but I wanted this chapter to focus on getting more experience with the scene graph.)

We'll also look at using the media classes to play videos from the local hard disk. To try out the project (see figure 6.1) you'll need a directory of movie files, such as MPEG and WMV files.

The video player we'll be developing is very primitive, lacking much of the functionality of full-size professional players like Windows Media Player or QuickTime. A full player application would have been 10 times the size with little extra educational value. Although primitive in function, our player will require a couple of custom controls, each demonstrating a different technique or skill.

We'll also be adding a gradient fill to the background, and a real-time reflection effect will be applied to the video itself, making it look like it's resting on a shiny surface.

DOWNLOAD NEEDED This project requires a few images, which can be downloaded along with the source code from the book's website: http://www.manning.com/JavaFXinAction.

Over the coming pages you'll learn about working with images and video, creating controls from scene graph shapes, and applying fancy color fills and effect. This is quite a busy project, with a lot of interesting ground to cover, so let's get started.

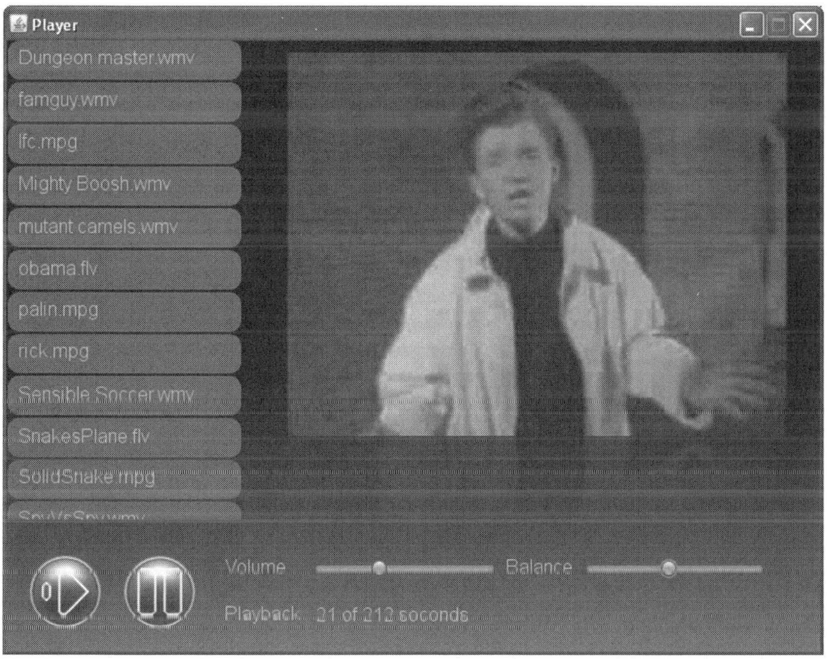

Figure 6.1 A preview of the simple video player we'll be building in this chapter

6.1 *Taking control: Video Player, version 1*

In this version of the player software we're focusing mainly on building the UI we'll need when we manipulate our video later on. Before JavaFX came along, getting video to work under Java would have deserved an entire book in itself. Thankfully, JavaFX makes things a lot easier. JavaFX's video classes are easy to use, so we don't have to devote the entire chapter to just getting video on screen.

You can see what this stage of the project looks like in figure 6.2.

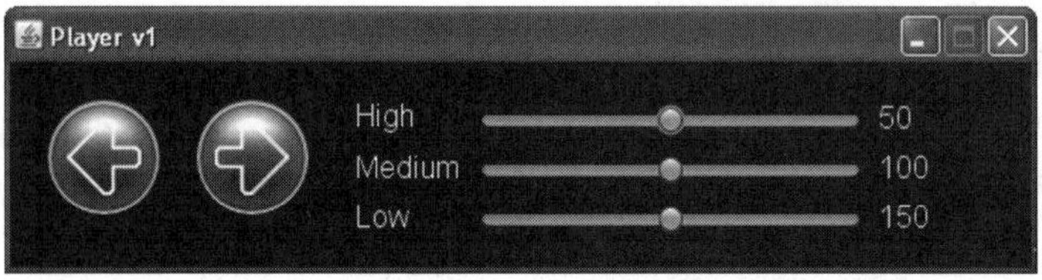

Figure 6.2 The interface for version 1 of our application

We'll begin simply enough, with the control panel that sits at the foot of the video player. It includes two examples of custom UI classes. The first is an image button, demonstrated to the left in figure 6.2; the second is a layout node, positioning the sliders and text to the right in figure 6.2.

We'll tackle the button first.

6.1.1 *The Util class: creating image nodes*

As before, the code is broken up into several classes and source files. But before we look at the button class itself, we'll take a short detour to consider a utility class. Quite often when we build software, the same jobs seem to keep coming up time and again, and sometimes it's useful to write small utility functions that can be called on by other parts of the code.

In our case the button we're writing needs to load images from a directory associated with the program—these are not images the user would choose but icons that come bundled with our player application. The code is shown in listing 6.1.

Listing 6.1 Util.fx

```
package jfxia.chapter6;

import javafx.scene.image.Image;

import java.io.File;
import java.net.URL;

package function appImage(f:String) : Image {
    Image {
        url: (new URL("{__DIR__}../../images/{f}")).toString();
    };
}
```

The script-level (static) function `appImage()` is used to load an application image from the project's images directory, such as icons, backgrounds, and other paraphernalia that might constitute our UI. It accepts a string—the filename of the image to load—and returns a JavaFX `Image` class representing that image. The JavaFX `Image` class uses a URL as its source parameter, explaining the presence of the Java `URL` class. Have you noticed that strange symbol in the middle of the code: `__DIR__`? What does it do?

It's an example of a predefined variable for passing environment information into our running program.

- `__DIR__` returns the location of the current class file as a URL. It may point to a directory if the class is a `.class` bytecode file on the computer's hard disk, or it may point to a JAR file if the class has been packaged inside a Java archive.
- `__FILE__` returns the full filename and path of the current class file as a URL.
- `__PROFILE__` returns either `browser`, `desktop`, or `mobile`, depending on the environment the JavaFX application is running in.

Note how both `__FILE__` and `__DIR__` are URLs instead of files. If the executing class lives on a local drive, the URL will use the file: protocol. If the class was loaded from across the internet, it may take the form of an http:-based address.

Most of you should have realized the `appImage()` function isn't the most robust piece of code in the world. It relies on the fact that our classes live in a package called `jfxia.chapter6`, which resolves to two directories deep from the application's root directory. It backs out of those directories and looks for an images directory living directly off the application root. If we were to package the whole application into a JAR, this brittle assumption would break. But for now it's enough to get us going.

6.1.2 The Button class: scene graph images and user input

The `Button` class creates a simple push button of the type we saw in our Swing example in chapter 4. However, this one is built entirely using the scene graph and has a bit of animation magic when it's pressed. The `Button` is a very simple component, which offers an ideal introduction to creating sophisticated, interactive, custom nodes.

The button is constructed from two bitmap graphics: a background frame and a foreground icon. When the mouse moves over the button its color changes, and when clicked it changes again, requiring three versions of the background image: the *idle* mode image, the *hover* image, and the *pressed* (clicked) image. See figure 6.3.

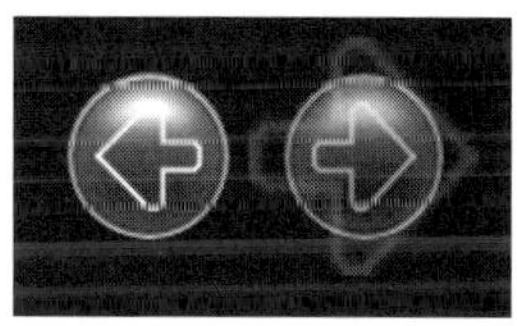

Figure 6.3 The button is constructed from two bitmap images: a background (blue circle) and icon (arrow). When the button is pressed, a ghost of its icon expands and fades.

When the button is pressed, the copy of the icon expands and fades, creating a pleasing ghosted zoom animation. Figure 6.3 demonstrates the effect: the arrow icon animates over the blue circle background. We'll be constructing the button from scratch, using a `CustomNode`, and implementing its animation as well as providing our own event handlers (because a button that stays mute when pressed is about as much use as the proverbial chocolate teapot).

Enough theory. Let's look at the code in listing 6.2.

BROKEN LISTINGS Because the button we're developing is a little more involved than the code we've seen thus far, I've broken its listing into two chunks, with accompanying text.

Listing 6.2 Button.fx (part 1)

```
package jfxia.chapter6;

import javafx.animation.Interpolator;
import javafx.animation.KeyFrame;
import javafx.animation.Timeline;
import javafx.lang.Duration;
import javafx.scene.CustomNode;
import javafx.scene.Group;
import javafx.scene.Node;
import javafx.scene.input.MouseEvent;
import javafx.scene.image.Image;
import javafx.scene.image.ImageView;
import javafx.scene.shape.Rectangle;
import javafx.util.Math;

def backIdleIm:Image = Util.appImage("button_idle.png");      // Button frame images
def backHoverIm:Image = Util.appImage("button_high.png");
def backPressIm:Image = Util.appImage("button_down.png");

package class Button extends CustomNode {
    public-init var iconFilename:String;                     // External interface variables
    public-init var clickAnimationScale:Number = 2.5;
    public-init var clickAnimationDuration:Duration = 0.25s;
    public-init var action:function(ev:MouseEvent);

    def foreImage:Image = Util.appImage(iconFilename);       // Private variables
    var backImage:Image = backIdleIm;
    def maxWidth:Number = Math.max (                         // Which is the bigger image?
        foreImage.width*clickAnimationScale ,
        backImage.width
    );
    def maxHeight:Number = Math.max (
        foreImage.height*clickAnimationScale ,
        backImage.height
    );

    var animButtonClick:Timeline;                            // Animation variables
    var animScale:Number = 1.0;
    var animAlpha:Number = 0.0;
    var iconVisible:Boolean = false;

    // ** Part 2 is listing 6.3
```

Listing 6.2 covers the first part of our custom button, including the variable definitions. The first thing we see are script variables to use as the button background images. Because these are common to all instances of our `Button` class, we save a few bytes by loading them just once.

Our `Button` class extends `javafx.scene.CustomNode`, which is the recognized way to create new scene graph nodes from scratch. Inside the class itself we find several external interface variables, used to configure its behavior:

- The iconFilename variable holds the filename of the icon image.
- The clickAnimationScale and clickAnimationDuration variables control the size and timing of the fade/zoom effect.
- The action function type is for a button press event handler.

There are also internal implementation variables:

- The foreImage and backImage are the button's current background and foreground images.
- Variables maxWidth and maxHeight figure out how big the button should be, based on whichever is larger, the foreground or the background image.
- The variables animButtonClick, animScale, animAlpha, and iconVisible all form part of the fade/zoom animation.

For CustomNode classes the create() function is called before the init block is run. This means we need to initialize the foreImage, backImage, maxWidth, and maxHeight variables as part of their definition, so they're ready to use when create() is called.

Custom node initialization

It's worth repeating: starting with JavaFX 1.2, create() is called before init and postinit; don't get caught! Give all key variables default values as part of their definition. Do not initialize them in the init block.

A quick tip: remember that object variables are initialized in the order in which they are specified in the source file, so if you ever need to preload private variables, make sure any public variables they depend on are initialized first.

Listing 6.3, the second half of the code, is where we create our button's scene graph.

Listing 6.3 Button.fx (part 2)

```
// ** Part 1 in listing 6.2
override function create() : Node {
    def n = Group {
        layoutX: maxWidth/2;
        layoutY: maxHeight/2;
        content: [
            Rectangle {                          <- Force dimensions
                x: 0-(maxWidth/2);
                y: 0-(maxHeight/2);
                width: maxWidth;
                height: maxHeight;
                opacity: 0;
            } ,
            ImageView {                          <- Background image
                image: bind backImage;
                x: 0-(backImage.width/2);
                y: 0-(backImage.height/2);
```

```
            onMouseEntered: function(ev:MouseEvent) {
                backImage = backHoverIm;
            }
            onMouseExited: function(ev:MouseEvent) {
                backImage = backIdleIm;
            }
            onMousePressed: function(ev:MouseEvent) {
                backImage = backPressIm;
                animButtonClick.playFromStart();
                if(action!=null)  action(ev);
            }
            onMouseReleased: function(ev:MouseEvent) {
                backImage = backHoverIm;
            }
        } ,
        ImageView {
            image: foreImage;
            x: bind (0-foreImage.width)/2;
            y: bind (0-foreImage.height)/2;
            opacity: bind 1-animAlpha;
        } ,
        ImageView {
            image: foreImage;
            x: bind 0-(foreImage.width/2);
            y: bind 0-(foreImage.height/2);
            visible: bind iconVisible;
            scaleX: bind animScale;
            scaleY: bind animScale;
            opacity: bind animAlpha;
        }
    ]
};

animButtonClick = Timeline {
    keyFrames: [
        KeyFrame {
            time: 0s;
            values: [
                animScale => 1.0  ,
                animAlpha => 1.0 ,
                iconVisible => true
            ]
        } ,
        KeyFrame {
            time: clickAnimationDuration;
            values: [
                animScale => clickAnimationScale
                    tween Interpolator.EASEOUT ,
                animAlpha => 0.0
                    tween Interpolator.LINEAR ,
                iconVisible => false
            ]
        }
    ];
};
```

Mouse enters node (onMouseEntered)

Mouse leaves node (onMouseExited)

Mouse button down (onMousePressed)

Mouse button up (onMouseReleased)

Icon image (first ImageView)

Animation image (second ImageView)

Animation timeline (animButtonClick)

```
        return n;
    }
}
```

At the top of listing 6.3 is the `create()` function, where the scene graph for this node is constructed. This is a function inherited from `CustomNode`, which is why `override` is present, and it's the recognized place to build our graph.

As we've come to expect, the various elements are held in place with a `Group` node. Moving the button's x and y coordinate space (`layoutX` and `layoutY`) into the center makes it easier to align the elements of the button. The `Group` is constructed from one `Rectangle` and three `ImageView` objects (figure 6.4). The `Rectangle` is invisible and merely forces the dimensions of the button to the maximum required size to prevent resizing (and jiggling neighboring nodes around) during animations.

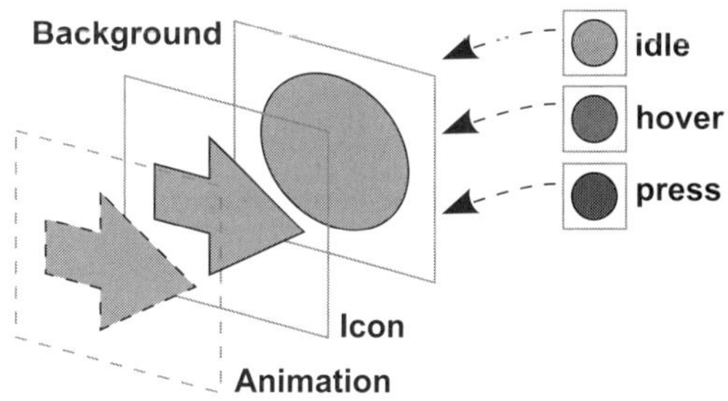

Figure 6.4 Ignoring the invisible `Rectangle` (used for sizing), there are three layers in our button.

In front of the rectangle there are three `ImageView` objects. What's an `ImageView`? It's yet another type of scene graph node. This one displays `Image` objects; the clue is in the class name. Our button requires three images (figure 6.4):

- The button background image, which changes when the mouse hovers over or clicks the button.
- The icon image, which displays the actual button symbol.
- The animation image, which is used in the fade/zoom effect when the button is pressed. This is a copy of the icon image, hidden when the animation isn't playing.

Look at the code for the first `ImageView` declaration. Like other `Node` subclasses, the `ImageView` can receive events and has a full complement of event-handling function types into which we can plug our own code. In the case of the background `ImageView`, we've wired up handlers to change its image when the mouse rolls into or out of the node and when the mouse button is pressed and released. The button press is by far the most interesting handler, as it not only changes the image but launches the fade/zoom animation and calls any `action` handler that might be linked to our `Button` class.

The second `ImageView` in the sequence displays the regular icon—the only cleverness is that it will fade into view as the animating fade/zoom icon fades out. Subtracting the current animation opacity from 1 means this image always has the opposite opacity to the animation icon image, so as the zooming icon fades out of view, the regular icon reappears, creating a pleasing full-circle effect.

The third ImageView in the sequence is the animation icon. It performs the fabled fade/zoom, and as you'd expect it's heavily bound to the object variables, which are manipulated by the animation's timeline.

And speaking of timelines, the create() function is rounded off by a classic start/finish key frame example, not unlike the examples we saw in chapter 5. The animation icon's size (scale) and opacity (alpha) are transitioned, while the animation ImageView is switched on at the start of the animation and off at the end. Simple stuff!

And so that, ladies and gentlemen, boys and girls, is our Button class. It's not perfect (indeed it has one minor limitation we'll consider later, when plugging it into our application), but it shows what can be achieved with only a modest amount of effort.

6.1.3 The GridBox class: lay out your nodes

Our button class is ready to use. Now it's time to turn our attention to the other piece of custom UI code in this stage of the application: the layout node. Figure 6.5 shows the effect we're after: the text and slider nodes in that screen shot are held in a loose grid, with variable-size columns and rows that adapt to the width or height of their contents.

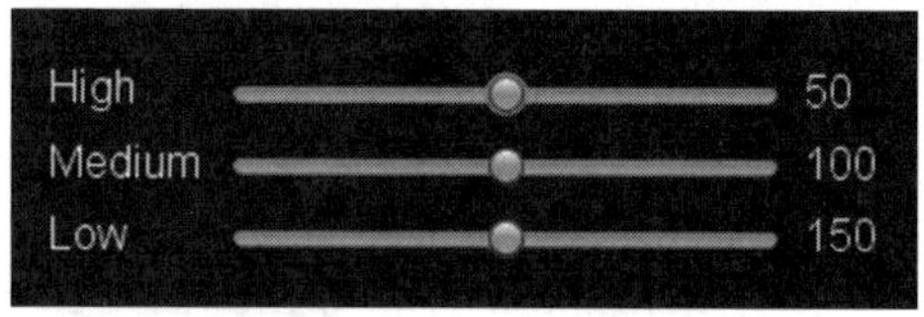

Figure 6.5 The GridBox node positions its children into a grid, with flexible column and row sizes.

This is not an effect we can easily construct with the standard layout classes in javafx.scene.layout. If you check the API documentation, you'll see there's a really handy Tile class that lays out its contents in a grid. But Tile likes to have uniform column and row sizes, and we want our columns and rows to size themselves individually around their largest element. So we have no option but to create our own layout node, and that's just what listing 6.4 does.

Listing 6.4 GridBox.fx

```
package jfxia.chapter6;

import javafx.geometry.HPos;
import javafx.geometry.VPos;
import javafx.scene.Node;
import javafx.scene.layout.Container;

package class GridBox extends Container {
    public-init var columns:Integer = 5;                 // Width in columns
    public-init var nodeHPos:HPos = HPos.LEFT;           // Alignment
    public-init var nodeVPos:VPos = VPos.TOP;
    public-init var horizontalGap:Number = 0.0;          // Gap between nodes
    public-init var verticalGap:Number = 0.0;

    override function doLayout() : Void {
        def nodes = getManaged(content);                 // Content to lay out

        def sz:Integer = sizeof nodes;                   // How many rows?
        var rows:Integer = (sz/columns);
        rows += if((sz mod columns) > 0) 1 else 0;
```

```
        var colSz:Number[] = for(i in [0..<columns]) 0.0;
        var rowSz:Number[] = for(i in [0..<rows]) 0.0;
        for(n in nodes) {
            def i:Integer = indexof n;
            def c:Integer = (i mod columns);
            def r:Integer = (i / columns).intValue();          Find maximum
            def w:Number = getNodePrefWidth(n);                 col/row size
            def h:Number = getNodePrefHeight(n);
            if(w > colSz[c])  colSz[c]=w;
            if(h > rowSz[r])  rowSz[r]=h;
        }

        var x:Number = 0;
        var y:Number = 0;
        for(n in nodes) {
            def i:Integer = indexof n;
            def c:Integer = (i mod columns);
            def r:Integer = (i / columns).intValue();

            layoutNode(n , x,y,colSz[c],rowSz[r] ,          Position
                nodeHPos,nodeVPos);                         node

            if(c < (columns-1)) {
                x+=(colSz[c] + horizontalGap);
            }                                               Next
            else {                                          position
                x=0;  y+=(rowSz[r] + verticalGap);
            }
        }
    }
}
```

There are two ways to create custom layouts in JavaFX: one produces layout nodes that can be used time and time again, and the other is useful for case-specific one-shot layouts. In listing 6.4 we see the former (reusable) approach.

To create a layout node we subclass `Container`, a type of `Group` that understands layout. As well as proving a framework to manage node layout, `Container` has several useful utility functions we can use when writing node-positioning code.

Our `Container` subclass is called `GridBox`, and has these public variables:

- `columns` determines how many columns the grid should have. The number of rows is calculated based on this value and the number of managed (laid-out) nodes in the `content` sequence.
- `nodeHPos` and `nodeVPos` determine how nodes should be aligned within the space available to them when being laid out.
- `horizontalGap` and `verticalGap` control the pixel gap between rows and columns.

To make the code simpler, all the configuration variables are `public-init` so they cannot be modified externally once the object is created. The `doLayout()` function is overridden to provide the actual layout code. Code inherited from the `Container` class will call `doLayout()` whenever JavaFX thinks a layout refresh is necessary.

To perform the actual layout, first we scan our child nodes to work out the width of each column and the height of each row. Rather than read the `content` sequence directly, we use a handy function inherited from `Container`, `getManaged()`, to process only those nodes that require layout. Two more inherited functions, `getNodePrefWidth()` and `getNodePrefHeight()`, extract the preferred size from each node. Having worked out the necessary column/row sizes, we do a second pass to position each node. Yet another inherited function, `layoutNode()`, positions the node within a given area (x, y, width and height) using the node's own layout preferences (if specified) or `nodeHPos` and `nodeVPos`. The result is the flexible grid we want, with each node appropriately aligned within its cell.

Layout using the object literal syntax

The `GridBox` class is an example of a layout node: a fully fledged subclass of `Container` that can be used over and over. But what if we want a specific, one-time-only layout; do we need to create a subclass every time?

The `Container` class has a sibling called `Panel`. It does the same job as `Container`, except its code can be plugged in via function types. We can drop a `Panel` into our scene graph with an anonymous function to provide the layout code, allowing us to create one-shot custom layouts without the use of a subclass. A full example of `Panel` in action will be presented in the next chapter.

Now we have a functioning grid layout node class; all we need are nodes to use it with, a problem we'll remedy next.

6.1.4 *The Player class, version 1*

We have our two custom classes, one a control node, the other a layout node. Before going any further we should give them a trial run in a prototype version of our video player. Listing 6.5 will do this for us.

Listing 6.5 Player.fx (version 1)

```
package jfxia.chapter6;

import javafx.geometry.VPos;
import javafx.scene.Group;
import javafx.scene.Scene;
import javafx.scene.control.Slider;
import javafx.scene.input.MouseEvent;
import javafx.scene.layout.LayoutInfo;
import javafx.scene.paint.Color;
import javafx.scene.text.Font;
import javafx.scene.text.Text;
import javafx.scene.text.TextOrigin;
import javafx.stage.Stage;

def font = Font { name: "Helvetica";  size: 16; };      <- Handy font declaration

Stage {
```

```
    scene: Scene {
        content: [
            Button {                                    // Left button
                iconFilename: "arrow_l.png";
                action: function(ev:MouseEvent) {
                    println("Back");
                };
            } ,
            Button {                                    // Right button (note the layoutX)
                layoutX: 80;
                iconFilename: "arrow_r.png";
                action: function(ev:MouseEvent) {
                    println("Fore");
                };
            } ,
            GridBox {                                   // Our GridBox in action
                layoutX: 185;  layoutY: 20;
                columns: 3;
                nodeVPos: VPos.CENTER;
                horizontalGap: 10;  verticalGap: 5;
                var max:Integer=100;
                content: for(l in ["High","Medium","Low"]) {   // Loop to add rows
                    var sl:Slider;
                    var contentArr = [
                        Text {                          // Left-hand label
                            content: l;
                            font: font;
                            fill: Color.WHITE;
                            textOrigin: TextOrigin.TOP;
                        } ,
                        sl = Slider {                   // The slider itself
                            layoutInfo:
                                LayoutInfo { width: 200; }
                            max: max;
                            value: max/2;
                        } ,
                        Text {                          // Bound display value
                            content: bind sl.value
                                .intValue().toString();
                            font: font;
                            fill: Color.WHITE;
                            textOrigin: TextOrigin.TOP;
                        }
                    ];
                    max+=100;
                    contentArr;                         // Add row to GridBox
                }
            }
        ];
        fill: Color.BLACK;
    };
    width: 550;  height: 140;
    title: "Player v1";
    resizable: false;
}
```

The code displays the two classes we developed: two image buttons are combined with JavaFX slider controls, using our grid layout.

I mentioned very briefly at the end of the section dealing with the `Button` class that our button code has a slight limitation, which we'd discuss later. Now is the time to reveal all. The click animation used in our `Button` class introduces a slight headache: the animation effect expands beyond the size of the button itself. Although it creates a cool zoom visual, it means padding is required around the perimeter, accommodating the effect when it occurs. This is the purpose of the transparent `Rectangle` that sits behind the other nodes in the `Button`'s internal scene graph. Without this padding the button would grow in size as the animation plays, which might cause its parent layout node to continually reevaluate its children, resulting in a jostling effect on screen as other nodes move to accommodate the button.

To solve this problem we need to absolutely position our buttons, overlapping them so they mask their oversized padding. And this is what listing 6.5 does, by using the `layoutX` variable.

Following the two buttons in the listing we find an example of our `GridBox` in use. Its content is formed using a `for` loop, adding three nodes (one whole row) with each pass. The first and last are `Text` nodes, while the middle is a `Slider` node. The `javafx.scene.text.Text` nodes simply display a string using a font, not unlike the `SwingLabel` class. However, because this is a scene graph node, it has a `fill` (body color) and a `stroke` (perimeter color), as well as other shape-like capabilities. By default a `Text` node's coordinate origin is measured from the font's baseline (the imaginary line on which the text rests, like the ruled lines on writing paper), but in our listing we relocate the origin to the more convenient top-left corner of the node.

The `Slider`, as its name suggests, allows the user to pick a value between a given minimum and a maximum by dragging a thumb along a track. We explicitly set the layout width of the control by assigning a `LayoutInfo` object. When our `GridBox` class uses `getNodePrefWidth()` and `getNodePrefHeight()` to query each node's size, this layout data is what's being consulted (if the `LayoutInfo` isn't set, the node's `getPrefWidth()` and `getPrefHeight()` functions are consulted.) The final `Text` node on each row is bound to the current value of this slider, and its text content will change when the associated slider is adjusted.

Version 1 of our application is complete!

6.1.5 Running version 1

Running version 1 gives us a basic control panel, as revealed by figure 6.6. Although the code is compact, the results are hardly crude. The buttons are fully functional,

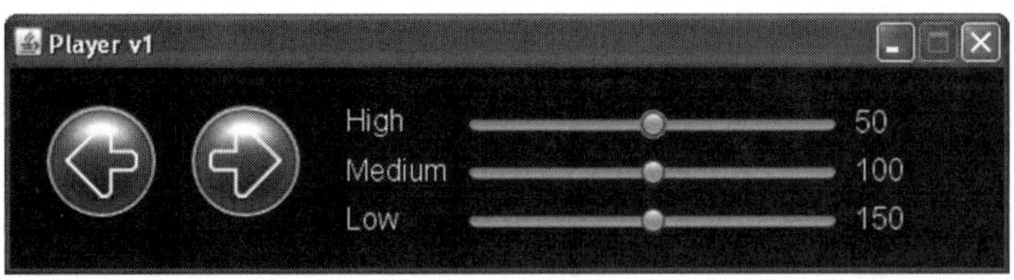

Figure 6.6 Our custom button and layout nodes on display

have their own event handler into which code can be plugged, and sport a really cool animation effect when pressed. The layout node makes building the slider UI much easier, yet it's still appropriately configurable.

I'll leave it up to you, the reader, to polish off our custom classes with your own bells and whistles. The `GridBox` in particular could become a really powerful layout class with not a great deal of extra work. The additional code wouldn't be of value from a demonstration viewpoint (that's why I didn't add it myself), but I encourage you to use version 1 as a test bed to try out your own enhancements.

So much for custom buttons. Did I hear someone ask when we will start playing with video? Good question. In the second, and final, part of this project we develop our most ambitious custom node yet—and, yes, finally we get to play with some video.

6.2 Making the list: Video Player, version 2

In this part of the chapter we have two objectives. The first is to incorporate a video playback node into our scene graph; the second is to develop a custom node for listing and choosing videos. Figure 6.7 shows what we're after.

Figure 6.7 shows the two new elements in action. The list allows the user to pick a video, and the video playback node will show it. Our control panel will interact with the video as it plays, pausing or restarting the action and adjusting the sound. The list display down the side will use tween-based animations, to control not only rollover effects but also its scrolling.

Figure 6.7 Lift off! Our control panel (bottom) is combined with a new list (left-hand side) and video node (center) to create the final player.

We need to develop this list node first, so that's where we'll head next.

6.2.1 *The List class: a complex multipart custom node*

The `List/ListPane` code is quite complex, indeed so complex that it's been broken into two classes. `List` is an interior node for displaying a list of strings and firing `action` events when they are clicked. `ListPane` is an outer container node that allows the `List` to be scrolled. In figure 6.8 you can see how the list parts fit together.

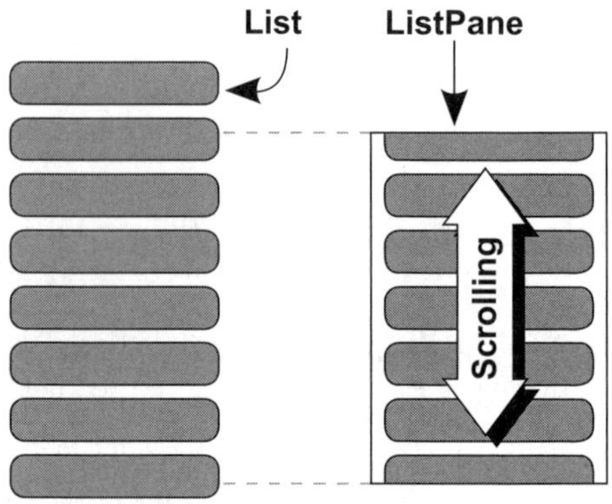

Figure 6.8 The `List` and `ListPane` classes will allow us to present a selection of movie files for the user to pick from.

Rather than using a scrollbar, I thought we might attempt something a little different; the list will work in a vaguely iPhone-like fashion. A press and drag will scroll the list, with inertia when we let go, while a quick press and release will be treated as a click on a list item. We start with just the inner `List` node, which I've broken into two parts to avoid page flipping. The first part is listing 6.6.

Listing 6.6 List.fx (part 1)

```
package jfxia.chapter6;

import javafx.animation.Interpolator;
import javafx.animation.KeyFrame;
import javafx.animation.Timeline;
import javafx.scene.CustomNode;
import javafx.scene.Group;
import javafx.scene.Node;
import javafx.scene.input.MouseEvent;
import javafx.scene.layout.VBox;
import javafx.scene.paint.Color;
import javafx.scene.shape.Rectangle;
import javafx.scene.text.Font;
import javafx.scene.text.Text;
import javafx.scene.text.TextOrigin;

package class List extends CustomNode {
    package var cellWidth:Number = 150;
    package var cellHeight:Number = 35;

    public-init var content:String[];
    public-init var font:Font = Font {};
    public-init var foreground:Color = Color.LIGHTBLUE;
    public-init var background:Color = Color.web("#557799");
    public-init var backgroundHover:Color = Color.web("#0044AA");
    public-init var backgroundPressed:Color = Color.web("#003377");
```

List item dimensions

```
public-init var action:function(n:Integer);

def border:Number = 1.0;
var totalHeight:Number;

override function create() : Node {          // Create scene graph
    VBox { content: build(); }
}
// ** Part 2 is listing 6.7
```

At the head of the code is our usual collection of variables for controlling the class:

- `cellWidth` and `cellHeight` are the dimensions of the items on screen. They need to be manipulated by the `ListPane` class, so we've given them package visibility.
- `content` holds the strings that define the list labels.
- `font`, `foreground`, `background`, `backgroundHover`, and `backgroundPressed` control the font and colors of the list.
- The function type `action` is our callback function.
- `border` holds the gap around items in the list, and `totalHeight` stores the pixel height of the list. Both are private variables.

Looking at the `create()` code, we see a `VBox` being fed content by a function called `build()`. `VBox` is a layout node that stacks its contents one underneath the other—precisely the functionality we need. But what about the `build()` function, which creates its contents? Look at the next part of the code, in listing 6.7.

Listing 6.7 List.fx (part 2)

```
// ** Part 1 is in listing 6.6
function build() : Node[] {
    for(i in [0..<sizeof content]) {             // For each list item
        var t:Text;
        var r:Rectangle;
        def g = Group {
            content: [
                Rectangle {                      // Hidden sizing rectangle
                    width: bind cellWidth;
                    height: bind cellHeight;
                    opacity: 0.0;
                },
                r = Rectangle {                  // List rectangle
                    x:border;  y:border;
                    width: bind cellWidth-border*2;
                    height: bind cellHeight-border*2;
                    arcWidth:20;  arcHeight:20;
                    fill: background;
                    onMouseExited: function(ev:MouseEvent) {
                        anim(r,background);
                    };
                    onMouseEntered: function(ev:MouseEvent) {
                        r.fill = backgroundHover;
                    }
```

```
                onMousePressed: function(ev:MouseEvent) {
                    r.fill = backgroundPressed;
                }
                onMouseClicked: function(ev:MouseEvent) {
                    r.fill = backgroundHover;
                    if(action!=null) { action(i); }
                }
            } ,
            t = Text {                              <-- Label text
                x: 10;  y: border;
                content: bind content[i];
                font: bind font;
                fill: bind foreground;
                textOrigin: TextOrigin.TOP;
            }
        ];
    };
    t.y += (r.layoutBounds.height-                  | Center text
        t.layoutBounds.height)/2;                   | vertically
    totalHeight += g.layoutBounds.height;
    g;
  }
}
                                                    Animate background
function anim(r:Rectangle,c:Color) : Void {     <--
    Timeline {
        keyFrames: [
            KeyFrame {
                time: 0.5s;
                values: [
                    r.fill => c
                        tween Interpolator.LINEAR
                ];
            }
        ]
    }.playFromStart();
}
}
```

The build() function returns a sequence of nodes, each a Group consisting of two Rectangle nodes and a Text node. The first node enforces an empty border on all four sides of each item. The second Rectangle is the visible box for our item; it also houses all the mouse event logic. Finally, we have the label itself, as a Text node. For easy handling we use the top of the text as its coordinate origin, rather than its baseline.

Both the background Rectangle and Text are assigned to variables (since JavaFX Script is an expression language, this won't prevent them from being added to the Group). But why? Take a look at the code immediately after the Group declaration; using those variables we vertically center the Text within the Rectangle, and that's why we needed references to them.

Now let's consider the mouse handlers. Entering the item sets the background rectangle fill color to backgroundHover, while exiting the item kicks off a Timeline (via the anim() function) to slowly return it to background. This slow fade creates a pleasing trail effect as the mouse moves across the list.

Pressing the mouse button sets the color to backgroundPressed, but we don't bother with the corresponding button release event; instead, we look for the higher-level clicked event, created when the user taps the button as opposed to a press and hold. The click event fires off our own action function, which can be assigned by outside code to respond to list selections.

The List class is only half of the list display; it's almost useless without its sibling, the ListPane class. That's where we're headed next.

6.2.2 The ListPane class: scrolling and clipping a scene graph

Now that we've seen the List node, let's consider the outer container that scrolls it. Check out listing 6.8.

Listing 6.8 ListPane.fx (part 1)

```
package jfxia.chapter6;

import javafx.animation.Interpolator;
import javafx.animation.KeyFrame;
import javafx.animation.Timeline;
import javafx.scene.CustomNode;
import javafx.scene.Group;
import javafx.scene.Node;
import javafx.scene.input.MouseEvent;
import javafx.scene.paint.Color;
import javafx.scene.shape.Rectangle;

package class ListPane extends CustomNode {
    public-init var content:List;

    package var width:Number = 150.0
        on replace oldVal = newVal {
            if(content!=null)
                content.cellWidth = newVal;
        };
    package var height:Number = 300.0;
    package var scrollY:Number = 0.0
        on replace oldVal = newVal {
            if(content!=null)
                content.translateY = 0-newVal;
        };

    var clickY:Number;
    var scrollOrigin:Number;
    var buttonDown:Boolean = false;
    var dragDelta:Number;
    var dragTimeline:Timeline;
    var noScroll:Boolean =
        bind content.layoutBounds.height < this.height;
    // ** Part 2 is listing 6.9
```

Annotations: Pass width on to List (width block); Position List within pane (scrollY block); Drag variables (clickY, scrollOrigin, buttonDown); Inertia animation variables (dragDelta, dragTimeline).

Listing 6.8 is the first part of our ListPane class, designed to house the List we created earlier. The exposed variables are quite straightforward:

- `content` is our `List`.
- `width` and `height` are the dimensions of the node. `width` is passed on to the `List`, where it's used to size the list items.
- `scrollY` is the scroll position of the `List` within our pane. The value is the `List` position relative to the `ListPane`, which is why it's negative. To scroll to pixel position 40, for example, we position the `List` at -40 compared to its container pane.

The private variables control the drag and the animation effect:

- To move the `List` we need to know how far we've dragged the mouse during this operation and where the `List` was before we started to drag. The private variable `clickY` records where inside the pane the mouse was when its button was pressed, and `scrollOrigin` records its scroll position at that time. `buttonDown` is a handy flag, recording whether or not we're in the middle of a drag operation.
- To create the inertia effect we must know how fast the mouse was traveling before its button was released, and `dragDelta` records that for us. We also need a `Timeline` for the effect, hence `dragTimeline`.
- If the `List` is smaller than the `ListPane`, we want to disable any scrolling or animation. The flag `noScroll` is used for this very purpose.

So much for the class variables. What about the actual scene graph and mouse event handlers? For those we need to look at listing 6.9.

Listing 6.9 ListPane.fx (part 2)

```
// ** Part 1 in listing 6.8
override function create() : Node {
    Group {
        content: [
            this.content ,                      <- List node
            Rectangle {                         <- Background and mouse events
                width: bind this.width;
                height: bind this.height;
                opacity: 0.0;
                onMousePressed: function(ev:MouseEvent) {
                    animStop();
                    clickY = ev.y;
                    scrollOrigin = scrollY;
                    buttonDown = true;
                };
                onMouseDragged: function(ev:MouseEvent) {
                    def prevY = scrollY;
                    updateY(ev.y);
                    dragDelta = scrollY-prevY;
                };
                onMouseReleased: function(ev:MouseEvent) {
                    updateY(ev.y);
                    animStart(dragDelta);
                    dragDelta = 0;
```

```
                    buttonDown = false;
                };
                onMouseWheelMoved: function(ev:MouseEvent) {
                    if(buttonDown == false) {
                        scrollY = restrainY (
                            scrollY + ev.wheelRotation
                                * content.cellWidth
                        );
                    }
                };
            }
        ];
        clip: Rectangle {
            x:0;  y:0;
            width: bind this.width;
            height: bind this.height;
        }
    }
}

function updateY(y:Number) : Void {
    if(noScroll) { return; }
    scrollY = restrainY( scrollOrigin-(y-clickY) );
}
function restrainY(y:Number) : Number {
    def h = content.layoutBounds.height-height;
    return
        if(y<0)  0
        else if(y>h)  h
        else  y;
}

function animStart(delta:Number) : Void {
    if(dragDelta>5 and dragDelta<-5) { return; }
    if(noScroll) { return; }

    def endY = restrainY(scrollY+delta*15);
    dragTimeline = Timeline {
        keyFrames: [
            KeyFrame {
                time: 1s;
                values: [
                    scrollY => endY
                        tween Interpolator.EASEOUT
                ];
            }
        ]
    },
    dragTimeline.playFromStart();
}
function animStop() : Void {
    if(dragTimeline!=null) {
        dragTimeline.stop();
    }
}
```

Constrain visible area

Limit scroll to list size

Inertia time line

The scene graph for `ListPane` consists of two nodes: the `List` itself and a `Rectangle` that handles our mouse events.

- When `onMousePressed` is triggered, we stop any inertia animation that may be running, store the initial mouse y coordinate and the current list scroll position, then flag the beginning of a drag operation.
- When `onMouseDragged` is called, we update the `List` scroll position and store the number of pixels we moved this update (used to calculate the speed of the inertia when we let go). The `restrainY()` function prevents the `List` from being scrolled off its top or bottom.
- When the `onMouseReleased` function is called, it updates the `List` position, kicks off the inertia animation, and resets the `dragDelta` and `buttonDown` variables so they're ready for next time.
- There's also a handler for the mouse scroll wheel, `onMouseWheelMoved()`, which should work only when we're not in the middle of a drag operation (we can drag or wheel, but not both at the same time!)

You'll note that the `Group` employs a `Rectangle` as a clipping area. Clipping areas are the way to show only a restricted view of a scene graph. Without this, the `List` nodes would spill outside the boundary of our `ListPane`. The clipping assignment creates the view port behavior our node requires, as demonstrated in figure 6.8.

Let's look at the `animStart()` function, which kicks off the inertia animation. The `delta` parameter is the number of pixels the pointer moved in the mouse-dragged event immediately before the button release. We use this to calculate how far the list will continue to travel. If the mouse movement was too slow (less than 5 pixels), or the `List` too small to scroll, we exit. Otherwise a `Timeline` animation is set up and started.

The list was our most ambitious piece of scene graph code yet. The result, complete with hover effect as the mouse moves over the list, is shown in figure 6.9. Even though it supports a lavish smooth scroll and animated reactions to the mouse pointer, it didn't take much more than a couple of hundred lines of code to write. It just shows how easy it is to create impressive UI code in JavaFX.

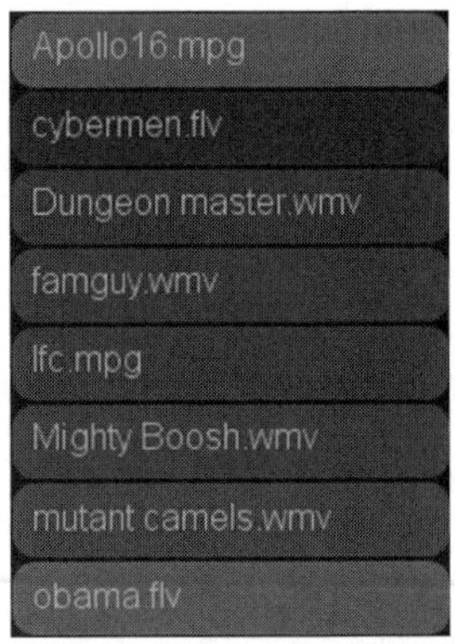

Figure 6.9 A closer look at our `List` and `ListPane`, with hover effect visible on the background of the list items

In the next section we'll delve into the exciting world of multimedia, as we plug our new list into the project application and use it to trigger video playback.

6.2.3 *Using media in JavaFX*

The time has come to learn how JavaFX handles media, such as the video files we'll be playing in our application. Before we look at the JavaFX Script code itself, let's invest time in learning about the theory. We'll start with figure 6.10.

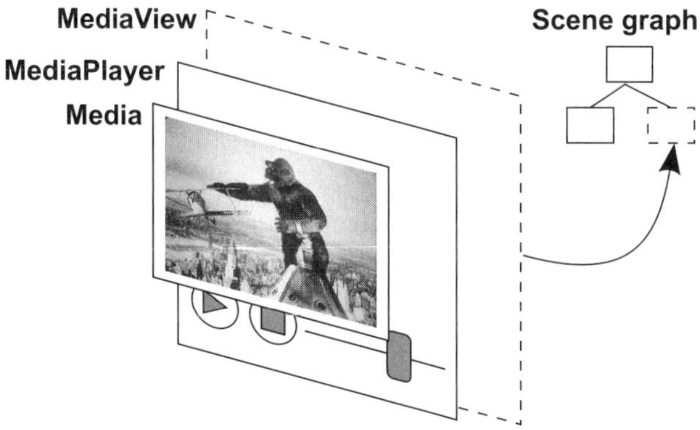

Figure 6.10 Like other JavaFX user interface elements, video is played via a dedicated `MediaView` scene graph node. (Note: `MediaPlayer` is not a visual element; the control icons are symbolic.)

To plug a video into the JavaFX scene graph takes three classes, located in the `javafx.scene.media` package. They are demonstrated in figure 6.10; starting from the outside, and working in, they are:

- The `MediaView` class, which acts as a bridge between the scene graph and any visual media that needs to be displayed within it. `MediaView` isn't needed to play audio-only media, because sound isn't displayed in the scene graph.
- The `MediaPlayer` class, which controls how the media is played; for example, stopping, restarting, skipping forward or backward, slowed down or sped up. `MediaPlayer` can be used to control audio or video. Important: `MediaPlayer` merely permits programmatic control of media; it provides no actual UI controls (figure 6.10 is symbolic). If you want play/pause/stop buttons, you must provide them yourself (and have them manipulate the `MediaPlayer` object).
- The `Media` class, which encapsulates the actual video and/or audio data to be played by the `MediaPlayer`.

As with images, JavaFX prefers to work with URLs rather than directly with local directory paths and filenames. If you read the API documentation, you'll see that the classes are designed to work with different types of media and to make allowances for data being streamed across a network.

The data formats supported fall into two categories. First, JavaFX will make use of the runtime operating system's media support, allowing it to play formats supported on the current platform. Second, for cross-platform applications JavaFX includes its own codec, available no matter what the capabilities of the underlying operating system.

Table 6.1 shows the support on different platforms. At the time this book was written, the details for Linux media support were not available, although the same mix of native and cross-platform codecs is expected.

The cross-platform video comes from a partnership deal Sun made with On2 for its Video VP6 decoder. On2 is best known for providing the software supporting Flash's own video decoder. The VP6 decoder plays FXM media on all JavaFX platforms, including mobile (and presumably TV too, when it arrives) without any extra

Table 6.1 JavaFX media support on various operating systems

Platform	Codecs	Formats
Mac OS X 10.4 and above (Core Video)	**Video:** H.261, H.263, and H.264 codecs. MPEG-1, MPEG-2, and MPEG-4 Video file formats and associated codecs (such as AVC). Sorenson Video 2 and 3 codecs. **Audio:** AIFF, MP3, WAV, MPEG-4 AAC Audio (.m4a, .m4b, .m4p), MIDI.	3GPP / 3GPP2, AVI, MOV, MP4, MP3
Windows XP/Vista (DirectShow)	**Video:** Windows Media Video, H264 (as an update). **Audio:** MPEG-1, MP3, Windows Media Audio, MIDI.	MP3, WAV, WMV, AVI, ASF
JavaFX (cross platform)	**Video:** On2 VP6. **Audio:** MP3.	FLV, FXM (Sun defined FLV subset), MP3

software installation. Regrettably, the only encoder for the On2 format at the time of writing seems to be On2 Flix, a proprietary commercial product.

Now that you understand the theory, let's push on to the final part of the project, where we build a working video player.

6.2.4 *The Player class, version 2: video and linear gradients*

We now have all the pieces; all that remains is to pull them together. The listing that follows is our largest single source file yet, almost 200 lines (be thankful this isn't a Java book, or it could have been 10 times that). I've broken it up into three parts, each dealing with different stages of the application. The opening part is listing 6.10.

Listing 6.10 Player.fx (version 2, part 1)

```
package jfxia.chapter6;

import javafx.geometry.HPos;
import javafx.geometry.VPos;
import javafx.scene.Group;
import javafx.scene.Scene;
import javafx.scene.control.Slider;
import javafx.scene.effect.Reflection;
import javafx.scene.input.MouseEvent;
import javafx.scene.layout.LayoutInfo;
import javafx.scene.layout.Stack;
import javafx.scene.media.Media;
import javafx.scene.media.MediaPlayer;
import javafx.scene.media.MediaView;
import javafx.scene.paint.Color;
import javafx.scene.paint.LinearGradient;
import javafx.scene.paint.Stop;
import javafx.scene.shape.Rectangle;
import javafx.scene.text.Font;
import javafx.scene.text.Text;
import javafx.scene.text.TextOrigin;
```

```
import javafx.stage.Stage;

import java.io.File;
import javax.swing.JFileChooser;

var sourceDir:File;
var sourceFiles:String[];

def fileDialog = new JFileChooser();
fileDialog.setFileSelectionMode(
   JFileChooser.DIRECTORIES_ONLY);
def ret = fileDialog.showOpenDialog(null);
if(ret == JFileChooser.APPROVE_OPTION) {
    sourceDir = fileDialog.getSelectedFile();
    if(sourceDir.isDirectory() == false) {
        println("{sourceDir} is not a directory");
        FX.exit();
    }
    def files:File[] = sourceDir.listFiles();
    for(i in [0 ..< sizeof files]) {
        def fn:String = files[i].getName().toLowerCase();
        if(fn.endsWith(".mpg") or fn.endsWith(".mpeg")
            or fn.endsWith(".wmv") or fn.endsWith(".flv")) {
            insert files[i].getName() into sourceFiles;
        }
    }
}
else {
    FX.exit();
}
// ** Part 2 is in listing 6.11; part 3 in listing 6.12
```

Select a directory

Check valid selection

Create video file list

When run, the program asks for a directory containing video files using Swing's own `JFileChooser` class. This time we're not using JavaFX wrappers around a Swing component; we're creating and using the raw Java class itself. Having created the chooser, we tell it to list only directories, then show it, and wait for it to return. Assuming the user selected a directory, we run through all its files, looking for potential videos based on their filename extension, populating the `sourceFiles` sequence when found.

Assuming we continue running past this piece of code, the next step (listing 6.11) is to set up the scene graph for our video player.

Listing 6.11 Player.fx (version 2, part 2)

```
// ** Part 1 is in listing 6.10; part 3 in listing 6.12
def margin = 10.0;
def videoWidth = 480.0;
def videoHeight = 320.0;
def reflectSize = 0.25;
def font = Font { name: "Helvetica"; size: 16; };
def listWidth = 200;
def listHeight =
    videoHeight*(1.0+reflectSize) + margin*2;

var volumeSlider:Slider;
var balanceSlider:Slider;
```

Video display dimensions

Height matches media area

Volume/balance sliders

```
def list:ListPane = ListPane {                    List display
    content: List {
        content: sourceFiles;
        font: font;
        action: function(i:Integer) {
            player.media = Media {
                source: getVideoPath(i);              Action: create
            }                                         then play media
            player.play();
        };
    };
    width: listWidth;
    height: listHeight;
}

var player:MediaPlayer = MediaPlayer {
    volume:  bind volumeSlider.value / 100.0;
    balance: bind balanceSlider.value / 100.0;        Control video
    onEndOfMedia: function() {                        with player
        player.currentTime = 0s;
    }
}
def view:Stack = Stack {
    layoutX: listWidth + margin;
    layoutY: margin;
    nodeHPos: HPos.CENTER;                        Always rests on
    nodeVPos: VPos.BASELINE;                      area baseline
    content: [
        Rectangle {
            width: videoWidth;                    Spacer
            height: videoHeight;                  rectangle
            opacity: 0;
        } ,
        MediaView {
            fitWidth: videoWidth;
            fitHeight: videoHeight;
            preserveRatio: true;
            effect: Reflection {
                fraction: reflectSize;            Reflection
                topOpacity: 0.25;                 under video
                bottomOpacity: 0.0;
            };
            mediaPlayer: player;
        }                                                     Video
    ]                                         position/duration (handy)
}
def vidPos = bind player.currentTime.toSeconds() as Integer;

def panel:Group = Group {                     Control
    layoutY: listHeight;                      panel
    content: [                                        Play
        Button {                                      button
            iconFilename: "play.png";
            action: function(ev:MouseEvent) {
                player.play();
            }
```

```
        } ,
        Button {                                        Pause
            layoutX: 80;                                button
            iconFilename: "pause.png";
            action: function(ev:MouseEvent) {
                player.pause();
            };
        } ,                                             GridBox
        GridBox {                                       layout
            layoutX:185;  layoutY:20;
            columns:4;
            nodeVPos: VPos.CENTER;
            horizontalGap:10;  verticalGap:20;
            content: [
                makeLabel("Volume") ,
                volumeSlider = Slider {                             Volume
                    layoutInfo: LayoutInfo { width:150 }            slider
                    value: 100;  max: 100;
                } ,

                makeLabel("Balance") ,
                balanceSlider = Slider {                            Balance
                    layoutInfo: LayoutInfo { width:150 }            slider
                    value: 0;  min: -100;  max: 100;
                } ,

                makeLabel("Playback") ,
                Text {
                    content: bind
                        if(player.media!=null)
                            "{vidPos} seconds"                  Position
                        else                                    display
                            "No video";
                    font: font;
                    fill: Color.LIGHTBLUE;
                    textOrigin: TextOrigin.TOP;
                }
            ];
        }
    ];
};
// ** Part 1 is in listing 6.10; part 3 is in listing 6.12
```

In listing 6.11 we create the parts of our scene graph, which will be plugged into the application's Stage in part 3 (listing 6.12). There are three main parts: list is the scrolling list of videos from which the user can select, view is the video display area itself, and panel is the control panel that runs along the bottom of the window. You'll notice that the MediaPlayer is also given its own variable, player.

The list is constructed from the two classes, List and ListPane, we developed earlier. Its contents are the filenames from the directory returned by JFileChooser. The action event takes the selected list index and turns it into a URL (thanks to the get-VideoPath() function we'll see later), creates a new Media object from it, plugs the Media object into player, and starts it playing.

The `player` node itself is quite simple. Its `volume` and `balance` variables are bound to sliders in the control panel, and it has an event handler (`onEndOfMedia`) that rewinds the video back to the start once it reaches the end.

The video area, `view`, uses another of JavaFX's standard layout nodes: `Stack`. `Stack` overlaps its children on top of each other, earlier nodes in the `content` sequence appearing below later nodes. Because children may be different sizes, the `nodeHPos` and `nodeVPos` properties determine how smaller nodes should be aligned. In our case we use a transparent spacer `Rectangle` to enforce the maximum size of our video area and then add the `MediaView` so it always rests against the bottom (baseline) of this area.

Figure 6.11 shows relationship of the key variables.

The script-level variables `videoWidth` and `videoHeight` determine the pixel size of the actual video node, `reflectSize` is the proportion of the node that gets reflected below it (see figures 6.1 and 6.7), and `margin` is the border around the whole area. Because the scrolling list extends for the full height of the video area, `listHeight` is calculated using `videoHeight`, including its `reflectSize`, plus the top and bottom `margin`.

The `fitWidth` and `fitHeight` parameters are set on the `MediaView` node, causing any video to be scaled to the `videoWidth/videoHeight` area, but `preserveRatio` is set so the video is never stretched out of proportion. Because a given video may be smaller, when scaled, than either `videoWidth` or `videoHeight`, we use the `Stack` node's `nodeHPos` and `nodeVPos` variables to fix the video centrally along the baseline of the area.

The reflection effect may look impressive, but in JavaFX applying any visual effect to a section of the scene graph is as easy as assigning the given node's `effect` variable. If you look in the API documentation for the `javafx.scene.effect` package, you'll see all manner of different effects you can apply; we'll be looking at more of them in future chapters. The `Reflection` effect adds a mirror below its node, with a given top/bottom opacity.

Finally, the control panel, aka the `panel` variable, will be familiar from version 1 of the project. The only substantial difference is that now the sliders are plugged into actual video player variables. The `makeLabel()` function is simply a convenience for creating label text; it appears in part 3 of the code. And speaking of part 3, here's listing 6.12.

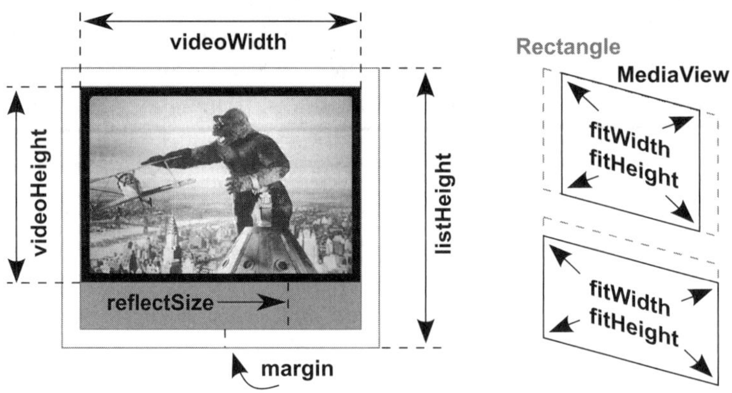

Figure 6.11 The video area layout and sizing are controlled by variables, some at the script level and others local to the scene graph node itself.

Listing 6.12 Player.fx (version 2, part 3)

```
// ** Part 1 is in listing 6.10; part 2 in listing 6.11
Stage {
    scene: Scene {
        content: [
            list,view,panel
        ];
        fill: LinearGradient {
            endX:0;  endY:1;
            proportional: true;
            stops: [
                Stop {
                    offset:0.55;  color:Color.BLACK;
                } ,
                Stop {
                    offset:1;  color:Color.STEELBLUE;
                }
            ];
        };
    };
    title: "Player v2";
    resizable: false;
}

function makeLabel(str:String) : Text {
    Text {
        content: str;
        font: font;
        fill: Color.LIGHTBLUE;
        textOrigin: TextOrigin.TOP;
    };
}

function getVideoPath(i:Integer) : String {
    def f = new File(sourceDir,sourceFiles[i]);
    return f.toURI().toString();
}
```

Scene graph bits

Linear gradient background

Handy label maker function

Convert list filename to URL

The final part of our application. Whew!

We see here that the three nodes we created in the second part (`list`, `view`, and `panel`) are hooked into our scene. At the bottom of the listing we see the `makeLabel()` and `getVideoPath()` convenience functions we used previously. But what's that in the middle of the listing, plugged into the scene's `fill` parameter? That's a `LinearGradient`, and it's responsible for the graduated fill color that sits behind the whole window's contents. If you think it looks rather odd, don't worry; I've devoted an entire section to unlocking its secrets, up next.

6.2.5 Creating varying color fills with LinearGradient

Instead of using a boring flat color for the window background, in listing 6.12 we create a `LinearGradient` and use it as the scene's fill. We can do this because the `Scene` class accepts a `javafx.scene.paint.Paint` instance as its background fill. The `Paint` class is a base for any object that can be used to determine how the pixels in a shape will be drawn; the flat colors we used in previous examples are also types of `Paint`, albeit not very exciting ones.

A gradient paint is one that transitions between a set of colors as it draws a shape. Good examples of linear gradients might include a color spectrum or a chrome metal effect, as shown in figure 6.12.

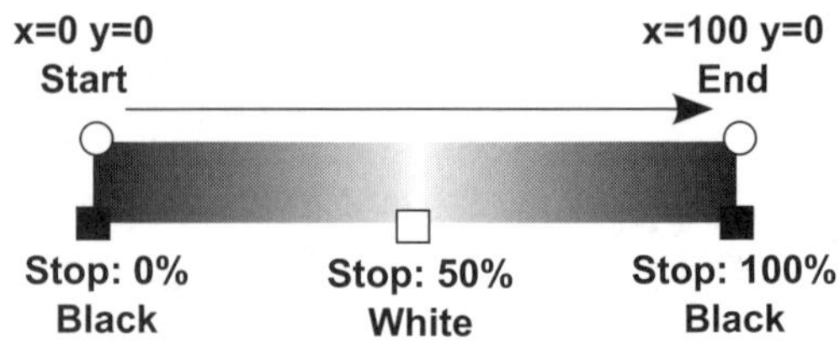

Figure 6.12 A gradient paint is one where the pixel tone changes over the course of a given area. Colors are set at stops along a line, and the paint transitions between them as a shape is drawn.

Think about how the color gradually changes across the painted area. To define a linear gradient we need two things: a line with start and end points (a path to follow) and a list of colors on the line plus where they are positioned. For a simple rainbow spectrum we might define a horizontal (or vertical) line, with each color stop spaced equally along its length.

The line can function either with proportional sizing or via absolute pixel coordinates. What's the difference? Take a look at the examples in figure 6.13.

When `proportional` is true, the line coordinates (`startX`, `startY`, `endX`, and `endY`) are scaled across a virtual coordinate space from 0 to 1, which is stretched to fit the actual painted area whenever the paint is applied. Without `proportional` set, the line start and end coordinates are absolute pixel positions. This means if you define a vertical gradient line of (0,0) to (0,100) but then paint an area of 200 x 200 pixels, the transition will not cover the entire painted area. By setting a parameter called `cycleMethod` we can control how the remainder will paint. The default option extends the color at either end of the gradient line. Alternatively we can repeat the gradient or reflect it by painting it backwards.

Incidentally, `LinearGradient` creates stripes of color along a gradient line, but you might also want to check out its cousin, `RadialGradient`, which paints circular patterns. It can be particularly useful for creating pleasing 3D ball effects.

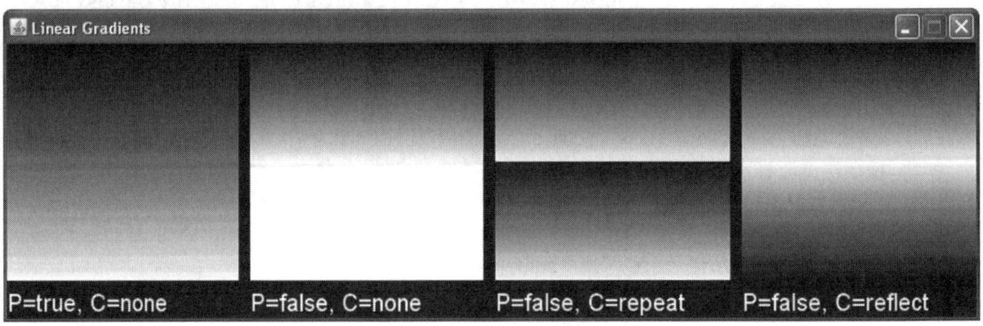

Figure 6.13 A proportional (P) gradient scaled to full height. Then three nonproportional examples, gradient (0,0) to (0,100), painted onto 200 x 200 sized rectangles with various cycle (C) methods.

6.2.6 *Running version 2*

Running version 2 of the project gives us our video player. Selecting a file from the list on the left will play it in the central area, complete with snazzy reflection over the shaded floor. Figure 6.14 shows what you should expect when firing up the application, selecting a directory, and playing a video (especially if you're a Mighty Reds fan).

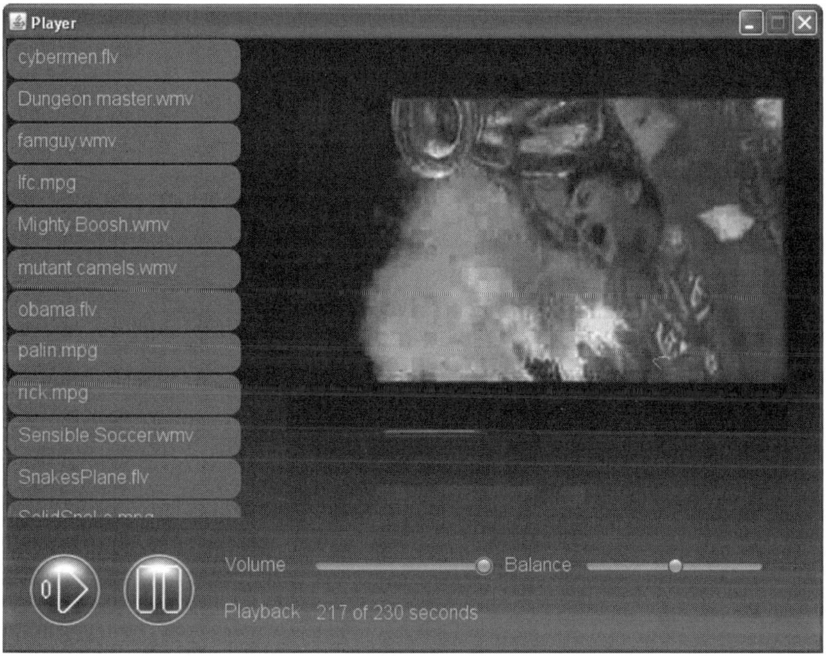

Figure 6.14 You'll never walk alone: relive favorite moments with your own homemade video player (like your soccer team lifting the Champion's League trophy).

Okay, so perhaps it's not the most functional player in the world, but it's still very impressive when you consider how little work we needed to pull it off. Think how long it would have taken to code all the UI and effects using Java or C++. And that's before we even *think* about getting video playback working.

6.3 *Bonus: taking control of fonts*

Time for another detour section. This one doesn't directly relate to the material in this chapter, but it's a very useful UI trick, and this seems an opportune moment to mention it.

Like Java, JavaFX has a small set of standard fonts with dependable names and appearances. It can also use fonts available on the local computer, although there's no guarantee which fonts will be installed or precisely what they'll look like. So, what if we need a specific font, not guaranteed to be available on every computer? Fortunately,

JavaFX allows us to embed fonts directly inside our application, guaranteeing availability and appearance. Figure 6.15 shows an example.

Figure 6.15 Text rendered using an embedded TrueType font file

To embed a typeface we need a font file in a format such as TrueType. The file is not loaded directly from a URL or an input stream but assigned an alias from which it can be referenced like any standard or operating system font. This is a two-step process:

1. The font file should be placed somewhere under the build directory of your project, so it is effectively *inside* the application (and ultimately inside the application's JAR file, when we package it—see chapter 9).
2. A file named META-INF/fonts.mf should be created/edited. This will provide mappings between font names and their associated embedded files. The META-INF directory should be familiar to you as the place where Java stores metadata about resources and JARs. Most JAR files have a META-INF directory, often created by the `jar` utility if not already part of the project.

When a JavaFX application needs to resolve a font name, it first checks the embedded fonts for a match; then it checks the standard JavaFX fonts and then the operating system's fonts. If no match can be found, it uses a default fallback font. So, by creating a fonts.mf file we can get our own fonts used in preference to other fonts, but what does this file look like? Listing 6.13 demonstrates.

Listing 6.13 fonts.mf

```
Data\ Control = /ttf/data-latin.ttf
```

This single line creates a mapping between the name `Data Control` (the backslash escapes the space) and a TrueType font file called data-latin.ttf, living in a directory called ttf off the build directory. Having created a font mapping, we can reference it in our code like any other font, as shown in listing 6.14.

Listing 6.14 FontTest.fx

```
import javafx.scene.Scene;
import javafx.scene.text.*;
import javafx.stage.Stage;

Stage {
    scene: Scene {
        content: Text {
            textOrigin: TextOrigin.TOP;
            font: Font {
                name: "Data Control";
                size: 40;
            }
            content: "Some text using an\nembedded font.";
```

```
        }
    }
}
```

Listing 6.14 is a simple program consisting of a text node in a window. It looks like figure 6.15 when run. The `Font` declaration references `Data Control` like it was a standard JavaFX or operating system font, which resolves via the fonts.mf file to our embedded font. When compiled, our application's build directory should feature the following files:

- FontTest.class
- META-INF/fonts.mf
- ttf/data-latin.ttf

The FontTest.fx source didn't specify a package, so its class file will compile into the root (I've omitted compiler implementation classes for readability). Also off the root is the META-INF directory with our font mapping file and the ttf directory where we deposited the font data file. Actually, it doesn't matter where we put the font file, so long as it lives under the build directory and the correct location is noted in the mapping file.

With this simple technique we can bundle any unusual fonts we need inside the application (and ultimately inside its JAR file), guaranteeing that they are available no matter where our code runs. A very useful UI trick indeed!

> **Credit where credit's due**
>
> I'm indebted to Rakesh Menon, who was the first (as far as I know) to reveal this method of embedding fonts into a JavaFX application. His blog post is located here:
>
> http://blogs.sun.com/rakeshmenonp/entry/javafx_custom_fonts

6.4 Summary

In this chapter we've seen in greater depth how to use the standard scene graph nodes to build fairly sophisticated pieces of UI, we've looked at how to include images and video in our JavaFX applications, and we've played around with gradient paints. We've also seen our first example of plugging an effect (reflection) into the scene graph.

Writing good scene graph code is all about planning. JavaFX gives you some powerful raw building blocks; you have to consider the best way to fit them together for the effect you're trying to achieve. Always be aware that a scene graph is a different beast than something like Swing or Java 2D. It's a structured representation of the graphics on screen, and as such we need to ensure it includes layout and spacing information, because we don't have direct control of the actual pixel painting as we do in Java 2D. Transparent shapes can be used to enforce spacing around parts of our scene graph, but they can also be used as a central event target.

Hopefully the source code in this chapter has given you ideas about how to write your own UI nodes. Feel free to experiment with the player, filling in its gaps and adding new features. Or take the custom nodes and develop them further in your own applications.

In the next chapter we're shifting focus from simple interactive scene graph nodes to full blown controls, as we explore JavaFX's standard user interface APIs. We'll also discover another powerful way to customize node layout.

But for now, enjoy the movie!

7 Controls, charts, and storage

This chapter covers

- Creating forms using standard controls
- Storing data (even on applets and phones)
- Playing with 3D charts and graphs
- Writing our own skinnable control

There can't be many programmers who haven't heard of the Xerox Alto, if not by name then certainly by reputation. The Alto was a pioneering desktop computer created in the 1970s at the Xerox's Palo Alto Research Center (PARC). It boasted the first modern-style GUI, but today it's probably best remembered as the inspiration behind the Apple Macintosh. Although graphics have become more colorful since those early monochrome days, fundamentally the GUI has changed very little. A time traveler from 1985 (perhaps arriving in a DeLorean sports car?) may be impressed by the beauty of modern desktop software but would still recognize the majority of UI widgets. UI stalwarts like buttons, lists, and check boxes still dominate. The World Wide Web popularized the hypertext pane, but that aside, very few innovations have really caught on. But then, if something works, why fix it?

But one problem *did* need fixing. The Xerox PARC GUI worked well for a desktop computer like the Alto but was wholly inappropriate for small-screen devices like a cell phone. So mobile devices found their own ways of doing things, creating *little-brother* equivalents to many standard desktop widgets. But, inevitably, little brothers grow up: mobile screens got better, graphics performance increased, and processing power seemed to leap with each new product release. Suddenly phones, media players, games consoles, and set-top boxes started to sport UIs looking uncannily like their desktop siblings, yet independent UI toolkits were still used for each.

One remit of the JavaFX project was to unite the different UI markets—PCs, Blu-ray players, cell phones, and other devices—under one universal toolkit, to create (as Tolkien might have put it) *one toolkit to rule them all.* Java had always had powerful desktop UI libraries (Abstract Windows Toolkit [AWT] and Swing), but they were far too complex for smaller devices. Neither used the *retained-mode* graphics favored by JavaFX's scene graph, and neither was designed to be constructed declaratively, making them alien to the way JavaFX would like to work.

The JavaFX team planned a new library of UI widgets: universal, lightweight, modern, and easily restyled. The result of their labor was the *controls* API introduced in JavaFX 1.2, designed to complement (and eventually replace) the desktop-only Swing wrappers in `javafx.ext.swing`, which had shipped with earlier JavaFX versions.

In this chapter we're going to learn how to use the new controls API, along with other features that debuted in 1.2. So far we've had a lot of fun with games, animations, and media, but JavaFX's controls permit us to write more serious applications, so that's what we'll be doing in this chapter's project. Let's begin by outlining the application we're building.

7.1 Comments welcome: Feedback, version 1

In this chapter we'll develop a small feedback form using JavaFX controls. Different control types will collect the answers to our questions, a persistent storage API will save this data, and some chart/graph controls will display the resulting statistics (see figure 7.1). Along the way we'll also expand our knowledge of JavaFX's container nodes.

There are just two classes in this project, but they pack quite a punch in terms of new material covered. As with previous projects, the code has been broken into versions. Version 1 will focus on building the input form using the new JavaFX 1.2 controls, and version 2 will save the data and create charts from it.

Although we'll be covering only a subset of the controls available under JavaFX 1.2—buttons, text fields, radio buttons, and sliders—there's enough variety to give you a taste of the controls library as a whole. We begin not with the controls but with a model class to bind our UI against.

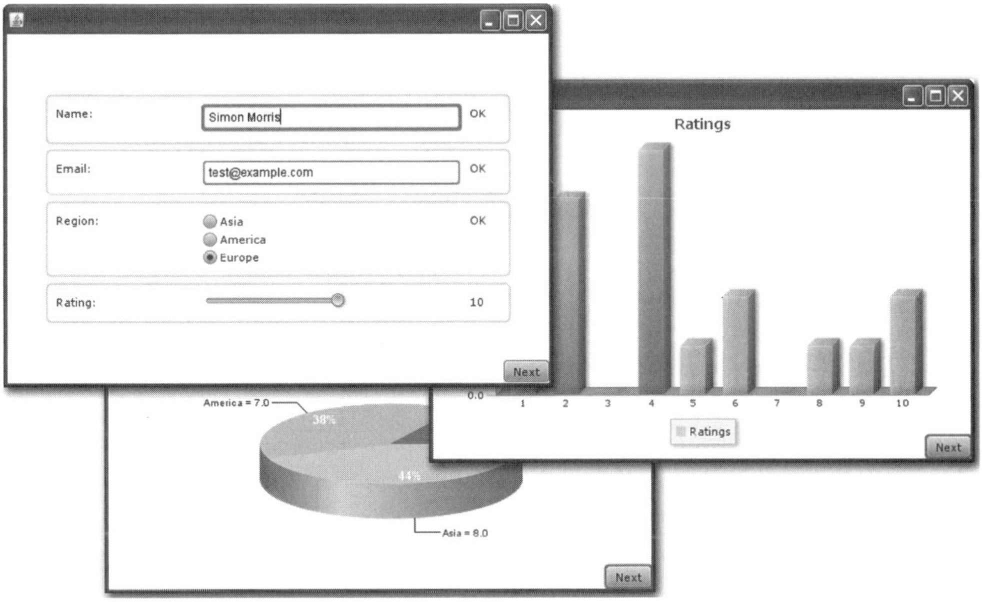

Figure 7.1 A bar chart, with 3D effect, showing feedback scores from contributors

7.1.1 *The Record class: a bound model for our UI*

To hold the data we're collecting for our form we need a class, such as the one in listing 7.1. Variables store the data for each field on the form, and a set of corresponding booleans reveals whether each value is valid. From a design point of view, it's useful to keep the logic determining the validity of a given field close to its data storage. In *ye olde times* (when AWT and Swing were all we had) this logic would be scattered across several far-flung event handlers, but not with JavaFX Script.

Listing 7.1 Record.fx (version 1)

```
package jfxia.chapter7;

package def REGIONS:String[] = [ "Asia","America","Europe" ];

package class Record {
    package var name:String;
    package var email:String;
    package var region:Integer = -1;
    package var rating:Number = 0;

    package def validName:Boolean = bind (       <-- Name valid?
        name.length() > 2
    );
    package def validEmail:Boolean = bind (      <-- Email address valid?
        (email.length() > 7) and
        (email.indexOf("@") > 0)
    );
    package def validRegion:Boolean = bind (     <-- Region set?
```

```
        region >= 0
    );
    package def validRating:Boolean = bind (     <— Rating set?
        rating > 0
    );
    package def valid:Boolean = bind (     <— All fields valid?
        validName and validEmail and
        validRegion and validRating
    );
}
```

This is our initial data class: a model to wire into our UI's view/controller—recall the Model/View/Controller (MVC) paradigm. The class consists of four basic feedback items, each with a corresponding `Boolean` variable bound to its validity, plus a master validity boolean:

- The `name` variable holds the name of the feedback user, and the `validName` variable checks to see if its length is over two characters.
- The `email` variable holds the email address of the feedback user, and the `validEmail` variable checks to see if it is at least eight characters long and has an `@` (at) symbol somewhere after the first character.
- The `region` variable stores the location of the user. A sequence of valid region names, `REGIONS`, appears at the head of the code, in the script context. The `validRegion` variable checks to see that the default, -1, is not set.
- The `rating` variable holds a feedback score, between 1 and 10. The `validRating` variable checks to see whether the default, 0, is not set.

An extra variable, `valid`, is a kind of *master boolean*, depending on the validity of all the other variables. It determines whether the `Record` as a whole is ready to be saved.

This four-field data class is what we'll base our UI on. Sure, we could ask more than four questions (in the real world we certainly would), but this wouldn't really teach us anything new. The four we have will be more than enough for this project, but feel free to add your own if you want.

We have a class to store the data; all we need now is a user interface.

7.1.2 The Feedback class: controls and panel containers

Java calls them *components*; I sometimes call them by the generic term *widgets*, but the new (official) JavaFX name for UI elements is *controls*, it seems. Controls are buttons, text fields, sliders, and other functional bits and pieces that enable us to collect input from the user and display output in return. In our feedback form we'll use a text field to collect the respondents' name and email address, we'll use radio buttons to allow them to tell us where they live, and we'll use a slider to let them provide a score out of 10. Figure 7.2 shows what the interface will look like.

A Next button sits in the corner of the window, allowing the user to move to the next page of the application. In the finished project the button will initially submit the feedback form (assuming all fields are valid) and then become a toggle, so users can

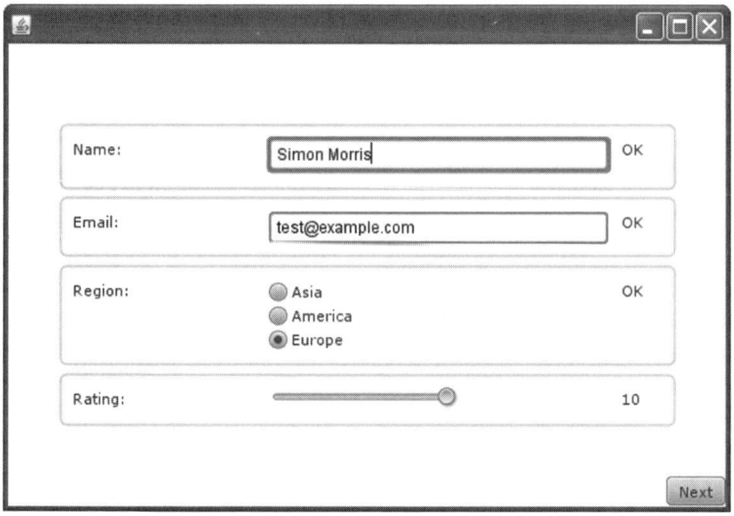

Figure 7.2 Our project's simple feedback form, complete with text fields, radio buttons, and sliders. Oh, and a Next button in the corner!

jump between a bar chart and a pie chart that summarize the data already collected. In version 1, however, the charts aren't available, so we'll just use the button to print the current data in the model object.

Because the UI code is quite long, I've broken it into four smaller listings (listings 7.2-7.5), each dealing with a different part of the interface. The first part, listing 7.2, begins with a long shopping list of classes (many for control and layout) that need to be imported.

Listing 7.2 Feedback.fx (version 1, part 1)

```
package jfxia.chapter7;

import javafx.scene.Group;
import javafx.scene.Node;
import javafx.scene.Scene;
import javafx.scene.control.Button;
import javafx.scene.control.Label;
import javafx.scene.control.RadioButton;
import javafx.scene.control.Slider;
import javafx.scene.control.TextBox;
import javafx.scene.control.ToggleGroup;
import javafx.scene.layout.Panel;
import javafx.scene.layout.Tile;
import javafx.scene.layout.VBox;
import javafx.scene.paint.Color;
import javafx.scene.shape.Rectangle;
import javafx.stage.Stage;
import javafx.util.Sequences;

def record:Record = Record {};        <-- Our data model

def winW:Number = 550;
def winH:Number = 350;
// Part 2 is listing 7.3; part 3, listing 7.4; part 4, listing 7.5
```

At the start of the code we see a new `Record` object being declared. Recall that this is the model class our UI will plumb itself into. The next two lines define a couple of constants that will be used as `Scene` dimensions in the part 2 of the code. And speaking of part 2, listing 7.3 is next.

Listing 7.3 Feedback.fx (version 1, part 2)

```
// Part 1 is listing 7.2
def nextButton = Button {                          <- Button in southeast corner
    text: "Next";
    action: function() {
        println("{record.name} {record.email} "
            "{record.region} {record.rating}");     Just print record details
    }
}

var mainPan:Panel;
Stage {
    scene: Scene {                                  Declarative custom layout
        content: mainPan = Panel {                  <-
            prefWidth: function(w:Number) { winW };
            prefHeight: function(h:Number) { winH };   Called to lay out children
            onLayout: function() {                  <-
                mainPan.resizeContent();
                var c = mainPan.content;
                for(n in mainPan.getManaged(c)) {
                    def node:Node = n as Node;
                    var x = winW-node.layoutBounds.width;
                    var y = winH-node.layoutBounds.height;
                    if(not (node instanceof Button)) {
                        x/=2;  y/=2;                Don't center nextButton
                    }
                    mainPan.positionNode(node , x,y);   <- Position node
                }
            }
            content: [
                createFeedbackUI() ,                Create window's scene graph
                nextButton
            ]
        }
        width: winW;  height: winH;
    }
    resizable: false;
}
// Part 3 is listing 7.4; part 4, listing 7.5
```

The `Button` class creates a standard button control, like the Swing buttons we saw in previous chapters, except entirely scene-graph based and therefore not confined to the desktop. Our `nextButton` object is very simple: text to display and an `action` function to run when clicked. In version 2 this button will permit users to move between pages of the application, but for version 1 all it does is print the data in our `Record`.

The most interesting part of listing 7.3 is the `Panel` class—clearly it's some kind of scene graph node, but it looks far more complex than the nodes we've encountered so far. You may recall that when we built the video player project, we created our own custom layout node by extending `javafx.scene.layout.Container`. Because we created a full container class, we could use it over and over in different places. But what if we wanted a one-shot layout? Do we have to go to all the hassle of writing a separate class each time?

No, we don't. The `javafx.scene.layout.Panel` class is a lightweight custom layout node. Its mechanics can be plugged in declaratively, making it ideal for creating one-shot containers, without the pain of writing a whole new class. The class has several variables that can be populated with anonymous functions to report its minimum, maximum, and preferred size, plus the all-important `onLayout` function, for actually positioning its children. Let's refresh our memory of the layout code in listing 7.3.

```
onLayout: function() {
    mainPan.resizeContent();
    var c = mainPan.content;
    for(n in mainPan.getManaged(c)) {
        def node:Node = n as Node;
        var x = winW-node.layoutBounds.width;
        var y = winH-node.layoutBounds.height;
        if(not (node instanceof Button)) { x/=2;  y/=2; }
        mainPan.positionNode(node , x,y);
    }
}
```

The `mainPan` variable is a reference to the `Panel` object itself, so `mainPan.resizeContent()` will resize the `Panel`'s own children to their preferred dimensions. The code then loops over each node requiring layout, centering it within the `Scene` (or rather, the constants used to size our `Scene`). Note, however, that we do not center any node of type `Button`—this is why the Next button ends up in corner of the window.

At the end of listing 7.3 you'll notice that, aside from the `nextButton`, the contents of the panel are populated by a function called `createFeedbackUI()`. Listing 7.4 shows us its detail.

Listing 7.4 Feedback.fx (version 1, part 3)

```
// Part 2 is listing 7.3; part 1, listing 7.2
function createFeedbackUI() : Node {              <-- Function builds feedback form
    def ok:String = "OK";
    def bad:String = "BAD";

    var togGrp = ToggleGroup {};                   <-- RadioButton group
    def selected = bind togGrp.selectedButton
        on replace {
            if(togGrp.selectedButton != null) {
                record.region = Sequences.indexOf
                    (togGrp.buttons , togGrp.selectedButton);
            }
        }

    VBox {
        var sl:Slider;
```

```
spacing: 4;
content: [
    createRow(       <-- Name row
        "Name:" ,
        TextBox {
            columns:30;
            text: bind record.name with inverse;
        } ,
        Label {
            text: bind
                if(record.validName) ok else bad;
        }
    ) ,
    createRow(       <-- Email row
        "Email:" ,
        TextBox {
            columns: 30;
            text: bind record.email with inverse;
        } ,
        Label {
            text: bind
                if(record.validEmail) ok else bad;
        }
    ) ,
    createRow(       <-- Region row
        "Region:" ,
        Tile {
            columns: 1;
            content: for(r in Record.REGIONS) {
                def idx:Integer = (indexof r);
                RadioButton {
                    text: r;
                    toggleGroup: togGrp;          <-- Assign to ToggleGroup
                    selected: (record.region==idx);

                }
            }
        } ,
        Label {
            text: bind
                if(record.validRegion) ok else bad;
        }
    ) ,
    createRow(       <-- Rating row
        "Rating:" ,
        sl = Slider {
            max: 10;
            value: bind record.rating with inverse;
        } ,
        Label {
            text: text: bind if(record.validRating)
                "{sl.value as Integer}" else bad;
        }
    )
]
```

```
    }
}
// Part 4 in listing 7.5
```

Each *page* in the application has its own function to create it. Separating each part of the scene graph into functions makes things more manageable. Listing 7.4 shows the function that creates the feedback form itself. It adds a row for each input field in the form, using a function called `createRow()` that we'll look at in the final listing for this source file. Each row consists of a string to act as the field's label, the control being used to collect the data, and a `Label` to display the validity of the current data.

A set of unfamiliar controls has been introduced in listing 7.4: `TextBox` provides a simple text entry field, `Slider` permits the user to choose a value within a given range (we saw it briefly in the last chapter), and `RadioButton` allows the user to make a choice from a given set of options. (Legend has it radio buttons got their name from the old-fashioned car radios, with mechanical push-button tuning.)

The `RadioButton` controls are added, via a `for` loop, to a `Tile` container, configured to position them in a single row. Because the `RadioButton` controls have to cooperate, they refer to a common `ToggleGroup` object. All `RadioButton` controls added to a given group will work together to ensure only one button is ever selected at any given time. Each grouping of radio buttons in a UI must have its own `ToggleGroup` object to manage it, or the buttons won't be able to cooperate.

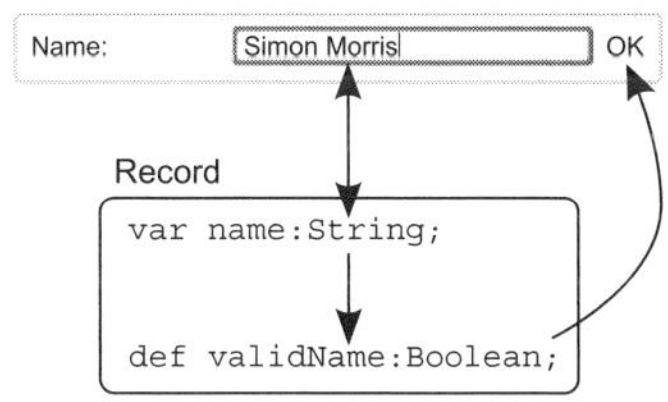

Figure 7.3 The flow of updates between the model and the UI: the data and text box are bidirectionally bound, the validity boolean is bound to the data, and the validity label is bound to the validity boolean.

Figure 7.3 shows the flow of data that connects the model to the UI. These connections are made through binds. Each control (with the exception of the radio buttons) has a bidirectional bind to its associated data in the model. If the model changes, the control updates; likewise, if the control changes, the model updates. The `Label` at the end of each row is also bound to the model; whenever any data in the model changes, the associated validity boolean updates, and this in turn causes the `Label` to update.

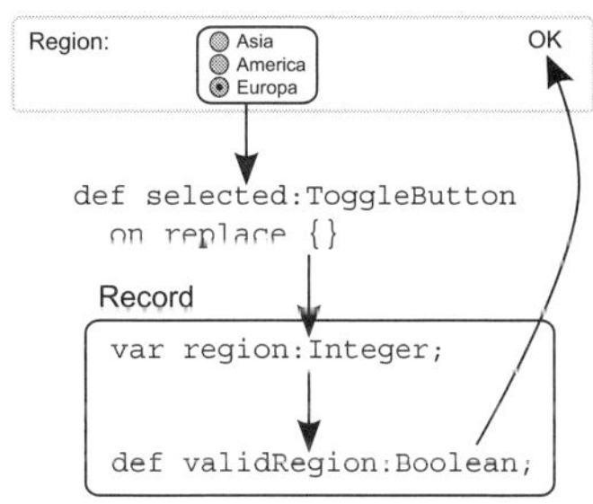

Figure 7.4 To update the model from a `ToggleGroup` we bind a variable against the group's selected button and then use a trigger to translate any changes into the button's index value.

Unfortunately the `ToggleGroup` that controls our radio buttons isn't so easy to bind against. It has a variable to tell us which `RadioButton` is currently selected but not the index of the button—the index is what we really need to know. Figure 7.4 shows the workaround we employ to convert the `RadioButton` into an index. We create a variable (`selected`) that binds against `ToggleGroup`'s `selectedButton` field, running a trigger each time it changes. The trigger translates the selected `ToggleButton` (a superclass of

RadioButton) into an index and pushes the value into the model. This causes the familiar validity boolean updates.

Regrettably, because the relationship between control and model is not bidirectional, a change to the model is not automatically reflected in the UI. (Hopefully future enhancements to the ToggleGroup class will make this type of binding easier.)

The final listing for this source code file is presented in listing 7.5. It shows the createRow() function we saw producing each row of the feedback form.

Listing 7.5 Feedback.fx (version 1, part 4)

```
// Part 3 is listing 7.4; part 2, listing 7.3; part 1, listing 7.2
function createRow(lab:String,n:Node,v:Node) : Node {
    def margin:Number = 10;

    n.layoutX = 150;                    // Position control and label
    v.layoutX = 420;

    var grp:Group = Group {             // Build controls group
        layoutX: margin;
        layoutY: margin;
        content: [ Label{text:lab} , n , v ]
    }
    Group {
        content: [
            Rectangle {
                fill: null;
                stroke: Color.POWDERBLUE;
                strokeWidth: 2;
                width: 450 + margin*2;
                height: bind
                    grp.layoutBounds.height + margin*2;
                arcWidth: 10;  arcHeight: 10;
            } ,
            grp    <-- Use group inside border
        ]
    }
}
```

This function is a convenience for positioning each row of the feedback form. It accepts a String and two Node objects: the String is turned into a Label, and the two nodes are positioned at set points horizontally (so the overall effect is three columns running down the form). Absolute positioning of nodes like this is less flexible than using a layout container but can be worthwhile if the UI is static and would otherwise demand custom layout code. In the sample code the rectangles grouping each row rule out the use of something like the standard Tile container. Figure 7.5 shows the relationship between the function parameters and the chunk of scene graph the function creates.

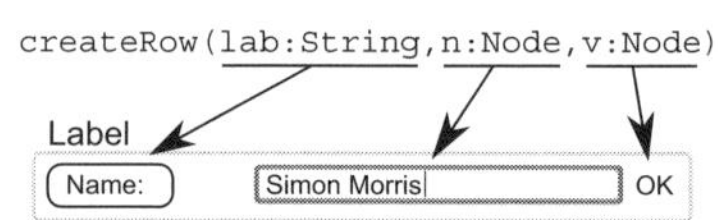

Figure 7.5 The createRow() function is a convenience for manufacturing each part of the feedback form. Each row consists of three parts: a text label and two nodes (controls).

The three nodes are gathered inside a `Group` and then added to another `Group` that provides a pin-line border by way of a `Rectangle` node.

The `createRow()` function draws to a close version 1 of the source code for our feedback form. These two simple classes, `Record` and `Feedback`, provide the entirety of the application. Now it's time to test the code.

7.1.3 Running version 1

Building and running version 1 of the project results in the window shown in figure 7.6.

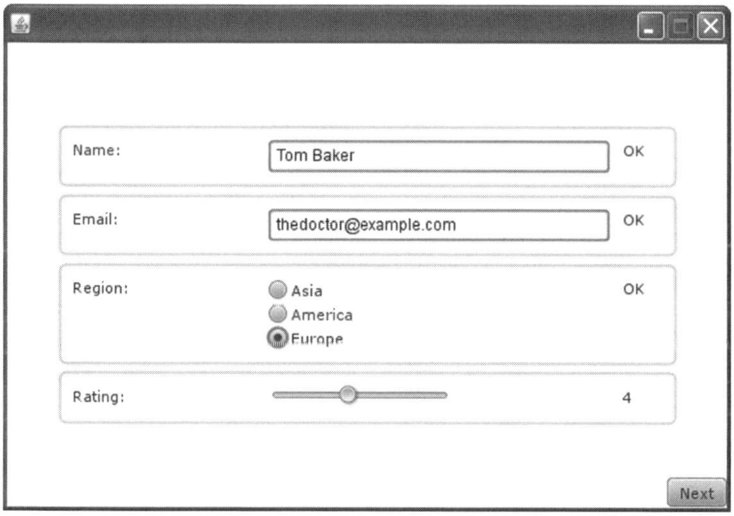

Figure 7.6 Version 1 of the application, running

We can edit the four data fields of the form, and their corresponding labels will change to reflect their content's validity. Clicking the Next button merely prints the details in the model, `Record`, to the console. Obviously this isn't particularly useful, unless we intend to deliberately ignore our users' feedback (which, of course, no self-respecting company would ever do!), so in the next part of this chapter we'll store the data from the form and produce some statistics.

7.2 Chart topping: Feedback, version 2

So we have a simple feedback form; it asks only four questions, but that's enough to derive some statistics from. In order to create those statistics, we need to record the details provided by each user. On a desktop application this would be as simple as opening a file and writing to it, but JavaFX applications might need to run on cell phones or inside a web page, where writing to a disk isn't usually an option. Fortunately JavaFX 1.2 provides its own persistent storage solution, which we'll explore in the coming section.

Once the data is stored safely, we need to find something to do with it. And again JavaFX provides an answer, in the form of its chart controls. All manner of graphs and charts can be created from collections of data and displayed in suitably impressive ways. We'll be using a couple of simple 3D charts to display the region and rating data from our form. So that's the plan; now let's get started.

7.2.1 Cross-platform persistent storage

Almost every application needs to record data—even games like to save their high-score tables. In a thin-client environment, working exclusively against data on a network, we have the luxury of not worrying about the storage capabilities of the host device, but fatter clients aren't so lucky. A problem arises about how to persist data across all the devices JavaFX supports. On the desktop we can fall back to Java's I/O classes to read and write files on the host's hard disk, but what happens if our code finds itself running as an applet, or on a cell phone, or on a Blu-ray player—where can it save its data then?

The `javafx.io` package provides a clean, cross-platform, persistence mechanism for that very purpose. It allows us to read and write files in a managed way across a variety of devices. By *managed*, I mean these files are firmly associated with the running application. In effect, they behave like a cross between the files of a regular desktop application and the cookies of a web page. Let's take a look at a demonstration, by way of listing 7.6.

Listing 7.6 Record.fx (version 2)

```
package jfxia.chapter7;

import javafx.io.Resource;
import javafx.io.Storage;
import javafx.io.http.URLConverter;

import java.io.BufferedReader;
import java.io.InputStreamReader;
import java.io.PrintStream;

package def REGIONS:String[] = [ "Asia","America","Europe" ];

package class Record {
    package var name:String;
    package var email:String;
    package var region:Integer = -1;
    package var rating:Number = 0;

    package def validName:Boolean = bind (
        name.length() > 2
    );
    package def validEmail:Boolean = bind (
        (email.length() > 7) and
        (email.indexOf("@") > 0)
    );
    package def validRegion:Boolean = bind (
        region >= 0
    );
    package def validRating:Boolean = bind (
        rating > 0
    );
```

```
    package def valid:Boolean = bind (
        validName and validEmail and
        validRegion and validRating
    );
}
                                                     Encode record
package function encode(r:Record) : String {     <-- into string
    def conv = URLConverter{}
    "{conv.encodeString(r.name)}&"
        "{conv.encodeString(r.email)}&"
        "{r.region}&"
        "{r.rating as Integer}"
}
                                                     Decode record
package function decode(s:String) : Record {     <-- from string
    def conv = URLConverter{}
    def arr:String[] = s.split("&");
    if(sizeof arr < 4) {
        null                                    Error: too
    }                                           few fields
    else {
        Record {
            name: conv.decodeString(arr[0]);
            email: conv.decodeString(arr[1]);
            region: Integer.parseInt(              Create Record
                conv.decodeString(arr[2]));        object
            rating: Integer.parseInt(
                conv.decodeString(arr[3]));
        }
    }
}
                                                Filename
def FILENAME:String = "feedback.txt";      <-- for data
package function load() : Record[] {            <-- Load all
    var recs:Record[] = [];                         records

    def data:Storage = Storage { source: FILENAME; }
    def resource:Resource = data.resource;

    if(resource.readable) {
        def br:BufferedReader = new BufferedReader(
            new InputStreamReader(                     Use Java's
                resource.openInputStream()             BufferedReader
            )                                          class
        );
        var in:String = br.readLine();
        while(in!=null) {
            insert Record.decode(in) into recs;    <-- Call our decode()
            in = br.readLine();                        function
        }
        br.close();
    }

    recs;
}                                                   Save all
package function save(recs:Record[]) : Void {   <-- records
    def data:Storage = Storage { source: FILENAME; }
    def resource:Resource = data.resource;
```

```
    if(resource.writable) {
        def ps:PrintStream =  new PrintStream(
            resource.openOutputStream(true)
        );
        for(r in recs) {
            ps.println(Record.encode(r));      <-- Call our encode() function
        }
        ps.close();
    }
}
```

This listing adds a mass of code to load and save the Record objects our UI populates. At the head of the file we see six I/O-related classes being imported. The first three are from JavaFX and the final three are from Java. (I'll explain why we need the Java classes later.)

Below the Record class itself (unchanged from the last version) we find four brand-new script-level functions. The first two are named encode() and decode(), and they translate our data to and from a String, using the javafx.io.http.URLConverter class. This class provides useful functions for working with web addresses, specifically encoding and decoding the parameters on HTTP GET requests (when query data is encoded as part of the URL). The encode() function uses URLConverter to turn a Record object into a String, so whitespace and other potentially troublesome characters are taken care of. Its companion reverses the process, reconstructing a Record from an encoded String.

The second two functions in listing 7.6, named load() and save(), make use of this encode/decode functionality to store and later re-create an entire bank of Record objects to a file. To locate the file we create a Storage object with the required filename and use its embedded Resource object to work with the data. Let's remind ourselves of the body of the load() function:

```
def data:Storage = Storage { source: FILENAME; }
def resource:Resource = data.resource;
if(resource.readable) {
    def br:BufferedReader = new BufferedReader(
        new InputStreamReader(
            resource.openInputStream()
        )
    );
    var in:String = br.readLine();
    while(in!=null) {
        insert Record.decode(in) into recs;
        in = br.readLine();
    }
    br.close();
}
```

Variables in the Resource class allow us to check on the state of the file (for example, its readability) and access its input stream. In the example, we use Java's BufferedReader, wrapped around an InputStreamReader, to pull data from the input stream as text. Java's reader classes know how to interpret different character encodings and deal with non-English characters (like letters with accents). The `decode()` function we saw earlier is then used to translate this text into a `Record` object.

> **Using Java's I/O classes**
> It's a shame we have to use Java's reader/writer classes, as we can't be sure those classes will be available outside the desktop environment. JavaFX 1.2 doesn't yet have a full complement of its own readers and writers, so for the time being we either have to handle the raw byte stream ourselves, use JavaScript Object Notation (JSON)/eXtensible Markup Language (XML), or revert to Java's I/O classes.

Now let's turn our attention to the body of the `save()` function:

```
def data:Storage = Storage { source: FILENAME; }
def resource:Resource = data.resource;
if(resource.writable) {
    def ps:PrintStream =  new PrintStream(
        resource.openOutputStream(true)
    );
    for(r in recs) {
        ps.println(Record.encode(r));
    }
    ps.close();
}
```

Again `Storage` and `Resource` are used to establish a link to the data, and Java classes are used to write it, combined with the `encode()` function to turn each `Record` into a `String`.

Using JavaFX's persistence API we can save and recover data to the host device, regardless of whether it's a phone, a games console, or a PC. Although the entry point into the data is described as a filename, we cannot use the API to access arbitrary files on the host. A bit like cookies on a website, the mechanism links data to the application that wrote it, a process that deserves a little further explanation.

7.2.2 How Storage manages its files

The `Storage` class segregates the files it saves using the application's URL domain and path. In listing 7.6 we saw the `Storage` class being used to access a file with a basic filename, feedback.txt, but it's also possible to prefix a filename with a path, like /JFX/FeedbackApplet/feedback.txt. To explain what impact this has on how the data is stored and accessed, we need to look at some example web addresses:

- http://www.jfxia.com/Games/PacmanGame/index.html
- http://www.jfxia.com/Games/SpaceInvaders/index.html

For JavaFX code from the above URLs, the persistence API would create an original space for the www.jfxia.com domain within its storage area (exactly where this is doesn't concern us; indeed it might be different for each device and/or manufacturer). This ensures files associated with applets/applications from different organizations or authors are kept apart. Within that space, files can be further managed by using the path element of the URL. The location of the HTML, JAR, or WebStart JNLP file (depending on what is being referenced by the URL) is taken to be the default directory of the application, and permission is granted to read or write files using that directory path or any path that's a direct or indirect parent or descendant.

Let's decipher that rather cryptic last sentence by using the two example URLs.

- If the applet at /Games/PacmanGame/index.html used the `Storage` class to create a file called scores.dat, the persistence API would write it into /Games/PacmanGame/scores.dat, within its area set aside for the www.jfxia.com domain. Because the applet didn't specify a path prefix for the filename, the API used the path of the HTML page the applet was on.
- The applet could alternatively specify the absolute path, /Games/PacmanGame/scores.dat, resulting in the same effect as scores.dat on its own.
- The applet could also have specified a subdirectory off of its *home directory*, such as /Games/PacmanGame/Data/scores.dat. As a descendant of the home directory, it would be granted permission for reading and writing. (Note: no such physical directory has to exist on the www.jfxia.com web server. These file paths are merely data source identifiers, and the data isn't being stored on the server side anyway!)
- The applet could alternatively have used the /Games/ or / (root) directory. Because both are parents of the applet's home directory, they would also have been permitted. But here's the important part: while both /Games/SpaceInvaders/index.html and /Games/PacmanGame/index.html can access the root and the Games directory, they cannot access each other's directories or any subdirectories therein.

  In other words, if either game writes its data *above* its home directory, that data is available to other applications living (directly or indirectly) off that directory. So, if the data was written into the root directory, then all JavaFX programs on www.jfxia.com could read or write it.

By using a full path prefix, different JavaFX programs can choose to share or hide their data files using the `Storage` mechanism. Subdirectories (below home) help us to organize our data; parent directories (above home) help us to share it. It's *that* simple!

7.2.3 Adding pie and bar charts

For every Dilbert, there's a Pointy-Haired Boss, or so it seems. As programmers interested in graphics, we naturally want to spend our time writing video effects, UI controls, and Pac-Man clones; unfortunately, our bosses are unlikely to let us. When bosses say "graphics" they generally mean charts and graphs, and that's probably why the 1.2 release of JavaFX came with a collection of ready-made pie, bar, line, and other chart controls (like the 3D pie chart in figure 7.7).

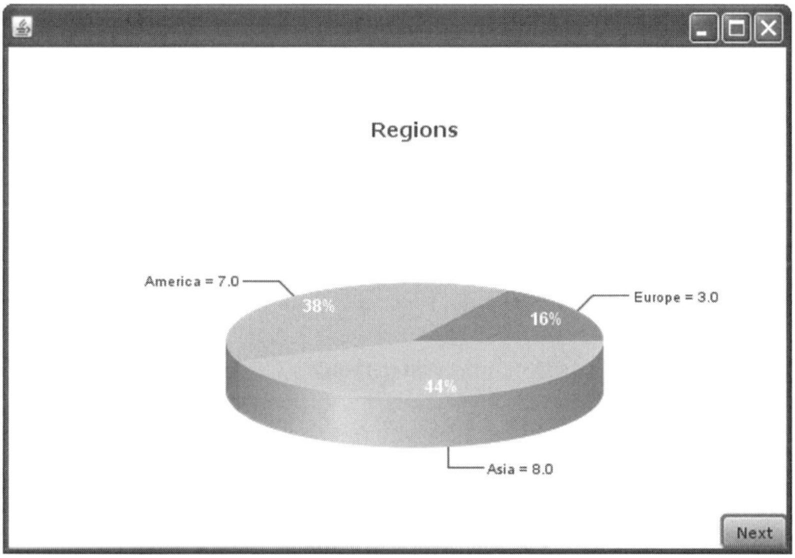

Figure 7.7 JavaFX has a powerful library of chart controls, including a 3D pie chart.

The next update of the feedback application will take the region and rating data collected from each user (and stored using the new persistent `Record` class) and produce a pie chart and a bar graph from it. The first part of the new `Feedback` class is shown in listing 7.7. The code continues in listings 7.8 and 7.9.

Listing 7.7 Feedback.fx (version 2, part 1)

```
package jfxia.chapter7;

import javafx.scene.Group;
import javafx.scene.Node;
import javafx.scene.Scene;
import javafx.scene.chart.BarChart;
import javafx.scene.chart.BarChart3D;
import javafx.scene.chart.PieChart;
import javafx.scene.chart.PieChart3D;
import javafx.scene.chart.part.CategoryAxis;
import javafx.scene.chart.part.NumberAxis;
import javafx.scene.control.Button;
import javafx.scene.control.Label;
import javafx.scene.control.RadioButton;
import javafx.scene.control.Slider;
import javafx.scene.control.TextBox;
import javafx.scene.control.ToggleGroup;
import javafx.scene.layout.Panel;
import javafx.scene.layout.Tile;
import javafx.scene.layout.VBox;
import javafx.scene.paint.Color;
import javafx.scene.shape.Rectangle;
import javafx.stage.Alert;
```

```
import javafx.stage.Stage;
import javafx.util.Sequences;

var recordStore = Record.load();
def record:Record = Record {};
insert record into recordStore;

def winW:Number = 550;
def winH:Number = 350;
var showCharts:Boolean = false;                    Show form or charts?
var showPie:Boolean = false;                       Show pie or bar?

def nextButton = Button {
    text: "Next";
    action: function() {
        if(not showCharts) {          If form showing
            if(record.valid) {
                delete mainPan.content[0];         Remove form from scene graph

                Record.save(recordStore);          Save form data

                insert createChartUI()
                    before mainPan.content[0];     Insert charts into scene graph
                showCharts=true;
            }
            else {
                Alert.confirm("Error","Form incomplete.");     Form invalid
            }
        }
        else {
            showPie = not showPie;         Toggle between charts
        }
    }
}
// Part 2 is listing 7.8; part 3, listing 7.9
```

This listing focuses on the introduction of the record store and the changes to the Next button. The `recordStore` variable is a sequence of `Record` objects, one of each feedback entry recorded in the application's persistent storage. Having loaded past records, we append the virgin record created as a model for our feedback UI.

After the user completes the feedback form, clicking the Next button will record the data and take the user to the charts. Subsequent clicks of the Next button toggle between the Regions pie chart and the Ratings bar chart. Therefore, the `nextButton` control needs to be aware of whether it's moving from the form to the charts or toggling between the two charts. The `showCharts` and `showPie` variables are used for that very purpose.

Within the `nextButton` action handler the code first checks, courtesy of `showCharts`, which mode the UI is currently in (form or charts). If the form is currently displayed, the form UI is deleted from the scene graph, the `Record` sequence is saved to persistent storage (including the `Record` just populated by the form), and the chart UI is created and added to the scene graph. Finally `showCharts` is set to mark the switch from form to charts. If `nextButton` is clicked when `showCharts` is already set, the `showPie` variable is toggled, causing a different chart to be displayed.

Listing 7.7 contains all the necessary updates to the application, except the crucial step of creating the charts themselves. To find out how that's done, we need to consult listing 7.8, which holds the first part of the createChartUI() function. Because large parts of the class are unchanged, I've replaced the details with comments in bold.

Listing 7.8 Feedback.fx (version 2, part 2)

```
// Part 1 is listing 7.7
var mainPan:Panel;
Stage {
    // Stage details unchanged from previous
    // version
}

function createFeedbackUI() : Node {
    // createFeedbackUI() details unchanged from
    // previous version
}

function createRow(lab:String,n:Node,v:Node) : Node {
    // createRow() details unchanged from previous
    // version
}

function createChartUI() : Node {
    def regionData:PieChart.Data[] =
        for(r in Record.REGIONS) {
            var regIdx:Integer  = indexof r;
            var cnt:Integer = 0;
            for(rc in recordStore) {
                if(rc.region == regIdx) cnt++;
            }

            PieChart.Data {
                label: r;
                value: cnt;
            }
        }

    var highestCnt:Integer = 0;
    def ratingData:BarChart.Data[] =
        for(i in [1..10]) {
            var cnt:Integer = 0;
            for(rec in recordStore) {
                def rat = rec.rating as Integer;
                if(rat == i) cnt++;
            }
            if(cnt>highestCnt) highestCnt=cnt;

            BarChart.Data {
                category: "{i}";
                value: cnt;
            }
        }
```

Annotations:
- Refer to previous Feedback.fx version
- Count respondents for given region
- Create PieChart.Data for region
- Highest rating in data
- Count respondents for given rating
- Create BarChart.Data for rating

This is only the first half of the function, not the entire thing. It deals with creating the data required by the pie and bar chart controls. The first block of code builds the data for the regions pie chart, the second block deals with the ratings bar chart.

```
def regionData:PieChart.Data[] =
    for(r in Record.REGIONS) {
        var regIdx:Integer  = indexof r;
        var cnt:Integer = 0;
        for(rc in recordStore) {
            if(rc.region == regIdx) cnt++;
        }
        PieChart.Data {
            label: r;
            value: cnt;
        }
    }
```

The first block, reprised here, creates a `PieChart.Data` object for each region named in the `Record.REGIONS` sequence. These objects collect to create a sequence called `regionData`. For each region we walk over every record in `recordStore`, building a count of the responses for that region—the `regIdx` variable holds the region index, and the inner `for` loop looks for records matching that index. Once we have the count, we use it with the region name to create a new `PieChart.Data` object, which gets added to the `regionData` sequence.

```
var highestCnt:Integer = 0;
def ratingData:BarChart.Data[] =
    for(i in [1..10]) {
        var cnt:Integer = 0;
        for(rec in recordStore) {
            def rat = rec.rating as Integer;
            if(rat == i) cnt++;
        }
        if(cnt>highestCnt) highestCnt=cnt;
        BarChart.Data {
            category: "{i}";
            value: cnt;
        }
    }
```

The bar chart code, reproduced here, is very similar to the pie chart code. This time we're dealing with numeric ratings between 1 and 10; for each of the 10 possible ratings we scan the records, counting how many feedback responses gave that rating. We keep track of the size of the most popular (`highestCnt`) so we can scale the chart appropriately. Each rating's count is used to create a `BarChart.Data` object, used to populate the `ratingData` sequence.

Now that we've seen how the data in the record store is translated into sequences of `PieChart.Data` and `BarChart.Data` objects, we can turn our attention to the actual creation of the chart controls themselves. Listing 7.9 shows how it's done.

Listing 7.9 Feedback.fx (version 2, part 3)

```
    Group {
        content: [
            PieChart3D {                                  <-- Pie chart control
                width: 500;  height: 350;
                visible: bind showPie;                    <-- Control its visibility
                title: "Regions";
                titleGap: 0;
                data: regionData;                         <-- Plug in data sequence
                pieLabelVisible: true;
                pieValueVisible: true;
            } ,
            BarChart3D {                                  <-- Bar chart control
                width: 500;  height: 350;
                visible: bind not showPie;                <-- Control its visibility
                title: "Ratings";
                titleGap: 10;
                data: BarChart.Series {                   Wrap data sequence
                    name: "Ratings";
                    data: ratingData;
                }
                categoryAxis: CategoryAxis {              Labels for category axis
                    categories: for(r in ratingData)
                        r.category;
                }
                valueAxis: NumberAxis {                   Bounds and unit for value axis
                    lowerBound: 0;
                    upperBound: highestCnt;
                    tickUnit: 1;
                }
            }
        ]
    }
}
```

The final part of the `createChartUI()` function manufactures the chart scene graph. Both chart controls are held inside a simple `Group`. The first, `PieChart3D`, has its visibility bound to show whenever `showPie` is true; the second, `BarChart3D`, has its visibility bound to show whenever `showPie` is false. Figure 7.8 reveals how both charts look when displayed.

The `PieChart3D` control's declaration is quite simple to understand: the `title` and `titleGap` properties control the label that appears over the chart and how far away it is from the bounds of the pie graphic itself. The `regionData` sequence we created in listing 7.8 is referenced via `data`. The `pieLabelVisible` and `pieValueVisible` variables cause the values and labels of each pie slice (set in each `PieChart.Data` object, as you recall) to be drawn.

The `BarChart3D` control's declaration is more complicated. As well as the familiar `title` and `titleGap` properties, objects controlling each axis are created, and the `ratingData` sequence (created in listing 7.8) is wrapped inside a `BarChart.Series`

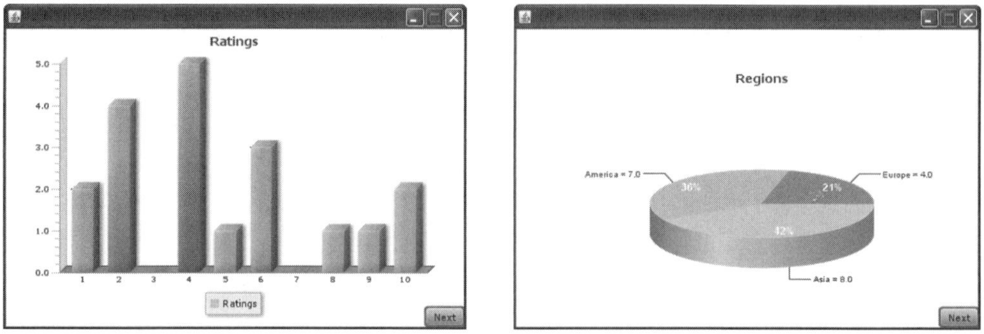

Figure 7.8 A bar chart and a pie chart, as drawn in 3D by the JavaFX 1.2 chart library

object rather than being plugged directly into the control. But what is a `BarChart.Series`, and why is it necessary?

JavaFX's bar charts are quite clever beasts—they can display several sets of data simultaneously. Suppose our application had allowed the user to set two ratings instead of just one; we could display both sets (or *series*) in one chart, looking like figure 7.9.

Each category in the chart (1 to 10 along the horizontal axis) has two independent bars, one from each series of data.

```
data: [
    BarChart.Series {
        name: "Ratings";
        data: ratingData;
    } ,
    BarChart.Series {
        name: "Ratings 2";
        data: reverse ratingData;
    }
]
```

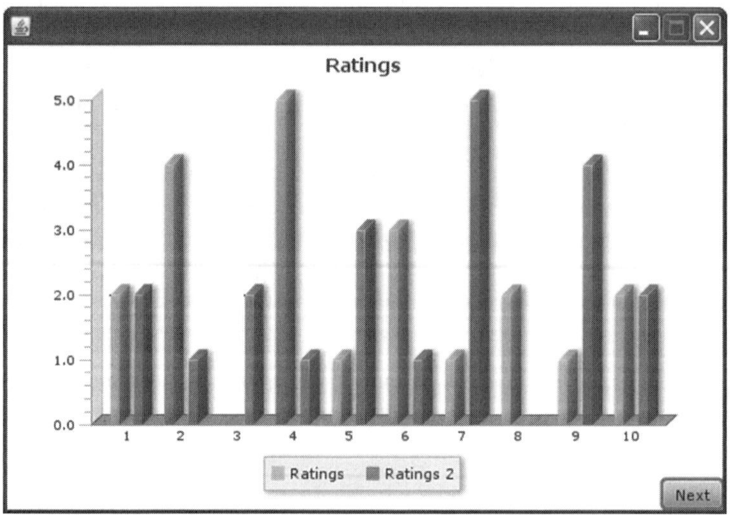

Figure 7.9 This is what the project's bar chart would look like if it used two data series rather than one. Each category has two bars, and the key at the foot of the chart shows two labels.

The data property in BarChart3D accepts a sequence of type BarChart.Series rather than just a single object. The example quick-'n'-dirty code snippet proves this, by adding a second series that mirrors the first (this was how figure 7.9 was created). Each BarChart.Series object contains a BarChart.Data object holding its data, and a label to use in the key at the foot of the chart.

With that explained, only the categoryAxis and valueAxis variables remain a mystery. We'll look at those in the next section.

7.2.4 Taking control of chart axes

If you've checked out the JavaFX API documentation, you'll have noticed that the chart classes are grouped into three packages. The main one, javafx.scene.chart, contains the chart controls themselves, plus their associated data and series classes. The javafx.scene.chart.data package holds the superclasses for these data and series classes (unless you code your own charts, you're unlikely to work directly with them). javafx.scene.chart.part contains classes to model common chart elements, such as the axes. This package is home to the CategoryAxis and NumberAxis used in listing 7.9. Here's a reminder of that code:

```
categoryAxis: CategoryAxis {
    categories: for(r in ratingData)
        r.category;
}
valueAxis: NumberAxis {
    lowerBound: 0;
    upperBound: highestCnt;
    tickUnit: 1;
}
```

These variables (part of the BarChart3D control, as you recall) determine how the horizontal (category) and vertical (value) axes will be drawn. Although many different types of charts exist, there are only a handful of different axis *flavors*. An axis can represent a linear (analog) range of values, or it can represent a finite set of groups. For example, if we drew a line chart of temperature readings over a 24-hour period, it might have *ticks* (or labels) every 5 degrees Centigrade on the temperature axis and every hour on the time axis, but the data is not necessarily constrained by these markings. We might plot a temperature of 37 degrees (which is not a multiple of 5) at 9:43 a.m. (which is not on the hour). If we then drew a bar chart of average daily temperatures for each month in a year, while the temperature axis would still be analog, the time axis would now be grouped into 12 distinct categories (January, February, etc.).

CategoryAxis and NumberAxis (plus the abstract ValueAxis) model those axis types. The first handles grouped data and the second linear data. Each has a host of configuration options for controlling what gets drawn and how. One particularly useful example is NumberAxis.formatTickLabel(), a function type that allows us to control how the values on an axis are labeled. To convert the values 0 to 11 into calendar names, we would use the following NumberAxis code:

```
NumberAxis {
    label: "Months";
    lowerBound:0;  upperBound:12;
    tickUnit: 1;
    formatTickLabel: function(f:Float) {
        def cal = ["Jan","Feb","Mar","Apr","May","Jun" ,
            "Jul","Aug","Sep","Oct","Nov","Dec" ];
        cal[f as Integer];
    }
}
```

The `lowerBound` and `upperBound` variables constrain the axis to values between 0 to 11 (inclusive), while `tickUnit` determines the frequency of labels on the axis (one label for every integer value). The `formatTickLabel` code converts a label value into text, using a lookup table of calendar month names. (The `cal` sequence is a local variable merely for the sake of brevity; in real-world code it would be declared at the script or class level, thereby avoiding a rebuild every time the function runs.)

You can see more examples of these axis classes at work in the next section, where we look at the other types of chart supported by JavaFX.

7.2.5 Other chart controls (area, bubble, line, and scatter)

Bar charts and pie charts are staples of the charting world, but JavaFX offers far more than just these two. In this section we'll tour alternatives, beginning with the two charts in figure 7.10.

The `AreaChart` class accepts a collection of x and y values, using them as points defining a polygon. The effect looks like a mountain range, and it's a useful alternative to the simple line chart (see later).

As well as the 3D bar chart we witnessed in the feedback project, JavaFX has a 2D alternative. The `BarChart` control has the same data requirements as its `BarChart3D` sibling; both accept a collection of values defining the height of each bar.

Two more chart types are demonstrated in figure 7.11.

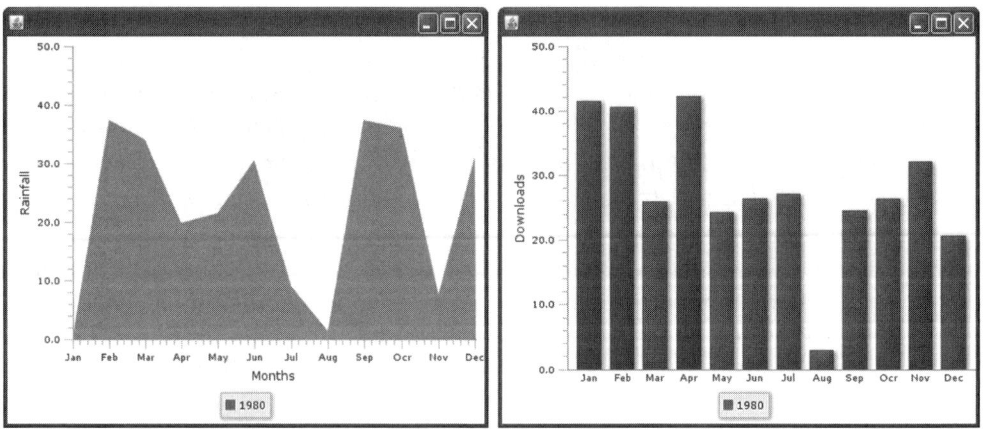

Figure 7.10 An area chart (left) and a standard 2D bar chart (right)

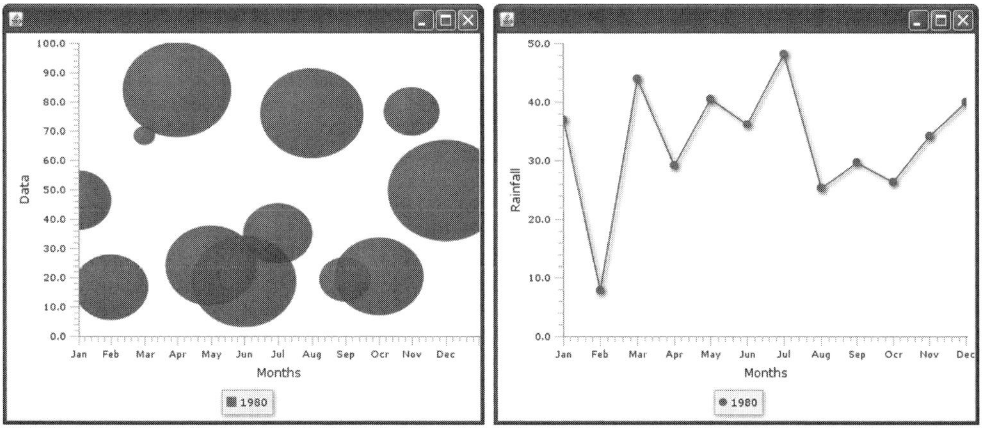

Figure 7.11 A bubble chart (left) and a line chart (right)

The BubbleChart is rarely used, but it can be a real lifesaver when necessary. As well as x and y values, each point can contain a radius, giving effectively a third dimension of data.

The LineChart is the familiar graph we all remember from school. Using x and y values, it plots a line to connect the dots.

The two final chart types are shown in figure 7.12.

Just as the bar chart comes in 2D and 3D flavors, so the pie chart also has 2D and 3D variations. Both PieChart and PieChart3D are unusual, as (understandably) they do not support multiple series of data like the other charts; only one set of values can be plugged in.

The ScatterChart, although graphically the simplest of all JavaFX charts, is incredibly useful for revealing patterns within a given body of data. It plots x and y values anywhere within its coordinate space.

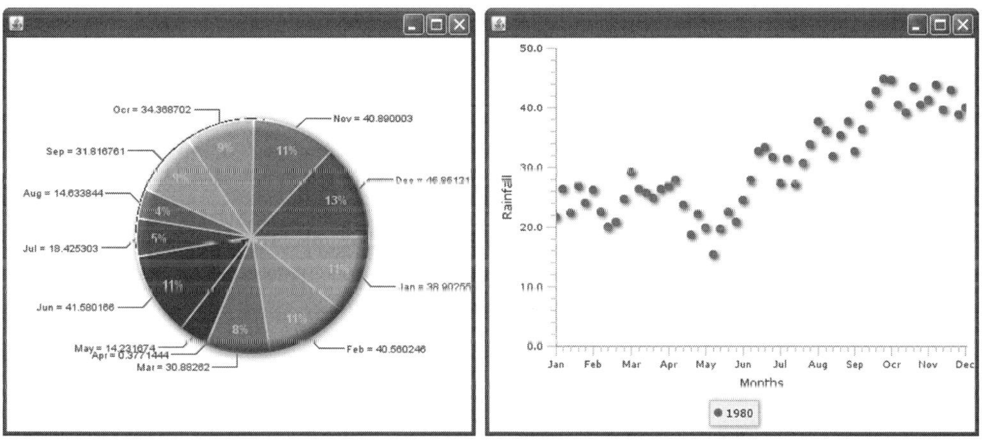

Figure 7.12 A standard 2D pie chart (left) and a scatter chart (right)

That completes our whistle-stop tour of the JavaFX charting controls. All that remains is to compile and try our new feedback application.

7.2.6 Running version 2

Starting up the project gives us the same form UI from version 1, but now the Next button has been rewired to save the data and replace the form UI with a couple of charts. The result should look like figure 7.13. Depending on how powerful your computer is, the flip between form and charts may not be instantaneous. I ran the code on an old laptop, and there was a slight (0.5s to 1s) delay before the charts appeared. A brief investigation revealed the delay emanated from building the chart UI. (Perhaps a simple *processing* animation is needed, giving an instance response to a Next button click?)

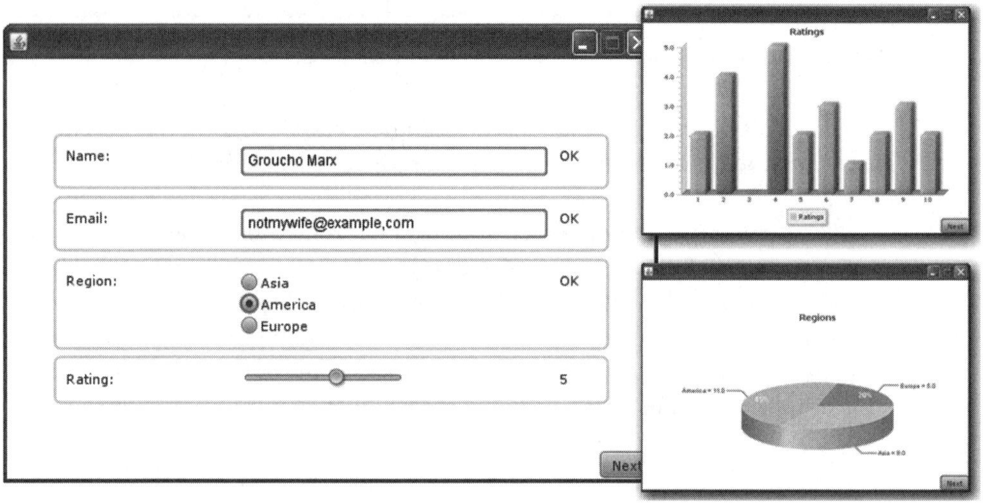

Figure 7.13 Version 2 of the Feedback application runs, complete with form (main image) and two charts (thumbnails).

Once the form has been submitted, to enter another record you need to quit and restart the application. I could have added logic to reset the UI and add a new `Record` to the `recordStore`, but the listings would have been longer, with little extra educational value. You can add the code yourself if you want. (Hint: you need to make sure the UI is bound against a new `Record` object; either rebuild a fresh UI for each `Record` or devise an abstraction, so the UI isn't plumbed directly into a specific `Record`.)

In the final part of this chapter, we finish with a super-sized bonus section, all about creating our own controls and skinning them.

7.3 Bonus: creating a styled UI control in JavaFX

In this chapter's project we saw JavaFX controls in action; now it's time to write our own control from scratch. Because much of the detail in this section is based on research and trial and error rather than official JavaFX documentation, I've separated it from the main project in this chapter and turned it into a (admittedly, rather lengthy) bonus project.

As already explained, JavaFX's controls library, in stark contrast to Java's Swing library, can function across a wide range of devices and environments—but that's not all it can do. Each control in the library can have its appearance customized through skins and stylesheets. This allows designers and other nonprogrammers to radically change the look of an application, without having to write or recompile any code.

In this section we'll develop our own very simple, style-aware control. Probably the simplest of all widget types is the humble progress bar; it's a 100% visual element with no interaction with the mouse or keyboard, and as such it's ideal for practicing skinning. The standard controls API already has a progress control of its own (we'll see it in action in the next chapter), but it won't hurt to develop our own super-sexy version.

WARNING *Check for updates* This section was written originally against JavaFX 1.1 and then updated for the 1.2 release. Although the latter saw the debut of the controls library, at the time of writing much of the details on how skins and Cascading Style Sheets (CSS) support works is still largely undocumented. The material in this section is largely based on what little information there is, plus lots of investigation. Sources close to the JavaFX team have hinted that, broadly speaking, the techniques laid out in the following pages are correct. However, readers are urged to search out fresh information that may have emerged since this chapter was written, particularly official tutorials, or best practice guides for writing skins.

Let's look at stylesheets.

7.3.1 What is a stylesheet?

Back in the old days (when the web was in black and white) elements forming an HTML document determined both the logical meaning of their content and how they would be displayed. For example, a `<p>` element indicated a given node in the DOM (Document Object Model) was of paragraph type. But marking the node as a paragraph also implied how it would be drawn on the browser page, how much whitespace would appear around it, how the text would flow, and so on. To counteract these presumptions new element types like `<font>` and `<center>` were added to browsers to influence display. With no logical function in the document, these new elements polluted the DOM and made it impossible to render the document in different ways across different environments.

CSS is a means of fixing this problem, by separating the logical meaning of an element from the way it's displayed. A *stylesheet* is a separate document (or a self-contained section within an HTML document) defining *rules* for rendering the HTML elements. By merely changing the CSS, a web designer can specify the display settings of a paragraph (for example), without need to inject extra style-specific elements into the HTML. Stylesheet rules can be targeted at every node of a given type, at nodes having been assigned a given class, or at a specific node carrying a given ID (see figure 7.14). Untangling the logical structure of a document from how it should be displayed allows the document to be shown in many different ways, simply by changing its stylesheet.

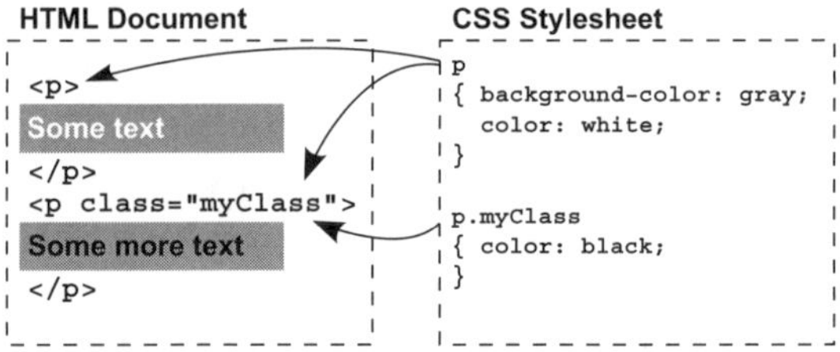

Figure 7.14 Two style rules and two HTML paragraph elements. The first rule applies to both paragraphs, while the second applies only to paragraphs of class `myClass`.

What works for web page content could also work for GUI controls; if buttons, sliders, scrollbars, and other controls deferred to an external stylesheet for their display settings, artists and designers could change their look without having to write a single line of software code. This is precisely the intent behind JavaFX's style-aware controls library.

JavaFX allows both programmers and designers to get in on the style act. Each JavaFX control defers not to a stylesheet directly but to a skin. Figure 7.15 shows this relationship diagrammatically. The skin is a JavaFX class that draws the control; it can expose various properties (public instance variables), which JavaFX can then allow designers to change via a CSS-like file format.

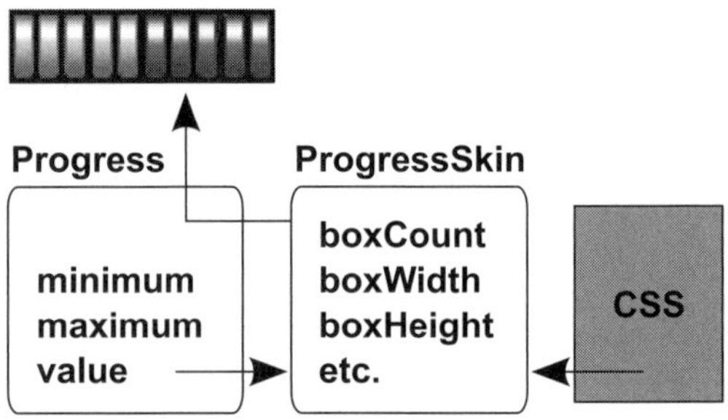

Figure 7.15 The data from the control (`Progress`) and the CSS from the stylesheet are combined inside the skin (`ProgressSkin`) to produce a displayable UI control, in this example, a progress bar.

In a rough sense the control acts as the *model* and the skin as the *view*, in the popular Model/View/Controller model of UIs. But the added JavaFX twist is that the skin can be configured by a stylesheet. Controls are created by subclassing `javafx.scene.control.Control` and skins by subclassing `Skin` in the same package. Another class, `Behavior`, is designed to map inputs (keystrokes, for example) to host-specific actions on the control, effectively making it a type of MVC *controller*.

Now that you understand the theory, let's look at each part in turn as actual code.

7.3.2 Creating a control: the Progress class

We're going to write our own style-compliant control from scratch, just to see how easy it is. The control we'll write will be a simple progress bar, like the one that might appear during a file download operation. The progress bar will take minimum and maximum bounds, plus a value, and display a series of boxes forming a horizontal bar, colored to show where the value falls in relation to its bounds. To keep things nice and simple our control won't respond to any mouse or keyboard input, allowing us to focus exclusively on the interaction between model (control) and view (skin), while ignoring the controller (behavior).

Listing 7.10 shows the control class itself. This is the object other software will use when wishing to create a control declaratively. It subclasses the `Control` class from `javafx.scene.control`, a type of `CustomNode` designed to work with styling.

Listing 7.10 Progress.fx

```
package jfxia.chapter7;

import javafx.scene.control.Control;

public class Progress extends Control
{   public var minimum:Number = 0;
    public var maximum:Number = 100;
    public var value:Number = 50 on replace {
        if(value<minimum) { value=minimum; }
        if(value>maximum) { value=maximum; }
    };

    override var skin = ProgressSkin{};
}
```

The control's data (annotates the three public variables)

Override the skin (annotates the `override var skin` line)

Our `Progress` class has three variables: `maximum` and `minimum` determine the range of the progress (its high and low values), while `value` is the current setting within that range. We override the `skin` variable inherited from `Control` to assign a default skin object. The skin, as you recall, gives our control its face and processes user input. It's a key part of the styling process, so let's look at that class next.

7.3.3 Creating a skin: the ProgressSkin class

In itself the `Progress` class does nothing but hold the fundamental data of the progress meter control. Even though it's a `CustomNode` subclass, it defers all its display and input to the skin class. So, what does this skin class look like? It looks like listing 7.11.

Listing 7.11 ProgressSkin.fx (part 1)

```
package jfxia.chapter7;

import javafx.scene.Group;
import javafx.scene.control.Skin;
import javafx.scene.input.MouseEvent;
import javafx.scene.layout.HBox;
import javafx.scene.paint.Color;
import javafx.scene.paint.LinearGradient;
import javafx.scene.paint.Paint;
import javafx.scene.paint.Stop;
import javafx.scene.shape.Rectangle;

public class ProgressSkin extends Skin {
    public var boxCount:Integer = 10;
    public var boxWidth:Number = 7;
    public var boxHeight:Number = 20;
    public var boxStrokeWidth:Number = 1;
    public var boxCornerArc:Number = 3;
    public var boxHGap:Number = 1;

    public var boxUnsetStroke:Paint = Color.DARKBLUE;
```

These properties can be styled with CSS (annotates the `public var box...` properties)

```
    public var boxUnsetFill:Paint = makeLG(Color.CYAN,
        Color.BLUE,Color.DARKBLUE);
    public var boxSetStroke:Paint = Color.DARKGREEN;
    public var boxSetFill:Paint = makeLG(Color.YELLOW,
        Color.LIMEGREEN,Color.DARKGREEN);

    def boxValue:Integer = bind {
        var p:Progress = control as Progress;
        var v:Number = (p.value-p.minimum) /
            (p.maximum-p.minimum);
        (boxCount*v) as Integer;
    }
// ** Part 2 is listing 7.12
```

These properties can be styled with CSS

How many boxes to highlight?

Listing 7.11 is the opening of our skin class, `ProcessSkin`. (The second part of the source code is shown in listing 7.12.) The `Progress` class is effectively the model, and this class is the view in the classic MVC scheme. It subclasses `javafx.scene.control.Skin`, allowing it to be used as a skin.

The properties at the top of the class are all exposed so that they can be altered by a stylesheet. They perform various stylistic functions.

- The `boxCount` variable determines how many progress bar boxes should appear on screen.
- The `boxWidth` and `boxHeight` variables hold the dimensions of each box, while `boxHGap` is the pixel gap between boxes.
- The variable `boxStrokeWidth` is the size of the trim around each box, and `boxCornerArc` is the radius of the rounded corners.
- For the public interface, we have two pairs of variables that colorize the control. The first pair are `boxUnsetStroke` and `boxUnsetFill`, the trim and body colors for *switched-off* boxes; the second pair is (unsurprisingly) `boxSetStroke` and `boxSetFill`, and they do the same thing for *switched-on* boxes. The `makeLG()` function is a convenience for creating gradient fills; we'll see it in the concluding part of the code.
- The private variable `boxValue` uses the data in the `Progress` control to work out how many boxes should be switched on. The reference to `control` is a variable inherited from its parent class, `Skin`, allowing us to read the current state of the control (model) the skin is plugged into.

One thing of particular note in listing 7.11: the `stroke` and `fill` properties are `Paint` objects, not `Color` objects. Why? Quite simply, the former allows us to plug in a gradient fill or some other complex pattern, while the latter would support only a flat color. And, believe it or not, JavaFX's support for styles actually extends all the way to patterned fills.

Moving on, the concluding part of the source code (listing 7.12) shows how these variables are used to construct the progress meter.

Listing 7.12 ProgressSkin.fx (part 2)

```
// ** Part 1 is listing 7.11
    override var node = HBox {
        spacing: bind boxHGap;
```

Override node in Skin class

```
        content: bind for(i in [0..<boxCount]) {
            Rectangle {
                width: bind boxWidth;
                height: bind boxHeight;
                arcWidth: bind boxCornerArc;
                arcHeight: bind boxCornerArc;
                strokeWidth: bind boxStrokeWidth;
                stroke: bind
                    if(i<boxValue) boxSetStroke
                    else boxUnsetStroke;
                fill: bind
                    if(i<boxValue) boxSetFill
                    else boxUnsetFill;
            };
        }
    };

    override function getPrefWidth(n:Number) : Number {
        boxCount * (boxWidth+boxHGap) - boxHGap;
    }
    override function getMaxWidth() { getPrefWidth(-1) }
    override function getMinWidth() { getPrefWidth(-1) }

    override function getPrefHeight(n:Number) : Number {
        boxHeight;
    }
    override function getMaxHeight() { getPrefWidth(-1) }
    override function getMinHeight() { getPrefWidth(-1) }

    override function contains
        (x:Number,y:Number) : Boolean {
        control.layoutBounds.contains(x,y);
    }
    override function intersects
        (x:Number,y:Number,w:Number,h:Number):Boolean {
        control.layoutBounds.intersects(x,y,w,h);
    }

    function makeLG(c1:Color,c2:Color,c3:Color) : LinearGradient {
        LinearGradient {
            endX: 0;  endY: 1;  proportional: true;
            stops: [
                Stop { offset:0;    color: c3; } ,
                Stop { offset:0.25; color: c1; } ,
                Stop { offset:0.50; color: c2; } ,
                Stop { offset:0.85; color: c3; }
            ];
        };
    }
}
```

Bind visible properties

Bind trim color to boxValue

Bind body color to boxValue

Inherited from Resizable

Gradient paint from three colors

We see how the style variables are used to form a horizontal row of boxes. An inherited variable from `Skin`, named `node`, is used to record the skin's scene graph. Anything plugged into `node` becomes the corporeal form (physical body) of the control the skin is applied to. In our case we've a heavily bound sequence of `Rectangle` objects, each tied to the instance variables of the class. This sequence is all it takes to create our progress bar.

Because our control needs to be capable of being laid out, our `Skin` subclass overrides functions to expose its maximum, minimum, and preferred dimensions. To keep the code small I've used the preferred size for all three, and I've ignored the available width/height passed in as a parameter (which is a bit naughty). Our skin also fills out a couple of abstract functions, `contains()` and `intersects()`, by deferring to the control. (Simply redirecting these calls to the control like this should work for the majority of custom controls you'll ever find yourself writing.) Remember, even though the control delegates its appearance to the skin, it is still a genuine scene graph node, and we can rely on its inherited functionality.

At the end of the listing is the `makeLG()` function, a convenience for creating the `LinearGradient` paints used as default values for the box fills.

All that remains, now that we've seen the control and its skin, is to take a look at it running with an actual style document.

7.3.4 Using our styled control with a CSS document

The `Progress` and `ProgressSkin` classes create a new type of control, capable of being configured through an external stylesheet document. Now it's time to see how our new control can be used and manipulated.

Listing 7.13 is a test program for trying out our new control. It creates three examples: (1) a regular `Progress` control without any *class* or *ID* (note, in this context the word *class* refers to the CSS-style class and has nothing to do with any class written in the JavaFX Script language), (2) another `Progress` control with an ID (`"testID"`), and (3) a final `Progress` assigned to a style class (`"testClass"`).

Listing 7.13 TestCSS.fx

```
package jfxia.chapter7;

import javafx.animation.KeyFrame;
import javafx.animation.Interpolator;
import javafx.animation.Timeline;
import javafx.scene.Scene;
import javafx.stage.Stage;
import javafx.scene.layout.VBox;
import javafx.scene.paint.Color;

var val:Number = 0;
Stage {
    scene: Scene {
        content: VBox {
            spacing:10;
            layoutX: 5;  layoutY: 5;
            content: [
                Progress {                         <-- Plain control, no ID or class
                    minimum: 0;  maximum: 100;
                    value: bind val;
                } ,
                Progress {              <-- Control with ID
```

```
                    id: "testId";
                    minimum: 0;  maximum: 100;
                    value: bind val;
                } ,
                Progress {
                    styleClass: "testClass";
                    style: "boxSetStroke: white";
                    minimum: 0;  maximum: 100;
                    value: bind val;
                }
            ];
        };
        stylesheets: [ "{__DIR__}Test.css" ]
        fill:  Color.BLACK;
        width: 230;  height: 105;
    };
    title: "CSS Test";
};

Timeline {
    repeatCount: Timeline.INDEFINITE;
    autoReverse: true;
    keyFrames: [
        at(0s)   { val => 0 } ,
        at(0.1s) { val => 0 tween Interpolator.LINEAR } ,
        at(0.9s) { val => 100 tween Interpolator.LINEAR } ,
        at(1s)   { val => 100 }
    ];
}.play();
```

Control with class

Assign stylesheets

Run val backward and forward

Note how the final progress bar also assigns its own local style for the boxSetStroke? This is important, as we'll see in a short while.

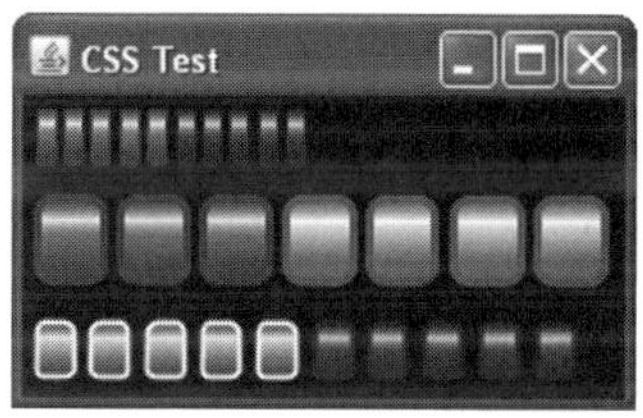

Figure 7.16 Three examples of our progress bar in action

Figure 7.16 shows the progress control on screen. All three `Progress` bars are bound to the variable `val`, which the `Timeline` at the foot of the code repeatedly increases and decreases (with a slight pause at either end), to make the bars shoot up and down from minimum to maximum.

The key part of the code lies in the `stylesheets` property of `Scene`. This is where we plug in our list of CSS documents (just one in our example) using their URLs. This particular example expects our docs to sit next to the TestCSS bytecode files. The `__DIR__` built-in variable returns the directory of the current class file as a URL, as you recall. If you downloaded the project's source code, you'll find the CSS file nested inside the res directory, off the project's root. When you build the project, make sure this file gets copied into the build directory, next to the TestCSS class file.

Now it's time for the grand unveiling of the CSS file that styles our component. Listing 7.14 shows the three style rules we've created for our test program. (Remember, it lives inside `jfxia.chapter7`, next to the `TestCSS` class.)

> **Classes and IDs**
>
> In stylesheets, classes and IDs perform similar functions but for use in different ways. Assigning an ID to an element in a document means it can be targeted specifically. IDs are supposed to be unique names, appearing only once in a given document. They can be used for more than just targeting stylesheet rules.
>
> What happens if we need to apply a style, not to a specific DOM element but to an entire subset of elements? To do this we use a class, a nonunique identifier designed primarily as a *type* identifier onto which CSS rules can bind.

Listing 7.14 Test.css

```
"jfxia.chapter7.Progress" {
    boxSetStroke: darkred;
    boxSetFill: linear (0%,0%) to (0%,100%) stops
        (0.0,darkred), (0.25,yellow), (0.50,red), (0.85,darkred);
    boxUnsetStroke: darkblue;
    boxUnsetFill: linear (0%,0%) to (0%,100%) stops
        (0.0,darkblue), (0.25,cyan), (0.50,blue), (0.85,darkblue);
}

"jfxia.chapter7.Progress"#testId {
    boxWidth: 25;  boxHeight: 30;
    boxCornerArc: 12;  boxStrokeWidth: 3;
    boxCount: 7;
    boxHGap: 1;

    boxUnsetStroke: dimgray;
    boxUnsetFill: linear (0%,0%) to (0%,100%) stops
        (0%,dimgray), (25%,white), (50%,silver), (75%,slategray);
}

"Progress".testClass {
    boxWidth: 14;
    boxCornerArc: 7;
    boxStrokeWidth: 2;
    boxHGap: 3;

    boxSetStroke: darkgreen;
    boxSetFill: linear (0%,0%) to (0%,100%) stops
        (0.0,darkgreen), (0.25,yellow), (0.50,limegreen), (0.85,darkgreen);
}
```

The first rule targets all instances of `jfxia.chapter7.Progress` controls. The settings in its body are applied to the skin of the control. The second is far more specific; like the first it applies to `jfxia.chapter7.Progress` controls, but only to that particular control with the ID of `testID`. The final rule targets the `Progress` class again (this time omitting the package prefix, just to show it's not necessary if the class name alone is not ambiguous), but it applies itself to any such control belonging to the style class `testClass`.

If multiple rules match a single control, the styles from all rules are applied in a strict order, starting with the generic (no class, no ID) rule, continuing with the class rule, then the specific ID rule, and finally any style plugged directly into the object literal inside the JavaFX Script code. Remember that explicit style assignment I said was important a couple of pages back? That was an example of overruling the CSS file with a style written directly into the JFX code itself. The styles for each matching rule are applied in order, with later styles overwriting the assignments of previous styles.

If absolutely nothing matches the control, the default styles defined in the skin class itself, `ProgressSkin` in our case, remain untouched. It's important, therefore, to ensure your skins always have sensible defaults.

You'll note how the class name is wrapped in quotes. If you were wondering, this is simply to stop the dots in the name from being misinterpreted as CSS-style class separators, like the one immediately before the name `"testClass"`.

> **Cascading Style Sheets**
>
> In this book we don't have the space to go into detail about the format of CSS, on which JavaFX stylesheets are firmly based. CSS is a World Wide Web Consortium specification, and the W3C website has plenty of documentation on the format at http://www.w3.org/Style/CSS/

Inside the body of each style rule we see the skin's public properties being assigned. The majority of these assignments are self-explanatory. Variables like `boxCount`, `boxWidth`, and `boxHeight` all take integer numbers, and color variables can take CSS color definitions or names, but what about the strange `linear` syntax?

7.3.5 Further CSS details

The exact nature of how CSS interacts with JavaFX skins is still not documented as this chapter is being written and updated, yet already several JFX devotees have dug deep into the class files and discovered some of the secrets therein.

In lieu of official tutorials and documentation, we'll look at a couple of examples to get an idea of what's available. An internet search will no doubt reveal further styling options, although by the time you read this the official documentation should be available.

Here is one of the linear paint examples from the featured stylesheet:

```
boxUnsetFill: linear (0%,0%) to (0%,100%) stops
    (0.0,dimgray), (0.25,white), (0.50,silver), (0.75,slategray);
```

The example creates, as you might expect, a `LinearGradient` paint starting in the top left corner (0% of the way across the area, 0% of the way down) and ending in the bottom left (0% of the way across, 100% of the way down). This results in a straightforward vertical gradient. To define the color stops, we use a comma-separated list of position/color pairs in parentheses. For the positions we could use percentages again or a fraction-based scale from 0 to 1. The colors are regular CSS color definitions (see the W3C's documentation for details).

The stylesheet in our example is tied directly to the `ProgressSkin` we created for our `Progress` control. The settings it changes are the publicly accessible variables inside the skin class. But we can go further than only tweaking the skin's variables; we can replace the entire skin class:

```
"Progress"#testID {
    skin: jfxia.chapter7.AlternativeProgressSkin;
}
```

The fragment of stylesheet in the example sets the skin itself, providing an alternative class to the `ProgressSkin` we installed by default. Obviously we haven't written such a class—this is just a demonstration. The style rule targets a specific example of the `Progress` control, with the ID `testID`, although if we removed the ID specifier from the rule it would target all `Progress` controls.

STYLING BUG The JavaFX 1.2 release introduced a bug: controls created after the stylesheet was installed are not styled. This means if your application dynamically creates bits of UI as it runs and adds them into the scene graph, styling will not be applied to those controls. A bug fix is on its way; in the meantime the only solution is to remove and reassign the `stylesheets` variable in `Scene` every time you create a new control that needs styling.

The `AlternativeProgressSkin` class would have its own public interface, with its own variables that could be styled. For this reason the rule should be placed before any other rule that styles variables of the `AlternativeProgressSkin` (indeed some commentators have noted it works best when placed in a separate rule, all on its own).

7.4 Summary

In this chapter we built a simple user interface, using JavaFX's controls API, and displayed some statistics, thanks to the charts API. We also learned how to store data in a manner that won't break as our code travels from device to device. Although the project was simple, it gave a solid grounding into controls, charts, and client-side persistence. However, we didn't get a chance to look at every type of control.

So, what did we miss? `CheckBox` is a basic opt-in/out control, either checked or unchecked. JavaFX check boxes also support a third option, *undefined*, typically used in check box trees, when a parent check box acts as a master switch to enable/disable all its children. `Hyperlink` is a web-like link, acting like a `Button` but looking like a piece of text. `ListView` displays a vertical list of selectable items. `ProgressBar` is a long, thin control, showing either the completeness of a given process or an animation suggesting work is being done; `ProgressIndicator` does the same thing but with a more compact *dial* display. `ScrollBar` is designed to control a large area displayed within a smaller viewport. `ToggleButton` flips between selected or unselected; it can be used in a `ToggleGroup`; however (unlike a `RadioButton`), a `ToggleButton` can be unselected with a second click, leaving the group with no currently selected button.

In the bonus project we created our own control that could be manipulated by CSS-like stylesheets. Although some of the styling detail was a little speculative because of the unavailability of solid documentation at the time of writing, the project should, at the very least, act as a primer.

With controls and charts we can build serious applications, targeted across a variety of platforms. With skins and styling they can also look good. And, since everything is scene graph–based, it can be manipulated just like the graphics in previous chapters.

In the next chapter we're sticking with the practical theme by looking at web services—but, of course, we'll also be having plenty of fun. Until then, why not try extending the main project's form with extra controls or charts? Experiment, see what works, and get some positive feedback.

8 Web services with style

This chapter covers

- Calling a web service
- Parsing an XML document
- Dynamically editing the scene graph
- Animating, with off-the-shelf transitions

In this chapter we're going to cover a range of exciting JavaFX features—and possibly the most fun project thus far. In previous chapters we were still learning the ropes, so to speak, but now that bind and triggers are becoming second nature and the scene graph is no longer a strange alien beast, we can move on to some of the power tools the JavaFX API has to offer.

We'll start by learning how to call a web service and parse its XML response. As more of our data is moving online and hidden behind web services, knowing how to exploit their power from within our own software becomes crucial. Then we'll turn our attention to taking the pain out of animation effects. As if the animation tools built into JavaFX Script weren't enough, JavaFX also includes a whole library of off-the-shelf *transition* classes. When we apply these classes to scene graph nodes, we can make them move, spin, scale, and fade with ease.

This chapter has a lot to cover, but by the time you reach its end you'll have experienced practical examples of most of the core JavaFX libraries. There are still plenty of juicy morsels in the remaining chapters. But after this we'll be focusing more on techniques and applications than on learning new API classes.

Let's get started.

8.1 Our project: a Flickr image viewer

Everyone and his dog are writing demos to exploit the Flickr web service API. It's not hard to understand why. Located at http://www.flickr.com, the site is an online photo gallery where the public can upload and arrange its digital masterpieces for others to browse. It's highly addictive trawling though random photos, some looking clearly amateur but others shockingly professional. Of course, as programmers we just want to know how cool the programming API is! As it happens, Flickr's API is pretty cool (which explains why everyone and his dog are using it).

Why did I decide to go with Flickr for this book? First, it's a well-known API with plenty of documentation and programmers who are familiar with it—important for anyone playing with the source code after the chapter has been read. Second, I wanted to show that photo gallery applications don't have to be boring (witness figure 8.1), particularly when you have a tool like JavaFX at your disposal.

The application we're going to build will run full screen. It will use a web service API to fetch details of a particular gallery then show thumbnails in a strip along the bottom of the screen, one page at a time. Selecting a thumbnail will cause the image

Figure 8.1 Our photo viewer will allow us to contact the online photo service, view thumbnails from a gallery, and then select and toss a full-sized image onto a desktop as if it were a real photo.

> **Thanks, Sally!**
>
> I'd like to thank Sally Lupton, who kindly allowed her gallery to be used to illustrate figures 8.1, 8.3, and 8.4 in this chapter. Her *Superlambanana* photos were certainly a lot nicer than anything your humble author could produce.

to spin onto the main desktop (the background) display, looking as if it's a printed photograph. The desktop can be dragged to move the photos, and as more pictures are dropped onto it, older ones (at the bottom of the heap) gracefully fade away.

8.1.1 The Flickr web service

A *web service* is a means of communicating between two pieces of software, typically on different networked computers. The client request is formulated using HTTP in a way that mimics a remote method invocation (RMI); the server responds with a structured document of data in either XML or JSON.

Flickr has quite a rich web service, with numerous functions covering a range of the site's capabilities. It also supports different web service data formats. In our project we'll use a lightweight ("RESTful") protocol to send the request, with the resulting data returned to us as an XML document. REST (Representational State Transfer) is becoming increasingly popular as a means of addressing web services; it generally involves less work than the heavily structured alternatives based on SOAP.

> **Not enough REST?**
>
> For more background information on REST take a look at its Wikipedia page. The official JavaFX site also hosts a Media Browser project that demonstrates a RESTful service.
>
> http://en.wikipedia.org/wiki/Representational_State_Transfer
> http://javafx.com/docs/tutorials/mediabrowser/

Before we can go any further, you'll need to register yourself as a Flickr developer, assuming you don't have an account already.

8.1.2 Getting registered with Flickr

You must register with Flickr so you can call its web service, which is a necessary part of this project. Signing up is relatively quick to do and totally free for nonprofessional use. Once your account is created you'll be assigned a key (a long hexadecimal string) for use in any software you write accessing the service. The necessity for a key, it seems, is primarily to stop a single developer from flooding the site with requests.

Go to http://www.flickr.com/services/api/ and click the Sign Up link at the head of the page to begin the process of creating your account. The site will walk you through what you need to do, which shouldn't take long. Once your account is created, a Your

API Keys link will appear at the head of the page whenever you're logged in. Click it to view your developer account details, including the all-important key.

The site contains plenty of API documentation and tutorials. We'll be using only a tiny subset of the full API, but once you've seen an example of one web service call, it should be clear how to apply the documentation to call another.

So, if you don't already have a Flickr developer account, put this book down and register one right now, before you read any further. You can't run the project code without one, and the very next section will throw us straight into web service coding.

8.2 Using a web service in JavaFX

At the heart of JavaFX's web service support are three classes. In the `javafx.io.http` package there's the `HttpRequest` class, used to make the HTTP request; in `javafx.data.pull` there's `PullParser` and `Event`, used to parse the reply.

Our application also uses three classes itself: `FlickrService` handles the request (using `HttpRequest`), `FlickrResult` processes the result (using `PullParser` and `Event`), and `FlickrPhoto` stores the details of the photos as they are pulled from the result.

In the sections ahead we'll examine each of these classes.

8.2.1 Calling the web service with HttpRequest

We'll start, naturally enough, with the `FlickrService`. You'll find it in listing 8.1. As in previous chapters, the listing has been broken into stages to aid explanation.

Listing 8.1 FlickrService.fx (part 1)

```
package jfxia.chapter8;

import javafx.io.http.HttpRequest;
import javafx.data.pull.PullParser;
import java.io.InputStream;
import java.lang.Exception;

def REST:String = "http://api.flickr.com/services/rest/";      <-- URL of web service

function createArgList(args:String[]) : String {               Create HTTP
    var ret="";                                                 query string
    var sep="";                                                 from keys/values
    for(i in [0..<sizeof args step 2]) {
        ret="{ret}{sep}{args[i]}={args[i+1]}";
        sep="&";
    }
    return ret;
}
// ** Part 2 is listing 8.2; part 3 is listing 8.3
```

We begin with one variable and one function, at the script level. The variable, `REST`, is the base URL for the web service we'll be addressing. Onto this we'll add our request and its parameters. The function `createArgList()` is a useful utility for building the argument string appended to the end of `REST`. It takes a sequence of key/value pairs and combines each into a query string using the format key=value, separated by ampersands.

Listing 8.2 shows the top of the FlickrService class itself.

Listing 8.2 FlickrService.fx (part 2)

```
// ** Part 1 is listing 8.1
public class FlickrService {
    public var apiKey:String;
    public var userId:String;
    public var photosPerPage:Integer = 10;
    public-read var page:Integer = 0;
    public var onSuccess:function(:FlickrResult);      | Callback
    public var onFailure:function(:String);            | functions

    var valid:Boolean;                           <-- Missing API key?

    init {
        valid = isInitialized(apiKey);          | Check for
        if(not valid)                           | API key
            println("API key required.");       |
    }
// ** Part 3 is listing 8.3
```

At the head of the class we see several variables:

- apiKey holds the developer key (the one associated with your Flickr account).
- userId is for the account identifier of the person whose gallery we'll be viewing.
- photosPerPage and page determine the page size (how many thumbs are fetched at once) and which page was previously fetched.
- onSuccess and onFailure are function types, permitting us to run code on the success or failure of our web service request.

In the init block we test for apiKey initialization; if it's unset we print an error message. A professional application would do something more useful with the error, of course, but for our project a simple error report like this will suffice (it keeps the class free of too much off-topic detail).

We conclude the code with listing 8.3.

Listing 8.3 FlickrService.fx (part 3)

```
// ** Part 1 is listing 8.1; part 2 is listing 8.2
    public function loadPage(p:Integer) : Void {
        if(not valid) throw new Exception("API key not set.");

        page = p;                                            | Request
                                                             | arguments
        var args = [                                     <---
            "method",     "flickr.people.getPublicPhotos",
            "api_key",    apiKey,
            "user_id",    userId,
            "per_page",   photosPerPage.toString(),
            "page",       page.toString()
        ];

        def http:HttpRequest = HttpRequest {    <-- Web call
```

```
            method: HttpRequest.GET;                          Method and
            location: "{REST}?{createArgList(args)}";         address
            onResponseCode: function(code:Integer) {      <-- Initial
                if(code!=200 and onFailure!=null)             response
                    onFailure("HTTP code {code}");
            }
            onException: function(ex:Exception) {      <-- I/O error
                if(onFailure!=null)
                    onFailure(ex.toString());
            }
            onInput: function(ip:InputStream) {      <-- Success!
                def fr = FlickrResult {};
                def parser = PullParser  {
                    documentType: PullParser.XML;
                    input: ip;
                    onEvent: fr.xmlEvent;                 Create and call
                };                                        XML parser
                parser.parse();
                parser.input.close();
                if(onSuccess!=null)  onSuccess(fr);
            }
        };
        http.start();
    }
}
```

In the final part of our service request code `loadPage()` function is where the action is; it takes a page number and accesses the Flickr service to fetch the photo details for that page. Each request ends in a call to either `onSuccess` or `onFailure` (if populated), allowing applications to run their own code when the process ends. (We'll deal with how our photo viewer uses these functions later.)

After (double) checking the `apiKey` and storing the selected page, `loadPage()` creates a sequence of key/value pairs to act as the arguments passed to the service call. The first list argument is the function we're calling on the web service, and the following arguments are parameters we're passing in.

Flickr's `flickr.people.getPublicPhotos` function returns a list of photos for a given user account, page by page. We need to pass in our own key, the ID of the person whose gallery we want to read, the number of photos we want back (the page size to break the gallery up into), and which page we want. See the web service API documentation for more details on this function.

After the argument list we have the `HttpRequest` object itself. The HTTP request doesn't execute immediately. Web service requests are commonly instigated from inside UI event handlers; if we performed the request immediately, it would hog the current thread (the GUI thread) and cause our application's interface to become temporarily unresponsive. Instead, when `start()` is called, the network activity is pushed onto another thread, and we assign callbacks to run when there's something ready to act upon (see figure 8.2).

The `HttpRequest` request declaratively sets a number of properties. The `method` and `location` variables tell `HttpRequest` how and where to direct the HTTP call. To form the web address we use the script function `createArgList()`, turning the `args`

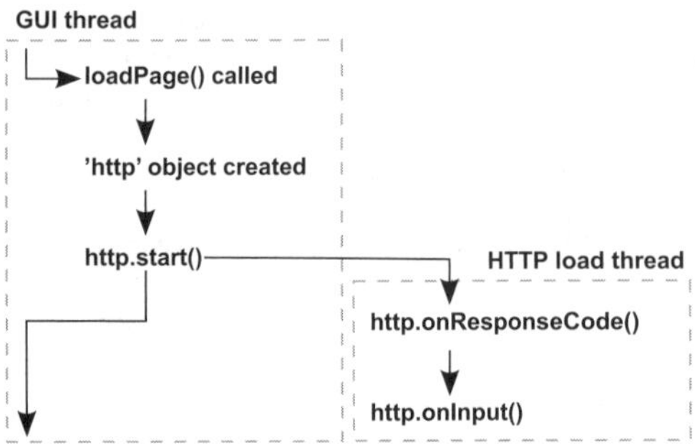

Figure 8.2 When `start()` is called on an `HttpRequest` object, a second thread takes over and communicates its progress through callback events, allowing the GUI thread to get back to its work.

sequence into a web-like query string, and append it to the `REST` base URL. The `onResponseCode`, `onException`, and `onInput` event function types will be called at different stages of the request life cycle. The `HttpRequest` class actually has a host of different functions and variables to track the request state in fine detail (check the API docs), but typically we don't need such fine-grained control.

The `onResponseCode` event is called when the initial HTTP response code is received (`200` means "ok"; other codes signify different results), `onException` is called if there's an I/O problem, while `onInput` is called when the result actually starts to arrive. The `onInput` call passes in a Java `InputStream` object, which we can assign a parser to. The JavaFX class `PullParser` is just such a parser. It reads either XML- or JSON-formatted data from the input stream and breaks it down into a series of events. To receive the events we need to register a function. But because our particular project needs to store some of the data being returned, I've written not just a single function but an entire class (the `FlickrResult` class) to interact with it. And that's what we'll look at next.

8.2.2 Parsing XML with PullParser

Because we need somewhere to store the data we are pulling from the web service, we'll create an entire class to interact with the parser. That class is `FlickrResult`, taking each XML element as it is encountered, extracting data, and populating its variables. The class also houses a `FlickrPhoto` sequence, to store details for each individual photo.

Listing 8.4 is the first part of our class to process and store the information coming back from the web service.

Listing 8.4 FlickrResult.fx (part 1)

```
package jfxia.chapter8;

import javafx.data.pull.Event;
import javafx.data.pull.PullParser;
import javafx.data.xml.QName;

public class FlickrResult {
    public-read var stat:String;
```

Status message from service

```
    public-read var total:Integer;
    public-read var perPage:Integer;
    public-read var page:Integer;
    public-read var pages:Integer;

    public-read var photos:FlickrPhoto[];

    public def valid:Boolean =  bind (stat == "ok");
// ** Part 2 is listing 8.5
```

Gallery details

Data for each photo in pages

Was request successful?

Let's have a closer look at the details:

- The `stat` variable holds the success/failure of the response, as described in the reply. If Flickr can fulfill our request, we'll get back the simple message "ok".
- The `total` variable holds the number of photos in the entire gallery, `perPage` contains how many there are per page (should match the number requested), and `pages` details the number of available pages (based on the total and number of photos per page).
- `page` is the current page (again, it should match the one we requested).
- The `valid` variable is a handy boolean for checking whether Flickr was able to respond to our request.

Listing 8.5 is the second half of our parser class. It contains the code that responds to the `PullParser` events. So we're not working blindly, the following is an example of the sort of XML the web service might reply with. Each opening element tag, closing element tag, and loose text content inside an element cause our event handler to be called.

```
<?xml version="1.0" encoding="utf-8" ?>
<rsp stat="ok">
  <photos page="1" pages="20" perpage="10" total="195">
    <photo id="3188821292" owner="12345678@N09" secret="cafebabe"
        server="3095" farm="4" title="Hello"
        ispublic="1" isfriend="0" isfamily="0" />
    <!-- Another nine photo elements appear here -->
  </photos>
</rsp>
```

And now, here is the code to parse this data.

Listing 8.5 FlickrResult.fx (part 2)

```
// ** Part 1 is listing 8.4
    public function xmlEvent(ev:Event) : Void {
        if(not (ev.type == PullParser.START_ELEMENT)) {
            return;
        }

        if(ev.level==0 and ev.qname.name == "rsp") {
            stat = readAttrS(ev,"stat");
        }
        else if(ev.level==1 and ev.qname.name == "photos") {
            total = readAttrI(ev,"total");
```

Not a start element? Exit!

Top level, <rsp>

2nd level, <photos>

```
            perPage = readAttrI(ev,"perpage");
            page = readAttrI(ev,"page");
            pages = readAttrI(ev,"pages");
        }
        else if(ev.level==2 and ev.qname.name == "photo") {    <-- 3rd level, <photo>
            def photo = FlickrPhoto {
                id: readAttrS(ev,"id");
                farm: readAttrS(ev,"farm");
                owner: readAttrS(ev,"owner");
                secret: readAttrS(ev,"secret");
                server: readAttrS(ev,"server");                 Create and store
                title: readAttrS(ev,"title");                   photo object
                isFamily: readAttrB(ev,"isfamily");
                isFriend: readAttrB(ev,"isfriend");
                isPublic: readAttrB(ev,"ispublic");
            };
            insert photo into photos;
        }
        else {                                                  <-- Didn't recognize element
            println("{ev}");
        }
    }

    function readAttrS(ev:Event,attr:String) : String {         <-- Read string attribute
        def qn = QName{name:attr};
        return ev.getAttributeValue(qn) as String;
    }
    function readAttrI(ev:Event,attr:String) : Integer {        <-- Read integer attribute
        return java.lang.Integer.parseInt(readAttrS(ev,attr));
    }
    function readAttrB(ev:Event,attr:String) : Boolean {        <-- Read boolean attribute
        return (readAttrI(ev,attr)!=0);
    }
}
```

The function `xmlEvent()` is the callback invoked whenever a node in the XML document is encountered (note: *node* in this context does *not* refer to a scene graph node). Both XML and JSON documents are nested structures, forming a tree of nodes. JavaFX's parser walks this tree, firing an event for each node it encounters, with an `Event` object to describe the type of node (text or tag, for example), its name, its level in the tree, and so on.

Our XML handler is interested only in starting tags; that's why we exit if the node type isn't an element start. The large `if/else` block parses specific elements. At level 0 we're interested in the `<rsp>` element, to get the status message (which we hope will be "ok"). At level 1 we're interested in the `<photos>` element, with attributes describing the gallery, page size, and so on. At level 2, we're interested in the `<photo>` element, holding details of a specific photo on the page we're reading. For any other type of element, we simply print to the console (handy for debugging) and then ignore.

The `<photo>` element is where we create each new `FlickrPhoto` object, with the help of three private functions for extracting named attributes from the tag in given data formats. Let's look at the `FlickrPhoto` class, in listing 8.6.

Listing 8.6 FlickrPhoto.fx

```
package jfxia.chapter8;

public def SQUARE:Number = 75;
public def THUMB:Number = 100;
public def SMALL:Number = 240;
public def MEDIUM:Number = 500;
public def LARGE:Number = 1024;

public class FlickrPhoto {
    public-init var id:String;
    public-init var farm:String;
    public-init var owner:String;
    public-init var secret:String;
    public-init var server:String;
    public-init var title:String;
    public-init var isFamily:Boolean;
    public-init var isFriend:Boolean;
    public-init var isPublic:Boolean;

    def urlBase:String = bind
        "http://farm{farm}.static.flickr.com/"
        "{server}/{id}_{secret}";
    public def urlSquare:String = bind "{urlBase}_s.jpg";
    public def urlThumb:String = bind "{urlBase}_t.jpg";
    public def urlSmall:String = bind "{urlBase}_m.jpg";
    public def urlMedium:String = bind "{urlBase}.jpg";
    //public def urlLarge:String = bind "{urlBase}_b.jpg";
    //public def urlOriginal:String = bind "{urlBase}_o.jpg";
}
```

Annotations: **Image pixel sizes** (the five script-level constants); **Photo data, provided by the XML** (the public-init variables); **Base image address** (urlBase); **Actual image URLs** (the url definitions).

Each Flickr photo comes prescaled to various sizes, accessible via slightly different filenames. You'll note that script-level constants are used to describe the sizes of these images.

- A square thumbnail is 75 x 75 pixels.
- A regular thumbnail is 100 pixels on its longest side.
- A small image is 240 pixels on its longest side.
- A medium image is 500 pixels on its longest side.
- A large image is 1024 pixels on its longest side.
- The original image has no size restrictions.

Inside the class proper we find a host of `public-init` properties that store the details supplied via the XML response. The `farm`, `secret`, and `server` variables are all used to construct the web address of a given image. The other variables should be self-explanatory.

At the foot of the class we have the web addresses of each scaled image. The different sizes of image all share the same basic address, with a minor addition to the filename for each size (except for medium). We can use these addresses to load our thumbnails and full-size images. In our project we'll be working with the thumbnail and medium-size images only. The class can load any of the images, but since extra steps and permissions may be required to load the larger-size images using the web service API, I've commented out the last two web addresses. The web service documentation explains how to get access to them.

That's all we require to make, and consume, a web service request. Now all that's needed is code to test it, but before we go there, let's recap the process, to ensure you understand what's happening.

8.2.3 A recap

The process of calling a web service may seem a bit convoluted. A lot of classes, function calls, and event callbacks are involved, so here's a blow-by-blow recap of how our project code works:

1. We formulate a web service request in `FlickrService`, using the service function we want to call plus its parameters.
2. Our `FlickrService` has two function types (event callbacks), `onSuccess` and `onFailure`, called upon the outcome of a web service request. We implement functions for these to deal with the data once it has loaded or handle any errors.
3. Now that everything is in place, we use JavaFX's `HttpRequest` to execute the request itself. It begins running *in the background*, allowing the current GUI thread to continue running unblocked.
4. If the `HttpRequest` fails, `onFailure` will be called. If we get as far as an `InputStream`, we create a parser (JavaFX's `PullParser`) to deal with the XML returned by the web service. The parser invokes an event callback function as incoming nodes are received, which we assign to a function, `xmlEvent()` in `FlickrResult`, a class designed to store data received from the web service.
5. The callback function in `FlickrResult` parses each start tag in the XML. For each photo it creates and stores a new `FlickrPhoto` object.
6. Once the parsing is finished, execution returns to `onInput()` in `FlickrService`, which calls `onSuccess` with the resulting data.
7. In the `onSuccess` function we can now do whatever we want with the data loaded from the service.

Now, at last, we need to actually see our web service in action.

8.2.4 Testing our web service code

Having spent the last few pages creating a set of classes to extract data from our chosen web service, we'll round off this part of the project with listing 8.7, showing how easy it is to use.

Listing 8.7 TestWS.fx

```
package jfxia.chapter8;

FlickrService {
    apiKey: "-";     // <== Your key goes here
    userId: "29803026@N08";                    <-- User's gallery to view
```

```
    photosPerPage: 10;

    onSuccess: function(res:FlickrResult) {
        for(photo in res.photos) {
            println("{photo.urlMedium}");
        }
    }
    onFailure: function(s:String) {
        println("{s}");
    }
}.loadPage(1);

javafx.stage.Stage { visible: true; }
```

Success, print photo URLs

Failure, print message

Prevent termination

Listing 8.7 is a small test program to create a web service request for photo details and print the URL of each medium-size image. To make the code work you'll need to supply the key you got when you signed up for a Flickr developer account.

As you can see, all that hard work paid off in the form of a nice and simple class we can use to get at our photo data.

Because the network activity takes place in the background, away from the main GUI thread, we need to stop the application from immediately terminating before Flickr has time to send back any details. We do this by creating a dummy window; it's a crude solution but effective. If all goes well, the code should spit out onto the console a list of 10 web addresses, one for each medium-size image in the first page of the gallery we accessed.

Now that our network code is complete, we can get back to our usual habit of writing cool GUI code.

8.3 Picture this: the PhotoViewer application

In this, the second part of the project, we're going to use the web service classes we developed earlier in an application to throw photos on screen. The application will be full screen—that is to say, it will not run in a window on the desktop but will take over the whole display. It will also use transitions to perform its movement and other animated effects.

The application has a bar of thumbnails along its foot, combined with three buttons, demonstrated in figure 8.3. One button moves the thumbnails forward by a page, another moves them back, and the final button clears the main display area (or *desktop*, as I'm calling it) of photos. As we move over the thumbnails in the bar, the associated title text, which the web service gave us, is displayed.

To get a photo onto the desktop, we merely click its thumbnail to see it spin dramatically onto the display scaled to full size. Initially we scale the tiny thumbnail up to the size of the photo, while we wait for the higher-resolution image to be loaded. As we wait, a progress bar appears in the corner of the photo, showing how much of the image has arrived over the network. When the high-resolution image finally finishes loading, it replaces the scaled-up thumbnail, and the progress bar vanishes.

We can click and drag individual images to move them around the desktop, or we can click on an empty part of the desktop and drag to move all the images at once.

Figure 8.3 Photos selected from the thumbnail bar fly onto the desktop.

The application itself is constructed from two further classes, weighing in at over 200 lines apiece. But don't worry, they still contain plenty of fresh JavaFX goodness for us to explore. As usual, they've been broken up into parts to aid explanation. We begin with the class that handles the thumbnail bar.

8.3.1 Displaying thumbnails from the web service: the GalleryView class

The `GalleryView` class is the visual component that deals with the Flickr web service, and it presents a horizontal list of thumbnails based on the data it extracts from the service. Figure 8.4 shows the specific part of the application we're building.

Figure 8.4 The custom scene graph node we are creating

That's what we want it to look like; let's dive straight into the source code with listing 8.8. GalleryView.fx is presented in four parts: listings 8.8, 8.9, 8.10, and 8.11. Here we see the variables in the top part of our `GalleryView` class.

Listing 8.8 GalleryView.fx (part 1)

```
package jfxia.chapter8;

import javafx.animation.Interpolator;
```

```
import javafx.animation.transition.TranslateTransition;
import javafx.scene.CustomNode;
import javafx.scene.Group;
import javafx.scene.Node;
import javafx.scene.image.Image;
import javafx.scene.image.ImageView;
import javafx.scene.input.MouseEvent;
import javafx.scene.paint.Color;
import javafx.scene.shape.Rectangle;
import javafx.scene.text.Font;
import javafx.scene.text.Text;

package class GalleryView extends CustomNode {
    def thumbWidth:Number = FlickrPhoto.THUMB;
    def thumbHeight:Number = FlickrPhoto.THUMB;
    def thumbBorder:Number =  10;

    public-init var apiKey:String;
    public-init var userId:String;
    package var width:Number = 0;
    package def height:Number = thumbHeight + thumbBorder*2;
    package var action:function(:FlickrPhoto,
        :Image,:Number,:Number);

    public-read var page:Integer = 1
        on replace {
            loadPage();
        };
    public-read var pageSize:Integer =
        bind {
            def aw:Number = width;
            def pw:Number = thumbWidth + thumbBorder*2;
            (aw/pw).intValue();
        }
        on replace {
            if(pageSize>0)  createUI();
            loadPage();

        };
    var service:FlickrService;
    var result:FlickrResult;
    var thumbImages:Image[];

    var topGroup:Group = Group{};
    var thumbGroup:Group;
    var textDisplay:Text;
// ** Part 2 is listing 8.9; part 3, listing 8.10; part 4 is listing 8.11
```

Annotations: Handy constants (thumbWidth, thumbHeight, thumbBorder); Flickr details (apiKey, userId); Thumbnail clicked event (action); New page means thumbs reload (page); Width determines thumbnail count (pageSize bind); Rebuild scene graph on change (createUI()); Flickr classes and fetched thumbs (service, result, thumbImages); Handy scene graph stuff (topGroup, thumbGroup, textDisplay)

At its head we see a few handy constants being defined: the maximum dimensions of a thumbnail (brought in from the `FlickrPhoto` class for convenience) and the gap between each thumbnail. The other variables are:

- `apiKey` and `userId` should be familiar from the first part of the project. We set these when we create a `GalleryView`, so it can access the Flickr service.
- The `height` of the bar we can calculate from the size of the thumbnails and their surrounding frames, but the `width` is set externally by using the size of the screen.

- The `action` function type holds the callback we use to tell the outside application that a thumbnail has been clicked. The parameters are the `FlickrPhoto` associated with this thumbnail, the thumb `Image` already downloaded, and the x/y location of the thumbnail in the bar.
- The `page` and `pageSize` variables control which page of thumbnails is loaded and how many thumbnails are on that page. Changing either causes an access to the web service to fetch fresh data, which is why both have an `on replace` block. A change to `pageSize` will also cause the contents of the scene graph to be rebuilt, using the function we created for this very purpose. The page size is determined by the number of thumbnails we can fit inside the `width`, which explains the bind.
- The private variables `service`, `results`, and `thumbImages` all relate directly to the web service. The first is the interface we use to load each page of thumbnails, the second is the result of the last page load, and finally we have the actual thumbnail images themselves.
- Private variables `topGroup`, `thumbGroup`, and `textDisplay` are all parts of the scene graph that need manipulating in response to events.

Now we'll turn to the actual code that initializes those variables. Listing 8.9 sets up the web service and returns the top-level node of our bit of the scene graph.

Listing 8.9 GalleryView.fx (part 2)

```
// ** Part 1 is listing 8.8
    init {
        service = FlickrService {          <- Flickr web service class
            apiKey: bind apiKey;
            userId: bind userId;
            photosPerPage: bind pageSize;
            onSuccess: function(res:FlickrResult)
            {   result = res;                     Do this on success
                assignThumbs(result);
            }
            onFailure: function(s:String)
            {   println("{s}");          Do this on failure
            }
        };
    }

    override function create() : Node {
        topGroup;                            Return scene graph node
    }
// ** Part 3 is listing 8.10; part 4, listing 8.11
```

The code shouldn't need too much explanation. We register two functions with the `FlickrService` class: `onSuccess` will run when data has been successfully fetched, and `onFailure` will run if it hits a snag. In the case of a successful load, we store the `result` object so we can use its data later, and we call a private function (see later for the code) to copy the URLs of the new thumbnails out of the `result` and into the `thumbImage` sequence, causing them to start loading.

Listing 8.10, the third part of the code, takes us to the scene graph for this class.

Listing 8.10 GalleryView.fx (part 3)

```
// ** Part 1 is listing 8.8; part 2, listing 8.9
    function createUI() : Void {
        def sz:Number = thumbWidth + thumbBorder*2;
        var thumbImageViews:ImageView[] = [];

        textDisplay = Text {
            font: Font { size: 30; }
            fill: Color.BROWN;
            layoutX: bind
                (width-textDisplay.layoutBounds.width)/2;
        }

        thumbGroup = Group {
            content: for(i in [0..<pageSize]) {
                var iv:ImageView = ImageView {
                    layoutX: bind i*sz + thumbBorder +
                        (if(iv.image==null) 0
                        else (thumbWidth-iv.image.width)/2);
                    layoutY: bind thumbBorder +
                        (if(iv.image==null) 0
                        else (thumbHeight-iv.image.height)/2);
                    fitWidth: thumbWidth;
                    fitHeight: thumbHeight;
                    preserveRatio: true;

                    image: bind if(thumbImages!=null)
                        thumbImages[i] else null;
                };
                insert iv into thumbImageViews;
                iv;
            };
        };

        def frameGroup:Group = Group {
            content: for(i in [0..<pageSize]) {
                def r:Rectangle = Rectangle {
                    layoutX: i*sz + 2;
                    width: sz-4;  height: sz - 4;
                    arcWidth: 25;  arcHeight: 25;
                    opacity: 0.15;
                    fill. Color.WHITE,

                    onMouseEntered: function(ev:MouseEvent) {
                        r.opacity = 0.35;
                        if(result!=null and
                            i<(sizeof result.photos)) {
                            textDisplay.content =
                                result.photos[i].title;
                        }
                    }
                    onMouseExited: function(ev:MouseEvent) {
                        r.opacity = 0.15;
                        textDisplay.content = "";
                    }
```

Annotations:

- **Create actual scene graph** (createUI)
- **Photo title banner text** (textDisplay)
- **Sequence of thumbnail images** (thumbGroup)
- **Center align thumb** (layoutX / layoutY)
- **Resize image** (fitWidth, fitHeight, preserveRatio)
- **Use image, if available** (image)
- **Background rectangle** (frameGroup)
- **Change opacity, show title text** (onMouseEntered)
- **Change opacity, clear title text** (onMouseExited)

```
                    onMouseClicked: function(ev:MouseEvent) {      Fire action
                        if(action!=null) {                         event
                            def f = result.photos[i];
                            def t = thumbImages[i];
                            def v = thumbImageViews[i];
                            def x:Number = v.layoutX;
                            def y:Number = v.layoutY;
                            action(f, t,x,y);
                        }
                    }
                };
            };
        };                                                         Center
                                                                   gallery view
        topGroup.layoutX = (width - pageSize*sz) / 2;
        topGroup.content = [
            frameGroup , thumbGroup , textDisplay              Create top-
        ];                                                     level node
    }
// ** Part 4 is listing 8.11
```

Listing 8.10 is the real meat of the scene graph. Whenever the pageSize variable is changed (assuming it's not the initial zero assignment), the createUI() function runs to repopulate the topGroup node, which is the root of our scene graph fragment.

The code constructs three layers of node, as shown in figure 8.5. We group the images separately from their background frames, so they can be animated independently. Whenever a new page of thumbnails is loaded, the current thumbnails will fall out of view; we can animate them separately only if they are grouped apart from their framing rectangles.

The textDisplay is used to show the title of each image as the mouse passes over it. We build the thumbGroup by adding an image at a time, scaled to fit the space available (which shouldn't be necessary if Flickr deliver the thumbs in the size we expect, but just in case this changes). We store each Image as we create it, because we'll need access to this thumbnail in the onMouseClicked() event handler.

The frameGroup is where we put all the mouse handling code. A rollover causes the photo's text to be displayed (entered) or cleared (exited), and the frame's opacity is changed. When the mouse is clicked it triggers an action event, with the appropriate FlickrPhoto object, its thumbnail image (we stored it earlier), and the coordinates within the bar, all bundled up and passed to the function assigned to action.

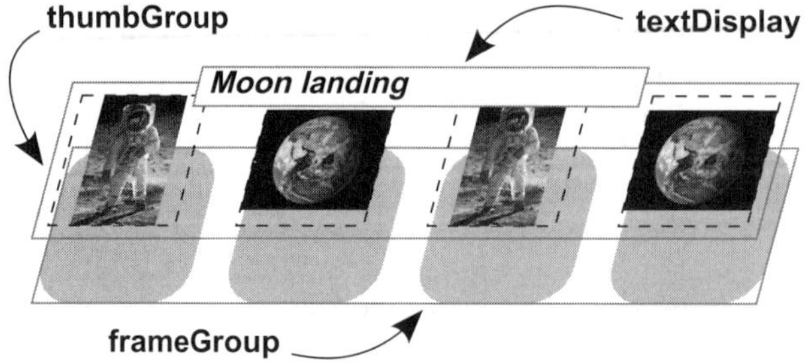

Figure 8.5 The thumbnail bar scene graph is made up on three core components: a group of frame rectangles in the background, a group of images over it, and a text node to display the thumb titles.

Almost there! Only one block of code left, listing 8.11, and it is has a surprise up its sleeve.

Listing 8.11 GalleryView.fx (part 4)

```
// ** Part 1 is listing 8.8; part 2, listing 8.9; part 3, listing 8.10
    package function next() : Void { setPage(page+1); }
    package function previous() : Void { setPage(page-1); }
    function setPage(p:Integer) : Void {
        if(result!=null) {
            page =
                if(p<=0)  result.pages
                else if(p>result.pages)  1
                else  p;
        }
    }

    function loadPage() : Void {
        if(service!=null and pageSize>0 and page>0) {
            TranslateTransition {
                node: thumbGroup;
                byX: 0;  byY: height;
                interpolator: Interpolator.EASEIN;
                duration: 0.5s;
                action: function() {
                    unassignThumbs();
                    thumbGroup.translateY = 0;
                    service.loadPage(page);
                }
            }.play();
        }
    }
    function assignThumbs(res:FlickrResult) : Void {
        thumbImages = for(i in [0..<sizeof res.photos]) {
            var im = Image {
                url: res.photos[i].urlThumb;
                backgroundLoading: true;
            };
        };
    }
    function unassignThumbs() : Void {
        thumbImages =  [];
    }
}
```

Make sure page is within range

Wrap around on over/underflow

Load page of thumbs

Move...

...this node...

...by this amount.

Do this, when finished

Run transition

URLs from result into ImageViews

Clear thumb image

The final part of our mammoth `GalleryView` class begins with three functions for manipulating the page variable, ensuring it never strays outside the acceptable range (Flickr starts its page numbering at 1, in case you were wondering). The `next()` and `previous()` functions will be called by outside classes to cause the gallery to advance or retreat.

We'll skip over `loadPage()` for now (we'll come back to it in a moment). The `assignThumbs()` and `unassignThumbs()` functions do what their name suggests. The first takes a `FlickrResult`, as retrieved from the web service, and populates the `ImageView` nodes in the thumbnail bar with fresh `Image` content. The second clears the `thumbImages` sequence, to remove the thumbnails from the bar.

The `loadPage()` function is the code ultimately responsible for responding to each request to fetch a fresh page of thumbnails from the web service. The entire function is based on a strange new type of operation called a *transition.* We've yet to see a transition in any of the projects so far, so let's stop and examine it in detail.

8.3.2 The easy way to animate: transitions

So far, whenever we wanted to animate something we had to build a `Timeline` and use it to manipulate the variables we wanted to change. It doesn't take a rocket scientist to realize a handful of common node properties (location, rotation, opacity, etc.) are frequent targets for animation. We could save a lot of unnecessary boilerplate if we created a library of prebuilt animation classes, pointed them at the nodes we wanted to animate, and then let them get on with the job.

If you haven't guessed by now, this is what *transitions* are. Let's have another look at the code in the last section:

```
TranslateTransition {
    node: thumbGroup;
    byX: 0;  byY: height;
    interpolator: Interpolator.EASEIN;
    duration: 0.5s;
    action: function() {
        unassignThumbs();
        thumbGroup.translateY = 0;
        service.loadPage(page);
    }
}.play();
```

The `TranslateTransition` is all about movement. It has a host of different configuration options that allow us to move a node *from* a given point, *to* a given point, or *by* a given distance. In our example we're moving the entire thumbnail group downward by the height of the thumbnail bar, which (one assumes) would have the effect of sending the thumbnails off the bottom of the screen.

When the transition is over, we have the opportunity to run some code. That's the purpose of the `action` function type. When this code runs, we know the thumbnails will be off screen, so we unassign them to get rid of the current images. Then we move the group we just animated back to its starting position, by resetting `translateY` (note: `translateY`, not `layoutY`, because `TranslateTransition` doesn't change its target node's layout position). And finally, we ask the web service to load a fresh page of thumbnails. This call will return immediately, as the web service interaction is carried out on another thread. In listing 8.9 we saw that the web service invokes `assignThumbs()` when its data has successfully loaded, so the images we just deleted with `unassignThumbs()` should start to be repopulated once the web service code is finished.

The call to `play()`, in case you haven't realized, fires the transition into action.

8.3.3 The main photo desktop: the PhotoViewer class

To round off our project we're going to look at clicking and dragging bits of the scene graph, and we'll play with even more types of transition. It all takes place in the `PhotoViewer` class, of which listing 8.12 is the first part. PhotoViewer.fx is divided into four parts; the final one in listing 8.15.

Listing 8.12 PhotoViewer.fx (part 1)

```
package jfxia.chapter8;

import javafx.animation.Interpolator;
import javafx.animation.transition.FadeTransition;
import javafx.animation.transition.ParallelTransition;
import javafx.animation.transition.ScaleTransition;
import javafx.animation.transition.RotateTransition;
import javafx.animation.transition.TranslateTransition;
import javafx.geometry.Bounds;
import javafx.scene.*;
import javafx.scene.control.Button;
import javafx.scene.control.ProgressBar;
import javafx.scene.image.*;
import javafx.scene.input.MouseEvent;
import javafx.scene.paint.*;
import javafx.scene.layout.LayoutInfo;
import javafx.scene.layout.Tile;
import javafx.scene.shape.Rectangle;
import javafx.stage.Stage;
import javafx.util.Math;

import java.lang.System;
import java.util.Random;

def buttonW:Number = 90;
def buttonH:Number = 35;
def maxImages:Integer = 6;
def rand:Random = new Random(System.currentTimeMillis());

var sc:Scene;

def exitButton = Button  {
    text: "Exit";
    layoutX: bind sc.width - buttonW;
    width: buttonW;  height: buttonH;
    action: function() { FX.exit(); }
};

def mouseHandler:Rectangle = Rectangle {
    var dragX:Number;
    var dragY:Number;
    width: bind sc.width;
    height: bind sc.height;
    opacity: 0;
    onMousePressed: function(ev:MouseEvent) {
        dragX=ev.x;  dragY=ev.y;
    }
```

Constants and utility objects

Exit button

Capture desktop click events

Remember initial position

```
        onMouseDragged: function(ev:MouseEvent) {
            var idx:Integer = 0;
            for(i in desktopGroup.content) {
                def v:Number = 1.0 + idx/3.0;
                i.layoutX += (ev.x-dragX) * v;
                i.layoutY += (ev.y-dragY) * v;
                idx++;
            }
            dragX=ev.x;  dragY=ev.y;
        }
}
def desktopGroup:Group = Group {}
// ** Part 2 is listing 8.13; part 3, listing 8.14; part 4, listing 8.15
```

Annotations: Move all photos with parallax; Photos added here

At the head of the source we define a few constants, such as the button size and maximum number of photos on the desktop. We also create an instance of Java's random number class, which we'll use to add a degree of variety to the animations. JFX's `javafx.util.Math` class has a `random()` function, but it only returns a `Double` between 0 and 1. (Although it has fewer options, our code would be able to run outside the desktop, where the full Java SE libraries aren't necessarily available.)

To get the dimensions of the screen we reference the application's `Scene`, which is what the `sc` variable is for. JavaFX has a class called `javafx.stage.Screen`, detailing all the available screens on devices that accommodate multiple monitors. We could tie the layout to the data in `Screen`, but referencing `Scene` instead makes it easier to adapt the code so it no longer runs full screen.

The exit button, imaginatively named `exitButton`, comes next. Then we define an invisible `Rectangle`, for capturing desktop mouse clicks and drag events. When the user clicks an empty part of the desktop, the event will be directed to this shape. On button down it stores the x/y position, and as drag events come in it moves all the nodes inside a `Group` called `desktopGroup`. This group is where all the desktop photos are stored. As each is moved, the code adds a small scaling factor, so more recent (higher) photos move farther than earlier (lower) ones, creating a cool parallax effect. (My friend Adam wasn't so keen on the parallax effect when I showed it to him, but what does he know?)

Moving on, listing 8.13 shows us our `GalleryView` class in action.

Listing 8.13 PhotoViewer.fx (part 2)

```
// ** Part 1 is listing 8.12
def galView:GalleryView = GalleryView
{   layoutY: bind (sc.height-galView.height);
    width: bind sc.width-100;

    apiKey: "-";  // <== Your key goes here
    userId: "29803026@N08";

    action: function(ph:FlickrPhoto ,
        im:Image,x:Number,y:Number) {
        def pv:Node = createPhoto(ph,im);
```

Annotations: Thumbnail bar; Position and size; Flickr details; Thumbnail clicked

```
        def pvSz:Bounds = pv.layoutBounds;
        def endX:Number = (sc.width-pvSz.width) / 2;
        def endY:Number = (sc.height-pvSz.height) / 2;
        ParallelTransition {
            node: pv;
            content: [
                TranslateTransition {
                    fromX: galView.layoutX + x;
                    fromY: galView.layoutY + y;
                    toX: endX;
                    toY: endY;
                    interpolator: Interpolator.EASEIN;
                    duration: 0.5s;
                } ,
                ScaleTransition {
                    fromX: 0.25;  fromY: 0.25;
                    toX: 1.0;  toY: 1.0;
                    duration: 0.5s;
                },
                RotateTransition {
                    fromAngle: 0;
                    byAngle: 360 + rand.nextInt(60)-30;
                    duration: 0.5s;
                }
            ];
        }.play();

        insert pv into desktopGroup.content;

        if((sizeof desktopGroup.content) > maxImages) {
            FadeTransition {
                node: desktopGroup.content[0];
                fromValue:1;  toValue:0;
                duration: 2s;
                action: function() {
                    delete desktopGroup.content[0];
                }
            }.play();
        }
    };
};
// ** Part 3 is listing 8.14; part 4, listing 8.15
```

Perform transitions together

Move: onto desktop from thumb bar

Scale: quarter to full

Rotate: Full 360, plus/minus random

Add photo to desktopGroup

Too many photos on desktop?

Here's a really meaty piece of code for us to chew on. The `action` event does all manner of clever things with transitions to spin the photo from the thumbnail bar onto the desktop. But let's look at the other definitions first. We need the thumbnail bar to sit along the bottom of the screen, so the `width` and `layoutY` are bound to the `Scene` object's size. We then plug in the familiar Flickr `apiKey` and `userID` (remember to provide your own key).

The `action` function runs when someone clicks a thumbnail in the `GalleryView`. It passes us the `FlickrPhoto` object, a copy of the thumbnail-size image (we'll use this as a stand-in while the full-size image loads), and the coordinates of the image within the bar so we can calculate where to start the movement transition.

We need a photo to work from, and the `createPhoto()` is a handy private function that creates one for us, complete with white border, shadow, loading progress bar, and the ability to be dragged around the desktop. We'll examine its code at the end of the listing; for now accept that `pv` is a new photo to be added to the desktop. The `endX` and `endY` variables are the destination coordinates on the desktop where the image will land. We use the photo's dimensions, from `layoutBounds`, to center it.

The `ParallelTransition` is another type of animation transition, except it doesn't have any direct effect itself. It acts as a group, playing several other transitions at the same time. In our code we use the `ParallelTransition` with three other transitions, represented in figure 8.6.

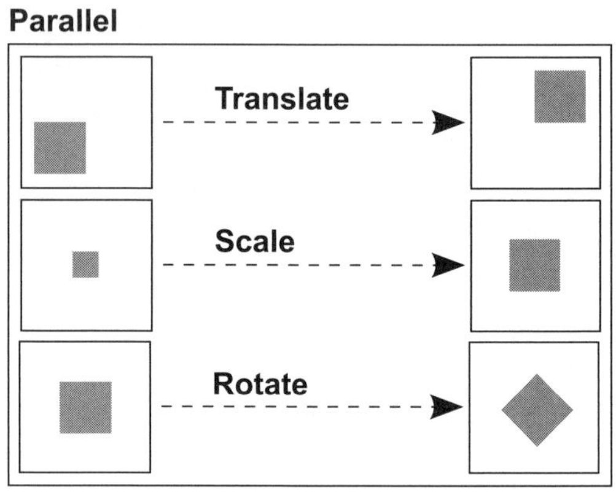

Figure 8.6 All three transitions, translate (movement), scale, and rotate, are performed at the same time to the same scene graph node.

The `TranslateTransition` you've already seen; it moves the image from the thumbnail bar into the center of the desktop. At the same time the `ScaleTransition` makes it grow from a quarter of its size to full size, over the same period of time. The `RotateTransition` spins the node by 360 degrees, plus or minus a random angle, no more than 30 degrees either way. Note how we only have to specify the actual target node at the `ParallelTransition` level, not at every transition contained within it. We fire off the transition to run in the background and add the new photo to the `desktopGroup`, to ensure it's displayed on the screen.

The final block of code uses yet another transition, this time a `FadeTransition`. We don't want too many photos on the desktop at a time, so once the maximum has been exceeded we kick off a fade to make the oldest photo gracefully vanish, and then (using an `action`) we delete it from the `desktopGroup`.

In the third part of the `PhotoViewer` code (listing 8.14) we'll tie off the loose ends, getting ready to build the scene graph.

Listing 8.14 PhotoViewer.fx (part 3)

```
// ** Part 1 is listing 8.12; part 2, listing 8.13
def controls:Tile = Tile {
    def li = LayoutInfo { width: buttonW;  height: buttonH }
    layoutX: bind sc.width - buttonW;
    layoutY: bind sc.height - controls.layoutBounds.height;
    hgap: 5;
    columns: 1;
    content: [
        Button {
            text: "Clear";
            layoutInfo: li;
```

Clear/prev/next buttons

Clear: empty desktopGroup

```
            action: function() { desktopGroup.content = []; }     Clear: empty
        } ,                                                          desktopGroup
        Button {
            text: "Next";
            layoutInfo: li;                                  Next:
            action: function() { galView.next(); }          next page
        } ,
        Button {
            text: "Previous";
            layoutInfo: li;                                  Previous:
            action: function() { galView.previous(); }      last page
        }
    ],
}

Stage {
    scene: sc = Scene {
        content: [
            mouseHandler, desktopGroup,                      Add to
            galView, controls, exitButton                    application scene
        ];
        fill: LinearGradient {
            endX: 1;  endY: 1;  proportional: true;
            stops: [
                Stop { offset: 0;  color: Color.WHITE; } ,
                Stop { offset: 1;  color: Color.GOLDENROD; }
            ];
        };
    }                                                        Full screen,
    fullScreen: true;                                        please
};
// ** Part 4 is listing 8.15
```

Listing 8.14 is quite tame compared to the previous two parts of PhotoViewer. Three JavaFX buttons allow the user to navigate the gallery using the exposed functions in GalleryView and to clear the desktop by emptying desktopGroup.contents. Then we build the actual Stage itself by combining the screenwide mouse hander, photo group, gallery, and buttons. The Scene background is set to a pleasant yellow/gold tint, a suitable backdrop for our photos. And speaking of photos, listing 8.15 has the final piece of code in this source file, a function to build our photo nodes.

Listing 8.15 PhotoViewer.fx (part 4)

```
// ** Part 1 is listing 8.12; part 2, listing 8.13; part 3, listing 8.14
function createPhoto(photo:FlickrPhoto, image:Image) : Node {
    var im:Image;
    var iv:ImageView;
    var pr:ProgressBar;

    def w:Number = bind iv.layoutBounds.width + 10;          Photo size
    def h:Number = bind iv.layoutBounds.height + 10;         (without shadow)

    def n:Group = Group {
        var dragOriginX:Number;                              Drag
        var dragOriginY:Number;                              variables
```

```
        content: [
            Rectangle {
                layoutX: 15;  layoutY: 15;
                width: bind w;  height: bind h;
                opacity: 0.25;
            } ,
            Rectangle {
                width: bind w;  height: bind h;
                fill: Color.WHITE;
            } ,

            iv = ImageView {
                layoutX: 5;  layoutY: 5;
                fitWidth: FlickrPhoto.MEDIUM;
                fitHeight: FlickrPhoto.MEDIUM;
                preserveRatio: true;
                //smooth:true;
                image: im = Image {
                    url: photo.urlMedium;
                    backgroundLoading: true;
                    placeholder: image;
                };
            } ,
            pr = ProgressBar {
                layoutX: 10;  layoutY: 10;
                progress: bind im.progress/100.0;
                visible: bind (pr.progress<1.0);
            }
        ];

        blocksMouse: true;
        onMousePressed: function(ev:MouseEvent) {
            dragOriginX=ev.x;  dragOriginY=ev.y;
        }
        onMouseDragged: function(ev:MouseEvent) {
            n.layoutX += ev.x-dragOriginX;
            n.layoutY += ev.y-dragOriginY;
        }
    };
}
```

Annotations: Shadow rectangle; White border rectangle; ImageView displays thumb or photo; Progress bar bound to loading; Mouse events stop here; Record click start coords; Update coordinates from drag

We've saved the best for last; this is real heavy-duty JavaFX Script coding! The `createPhoto()` function constructs a scene graph node to act as our full-size desktop photo, but it does more than just that. It:

- Creates a white border and shadow to fit around the photo, matched to the correct dimensions of the image.
- Displays a scaled thumbnail and kicks off the loading of the full-size image.
- Displays a progress meter while we wait for the full image to load.
- Allows itself to be dragged by the mouse, within its parent (the desktop).

At the top of the function we define some variables to reference parts of the scene graph we're creating. The variables `w` and `h` are the size of the photo, including its white border. The first `Rectangle` inside our `Group` is the shadow, using the default color (black) set to a quarter opacity. I experimented with using the `DropShadow` effect class inside `javafx.scene.effect` but found it had too much of a detrimental impact on the application's frame rate, so this `Rectangle` is a kind of poor man's alternative. The shadow is followed by the white photo border, and this in turn is followed by the `ImageView` to display our photo.

We make sure the image is sized to fit the proportions of Flickr's medium-size photo, and we point to the medium photo's URL from the `FlickrPhoto` object. Here's the clever part: we assign the thumbnail as the placeholder while we wait for the full-size image to load. This ensures we get *something* to display immediately, even if it's blocky.

The progress bar completes the scene graph contents. It will be visible only so long as there's still some loading left to be done.

That's the scene graph; now it's time to look at the event handlers.

```
blocksMouse: true;
onMousePressed: function(ev:MouseEvent) {
    dragOriginX=ev.x;  dragOriginY=ev.y;
}
onMouseDragged: function(ev:MouseEvent) {
    n.layoutX += ev.x-dragOriginX;
    n.layoutY += ev.y-dragOriginY;
}
```

The example is the chunk of code responsible for allowing us to drag the node around the desktop display. The `blocksMouse` setting is very important; without it we'd get all manner of bizarre effects whenever we moved a photo. When the mouse button goes down on a given part of the screen, there may be numerous scene graph nodes layered beneath it, so what gets the event? The highest node? The lowest node? All of them?

The answer is "all of them," working from front to back, unless we take action to stop it. If we allowed mouse events to be applied to both a photo and the underlying desktop, we'd get two sets of actions at once. With some applications this might be desirable, but in our case it is not; the event should go to either an individual photo or the desktop, but not both! The handy `blocksMouse` variable can be set to prevent mouse events from traveling any farther down the stack of nodes.

The remainder of the event code should be fairly obvious. When the mouse goes down we record its start position, relative to the top-left corner of the node. Even though the node will be rotated on the desktop, the mouse coordinates still work in sync with the rectangular shape of the photo, because the coordinates are local to the interior of the node (see figure 8.7). Drag events then

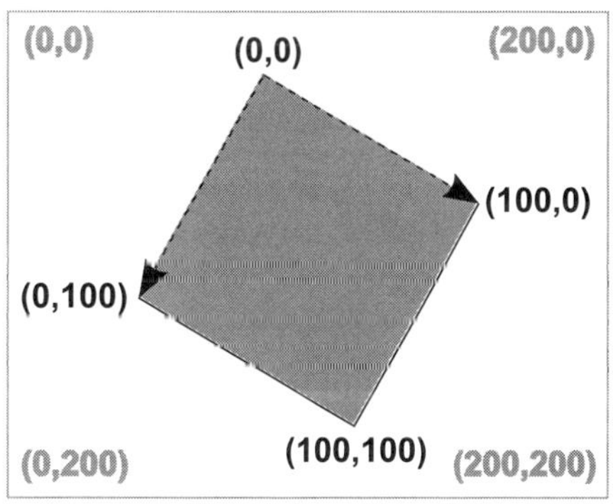

Figure 8.7 The coordinate system of a node always matches the rotation of the node itself. The gray rectangle has been rotated 30 degrees clockwise, yet its local coordinate system is unaffected.

update the layout position of the node within its parent, causing it to move inside the desktop.

Now that our JavaFX Script code is done and dusted, we can try running the application.

8.3.4 Running the application

Before running the application, make sure you've set your own Flickr API key (the one you got after registering) into the `apiKey` variable in listing 8.13. Failure to do so will mean the code will exit with an exception.

Once the application is running, the screen should look like figures 8.1 and 8.3. A paged thumbnail image display should appear at the foot of the screen, with clicked images flying onto the main desktop. Initially the full-size image will lack detail, as a copy of the thumbnail is scaled up to act as a placeholder while the high-res version loads. After a second or two, however, the scaled thumbnail should be replaced by the real image (depending on how fast your internet connection is).

Clicking and dragging the images on the desktop will move them around, while clicking and dragging an empty part of the desktop will move all the desktop images currently displayed. The desktop will show only a handful of images at a time; older images will fade away as new ones are added.

The application demonstrates a lot of manipulation of nodes, including scaling, rotation, and movement. This seems an ideal time to discuss how JavaFX calculates the size (bounds) of each part of the scene graph when various transformations are applied. So that's what we'll do next.

8.4 Size matters: node bounds in different contexts

In this project we had a lot of rotating and scaling of nodes, and we saw prominent use of `layoutBounds` and other node properties. If you browsed the JavaFX API documentation, you may have noticed that every node has several `javafx.geometry.Bounds` properties, publicizing its location and size. Each defines two x and y coordinates: top-left corner and bottom-right corner. But why so many `Bounds`—wouldn't one be enough, and how do they relate to each other?

The truth is they detail the location of the node at different points during its journey from abstract shape in a scene graph, to pixels on the video screen. The journey looks like this:

1. We start with the basic node.
2. At this point `layoutBounds` is calculated.
3. Any effects are performed (reflections, drop shadow, etc.), as specified by the node's `effect` property.
4. If the `cache` property is set to true, the node may be cached as a bitmap to speed future updates.
5. Opacity is applied next, as per the `opacity` property.
6. The node is clipped according to its `clip` property, if set.
7. At this point `boundsInLocal` is calculated.

8 Any `transforms` are then applied, translating, rotating, and scaling the node.
9 The node is scaled, by `scaleX` and `scaleY`.
10 The `rotate` property is now applied.
11 The node origin is moved within its parent, using `layoutX/translateX` and `layoutY/translateY`.
12 At this point `boundsInParent` is calculated.

In layperson's terms `layoutBounds` is the size the node thinks it is. Most of the time these are the bounds you'll use to read the node's size or lay it out. Next, `boundsInLocal` accommodates any nontransforming alterations (drop shadow, clip, etc.) applied to the node. Usually effects are ignored during layout (we usually want two nodes placed side by side to touch, even if they have surrounding drop shadows), so you'll probably find `boundsInLocal` is only infrequently needed in your code. Finally, `boundsInParent` exposes the true pixel footprint of the node inside its parent, once all effects, clips, and transformation operations have been applied. Since the scene graph translates coordinate spaces automatically, including for events, you'll likely find there are very few circumstances where you actually need to reference `boundsInParent` yourself.

8.5 Summary

This has been quite a long project, and along the way we've dealt with a lot of important topics. We started by looking at addressing a web service and parsing the XML data it gave back. This is a vital skill, as the promise of *cloud computing* is ever more reliance on web services as a means of linking software components. Although we addressed only one Flickr method, the technique is the same for all web service calls. You should be able to extend the classes in the first part of our project to talk to other bits of the Flickr API with ease. Why not give it a try?

In the main application we threw nodes around the screen with reckless abandon, thanks to our new friend the transition. Transitions take the sting out of creating beautiful UI animation, and as such they deserve prime place in any JavaFX programmer's toolbox. Why not experiment with the other types of transition `javafx.animation.transition` has to offer?

You'll be glad to know that not only do we now have a nice little application to view our own (or someone else's) photos with, but we've passed an important milestone on our journey to master JavaFX. With this chapter we've now touched on most of the important scene graph topics. Sure, we didn't get to use *every* transition, or try out *every* different effect, and we didn't even get to play with *every* different type of shape in the `javafx.scene.shape` package, but we've covered enough of a representative sample that you should now be able to find your way around the JavaFX API documentation without getting hopelessly lost.

In the next chapter we'll move away from purely language and API concerns to look at how designers and programmers can work together and how to turn our applications into applets. Until then, I encourage you make this project's code your own—add a text field for the ID of the gallery to view, and have a lot more fun with transitions.

9 From app to applet

This chapter covers

- Turning a desktop app into a web applet
- Explaining designer/programmer workflow
- Manipulating Adobe/SVG artwork
- Designing entire UIs in graphics programs

Previous chapters have concerned themselves with language syntax and programming APIs—the nuts and bolts of coding JavaFX. In this chapter we're focusing more on how JavaFX fits into the wider world, both at development time and at deployment time.

One of the goals of JavaFX was to recognize the prominent role graphic artists and designers play in modern desktop software and bring them into the application development process in a more meaningful way. To this end Sun created the JavaFX Production Suite, a collection of tools for translating content from the likes of Adobe Photoshop and Illustrator into a format manipulable by a JavaFX program.

Another key goal of JavaFX was to provide a single development technology, adaptable to many different environments (as mentioned in the introductory chapter). The 1.0 release concentrated on getting the desktop and web right; phones followed with 1.1 in February 2009, and the TV platform is expected sometime in 2009/10. The snappily titled "release 6 update 10" of the Java Runtime Environment (JRE) offers an enhanced experience for desktop applications and web applets. The new features mainly center on making it less painful for end users to install updates to the JRE, easier for developers to ensure the right version of Java is available on the end user's computer, and considerably easier for the end user to rip their favorite applet out of the browser (literally) and plunk it down on the desktop as a standalone application.

In this chapter we're going to explore how JavaFX makes life easier for nonprogrammers, focusing specifically on improvements in the designer and end-user experience. First we'll have some fun developing UI widgets from SVG (Scalable Vector Graphics) images, turning them into scene graph nodes, and manipulating them in our code. Then we'll transform the application into an applet to run inside a web browser. As with previous chapters, you'll be learning by example. So far most of our projects have centered on visuals; it's about time we developed something with a little more practical value. Increasingly serious applications are getting glossy UIs, and you don't get more serious than when the output from your program could change the fate of nations.

9.1 The Enigma project

These days practically everyone in the developed world has used encryption. From online shopping to cell phone calls, encryption is the oil that lubricates modern digital networks. It's interesting to consider, then, that machine-based encryption (as opposed to the pencil-and-paper variety) is a relatively recent innovation. Indeed, not until World War II did automated encryption achieve widespread adoption, with one technology in particular becoming the stuff of legend.

The Enigma machine was an electro-mechanical device, first created for commercial use in the early 1920s, but soon adopted by the German military for scrambling radio Morse code messages between commanders and their troops in the field. With its complex, ever-shifting encoding patterns, many people thought the Enigma was unbreakable, presumably the same people who thought the Titanic was unsinkable. As it happens, the Enigma cipher *was* broken, not once but twice!

Creating our own Enigma machine gives us a practical program with a real-world purpose, albeit one 60 years old. Its UI demands may be limited but offer a neat opportunity to cover important JavaFX techniques for turbocharging UI development (plus it's an excuse to write JFX code that isn't strictly UI related). Having reconstructed our own little piece of computing history, we'll be turning it from a desktop application into an applet and then letting the end user turn it back into a desktop application again with the drag and drop of a mouse.

9.1.1 The mechanics of the Enigma cipher

Despite its awesome power, the Enigma machine was blissfully simple by design. Predating the modern electronic computer, it relied on old-fashioned electric wiring and mechanical gears. The system consisted of four parts: three rotors and a reflector.

Each rotor is a disk with 52 electrical contacts, 26 on one face and another 26 on the other. Inside the disk each contact is wired to another on the opposite face. Electric current entering at position 1 might exit on the other side in position 8, for example. The output from one rotor was passed into the next through the contacts on the faces, forming a circuit.

In figure 9.1 current entering Rotor A in position 1 leaves in position 8. Position 8 in the next rotor is wired to position 3, and 3 in the last rotor is wired to 22. The final component, the reflector, directs the current back through the rotors in the reverse direction. This ensures that pressing A will give W and (more important, when it comes time to decode) pressing W will give A.

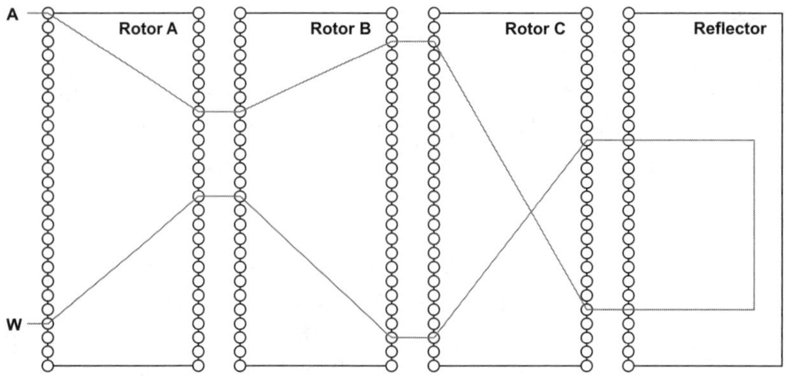

Figure 9.1 Tracing one path inside the Enigma, forming a circuit linking key A with lamp W and key W with lamp A. But as the rotors move, the circuit changes to provide a different link.

Each time a letter is encoded, one or more rotors turn, changing the combined circuit. This constant shifting of the circuit is what gives the Enigma part of its power; each letter is encoded differently with successive presses. To decode a message successfully, one must set the three rotor disks to the same start position as when the message was originally encoded. Failure to do so results in garbage.

9.2 Programmer/designer workflow: Enigma machine, version 1

The first stab we're going to have at an Enigma machine will put only the basic encryption and input and output components in place. In this initial version of the project we'll stick to familiar ground by developing a desktop application; the web applet will come later. You can see what the application will look like from figure 9.2. In the next version we'll flesh it out with a nicer interface and better features.

To create the key and lamp graphics we'll be using two SVG files, which we'll translate to JavaFX's own FXZ file format using the tools in the JavaFX Production Suite. In keeping with this book's policy of not favoring one platform or tool or IDE, I used the open source application Inkscape to draw the graphics and the SVG converter tool to

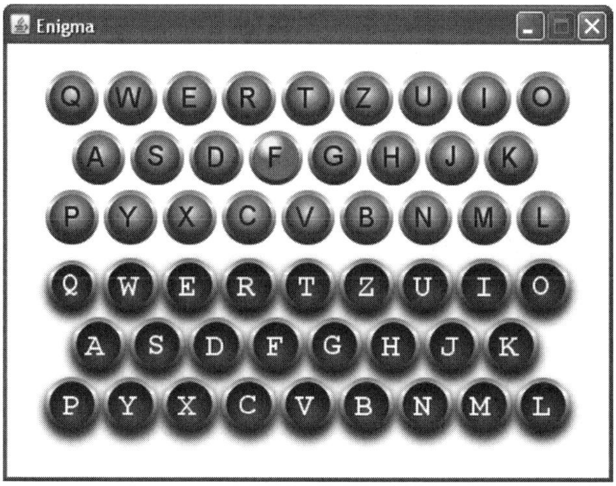

Figure 9.2 Our initial version of the Enigma machine will provide only basic encryption, input, and output, served up with a splash of visual flare, naturally!

turn them into JavaFX scene graph–compatible files. If you are lucky enough to own Adobe Photoshop CS3 or Illustrator CS3, you can use plug-ins available in the suite to export directly into JavaFX's FXZ format from inside those programs.

The SVG/IDE-agnostic route isn't that different from working with the Adobe tools and using the NetBeans JFX plug-in. For completeness I'll give a quick rundown of the Adobe/NetBeans shortcuts at the end of the first version.

9.2.1 *Getting ready to use the JavaFX Production Suite*

To join in with this chapter you'll need to download a few things. The first is the JavaFX Production Suite, available from the official JavaFX site; download this and install it. The JavaFX Production Suite is a separate download to the SDK because the suite is intended for use by designers, not programmers.

> **JavaFX v1.0 and the Production Suite**
>
> Are you being forced to use the old 1.0 version of JavaFX? If you find yourself maintaining ancient code, you need to be aware that JavaFX 1.0 did not include the FXD library by default, as its successors do. To use the FXZ/FXD format with a JavaFX 1.0 application, you'll need to download the Production Suite and include its javafx-fxd-1.0.jar file on your classpath. You'll also need to ship it with your application, along with other JARs your code depends on.

The second download is the project source code, including the project's SVG and FXZ files, available from this book's web page. Without this you won't have the graphics files to use in the project.

The final download is optional: Inkscape, an open source vector graphics application, which you can use to draw SVG files yourself. Because the SVG files are already available to you in the source code download, you won't need Inkscape for this project, but you may find it useful when developing your own graphics. As noted, you could alternatively use Photoshop CS3 (for bitmap images) or Illustrator CS3 (for vector images), if you have access to them.

> **The links**
> http://javafx.com/ *(follow the download link)*
> http://www.manning.com/JavaFXinAction
> http://www.inkscape.org/

If you downloaded the source code, you should have access to the SVG files used to create the images in this part of the project.

9.2.2 *Converting SVG files to FXZ*

Scalable Vector Graphics is a W3C standard for vector images on the web. Vector images, unlike their bitmap cousins, are defined in terms of geometric points and shapes, making them scalable to any display resolution. This fits in nicely with the way JavaFX's scene graph works.

There are two files supplied with the project, key.svg and lamp.svg, defining the vector images we'll need. They're in the svg directory of the project. Figure 9.3 shows the

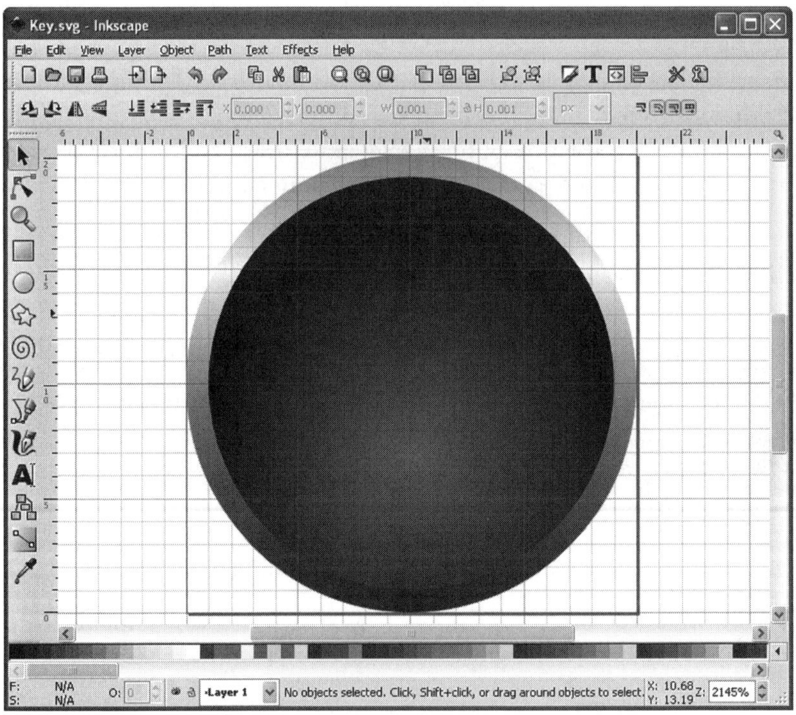

Figure 9.3 SVG images are formed from a collection of shapes; the key is two circles painted with gradient fills. JavaFX also supports layered bitmaps from Photoshop and vector images from Illustrator.

key image being edited by Inkscape. To bring these images into our JavaFX project we need to translate them from their SVG format into something closer to JavaFX Script. Fortunately for us, the JavaFX Production Suite comes with a tool to do just that.

The format JavaFX uses is called FXZ (at least, that's the three-letter extension its files carry), which is a simple zip file holding one or more components. Chief among these is the FXD file, a JavaFX Script scene graph declaration. There may also be other supporting files, such as bitmap images or fonts. (If you want to poke around inside an FXZ, just change its file extension from .fxz to .zip, and it should open in your favorite zip application.)

For each of our SVG files the converter parses the SVG and outputs the equivalent JavaFX Script code, which it stores in the FXD file. Any supporting files (for example, texture bitmaps) are also stored, and the whole thing is zipped up to form an FXZ file.

Once the JavaFX Production Suite is installed, the SVG to JavaFX Graphics Converter should be available as a regular desktop application (for example, via the Start menu on Windows). You can see what it looks like in figure 9.4.

To run the converter we need to provide the filenames of the source SVG and the destination FXZ. We can also choose whether to retain `jfx:` IDs during the conversion, which demands extra explanation.

While creating the original SVG file (and this is also true of Illustrator and Photoshop files), it is possible to mark particular elements and expose them to JavaFX after the conversion. We do this by assigning the prefix `jfx:` (that's jfx followed by a colon) to the layer or element's ID. When the conversion tool sees that prefix on an ID, it stores a reference to the element in the FXD, allowing us to later address that specific part of the scene graph in our own code. Later, when we play with the lamp graphic, we'll see an example of doing just that. In general you should ensure that the option is switched on when running the tool.

TIP *Check your ID* When I first attempted to use FXZ files in my JavaFX programs, the FXD reader didn't seem to find the parts of the image I'd carefully labeled with the `jfx:` prefix. After 15 minutes of frustration, I realized my schoolboy error: naming the layers of a SVG is not the same as setting their IDs. The JavaFX Production Suite relies on the ID only. So if, like me, you experience trouble finding parts of your image once it has been loaded into JavaFX, double-check the IDs on your original SVG.

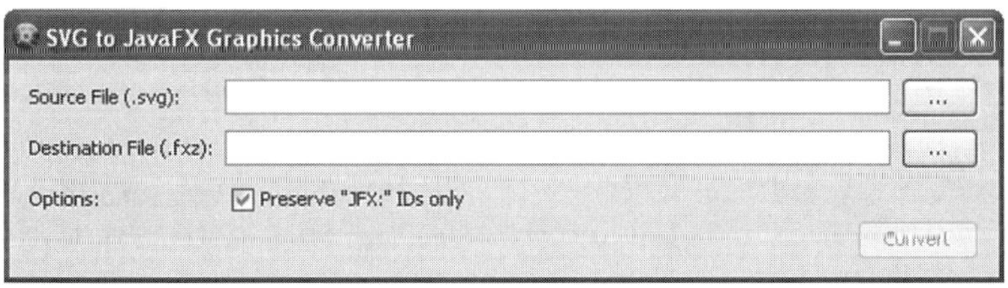

Figure 9.4 The SVG Converter takes SVG files, using the W3C's vector format, and translates them into FXZ files, using JavaFX's declarative scene graph markup.

The JavaFX Production Suite also comes with a utility to display FXZ files, called the JavaFX Graphics Viewer. After generating your FXZ, you can use it to check the output. If you haven't done so already, try running the converter tool and generating FXZ files from the project's SVGs; then use the viewer to check the results.

We'll use the resulting FXZ files when we develop the lamp and key classes. Right now you need to be aware that the FXZ files should be copied into the `jfxia.chapter9` package of the build, so they live next to the two classes that load them; otherwise the application will fail when you run it.

9.2.3 The Rotor class: the heart of the encryption

The `Rotor` class is the heart of the actual encryption code. Each instance models a single rotor in the Enigma. Its 26 positions are labeled A to Z, but they should not be confused with the actual letters being encoded or decoded. The assigning of a letter for each position is purely practical; operators needed to encode rotor start positions into each message but the machine had no digit keys, so rotors were labeled A–Z rather than 1–26. For convenience we'll also configure each rotor using the letter corresponding to each position. Since the current can pass in either direction through the rotor wiring, we'll build two lookup tables, one for left to right and one for right to left. Listing 9.1 has the code.

Listing 9.1 Rotor.fx (version 1)

```
package jfxia.chapter9;

package class Rotor {
    public-init var wiring:String;
    public-init var turnover:String;
    public-read var rotorPosition:Integer = 0;
    public-read var isTurnoverPosition:Boolean = bind
        (rotorPosition == turnoverPosition);

    var rightToLeft:Integer[];
    var leftToRight:Integer[];
    var turnoverPosition:Integer;

    init {
        rightToLeft = for(a in [0..<26]) { -1; }
        leftToRight = for(a in [0..<26]) { -1; }
        var i=0;
        while(i<26) {
            var j:Integer = chrToPos(wiring,i);
            rightToLeft[i]=j;
            leftToRight[j]=i;
            i++;
        }

        if(isInitialized(turnover))
            turnoverPosition = chrToPos(turnover,0);
    }

    package function encode(i:Integer,leftwards:Boolean) : Integer {
        var res = (i+rotorPosition) mod 26;
```

Wiring connections set as string

When should next rotor move?

Encode an input

```
        var r:Integer = if(leftwards) rightToLeft[res]
            else leftToRight[res];
        return (r-rotorPosition+26) mod 26;
    }
    package function nextPosition() : Boolean {
        rotorPosition = if(rotorPosition==25) 0
            else rotorPosition+1;
        return isTurnoverPosition;
    }
}

package function posToChr(i:Integer) : String {
    var c:Character = (i+65) as Character;
    return c.toString();
}
package function chrToPos(s:String,i:Integer) : Integer {
    var ch:Integer = s.charAt(i);
    return ch-65;
}
```

Encode an input

Step to next position, returning turnover

Convert between letter and position

Looking at listing 9.1 we can see the wiring is set using a `String`, making it easy to declaratively create new rotor objects. Other public variables control how the encryption works and how the rotors turn.

- The variable `wiring` is the source for two lookup tables, used to model the flow of current as it passes through the rotor. The tables created from `wiring` determine how the contacts on the rotor faces are linked: `rightToLeft` gives the outputs for positions A to Z (0 to 25) on one face, and for convenience `leftToRight` does the reverse path from the other face. If the first letter in `wiring` was D, for example, the first entry of `rightToLeft` would be 3 (labeled D because A = 0, B = 1, etc.), and the fourth entry of `leftToRight` would be 0 (labeled A). Thus 0 becomes 3 right to left, and 3 becomes 0 left to right.
- The variable `turnover` is the position (as a letter) at which the next rotor should step (like when a car odometer digit moves to 0, causing the next-highest digit to also move). The private variable `turnoverPosition` is the `turnover` in its more useful numeric form. One might have expected a rotor to do a full A-to-Z cycle before the next rotor ticks over one position, but the Enigma designers thought this was too predictable. The `isTurnoverPosition` variable is a handy bound flag for assessing whether this rotor is currently at its turnover position.
- The `rotorPosition` property is the current rotation offset of this rotor, as an `Integer`. If this were set to 2, for example, an input for position 23 would actually enter the rotor at position 25.

So that's our `Rotor` class. Each rotor provides one part of the overall encryption mechanism. We can use a `Rotor` object to create the reflector too; we just need to ensure the `wiring` string models symmetrical paths. Figure 9.5 show how this might look.

The regular rotors are symmetrical only by reversing the direction of current flow. Just because N (left input) results in A (right output), does not mean A will result in N

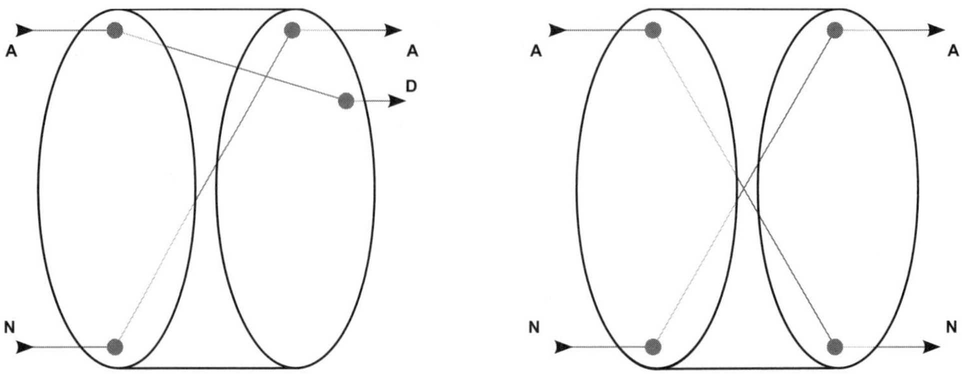

Figure 9.5 Two disks, with left/right faces. The rotor wiring is not symmetrical (left), but we can create a reflector from a rotor by ensuring 13 of the wires mirror the path of the other 13 (right).

when moving in the same left-to-right direction. Figure 9.5 shows this relationship in its left-hand rotor. We can, however, conspire to create a rotor in which these connections are deliberately mirrored (see figure 9.5's right-hand rotor), and this is precisely how we model the reflector. This convenience saves us from needing to create a specific reflector class.

9.2.4 A quick utility class

Before we proceed with the scene graph classes, we need a quick utility class to help position nodes. Listing 9.2, which does that, is up next.

Listing 9.2 Util.fx

```
package jfxia.chapter9;

import javafx.scene.Node;

package bound function center(a:Node,b:Node,hv:Boolean) : Number {
    var aa:Number = if(hv) a.layoutBounds.width
        else a.layoutBounds.height;
    var bb:Number = if(hv) b.layoutBounds.width
        else b.layoutBounds.height;
    return ((aa-bb) /2);
}
package bound function center(a:Number,b:Node,hv:Boolean) : Number {
    var bb:Number = if(hv) b.layoutBounds.width
        else b.layoutBounds.height;
    return ((a-bb) /2);
}
```

The two functions in listing 9.2 are used to center one node inside another. The first function centers node b inside node a; the second centers node b inside a given dimension. In both cases the boolean hv controls whether the result is based on the width (true) or the height (false) of the parameter nodes.

9.2.5 The Key class: input to the machine

The real Enigma machine used keys and lamps to capture input and show output. To remain faithful to the original we'll create our own `Key` and `Lamp` custom nodes. The `Key` is first; see listing 9.3.

Listing 9.3 Key.fx

```
package jfxia.chapter9;

import javafx.fxd.FXDNode;
import javafx.scene.Node;
import javafx.scene.CustomNode;
import javafx.scene.Group;
import javafx.scene.paint.Color;
import javafx.scene.input.MouseEvent;
import javafx.scene.text.Font;
import javafx.scene.text.FontWeight;
import javafx.scene.text.Text;
import javafx.scene.text.TextOrigin;

package class Key extends CustomNode {
    package def diameter:Number = 40;
    def fontSize:Integer = 24;

    public-init var letter:String on replace {        // Key's letter
        letterValue = letter.charAt(0)-65;
    }
    package var action:function(:Integer,:Boolean):Void;

    def scale:Number = bind if(pressed) 0.9 else 1.0;   // Animation scale
    def letterFont:Font = Font.font(
        "Courier", FontWeight.BOLD, fontSize
    );
    var letterValue:Integer;

    override function create() : Node {
        def keyNode = FXDNode {                       // Load FXZ file into node
            url: "{__DIR__}key.fxz";
        }

        keyNode.onMousePressed = function(ev:MouseEvent) {   // Assign mouse handlers
            if(action!=null)
                action(letterValue,true);
        };
        keyNode.onMouseReleased = function(ev:MouseEvent) {
            if(action!=null)
                action(letterValue,false);
        };

        Group {
            var k:Node;
            var t:Node;
            content: [
                k = keyNode ,                          // FXD node
                t = Text {
                    layoutX: bind Util.center(k,t,true);   // Key letter, centered
```

```
                layoutY: bind Util.center(k,t,false);
                fill: Color.WHITE;
                content: letter;
                font: letterFont;
                textOrigin: TextOrigin.TOP;
            }
        ];
        scaleX: bind scale;
        scaleY: bind scale;
    }
  }
}
```

Key letter, centered

The Key class is used to display an old-fashioned-looking manual typewriter key on the screen. Its variables are as follows:

- diameter and fontSize set the size of the key and its key font.
- letter is the character to display on this key. In order to convert the ASCII characters A to Z into the values 0 to 25, the String.toChar() function is called, and 65 (the value of ASCII letter A) is subtracted.
- action is the event callback by which the outside world can learn when our key is pressed or released.
- scale is bound to the inherited variable pressed. It resizes our key whenever the mouse button is down.
- letterFont is the font we use for the key symbol.

The overridden create() function is, as always, where the scene graph is assembled. It starts with an unfamiliar bit of code, reproduced here:

```
def keyNode = FXDNode {
    url: "{__DIR__}key.fxz";
}
```

The FXDNode class creates a scene graph node from an FXZ file. This isn't actually as complex as sounds, given the SVG to JavaFX Graphics Converter tool has already done all the heavy lifting of converting the SVG format into declarative JavaFX Script code. The class also has options to load the FXZ in the background (rather than tie up the GUI thread) and provide a placeholder node while the file is loaded and processed. But the FXDNode created from our file doesn't have any event handlers.

```
keyNode.onMousePressed = function(ev:MouseEvent) {
    if(action!=null)
        action(letterValue,true);
};
keyNode.onMouseReleased = function(ev:MouseEvent) {
    if(action!=null)
        action(letterValue,false);
};
```

Once our key image has been loaded as a node, we need to assign two mouse event handlers to it. Because the object is already defined, we can't do this declaratively, so we must revert to plain-old procedural code (à la Java) to hook up two anonymous functions. Both call the `action()` function type (if set) to inform the outside world a key has been pressed or released.

The rest of the scene graph code should be fairly clear. We need to overlay a letter onto the key, and that's what the `Text` node does. It uses the utility functions we created earlier to center itself inside the key. (There is actually a layout node called `Stack` that can center its contents; we saw it in listing 6.11.) At the foot of the scene graph the containing `Group` is bound to the `scale` variable, which in turn is bound to the inherited `pressed` state of the node. Whenever the mouse button goes down, the whole key shrinks slightly, as if being pressed.

NOTE *Don't forget to copy the FXZ files* The FXZ files for this project should be inside the directory representing the `jfxia.chapter9` package, so a reference to `__DIR__` can be used to find them. Once you've built the project code, make sure the FXZs are alongside the project class files.

Next we need to create the `Lamp` class to display our output.

9.2.6 *The Lamp class: output from the machine*

We've just developed a stylized input for our emulator; now we need a similar retro-looking output. In the original Enigma machine the encoded letters were displayed on 26 lamps, one of which would light up to display the output as a key was pressed, so that's what we'll develop next, in listing 9.4.

Listing 9.4 Lamp.fx

```
package jfxia.chapter9;

import javafx.fxd.FXDLoader;
import javafx.fxd.FXDContent;
import javafx.scene.Node;
import javafx.scene.CustomNode;
import javafx.scene.Group;
import javafx.scene.paint.Color;
import javafx.scene.text.Font;
import javafx.scene.text.FontWeight;
import javafx.scene.text.Text;
import javafx.scene.text.TextOrigin;

package class Lamp extends CustomNode {
    package def diameter:Number = 40;
    def fontSize:Integer = 30;

    public-init var letter:String;
    package var lit:Boolean = false on replace {
        if(lampOn!=null)  lampOn.visible = lit;
    }

    def letterFont:Font = Font.font(
        "Helvetic", FontWeight.REGULAR, fontSize
    );
```

Manipulate lamp FXD

```
    var lampOn:Node;                                    <— Our FXD node

    override function create() : Node {
        def lampContent:FXDContent = FXDLoader          | Load as
            .loadContent("{__DIR__}lamp.fxz");          | FXDContent type

        def lampNode = lampContent.getRoot();           <— Top level

        lampOn = lampContent.getNode("lampOn");         <— Specific layer

        var c:Node;
        var t:Node;
        Group {
            content: [                         Use in scene
                c = lampNode ,             <— graph
                t = Text {
                    content: letter;
                    font: letterFont;
                    textOrigin: TextOrigin.TOP;                    Letter text,
                    layoutX: bind Util.center(c,t,true);           centered
                    layoutY: bind Util.center(c,t,false);
                }
            ];
        }
    }
}
```

The Lamp class is a very simple binary display node. It has no mouse or keyboard input, just two states: lit or unlit. Once again we load an FXZ file and bring its content into our code. But this time, instead of using the quick-'n'-easy FXDNode class, we go the *long route* via FXDLoader and FXDContent. (There's no great advantage to this; I just thought a bit of variety in the example code wouldn't hurt!) Once the file is loaded, we extract references to specific parts of the scene graph described by the FXD.

If you load up the original SVG files, you'll find inside the lamp a layer with an alternative version of the center part of the image, making it appear lit up (see figure 9.6). The layer is set to be invisible, so it doesn't show by default. It has been given the ID jfx:lampOn, causing the converter to record a reference to it in the FXD.

In the code we extract that reference by calling FXDContent.getNode() with an ID of lampOn. We don't need the jfx: prefix with the FXZ/FXD; it was used in the original SVG only to tag the parts of the image we wanted to ID in the FXD. If the ID is found, we'll get back a scene graph node, which we'll store in a variable called lampOn (it doesn't *have* to share the same name). We can now manipulate lampOn in the code, by switching its visibility on or off whenever the status of lit changes.

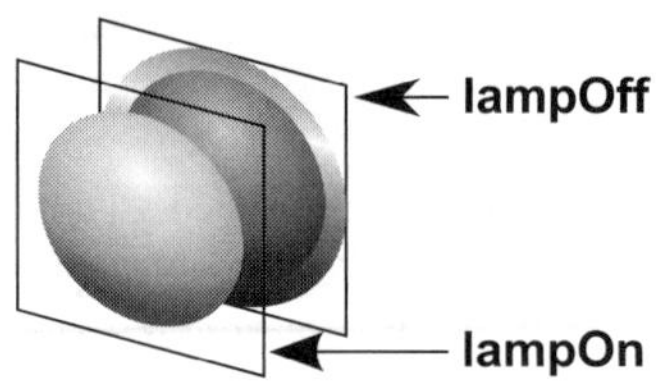

Figure 9.6 The lamp image is constructed from two layers. The lower layer shows the rim of the lamp and its dormant (off) graphic; the upper layer, invisible by default, shows the active (on) graphic.

This ability to design images in third-party applications, bring them into our JavaFX programs, and then reach inside and manipulate their constituent parts is very powerful. Imagine, for example, a chess game where the board and all the playing pieces are stored in one big SVG (or Photoshop or Illustrator) image, tagged with individual JFX IDs. To update the game's graphics the designer merely supplies a replacement FXZ file. Providing the IDs are the same, it should drop straight into the project as a direct replacement, without the need for a rebuild of the code.

9.2.7 The Enigma class: binding the encryption engine to the interface

Ignoring the utility class, we've seen three application classes so far: the `Rotor`, which provides the basis of our Enigma cipher emulation; the `Key`, which provides the input; and the `Lamp`, which displays the output. Now it's time to pull these classes together with an actual application class, the first part of which is listing 9.5.

Listing 9.5 Enigma.fx (version 1, part 1)

```
package jfxia.chapter9;

import javafx.scene.Group;
import javafx.scene.Node;
import javafx.scene.Scene;
import javafx.scene.effect.DropShadow;
import javafx.scene.layout.Tile;
import javafx.scene.layout.VBox;
import javafx.stage.Stage;

def rotors:Rotor[] = [
    Rotor { wiring: "JGDQOXUSCAMIFRVTPNEWKBLZYH";
        turnover: "R" } ,
    Rotor { wiring: "NTZPSFBOKMWRCJDIVLAEYUXHGQ";
        turnover: "F" } ,
    Rotor { wiring: "JVIUBHTCDYAKEQZPOSGXNRMWFL";
        turnover: "W" }
];
def reflector =
    Rotor { wiring: "QYHOGNECVPUZTFDJAXWMKISRBL"; }

def row1:String[] = [ "Q","W","E","R","T","Z","U","I","O" ];
def row2:String[] = [ "A","S","D","F","G","H","J","K" ];
def row3:String[] = [ "P","Y","X","C","V","B","N","M","L" ];

def dummyLamp = Lamp {};
var lamps:Lamp[] = for(i in [0..<26])  dummyLamp;

def innerWidth:Integer = 450;
def innerHeight:Integer = 320;
// Part 2 is listing 9.6; part 3, listing 9.7
```

Declare the rotors and reflector

Key and lamp layout

This is just the top part of our application class. The code mainly concerns itself with setting up the three rotors and single reflector, plus defining the keyboard and lamp layout. We'll use the Enigma's authentic keyboard layout, which is similar to but not quite the same as QWERTY. Because we need to manipulate the lamps, we create a sequence to hold the nodes alphabetically. We won't be creating the lamp node in ABC order, so 26 dummy entries pad the sequence to allow `lamps[letter]=node` later on.

Listing 9.6 is the second part of our project and shows the main scene graph code that builds the window and its contents.

Listing 9.6 Enigma.fx (version 1, part 2)

```
// Part 1 is listing 9.5
Stage {
    scene: Scene {
        var l:Node;
        content: Group {
            content: [
                l = VBox {                                    <- Lamp, centered
                    layoutX: bind
                        Util.center(innerWidth,l,true);
                    layoutY: 20;
                    spacing: 4;
                    content: [                                <- Three rows of lamps
                        createRow(row1,false,createLamp) ,
                        createRow(row2,true,createLamp) ,
                        createRow(row3,false,createLamp)
                    ];
                } ,
                VBox {                                        <- Keys, positioned using lamps
                    layoutX: bind l.layoutX;
                    layoutY: bind l.boundsInParent.maxY+10;
                    spacing: 4;
                    content: [                                <- Three rows of keys
                        createRow(row1,false,createKey) ,
                        createRow(row2,true,createKey) ,
                        createRow(row3,false,createKey)
                    ];
                    effect: DropShadow {                      Drop-shadow effect
                        offsetX: 0;  offsetY: 5;
                    };
                }
            ];
        };
        width: innerWidth;  height: innerHeight;              <- Window inner content
    }
    title: "Enigma";
    resizable: false;
    onClose: function() { FX.exit(); }
}
// Part 3 is listing 9.7
```

The structure is fairly simple: we have two VBox containers (they stack their contents in a vertical alignment, recall), each populated with three calls to createRow(). The top VBox is aligned centrally using the utility functions we developed earlier and 20 pixels from the top of the window's inner bounds. The second VBox has its X layout bound to its sibling and its Y layout set to 10 pixels below the bottom of its sibling.

The second VBox has an effect attached to it, javafx.scene.effect.DropShadow. We touched on effects briefly when we used a reflection in our video player project. Effects manipulate the look of a node, anything from a blur or a color tint to a reflection or even a pseudo 3D distortion. The `DropShadow` effect merely adds a shadow underneath the node tree it is connected to. This gives our keys a floating 3D effect.

The `createRow()` function manufactures a row of nodes from a sequence of letters, using a function passed into it (`createLamp` or `createKey`). Its code begins the final part of this source file, as shown in listing 9.7.

Listing 9.7 Enigma.fx (version 1, part 3)

```
// Part 1 is listing 9.5; part 2, listing 9.6
function createRow(row:String[] , indent:Boolean ,
    func:function(l:String):Node) : Tile {
    def h = Tile {
        hgap: 4;
        columns: sizeof row;
        content: for(l in [row]) { func(l); };
    };
    if(indent) {
        h.translateX =
            h.content[0].layoutBounds.width/2;
    }
    return h;
}
function createKey(l:String) : Node {
    Key {
        letter: l;
        action: handleKeyPress;
    };
}
function createLamp(l:String) : Node {
    def i:Integer = l.charAt(0)-65;
    def lamp = Lamp { letter: l; };
    lamps[i]=lamp;
    return lamp;
}

function handleKeyPress(l:Integer,down:Boolean) : Void {
    def res = encodePosition(l);
    lamps[res].lit = down;
    if(not down) {
        var b:Boolean;
        b=rotors[2].nextPosition();
        if(b) { b=rotors[1].nextPosition(); }
        if(b) { rotors[0].nextPosition(); }
    }
}

function encodePosition(i:Integer) : Integer {
    var res=i;
    for(r in rotors) { res=r.encode(res,false); }
    res=reflector.encode(res,false);
    for(r in reverse rotors) { res=r.encode(res,true); }
    return res;
}
```

Create rows of lamps or keys

Intent row, if required

Function used to create key

Function used to create lamp

Handle key up or down

Key release? Turn rotors

Encode key position

Forward then back through rotors

Here we see the `createRow()` function encountered in the previous part. Since the layout for both the keyboard and lamp board is the same, a single utility function is employed to position the nodes in each row. The `createKey()` and `createLamp()` functions are passed to `createRow()` to manufacture the nodes to be laid out. For that important authentic keyboard look, rows can be indented slightly, using the `indent` boolean.

Finally, we need to consider the `handleKeyPress()` and `encodePosition()` functions. The former uses the latter to walk forward, then backward across the rotors, with the deflector in the middle, performing each stage of the encryption. Once the input letter is encoded, it switches the associated lamp on or off (depending on the direction the key just moved) and turns any rotors that need turning (the `nextPosition()` function turns a rotor and returns `true` if it hits its *turnover* position).

And so, with the `Enigma` class itself now ready, we have version 1 of our simulated encryption machine.

9.2.8 Running version 1

What we have with version 1 is a functional, if not very practical, Enigma emulator. Figure 9.7 shows what to expect when the application is fired up.

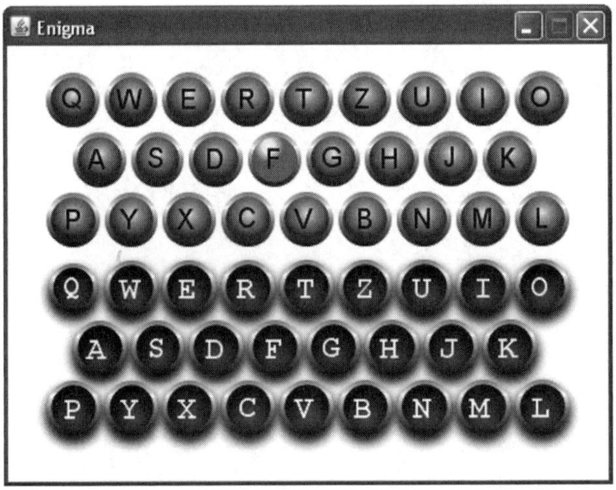

Figure 9.7 This is what we should see when compiling and running version 1. It works, but not in a very practical way. The stylized button and lamp nodes help lend the application an authentic feel.

Pressing a key runs its position through the rotors and reflector, with the result displayed on a lamp. There are two clear problems with the current version: first, we cannot see or adjust the settings of the rotors, and second (in a departure from the real Enigma), we cannot capture the output in a more permanent form.

In the second version of our Enigma we'll be fixing those problems, making the application good enough to put on the web for all to see.

9.2.9 Shortcuts using NetBeans, Photoshop, or Illustrator

The details in this chapter attempt to be as inclusive as possible. Inkscape was chosen as an example of an SVG editor precisely because it was free and did not favor a particular operating system. As mentioned previously, the JavaFX Production Suite does hold some benefits for users of certain well-known products. In this section we'll list those benefits.

If you are lucky enough to own Adobe Photoshop CS3 or Adobe Illustrator CS3, or you're working with someone who uses them, you'll be happy to know that the JavaFX Production Suite comes with plug-ins for these applications to save directly to FXZ (no need for external tools, like the SVG Converter). Obviously you need to install the Production Suite on the computer running Photoshop or Illustrator, and make sure there's an up-to-date JRE on there too, but you *don't* need to install the full JavaFX SDK.

Just as we saw with our SVG files, layers and sublayers in graphics created with these products can be prefixed with `jfx:` to preserve them in the FXD definition written into the FXZ file. Fonts, bitmaps, and other supporting data will also be included in the FXZ.

The good news isn't confined to designers; programmers using NetBeans also have an extra little tool included in the Production Suite. The *UI Stub Generator* is a convenience tool for NetBeans users to create JavaFX Script wrappers from FXZ files. Pointing the tool at any FXZ file results in a source code file being generated that extends `javafx.fxd.FXDNode`. Each exposed node in the FXZ (the ones with `jfx:` prefixes in the original image) is given a variable in the class, so it can be accessed easily. An `update()` method is written to do all the heavy lifting of populating the variables with successive calls to `getNode()`. Once the file is generated, NetBeans users can compile this class into their project and use it in preference to explicit `getNode()` calls.

The UI Stub Generator helps to keep your source files clean from the mechanics of reading FXD data; however, once the source code has been generated you may feel the need to edit it. The tool assumes everything is a `Node`, so if you plan on addressing a given part of the scene graph by its true form (for example, a `Text` node), you'll need to change the variable's type and add a cast to the relevant `getNode()` line.

All of these tools are fully documented in the help files that come bundled with the JavaFX Production Suite.

9.3 More cryptic: Enigma machine, version 2

Version 1 of the project has a couple of issues that need addressing. First, the user needs to be able to view and change the state of the rotors. Second, we need to introduce some way to capture the encoded output.

To fix the first problem we're going to turn the `Rotor` class into a node that can be used not only to encode a message but also to set the encryption parameters. To fix the second we'll develop a simple printout display, which looks like a teletype page, that records our output along with the lamps. You can see what it looks like at the top of figure 9.8.

As a glance at figure 9.8 reveals, each rotor will show its letter in a gradient-filled display, with arrow buttons constructed from scene graph polygons. The paper node we'll develop will be shaded at the top, giving the impression its text is vanishing over a curved surface. Changes to the `Enigma` class will tie the features into the application's interface, giving a more polished look.

Figure 9.8 Quite an improvement: the Enigma emulator acquires a printout display and rotors, as well as an attractive shaded backdrop.

9.3.1 *The Rotor class, version 2: giving the cipher a visual presence*

The `Rotor` class needs a makeover to turn it into a fully fledged custom node, allowing users to interact with it. Because this code is being integrated into the existing class, I've taken the liberty of snipping (omitting for the sake of brevity) the bulk of the code from the previous version, as you'll see from listing 9.8. (It may not save many trees, but it could help save a few branches.) The snipped parts have been marked with bold comments to show what has been dropped and where. Refer to listing 9.1 for a reminder of what's missing.

Listing 9.8 Rotor.fx (version 2—changes only)

```
package jfxia.chapter9;

import javafx.scene.Node;
import javafx.scene.CustomNode;
import javafx.scene.Group;
import javafx.scene.input.MouseEvent;
import javafx.scene.paint.Color;
import javafx.scene.paint.LinearGradient;
import javafx.scene.paint.Stop;
import javafx.scene.shape.Polygon;
import javafx.scene.shape.Rectangle;
import javafx.scene.text.Font;
```

```
import javafx.scene.text.FontWeight;
import javafx.scene.text.Text;
import javafx.scene.text.TextOrigin;

package class Rotor extends CustomNode {
    // [Snipped variables: see previous version]

    def fontSize:Integer = 40;
    def width:Number = 60;
    def height:Number = 60;
    def buttonHeight:Number = 20.0;
    def letterFont:Font = Font.font(
        "Helvetic" , FontWeight.BOLD, fontSize
    );

    // [Snipped init block: see previous version]

    override function create() : Node {
        var r:Node;
        var t:Node;
        Group {
            content: [
                Polygon {
                    points: [
                        width/2 , 0.0 ,
                        0.0 , buttonHeight ,
                        width , buttonHeight
                    ];
                    fill: Color.BEIGE;
                    onMouseClicked: function(ev:MouseEvent) {
                        rotorPosition = if(rotorPosition==0) 25
                            else rotorPosition-1;
                    }
                } ,
                r = Rectangle {
                    layoutY: buttonHeight;
                    width: width;
                    height: height;
                    fill: LinearGradient {
                        proportional: false;
                        endX:0;  endY:height;
                        stops: [
                            Stop { offset: 0.0;
                                color: Color.DARKSLATEGRAY; } ,
                            Stop { offset: 0.25;
                                color: Color.DARKGRAY; } ,
                            Stop { offset: 1.0;
                                color: Color.BLACK; }
                        ]
                    }
                } ,
                Rectangle {
                    layoutX: 4;
                    layoutY: buttonHeight;
                    width: width-8;
                    height: height;
                    fill: LinearGradient {
```

Sizing and font constants

Up arrow polygon

Move rotor back one

Rotor display rim

Rotor display body

```
                        proportional: false;
                        endX:0;  endY:height;
                        stops: [
                            Stop { offset: 0.0;
                                color: Color.DARKGRAY; } ,
                            Stop { offset: 0.25;
                                color: Color.WHITE; } ,
                            Stop { offset: 0.75;
                                color: Color.DARKGRAY; } ,
                            Stop { offset: 1.0;
                                color: Color.BLACK; }
                        ]
                    }
                } ,
                t = Text {                                    ◁ Rotor current letter
                    layoutX: bind Util.center(r,t,true);
                    layoutY: bind buttonHeight +
                        Util.center(r,t,false);
                    content: bind posToChr(rotorPosition);
                    font: letterFont;
                    textOrigin: TextOrigin.TOP;
                } ,
                Polygon {                                     ◁ Down arrow polygon
                    layoutY: buttonHeight+height;
                    points: [
                        0.0 , 0.0 ,
                        width/2 , buttonHeight ,
                        width , 0.0
                    ];
                    fill: Color.BEIGE;                        ◁ Move rotor forward one
                    onMouseClicked: function(ev:MouseEvent) {
                        rotorPosition = if(rotorPosition==25) 0
                            else rotorPosition+1;
                    }
                }
            ];
        }
    }

    // [Snipped encode(), nextPosition(): see previous version]
}
// [Snipped posToChr(), chrToPos(): see previous version]
```

The new Rotor class contains a hefty set of additions. The scene graph, as assembled by create(), brings together several layered elements to form the final image. The graph is structured around a Group, at the top and tail of which are Polygon shapes. As its name suggests, the Polygon is a node that allows its silhouette to be custom defined from a sequence of coordinate pairs. The values in the points sequence are alternate x and y positions. They form the outline of a shape, with the last coordinate connecting back to the first to seal the perimeter. Both of our polygons are simple triangles, with points at the extreme left, extreme right, and in the middle, forming up and down arrows.

The rest of the scene graph consists of familiar components: two gradient-filled rectangles and a text node, forming the rotor body between the arrows.

The arrow polygons have mouse handlers attached to them to change the current `rotorPosition`. As rotor positions form a circle, condition logic wraps `rotorPosition` around when it overshoots the start or end of its range. The `turnover` position is ignored, you'll note, because we don't want rotors *clocking* each other as we're manually adjusting them.

So that's the finished `Rotor`. Now for the `Paper` class.

9.3.2 The Paper class: making a permanent output record

The `Paper` class is a neat little display node, with five lines of text that are scaled vertically to create the effect of the lines vanishing over a curved surface. We're employing a fixed-width font, for that authentic manual typewriter look. Check out figure 9.9. You can almost hear the clack-clack-clack of those levers, hammering out each letter as the keys are pressed.

Figure 9.9 Each line of our `Paper` node is scaled to create the optical effect of a surface curving away, to accompany the shading of the background `Rectangle`.

The real Enigma didn't have a paper output. The machines were designed to be carried at the frontline of a battle, and their rotor mechanics and battery were bulky enough without adding a stationery cupboard full of paper and ink ribbons. But we've moved on a little in the 80-plus years since the Enigma was first developed, and while a 1200 dpi laser printer might be stretching credibility a little *too* far, we can at least give our emulator a period teletype display. The code is in listing 9.9.

Listing 9.9 Paper.fx

```
package jfxia.chapter9;

import javafx.scene.CustomNode;
import javafx.scene.Group;
import javafx.scene.Node;
import javafx.scene.effect.DropShadow;
import javafx.scene.input.MouseEvent;
import javafx.scene.layout.VBox;
import javafx.scene.paint.Color;
import javafx.scene.paint.LinearGradient;
import javafx.scene.paint.Stop;
import javafx.scene.shape.Rectangle;
import javafx.scene.text.Font;
```

```
import javafx.scene.text.FontWeight;
import javafx.scene.text.Text;
import javafx.scene.text.TextOrigin;

package class Paper extends CustomNode {
    package var width:Number = 300.0;
    public-read var height:Number;

    def lines:Integer= 5;
    def font:Font = Font.font(
        "Courier" , FontWeight.REGULAR , 20
    );

    def paper:Text[] = for(i in [0..<lines]) {          <- Sequence of text lines
        def y:Number = height;
        def scale:Number = 1.0 - ((lines-1-i)*0.15);    Scale and position to create curve
        def lineHeight:Number = 25*scale;
        height = height+lineHeight;
        Text {
            layoutY: y;
            font: font;
            textOrigin: TextOrigin.TOP;
            scaleY: scale;
            clip: Rectangle {
                width: width;  height: lineHeight;
            }
        };
    }

    override function create() : Node {
        Group {
            content: [
                Rectangle {                             <- Shaded paper backdrop
                    width: width;
                    height: height;
                    fill: LinearGradient {
                        proportional: true;
                        endX: 0;  endY: 1;
                        stops: [
                            Stop { offset:0.0;
                                color: Color.SLATEGRAY; } ,
                            Stop { offset:0.2;
                                color: Color.WHITE; } ,
                            Stop { offset:1.0;
                                color: Color.LIGHTGRAY; }
                        ];
                    }
                    effect: DropShadow {
                        offsetX: 0;  offsetY: 10;
                        color: Color.CHOCOLATE;
                    };
                } ,
                Group { content: paper; }               <- Text nodes expanded in place
            ];
            onMouseClicked: function(ev:MouseEvent) {   <- Scroll up when clicked
                add("\n");
            }
```

```
        };
    }
    package function add(l:String) : Void {        <- Add to bottom text line
        def z:Integer = lines-1;
        if(l.equals("\n")) {
            var i:Integer = 1;
            while(i<lines) {
                paper[i-1].content = paper[i].content;     Push
                i++;                                        paper up
            }
            paper[z].content="";
        }
        else {
            paper[z].content = "{paper[z].content}{l}";   <- Append to last line
        }
    }
}
```

The most interesting thing about listing 9.9 is the creation of the sequence `paper`. What this code does is to stack several `Text` nodes using `layoutY`, scaling each in turn from a restricted height at the top to full height at the bottom. The rather fearsome-looking code `1.0-((lines-1-i)*0.15)` subtracts multiples of 15 percent from the height of each line, so the first line is scaled the most and the last line not at all. The result is a curved look to the printout, just what we wanted!

The rest of the listing is unremarkable scene graph code, with the exception of the `add()` function at the end. This is what the outside world uses to push new letters onto the bottom line of the teletype display. Normally the character is appended to the end of the last `Text` node, but if the character is a carriage return, each `Text` node in `content` is copied to its previous sibling, creating the effect of the paper scrolling up a line. The last `Text` node is set to an empty string, ready for fresh output.

We now have all the classes we need for our finished Enigma machine; all that's left is to refine the application class itself to include our new graphical rotors and paper.

9.3.3 The Enigma class, version 2: at last our code is ready to encode

Having upgraded the `Rotor` class and introduced a new `Paper` class, we need to integrate these into the display. Listing 9.10 does just that.

Listing 9.10 Enigma.fx (version 2, part 1 – changes only)

```
package jfxia.chapter9;

import javafx.scene.Group;
import javafx.scene.Node;
import javafx.scene.Scene;
import javafx.scene.effect.DropShadow;
import javafx.scene.layout.Tile;
import javafx.scene.layout.VBox;
import javafx.scene.paint.Color;
import javafx.scene.paint.LinearGradient;
import javafx.scene.paint.Stop;
```

```
import javafx.scene.shape.Rectangle;
import javafx.stage.Stage;

// [Snipped defintions for rotors, reflector, row1, row2,
//   row3 and lamps: see previous version]

def innerWidth:Integer = 450;
def innerHeight:Integer = 520;

var paper:Paper;
// Part 2 is listing 9.11; part 3, listing 9.12
```

Listing 9.10 is the top part of the updated application class, adding little to what was already there in the previous version. That's why I've snipped parts of the content again, indicated (as before) with comments in bold. You can refresh your memory by glancing back at listing 9.5. As you can see, the window has been made bigger to accommodate the new elements we're about to add, and we've created a variable to hold one of them, paper.

The main changes come in the next part, listing 9.11, the scene graph.

Listing 9.11 Enigma.fx (version 2, part 2)

```
// Part 1 is listing 9.10
Stage {
    scene: Scene {
        content: Group {
            var p:Node;
            var r:Node;
            var l:Node;
            content: [
                p = paper = Paper {                        <- Our new Paper class
                    width: innerWidth-50;
                    layoutX: 25;
                } ,
                r = Tile {                                 <- Rotors in horizontal layout
                    columns: 3;
                    layoutX: bind Util.center(innerWidth,r,true);
                    layoutY: bind p.boundsInParent.maxY;
                    hgap: 20;
                    content: [
                        rotors[0], rotors[1], rotors[2]
                    ];
                } ,
                l = VBox {
                    layoutX: bind Util.center(innerWidth,l,true);
                    layoutY: bind r.boundsInParent.maxY+10;
                    spacing: 4;
                    content: [
                        createRow(row1,false,createLamp) ,
                        createRow(row2,true,createLamp) ,
                        createRow(row3,false,createLamp)
                    ];
                } ,
                VBox {
```

```
                    layoutX: bind l.layoutX;
                    layoutY: bind l.boundsInParent.maxY+10;
                    spacing: 4;
                    content: [
                        createRow(row1,false,createKey) ,
                        createRow(row2,true,createKey) ,
                        createRow(row3,false,createKey)
                    ];
                    effect: DropShadow {
                        offsetX: 0;  offsetY: 5;
                    };
                }
            ];
        };
        fill: LinearGradient {                              Gradient backdrop to window
            proportional: true;  endX: 0;  endY: 1;
            stops: [
                Stop { offset: 0.0;  color:  Color.BURLYWOOD; } ,
                Stop { offset: 0.05;  color:  Color.BEIGE; } ,
                Stop { offset: 0.2;  color:  Color.SANDYBROWN; } ,
                Stop { offset: 0.9;  color:  Color.SADDLEBROWN; }
            ];
        }
        width: innerWidth;  height: innerHeight;
    }
    title: "Enigma";
    resizable: false;
    onClose: function() { FX.exit(); }
}
// Part 3 is listing 9.12
```

Listing 9.11 is the meat of the new changes. I've preserved the full listing this time, without any snips, to better demonstrate how the changes integrate into what's already there. At the top of the scene graph we add our new `Paper` class, sized to be 50 pixels smaller than the window width. Directly below that we create a horizontal row of `Rotor` objects; recall that the new `Rotor` is now a `CustomNode` and can be used directly in the scene graph. The lamps have now been pushed down to be 10 pixels below the rotors. At the very bottom of the `Scene` we install a `LinearGradient` fill to create a pleasing shaded background for the window contents.

Just one more change to this class is left, and that's in the (on screen) keyboard handler, as shown in listing 9.12.

Listing 9.12 Enigma.fx (version 2, part 3 – changes only)

```
// Part 1 is listing 9.10; part 2 is listing 9.11

// [Snipped createRow(), createKey(),
//   createLamp(): see previous version]

function handleKeyPress(l:Integer,down:Boolean) : Void {
    def res = encodePosition(l);
    lamps[res].lit = down;
    if(not down) {
```

```
            var b:Boolean;
            b=rotors[2].nextPosition();
            if(b) { b=rotors[1].nextPosition(); }
            if(b) { rotors[0].nextPosition(); }
        }
        else {
            paper.add(Rotor.posToChr(res));
        }
    }
// [Snipped encodePosition(): see previous version]
```

Key down? Add to paper

At last we have the final part of the `Enigma` class, and once again the unchanged parts have been snipped. Check out listing 9.7 if you want to refresh your memory. Only one change to mention, but it's an important one: the `handleKeyPress()` now has some plumbing to feed its key into the new `paper` node. This is what makes the encoded letter appear on the printout when a key is clicked.

9.3.4 Running version 2

Running the `Enigma` class gives us the display shown in figure 9.10. Our keys and lamps have been joined by a printout/teletype affair at the head of the window and three rotors just below.

Clicking the arrows surrounding the rotors causes them to change position, while clicking the paper display causes it to jump up a line. As we stab away at the keys, our

Figure 9.10 Our Enigma machine in action, ready to keep all our most intimate secrets safe from prying eyes (providing they don't have access to any computing hardware made after 1940).

input is encoded through the rotors, flashed up on the lamps, and appended to the printout.

Is our Enigma machine finished then? Well, for now, yes, but there's plenty of room for new features. The Enigma we developed is a simplified version of the original, with two important missing elements. The genuine Enigma had rotors that could be removed and interchanged, to further hinder code breaking. It also featured a *plug board*: 26 sockets linked by 13 pluggable cables, effectively creating a configurable second reflector. That said, unless anyone reading this book is planning on invading a small country, the simplified emulator we've developed should be more than enough.

In the final part of this chapter we'll turn our new application into an applet, so we can allow the world and his dog to start sending us secret messages.

9.4 From application to applet

One of the banes of deploying Java code in the *bad old days* was myriad options and misconfigurations one might encounter. Traditionally Java relied on the end user (the customer) to keep the installed Java implementation up to date, and naturally this led to a vast range of runtime versions being encountered in the wild. The larger download size of the Java runtime, compared to the Adobe Flash Player, also put off many web developers. Java fans might note this is an apples-and-oranges comparison; the JRE is more akin to Microsoft's .NET Framework, and .NET is many times larger than the JRE. Yet still the perception of Java as large and slow persisted.

Starting with Java 6 update 10 at the end of 2008, a huge amount of effort was put behind trying to smarten up the whole Java deployment experience, for both the end user and the developer. In the final part of this chapter we'll be exploring some of these new features, through JavaFX. Although none of them are specifically JavaFX changes, they go hand in glove with the effort to brighten up Java's prospects on the desktop, something that JavaFX *is* a key part of.

9.4.1 The Enigma class: from application to applet

Having successfully created an Enigma application, we need to port it over to be an applet. If you've ever written any Java applets, this might send a chill down your spine. Although Java applications and applets have a lot in common, translating one to the other still demands a modest amount of reworking. But this is JavaFX, not Java, and our expectations are different. JavaFX was, after all, intended to ease the process of moving code between different types of user facing environments.

Listing 9.13 shows the extent of the changes. Astute readers (those who actually read code comments) will note that once again the unchanged parts of the listing have been omitted, showing only the new material and its context.

Listing 9.13 Enigma.fx (version 3 – changes only)

```
package jfxia.chapter9;

import javafx.scene.Group;
```

```
import javafx.scene.Node;
import javafx.scene.Scene;
import javafx.scene.effect.DropShadow;
import javafx.scene.input.MouseEvent;                    // Trap mouse events
import javafx.scene.layout.Tile;
import javafx.scene.layout.VBox;
import javafx.scene.paint.Color;
import javafx.scene.paint.LinearGradient;
import javafx.scene.paint.Stop;
import javafx.scene.shape.Rectangle;
import javafx.stage.AppletStageExtension;                // Import applet extension
import javafx.stage.Stage;

// [Snipped definitions for rotors, reflector, row1, row2, row3,
//   lamps, innerWidth, innerHeight and paper: see previous version]

Stage {
    // [Snipped Scene, title, resizable and
    //   onClose: see previous version]

    extensions: [
        AppletStageExtension {                           // Plug extension into Stage
            shouldDragStart: function(e: MouseEvent): Boolean {   // Condition to begin drag action
                return e.shiftDown and e.primaryButtonDown;
            }
            useDefaultClose: true;                       // Closing X button
        }
    ];
}

// [Snipped createRow(), createKey(), createLamp(),
//   handleKeyPress() and encodePosition(): see first version]
```

Your eyes do not deceive you: the entire extent of the modifications amount to nothing more than eight lines of new code and two extra class imports (only one of which specifically relates to applets). The modifications center on an enhancement to the `Stage` object. To accommodate specific needs of individual platforms and environments, JavaFX supports an extension mechanism, using subclasses of `javafx.stage.StageExtension`. The specific extension we're concerned with is the `AppletStageExtension`, which adds functionality for using the JavaFX program from inside a web page.

In truth, we're not obliged to use this extension. Most JavaFX desktop programs can be run as applets without any specific modifications, but the extension allows us to specify applet-specific behavior, thus making our application that little bit more professional.

As you can see from the code, `Stage` has an `extensions` property that accepts a sequence of `StageExtension` objects. We've used an instance of `AppletStageExtension`, which does two things. First, it specifies when a mouse event should be considered the start of a drag action to rip the applet out of the web page and onto the desktop. Second, it adds a close box to the applet when on the desktop. But simply changing our application isn't enough; for effective deployment on the web we need to package it into a JAR file. And that's just what we'll do next.

9.4.2 The JavaFX Packager utility

The JavaFX SDK comes with a neat little utility to help deploy our JavaFX programs. It can be used to package up our applications for all manner of different environments. For our project we want to use it to target the desktop platform and make the resulting program capable of running as an applet.

> **NetBeans users, take note**
>
> As always, I'm going to show you how the packaging process works under the hood, sans IDE. If you've using NetBeans, however, you may want to look over the following step-by-step tutorial for how to access the same functionality inside your IDE:
>
> http://javafx.com/docs/tutorials/deployment/

The `javafxpackager` utility can be called from the command line and has a multitude of options. Table 9.1 is a list of what's available.

Table 9.1 `JavaFXPackager` options

Option(s)	Function
`-src` or `-sourcepath`	The location of your JavaFX Script source code (mandatory).
`-cp` or `-classpath` or `-librarypath`	The location of dependencies, extra JAR files your code relies on.
`-res` or `-resourcepath`	The location of resources, extra data, and image files your code relies on.
`-d` or `-destination`	The directory to write the output.
`-workDir`	The temporary directory to use when building the output.
`-v` or `-verbose`	Print useful (debugging) information during the packaging process.
`-p` or `-profile`	Which environment to target. Either `DESKTOP` or `MOBILE` (desktop includes applets).
`-appName` and `-appVendor` and `-appVersion`	Meta information about the application: its name, creator's name, and version.
`-appClass`	The startup class name, including package prefix (mandatory).
`-appWidth` and `-appHeight`	Application width and height (particularly useful for applets).
`-appCodebase`	Codebase of where the application is hosted, if available on the web. This is the base address of where the JNLP, JAR, and other files are located.

Table 9.1 `JavaFXPackager` options *(continued)*

Option(s)	Function
`-draggable`	Make applet draggable from the browser and onto the desktop.
`-sign` and `-keystore` and `-keystorePassword` and `-keyalias` and `-keyaliasPassword`	Used to sign an applet to grant it extra permissions.
`-pack200`	Use Java-specific compression (usually much tighter than plain JAR).
`-help` and `-version`	Useful information about packager utility.

Now that you've familiarized yourself with the options, it's time to see the packager in action.

9.4.3 *Packaging up the applet*

Before we can run the packager for ourselves, we need to make one change. In previous versions of this project we simply copied the FXZ files into the package directory created by our compiler. For the `javafxpackager` to work, we need to put the files in their own resource directory. (Of course, if you're using an IDE you probably already have set up this directory, so your IDE could copy the necessary resources alongside the code during the build process.)

1. Next to the src directory that holds the project source code, create a new directory called res.
2. Inside the new res directory create one called jfxia and then one inside that called chapter9. You should end up with a directory structure of res/jfxia/chapter9 (or res\jfxia\chapter9 if you prefer DOS backslashes) inside the project directory.
3. Copy the two FXZ files we're using for our project into the chapter9 directory.

Now we're ready to run the packager. Open a new command console (such as an MS-DOS console on Windows) and change into the project directory, such that the src and res directories live off your current directory. Assuming the JavaFX tools are on your current command path, type (all on one line):

```
javafxpackager -src .\src -res .\res
  -appClass "jfxia.chapter9.Enigma"
  -appWidth 450 -appHeight 520
  -draggable -pack200 -sign
```

Alternatively, if you're running a Unix-flavored machine, try this:

```
javafxpackager -src ./src -res ./res
  -appClass "jfxia.chapter9.Enigma"
  -appWidth 450 -appHeight 520
  -draggable -pack200 -sign
```

I've broken the command over several lines; you might want to turn it into a script (or batch file) if you plan to run the packager from outside an IDE often. Let's look at the options, chunk by chunk:

- `-src` is the location of our source code files. The packager attempts to build the source code, so it needs to know where it lives.
- `-res` is the location of any resource, which in our case is the res directory housing copies of our FXZ files.
- `-appClass` is the startup class for our application.
- `-appWidth` and `-appHeight` are the size of the applet.
- `-draggable` activates the ability to drag the applet out of the browser (but our code controls what key/mouse events will trigger this).
- `-pack200` uses supertight compression on the resulting application archive.
- `-sign` signs the output so we can ask to be granted extra permissions when it runs on the end user's machine. Even though our applet doesn't do anything dangerous, we may trigger a security problem when running it directly from the computer's file system (using a file: URL location). Since we don't provide any keystore details, the packager will create a short-term self-signed certificate for us, which will be fine for testing purposes.
- `-cp` (classpath) informs the packager about any extra JAR dependencies, so they can be included in the build process and copied into the distribution output. We don't need any extra JARs, so I've not used this option (although remember, if you're building code under JavaFX 1.0, you may need to reference the Production Suite's javafx-fxd-1.0.jar file, because it wasn't shipped as standard).

If all went well, you should end up with a new directory, called dist. This name is the default when we don't specify a `-destination` option. Inside, we have all the files we need to run the Enigma applet.

- Enigma.jar and Enigma.jar.pack.gz, which contain our project's classes and resources in both plain JAR and Pack200 format.
- Enigma.jnlp and Enigma_browser.jnlp, which hold the Java Web Start (JWS) details for our Enigma machine in regular desktop and applet variants.
- Enigma.html, an HTML file we can use to launch our applet. We can copy the core markup from this file into any web page hosting the applet.
- If you package a project using the `-cp` option to list dependent JARs, a lib directory will be created to contain copies of them.

From the desktop, enter the `dist` directory and double-click (or otherwise open) the HTML file. Your favorite web browser should start, and eventually the Enigma applet should appear in all its glory. It may take some time initially, as the JavaFX libraries are not bundled in the distribution the package creates but loaded over the web from the `javafx.com` site. This is to ensure maximum efficiency—why should

> **Java Web Start, JNLP, and applet security**
>
> JWS is a way of packaging and distributing Java desktop applications, deployable from a single click. Although usually started from a web link in the first instance, a JWS program can install desktop icon shortcuts and uninstall options in appropriate places for the host OS, resembling any other locally installed application. Cached copies of the application JARs may be held locally for speed, but the application is tied firmly to its origin web address, with updates fetched as required.
>
> The JNLP file format (Java Network Launch(ing) Protocol) is at the heart of JWS. It provides metadata about an application the JRE needs to install and manage it. In Java 6 update 10 the reach of JNLP was extended to include applets, as this web page explains:
>
> http://java.sun.com/developer/technicalArticles/javase/newapplets/
>
> JavaFX doesn't change the underlying security model of Java, either for applets or JWS applications. Unsigned applets (those not requiring user permission to run) are typically restricted in their network access and ability to interact with local computer resources. Signed applets can use the JNLP file to request extra privileges, which the user can grant or deny. Expert end users can also edit a special policy file to automatically grant or deny permissions to Java programs, based on their origin.
>
> For an overview of JNLP and its security permissions, plus a quick tutorial on applet security, see the following web pages (split over two lines):
>
> http://java.sun.com/javase/6/docs/technotes/guides/javaws/
> developersguide/syntax.html
>
> http://java.sun.com/docs/books/tutorial/security/tour1/

every individual JFX application burden itself with local copies of the core API libraries, when they could be loaded (and maybe cached) from a single location across all JavaFX programs?

The javafx.com site holds independent copies of the JARs for each JavaFX release, and the `javafxpackager` utility writes files that target its own release, so code packaged under JavaFX 1.2 will continue to run once 1.3 is available. This enables the JavaFX team to make breaking changes to the APIs without upsetting currently deployed code.

Figure 9.11 shows the applet in action.

The Enigma machine looks just as it did when we ran it directly on the desktop, except now it's inside a browser window. Before we drag it back onto the desktop, let's look at the JNLP file and make a small modification.

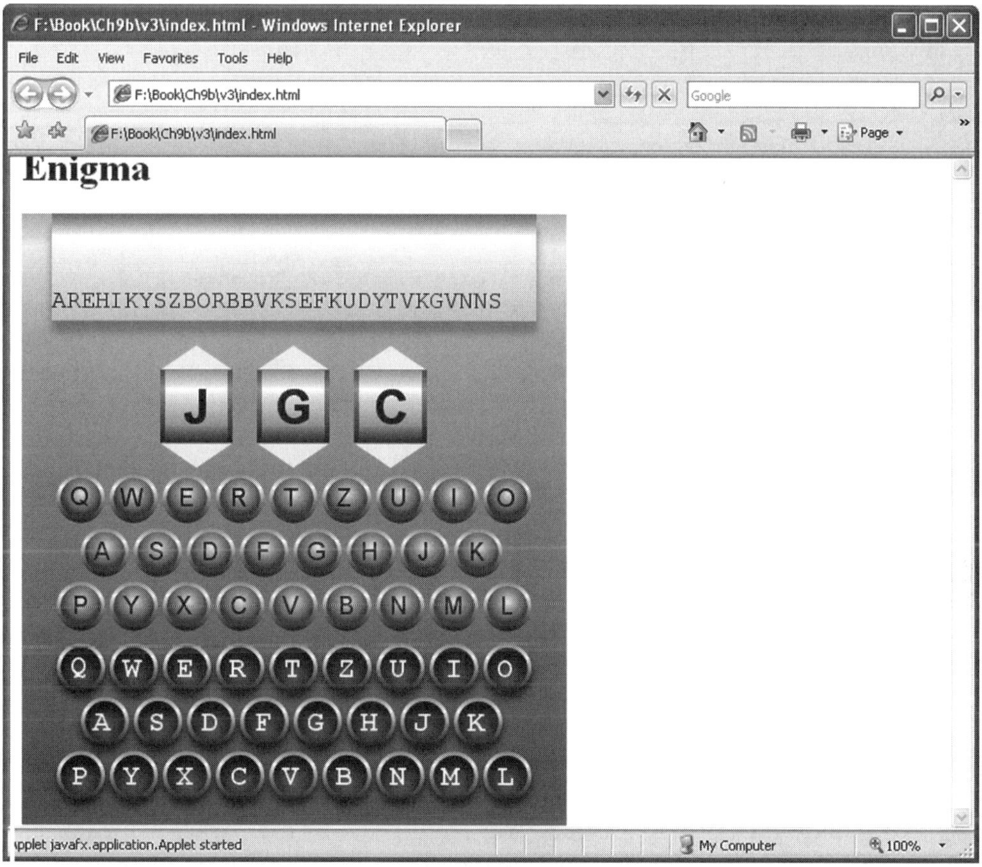

Figure 9.11 Our applet running inside Microsoft's Internet Explorer

9.4.4 Dragging the applet onto the desktop

Dragging the application out of the browser gives us the opportunity to put an icon on the desktop. By default JavaFX uses a boring generic logo, but fortunately we can change that. To do so we need to create icon files and link them into the JNLP file.

If you download the source code from the book's website, you'll find, inside this project's directory, a couple of GIF files: Enigma_32.gif and Enigma_64.gif. We'll use these as our icons (unless you fancy creating your own). Java Web Start allows us to specify icons of different sizes, for use in different situations. For the record: the first of the supplied icons is 32x32 pixels in size, and the second is 64x64 pixels in size.

Copy these two images into the dist directory, and we're ready to change the JNLP. Take a look at listing 9.14.

Listing 9.14 Enigma_browser.jnlp

```
<?xml version="1.0" encoding="UTF-8"?>
<jnlp spec="1.0+" codebase="file:/JavaFX_in_Action/dist/"
```

```
    href="Enigma_browser.jnlp">
    <information>
        <title>Enigma</title>
        <vendor>Simon</vendor>
        <homepage href=""/>
        <description>Enigma</description>
        <offline-allowed/>
        <shortcut>
            <desktop/>
        </shortcut>
        <icon href="./Enigma_32.gif" width="32" height="32" />
        <icon href="./Enigma_64.gif" width="64" height="64" />
    </information>
    <security>
        <all-permissions/>
    </security>
    <resources>
        <j2se version="1.5+"/>
        <property name="jnlp.packEnabled" value="true"/>
        <property name="jnlp.versionEnabled" value="true"/>
        <extension name="JavaFX Runtime"
            href="http://dl.javafx.com/1.2/javafx-rt.jnlp"/>
        <jar href="Enigma.jar" main="true"/>
    </resources>
    <applet-desc name="Enigma"
        main-class="com.sun.javafx.runtime.adapter.Applet"
        width="450" height="520">
        <param name="MainJavaFXScript" value="jfxia.chapter9.Enigma">
    </applet-desc>
</jnlp>
```

We have the `Enigma_browser.jnlp` file created by the packager for our application, complete with two extra lines (highlighted in bold) to hook up our icons. By studying the XML contents you can see how the details we passed into the packager were used to populate the JNLP configuration.

More JNLP information

Java Web Start supports all manner of options for controlling how Java applications behave as applets and on the desktop. Some of them are exposed by options on the JavaFX Packager, while others may require some post-packaging edits to the JNLP files. Unfortunately an in-depth discussion of JNLP is beyond the scope of this chapter. The lengthy web address below (split over two lines) points to a page with details and examples of the various JNLP options.

http://java.sun.com/javase/6/docs/technotes/
guides/javaws/developersguide/syntax.html

So much for the icons, now it's time to try dragging our applet out of the browser and turning it back into a desktop application.

Double-click the Enigma.html file inside dist to start it up again in the browser. Now hold down the Shift key on your computer, click and hold inside the applet with your mouse, and drag away from the browser. The applet should become unstuck from the browser page and float over the desktop. Remember, we specified the criteria for the start of a drag operation in the `shouldDragStart` function of the `AppletStageExtension` we plugged into our application's `Stage`.

Once it's floating free, you can let the applet go, and it will remain on the desktop. Figure 9.12 shows how it might look. In place of the applet on the web page there should appear a default Java logo, showing where the applet once lived. In the top-right corner of our floating applet there should be a tiny close button, a result of us specifying `useDefaultClose` in the extension.

We now have two courses of action:

- Clicking the applet's close button while the applet's web page is still open returns the applet to its original home, inside the web page.
- Clicking the web page's close button while the applet is outside the browser (on the desktop) causes the browser window (or tab) to close and the applet to be installed onto our desktop, including a desktop icon.

Even though the applet's web page may have vanished, the applet continues to run without a hitch. It is now truly independent of the browser. This means getting the

Figure 9.12 Starting life in a web page, our Enigma emulator was then dragged onto the desktop to become an application (note the desktop icon) and finally relaunched from the desktop.

Enigma emulator onto the desktop is as simple as pulling it from the browser window and closing the page. The applet will automatically transform into a desktop application, complete with startup icon (although in reality it remains a JWS application, it merely has a new home).

Removing the application should be as simple as following the regular uninstall process for software on your operating system. For example, Windows users can use the Add or Remove Programs feature inside Control Panel. Enigma will be listed along with other installed applications, with a button to remove it.

At last we have a fully functional JavaFX applet.

9.5 Bonus: Building the UI in an art tool

Before we get to the summing up, there's just enough time for another quick end-of-chapter detour. At the end of section 9.2.6, when we coded the Enigma's lamps, I mentioned the possibility of building an entire UI inside a design/art tool. In this section we're going to do just that. Figure 9.13 shows a UI constructed in Inkscape. The left-hand side of the window contains two buttons, each constructed from four layers stacked atop each other. The right-hand side indicates how those layers are formed.

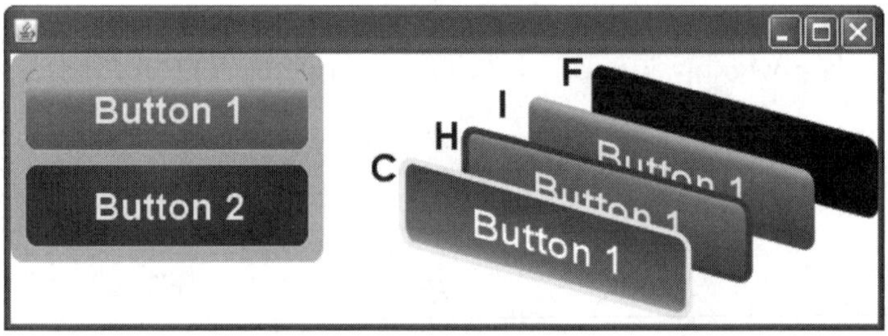

Figure 9.13 Two buttons (left), each formed using four carefully labeled layers (demonstrated right), which are manipulated by JavaFX code to create functioning buttons

Each button layer has an ID consisting of a base ID for that button, followed by a letter denoting the layer's function: either F (footprint), I (idle), H (hover), or C (clicked). The *idle* layer is shown when the button is idle (not hovered over or pressed), the *hover* layer is shown when the mouse is inside the button, and the *clicked* layer is shown when the button is pressed. Only one of these three layers is visible at any one time. The final layer, *footprint,* is used as a target for event handlers and to define the shape of the button; it is never actually displayed.

Listing 9.15 is sample code that loads the FXD created from the Inkscape file and manipulates the two buttons inside it. The first button has a base ID of `button1`, and the second has a base ID of `button2`.

Listing 9.15 UI.fx

```
import javafx.fxd.FXDNode;
import javafx.scene.Node;
import javafx.scene.input.MouseEvent;
import javafx.scene.Scene;
```

```
import javafx.stage.Stage;

def ui:FXDNode = FXDNode { url: "{__DIR__}ui.fxz" };
FXDButton {
    fxd: ui;
    id: "button1";
    action: function() { println("Button 1 clicked"); }
}
FXDButton {
    fxd: ui;
    id: "button2";
    action: function() { println("Button 2 clicked"); }
}

Stage {
    scene: Scene {
        content: ui;        <-- Root scene graph node of FXD
    }
}

class FXDButton {
    var footprintNode:Node;
    var idleNode:Node;
    var hoverNode:Node;
    var clickNode:Node;

    public-init var fxd:FXDNode;
    public-init var id:String;
    public-init var action:function():Void;

    init {
        footprintNode = fxd.getNode("{id}F");
        idleNode = fxd.getNode("{id}I");
        hoverNode = fxd.getNode("{id}H");
        clickNode = fxd.getNode("{id}C");
        makeVisible(idleNode);

        footprintNode.onMouseEntered = function(ev:MouseEvent) {
            makeVisible(
                if(footprintNode.pressed) clickNode
                    else hoverNode
            );
        }
        footprintNode.onMouseExited = function(ev:MouseEvent) {
            makeVisible(idleNode);
        }
        footprintNode.onMousePressed = function(ev:MouseEvent) {
            makeVisible(clickNode);
            if(action!=null) action();
        }
        footprintNode.onMouseReleased = function(ev:MouseEvent) {
            makeVisible(
                if(footprintNode.hover) hoverNode
                    else idleNode
            );
        }
    }
```

```
    function makeVisible(n:Node) : Void {
        for(i:Node in [idleNode,hoverNode,clickNode])
            i.visible = (i==n);
    }
}
```

The FXDButton class is the hub of the action, turning parts of the FXD scene graph into a button. It accepts an FXDNode object, a base ID, and an action function to run when the button is clicked. During initialization it locates the four required layer nodes inside the FXD structure and adds the necessary event code to make them function as a button. For example, a base ID of button1 extracts nodes with IDs of button1F, button1I, button1H, and button1C and then adds event handlers to the footprint node to control the visibility of the other three according to mouse events. (In the original Inkscape file the layers were labeled with IDs of jfx:button1F, jfx:button1I, etc.)

The beauty of this scheme is that a designer can create whole UI scene graphs inside Inkscape, Photoshop, or Illustrator, and then a programmer can turn them into functional user interfaces without having to recompile the code each time the design is tweaked. This brings us perilously close to the Holy Grail of desktop software programming: no more tedious and inflexible reconstructions of a designer's artwork using UI widgets and fiddly layout code; designers draw what they want, and programmers breathe life directly into their art.

I'm certainly not suggesting that in the future every UI will be constructed this way. This technique suits UIs resembling interactive photos or animations, an informal style previously used only in video games and children's software but now becoming increasingly trendy with other types of software too. I expect most UIs will become a fusion of the formal and informal—an audio production tool, for example, may have a main window looking just like a picture of a studio mixing desk, but *secondary* windows will still use familiar widgets (albeit styled).

As JavaFX (and its supporting tool set) continues to grow, we can expect more and more animation and transition capabilities to be shifted away from the source code and exposed directly to the designer. While highly sophisticated UIs will probably always need to be developed predominantly by a programmer, the ultimate goal of JFX is to allow simple (bold, fun, colorful) UIs to be developed in design tools and then plugged into the application at runtime. Updating the UI becomes as simple as exporting a new FXD/FXZ file.

9.6 Summary

In this chapter we looked at writing a practical application, with a swish front end, focusing on a couple of important JavaFX skills. First of all we looked at how to take the hard work of a friendly neighborhood graphic designer, bring it directly into our JavaFX project, and manipulate it as part of the JFX scene graph. Then we examined how to take our own hard work and magically transform it into an applet capable of being dragged from the browser and turned into a JWS application. (Okay, okay, it's not *actually* magic!)

I hope this chapter, as well as being a fun little project, has demonstrated how easy it is to move JavaFX software from one environment to another and how simple it is to move multimedia elements from artist to programmer. The addition of a `Stage` extension was all it took to add applet-specific capabilities to our Enigma machine, and conversion into FXZ files was all it took to turn our vector images into programmable elements in our project.

There are plans to bring JavaFX to many different types of device in the future. The ability to leap across environments in a single bound would be a welcome change to the current drudgery of moving applications between platforms. The bonus section revealed how entire UIs could be drawn by a designer and then hooked up directly into JavaFX code. Imagine if we could switch the whole design of our application for desktop, mobile, or TV by merely choosing which FXZ file was loaded on startup! It's this sense of freedom, in both *how* we work and *where* our code can run, that will be central to JavaFX as it evolves in years to come.

So much for the future. For now, I'll just set the Enigma rotors to an appropriate three letters (I'll let you guess what they might be) and leave you with the simple departing message "NIAA CHZ ZBPS DVD AWOBHC RKNAHI."

10 Clever graphics and smart phones

The chapter covers

- Constructing complex scene graphs
- Handling device-agnostic key input
- Going mobile, with the phone emulator
- Tuning apps, for better performance

Previous projects in this book have introduced a lot of fresh material and concepts, covering the core of the JavaFX Script language and its associated JavaFX APIs. Although we haven't explored every nook and cranny of JavaFX, by now you should have experienced a representative enough sample to navigate the remainder of the API without getting lost or confused. So this chapter is a deliberate shift down a gear or two.

Over the coming pages we won't be discovering any new libraries, classes, or techniques. Instead, this chapter's project will focus on a couple of goals. We'll start by reinforcing the skills you've acquired thus far, pushing the scene graph in directions you've previously not seen, and then end by moving our finished project onto the JavaFX Mobile platform.

This chapter is being written against JavaFX release 1.2 (June 2009), and, regrettably, at the time of this writing, the mobile emulator is bundled only with the Windows JavaFX SDK. This is an omission the JFX team is committed to address soon; hopefully the fruits of their labor will be available by the time this book reaches you. Despite the limitations of the mobile preview, there's still a lot of value in the project. The code has been written to run in both the desktop and the mobile environments, so non-Microsoft users can work through the majority of the project while waiting for the emulator to arrive on their platform.

The scene graph code we'll soon encounter is by far our most complex and imaginative yet, so once I've rattled through an outline of the project, we'll spend a little time on the secrets of how it's put together. But, first of all, we need to know what the project is.

10.1 Amazing games: a retro 3D puzzle

It's incredible to think, when looking at the sophistication of consoles like the PlayStation and Xbox, just how far graphics have come in the last few decades. I'm just about old enough to remember the thrill of the Atari 2600 and the novelty of controlling an image on the TV set. The games back then seemed every bit as exciting as the games today, although having replayed some of my childhood favorites thanks to modern-day emulators, I'm at a loss to explain why. Some games never lose their charm, however. I discovered this the hard way, after losing the best part of a day to a Rubik's Cube I discovered while clearing out old junk.

In this chapter we're going to develop a classic 3D maze game, like the ones that sprang up on the 8-bit computers a quarter of a decade before JavaFX was even a twinkle in Chris Oliver's eye. Retro games are fun, and they're popular with phone owners; not only is there an undeniable nostalgia factor, but their clean and simple game play fits nicely with the short bursts of activity typical of mobile device usage.

Figure 10.1 Get lost! This is our simple 3D maze game. The whole thing is constructed from the JavaFX scene graph, using basic shapes.

Figure 10.1 shows our retro maze game in action. The maze is really a grid, with some of the cells as walls and others as passageways. Moving through the maze is done one cell at a time, either forward, backward, left, or right. It's also possible to turn 90 degrees clockwise or counterclockwise. There's no swish true-3D movement here; the display simply jumps one block at a time, in true Dungeon Master fashion.

To aid the player we'll add a radar, similarly retro fashioned, giving an idea of where the player is in relation to the boundaries of the maze. We'll also add a compass, spinning to show which way the view is facing. A game needs a score, so we'll track the number of moves the player has made, the objective being to solve the maze in as few moves as possible.

The interface looks fairly simple, and that's because I want to spend most of the pages ahead concentrating on the 3D part of the game rather than on mundane control panel components. The 3D effect is quite an unusual use of the scene graph, and it demands careful forward thinking and node management. Let's start by looking at the theory behind how it works.

10.1.1 Creating a faux 3D effect

One evening, many years ago, I wandered up the road where I lived at the time, and found myself transported back to Victorian London. A most surreal moment! It happened that a film crew had spent the morning shooting scenes for an episode of *Sherlock Holmes*, and the nearby terrace housing had undergone a period makeover. If you've ever visited a Hollywood-style back lot, you'll be familiar with how looks can deceive. Everything from the brick walls to the paved sidewalks is nothing more than lightweight fabrications, painted and distressed to make them look authentic.

This may surprise some readers, but the walls in our project do not use any mind-bending 3D geometry. The maze is nothing more than the illusion of 3D, creating the effect without any of the heavy lifting or number crunching. Now it's time to reveal its secrets.

Picture five squares laid out side by side in a row. Now picture another row of squares, this time twice the size, overlaid and centered atop our original squares. And a third row, again twice as big (making them four times the size of the original row), and a fourth row (eight times the original size), all overlaid and centered onto the scene. If we joined the points from all these boxes, we might get a geometry like the one in figure 10.2.

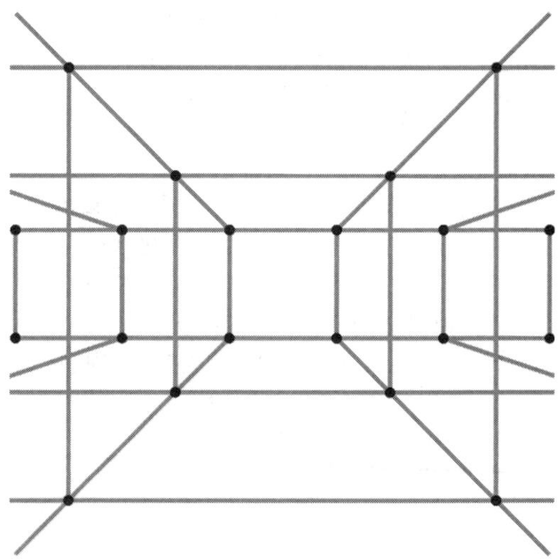

Figure 10.2 The 3D in our maze is all fake. The grid defines the maze geometry without using any complex mathematics.

Figure 10.2 has been clipped so that some of the squares are incomplete or missing. We can see the smallest row of squares, five in all, across the middle of the figure. The next row has three larger squares, the extremes of which are partially clipped. There are three even larger squares, so big only one fits fully within the clipped area, with just a fragment of its companions showing. And the final row of squares is so large they all fall entirely outside the clipping area, but we can see evidence for them in the diagonal lines leading off at the far corners of the figure. This collection of squares is all we need to construct the illusion of three dimensions.

10.1.2 Using 2D to create 3D

So, the 3D effect in our maze is entirely constructed from a plain and simple 2D grid, but how does that actually work? Figure 10.3 shows how the geometry of our 3D display is mapped to the 20 x 20 grid we're using to represent it.

By using rows of squares and connecting their points, we can build a faux 3D view. The visible area exposed in figure 10.2 fits within a grid, 20 x 20 points. Using a grid of that size we can express the coordinates of every square using integer values only. Figure 10.3 shows how those points are distributed inside (and outside) the 20 x 20 grid. Remember: even though the diagram *looks* 3D, the beauty is we're still dealing with 2D x/y points.

- Our five smallest squares (let's say they're the *farthest away*) are each 4 points wide, with the first one having its top-left and bottom-right coordinates at (0,8)-(4,12), the second at (4,8) (8,12), and so on.
- The next row of three squares is 8 points in size: (-2,6)-(6,14), then (6,6)-(14,14), and finally (14,6)-(22,14). The first and the last squares fall slightly outside the (0,0)-(20,20) viewport.
- The next row of three is 16 points in size: (-14,2)-(2,18), then (2,2)-(18,18), etc. The first and last squares fall predominantly outside the clipping viewport.
- The final row, not shown in figure 10.3, needs only one square, which falls entirely outside the clipped area, at (-6,-6)-(26,26).

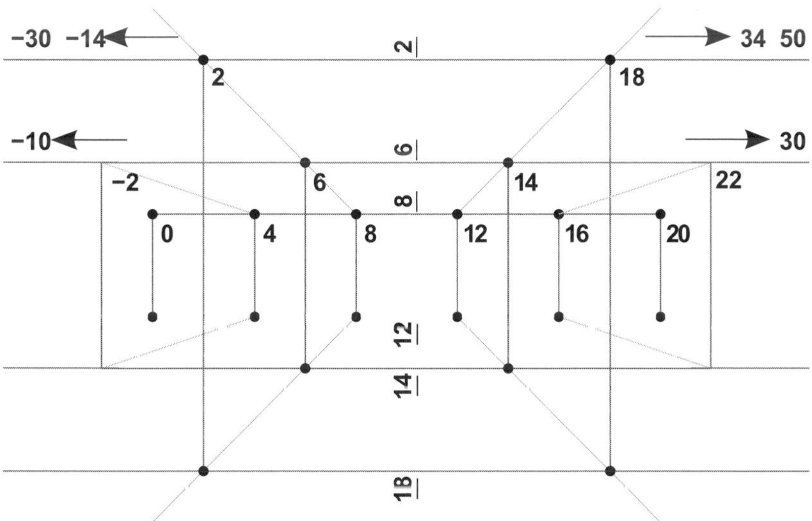

Figure 10.3 The geometry of our maze. Using a flat 20 x 20 grid as the viewport, the regular numbers describe x coordinates, and the rotated numbers (underlined) describe y coordinates.

This simple grid of points is the key behind the custom node that creates the 3D maze display. Now that we know the theory, we need to see how it works using code.

10.2 The maze game

The game we'll develop will be constructed from custom nodes, centered on a *model* class for the maze and player status. The scene graph code is simple, except for the 3D node, which is highly complex. The 3D custom node demonstrates just how far we can push JavaFX's *retained mode* graphics, with clever positioning and management of nodes, to create a display more typical of *immediate mode* (the model Swing and Java 2D use).

10.2.1 The MazeDisplay class: 3D view from 2D points

We might as well start with the most complex part of the UI, indeed probably the most involved piece of UI code you'll see in this book. The `MazeDisplay` class is the primary custom node responsible for rendering the 3D view. As with previous source code listings, this one has been broken into stages. The first of these is listing 10.1.

Listing 10.1 MazeDisplay.fx (part 1)

```
package jfxia.chapter10;

import javafx.scene.CustomNode;
import javafx.scene.Group;
import javafx.scene.Node;
import javafx.scene.paint.Color;
import javafx.scene.paint.LinearGradient;
import javafx.scene.paint.Stop;
import javafx.scene.shape.Polygon;
import javafx.scene.shape.Rectangle;

package class MapDisplay extends CustomNode {
    def xPos:Integer[] = [
         0,  4,  8, 12, 16, 20 ,
       -10, -2,  6, 14, 22, 30 ,
       -30,-14,  2, 18, 34, 50 ,
       -70,-38, -6, 26, 58, 90
    ];
    def yPos:Integer[] = [
         8,  6,  2, -6 ,
        12, 14, 18, 26
    ];

    public-init var map:Map;

    var wallVisible:Boolean[];
    def scale:Integer = 12;
// Part 2 is listing 10.2
```

Annotations: Horizontal points on faux 3D — Vertical points on faux 3D — Map data — Manipulates scene graph — Scale points on screen

We have the opening to our maze view class, and already we're seeing some pretty crucial code for making the 3D effect work.

The opening tables, `xPos` and `yPos`, represent the points on the 20 x 20 grid shown in figure 10.3. Each line in the `xPos` table represents the horizontal coordinate for five squares. Even though *nearer* (larger) rows require only three squares or one square, we use five consistently to balance the table and make it easier to access. Each line contains six entries because we need not just the left-side coordinate but the right side too; the final entry defines the right-hand side of the final square. The first line in the table represents the row of squares farthest away (smallest), with each successive line describing nearer (larger) rows.

The `yPos` table documents the vertical coordinate for each row. The first line describes the y positions for the tops of the farthest (smallest) row, through to the nearest (largest) row. The next line does the same for the bottoms. We'll be using the `xPos` and `yPos` tables when we build our scene graph, shortly. Meanwhile, let's consider the remainder of the variables:

- `map` variable is where we get our maze data from. It's an instance of the `Map` class, which we'll see later.
- The `wallVisible` boolean sequence is used to manipulate the scene graph once it has been created.
- `scale` decides how many pixels each point in our 20 x 20 grid is worth. Setting `scale` to 12 results in a maze display of 240 x 240 pixels, ideal for our mobile environment. Larger or smaller values allow us to size the maze to other display dimensions.

The next step is to create the application's scene graph. Listing 10.2 shows how it fits together.

Listing 10.2 MazeDisplay.fx (part 2)

```
// Part 1 is listing 10.1
    override function create() : Node {
        def n:Node = Group {
            content: [
                Rectangle {
                    width: 20*scale;
                    height: 20*scale;
                    fill: LinearGradient {          <-- Sky and floor gradient
                        proportional: true;
                        endX: 0.0;  endY: 1.0;
                        stops: [
                            Stop { offset: 0.0;
                                color: Color.color(0,0,.5); },
                            Stop { offset: 0.40;
                                color: Color.color(0,.125,.125); },
                            Stop { offset: 0.50;
                                color: Color.color(0,0,0); },
                            Stop { offset: 0.60;
                                color: Color.color(0,.125,0); },
                            Stop { offset: 1.0;
                                color: Color.color(.5,1,0); }
                        ];
                    };
                } ,
```

```
            _wallFront(0,4,0 , 0.15),                  Smallest row, fronts
            _wallSides(1,4,0 , 0.15,0.45),             Medium row, sides/fronts
            _wallFront(1,3,1 , 0.45),
            _wallSides(2,3,1 , 0.45,0.75),             Large row, sides/fronts
            _wallFront(1,3,2 , 0.75) ,
            _wallSides(2,3,2 , 0.75,1.00)              X-large sides
        ]
        clip: Rectangle {
            width: 20*scale;
            height: 20*scale;
        };
        cache: true;                                   Cache output
    };
    update();                                          Populate scene with map data

    n;
}
// Part 3 is listing 10.3
```

The `create()` function should, by now, be immediately recognizable as the code that creates our scene graph. It begins with a simple background `Rectangle`, using a `LinearGradient` to paint the sky and floor, gradually fading off to darkness as they approach the horizon. To populate the colors in the gradient we're using a script-level (static) function of `Color`, which returns a hue based on red, green, and blue values expressed as decimals between 0 and 1.

After the background, a series of function calls populates the graph with front-facing and side-facing walls. These are convenience functions that help keep `create()` looking nice and clean (I tend to prefix the name of such *refactored* functions with an underscore, although that's just personal style). We'll look at the mechanics of how the shapes are added to the scene in a moment, but for now let's just focus on the calls themselves. Here they are again:

```
_wallFront(0,4,0 , 0.15),
_wallSides(1,4,0 , 0.15,0.45),
_wallFront(1,3,1 , 0.45),
_wallSides(2,3,1 , 0.45,0.75),
_wallFront(1,3,2 , 0.75) ,
_wallSides(2,3,2 , 0.75,1.00)
```

The first call is to `_wallFront()`. It adds in the back row of five front-facing walls, which you can see in figure 10.4. The three-integer parameters all relate to the tables we saw in listing 10.1. The first two parameters are delimiters, from 0 to 4 (five walls), and the third parameter determines which parts of the `xPos` and `yPos` tables to use for coordinates. In this case we're using line 0 (the first six entries) in `xPos` and entry 0 in the top/bottom lines from `yPos`. In plain English this means we'll be drawing boxes 0 to 4 using horizontal coordinates 0, 4, 8, 12, 16, and 20 from `xPos` and vertical coordinates 8 and 12 from `yPos`. The final, fractional parameter determines how dark to make each wall. Because these walls are the farthest away, they are set to a very low brightness.

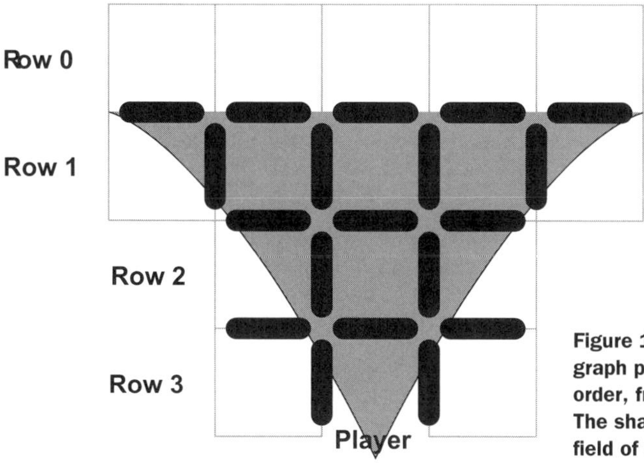

Figure 10.4 A plan view of the scene graph pieces that have to be added, in order, from back (row 0) to front (row 3). The shaded area represents the player's field of view.

The next line is a call to `_wallSides()`. It adds in the four side-facing walls, two left of center, two right of center. The first three parameters do pretty much the same thing, but there are two brightness parameters. This is because the *perspective* walls (the ones running *into* the screen) have a different brightness from their farthest to their nearest edge. The first parameter is for the farthest; the second is for the nearest.

The remaining function calls add in the other front and side walls, working from the back to the front of the 3D scene. Next, we see the actual function code (listing 10.3).

Listing 10.3 MazeDisplay.fx (part 3)

```
// Part 1 is listing 10.1; part 2 is listing 10.2
    function _wallFront(x1:Integer,x2:Integer , r:Integer,
    op:Number ) : Node[] {
        for(x in [x1..x2]) {                        <- For each wall
            insert false into wallVisible;             Add on/off
            def pos:Integer = sizeof wallVisible -1;   switch

            Polygon {                               <- Front wall polygon
                points: [
                    xPos[r*6+x+0]*scale , yPos[0+r]*scale , // UL
                    xPos[r*6+x+1]*scale , yPos[0+r]*scale , // UR
                    xPos[r*6+x+1]*scale , yPos[4+r]*scale , // LR
                    xPos[r*6+x+0]*scale , yPos[4+r]*scale   // LL
                ];
                fill: Color.color(0,op,0);
                visible: bind wallVisible[pos];     <- Bind to on/off
            };                                         switch
        }
    }

    function _wallSides(x1:Integer,x2:Integer , r:Integer,
    opBack:Number,opFore:Number) : Node[] {
        var half:Integer = x1 + ((x2-x1)/2).intValue();   For each
        for(x in [x1..x2]) {                           <- wall
```

```
            def rL:Integer = if(x>half) r else r+1;          Near/far edge?
            def rR:Integer = if(x>half) r+1 else r;
            def opL:Number = if(x>half) opBack else opFore;   Near/far
            def opR:Number = if(x>half) opFore else opBack;   brightness?

            insert false into wallVisible;                 Add on/off
            def pos:Integer = sizeof wallVisible -1;        switch

            Polygon {                                   <-- Side wall polygon
                points: [
                    xPos[rL*6+x]*scale , yPos[0+rL]*scale , // UL
                    xPos[rR*6+x]*scale , yPos[0+rR]*scale , // UR
                    xPos[rR*6+x]*scale , yPos[4+rR]*scale , // LR
                    xPos[rL*6+x]*scale , yPos[4+rL]*scale   // LL
                ];
                fill: LinearGradient {
                    proportional: true;
                    endX:1;  endY:0;
                    stops: [
                        Stop {
                            offset:0;                          Left edge
                            color:Color.color(0,opL,0);        color
                        } ,
                        Stop {
                            offset:1;                          Right edge
                            color:Color.color(0,opR,0);        color
                        }
                    ];
                };
                visible: bind wallVisible[pos];    <-- Bind to on/off
            };                                         switch
        }
    }
// Part 4 is listing 10.4
```

Listing 10.3 shows the two functions responsible for adding the walls into our scene graph. The first function, `_wallFront()`, adds the front-facing walls. It loops inclusively between two delimiters, parameters `x1` and `x2`, adding `Polygon` shapes. The `r` parameter determines which row in the view we're drawing, which in turn determines the parts of the `xPos` and `yPos` tables we should use. For example, when `r = 0` the table data for the farthest (smallest) row of walls is used; when `r = 3` the nearest (largest) row is used.

The polygon forms a square using the coordinate pairs upper-left, upper-right, lower-right, and lower-left, in that order. We could have used a `Rectangle`, but using a `Polygon` makes the code more consistent with its companion `_wallSides()` function.

Because the `xPos` and `yPos` tables are, in reality, linear sequences, we need to do a little bit of math to find the correct value. Each row of horizontal coordinates in `xPos` has six points, from left to right across the view. There are two sets of vertical coordinates (upper y and lower y) in `yPos`, each with four points (rows 0 to 3). For horizontal coordinates we multiply `r` up to the right row and then add on the wall index to find the left-hand side or its next-door neighbor for the right-hand side. The vertical coordinates, which define the top and bottom of the shape, are as simple as reading the `r`th value from the first and second line of `yPos`.

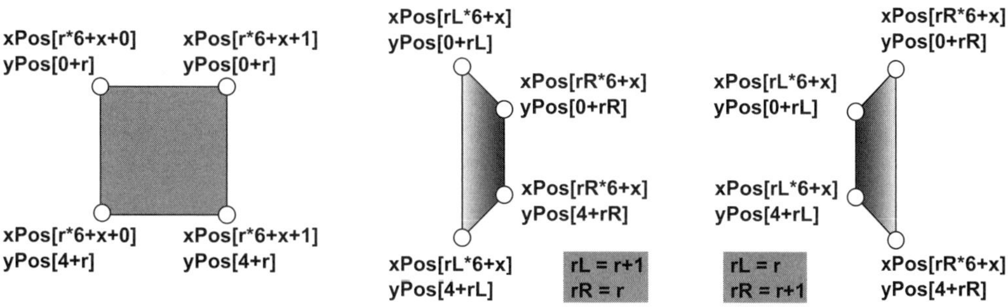

Figure 10.5 By plotting the points on our polygon, using the `xPos` and `yPos` tables for reference, we can created the illusion of perspective.

Figure 10.5 shows how the x and y coordinates are looked up inside the two tables. Remember, once we've used the tables to find the point in our 20 x 20 grid, we need to apply `scale` to multiply it up to screen-pixel coordinates.

Just before we create the polygon, we add a new boolean to `wallVisible`, and in the polygon itself we bind visibility to its index. This allows us to switch the wall on or off (visible or invisible) later in the code. This switch is key to updating the 3D view, as demonstrated in the final part of the code, in listing 10.4.

The `_wallSides()` function is a more complex variation of the function we've just studied. This time, one edge of the polygon is on one row, and the other edge is on another row. The left and right edges of the polygon are positioned depending on whether we're drawing a wall on the left side of the view or the right, in order to create the illusion of perspective. The `half` variable is used for that purpose, and instead of one `r` value we have two: one for the left and one for the right. We also have two color values for the edges of the polygon, to ensure it gets darker as it goes *deeper* into the display.

Once again we add a boolean to `wallVisible` and bind the polygon's visibility to it. But what do we do with all these booleans? The answer is in listing 10.4.

Listing 10.4 MazeDisplay.fx (part 4)

```
// Part 1 is listing 10.1; part 2, listing 10.2; part 3, listing 10.3
    package function update() : Void {
        def walls:Integer[] = [
            -2, 2,-3  ,
            -2,-1,-2  ,  1, 2,-2 ,
            -1, 1,-2  ,
            -1, 1, 1  ,  1, 1, 1 ,
            -1, 1,-1  ,
            -1,-1, 0  ,  1, 1, 0
        ];

        var idx:Integer = 0;
        var pos:Integer = 0;
        while(idx<sizeof walls) {
            var yOff:Integer = walls[idx+2];
            for(xOff in [walls[idx]..walls[idx+1]]) {
```

Row 0, fronts
Row 1, sides
Row 1, fronts
Row 2, sides
Row 2, fronts
Row 3, sides
(x1,y) to (x2,y)

```
                var rot:Integer[] = map.rotateToView(xOff,yOff);
                wallVisible[pos] = not map.isEmpty
                    (map.x+rot[0] , map.y+rot[1]);         Change visibility
                pos++;
            }
            idx+=3;        <-- Next xl, x2, y triple
        }
    }
}
```

This is our final chunk of the mammoth 3D code. Having put all our polygons in place, we need to update the 3D view by switching their visibility on or off, depending on which cells of the map inside our viewport are walls and which are empty (passageways). We do this each time the player moves, using the `update()` function.

A reminder: we added rows of polygons into our scene graph, in sequence, from farthest to nearest. At the same time we added booleans to `wallVisible` in the same order, tying them to the corresponding polygon's visibility. These booleans are the means by which we will now manipulate each wall polygon. As we move around the maze, different parts of the map fall inside our field of view (the viewport). The wall nodes never get moved or deleted, and when a given cell of the map has no wall block present, the corresponding polygons are simply made invisible (they're still there in the graph; they just don't get drawn).

The `update()` function looks at map positions, relative to the player's position and orientation (facing north, south, east, or west), and sets the visibility boolean on the corresponding node of the scene graph. Figure 10.6 shows how the relative coordinates relate to the player's position at (0,0).

We need to work through each polygon node in the scene graph, relate it to an x/y coordinate in the map, and set the corresponding `wallVisible` boolean to turn the polygon on or off. The `walls` table at the start of the code holds sets of x1, x2, and y

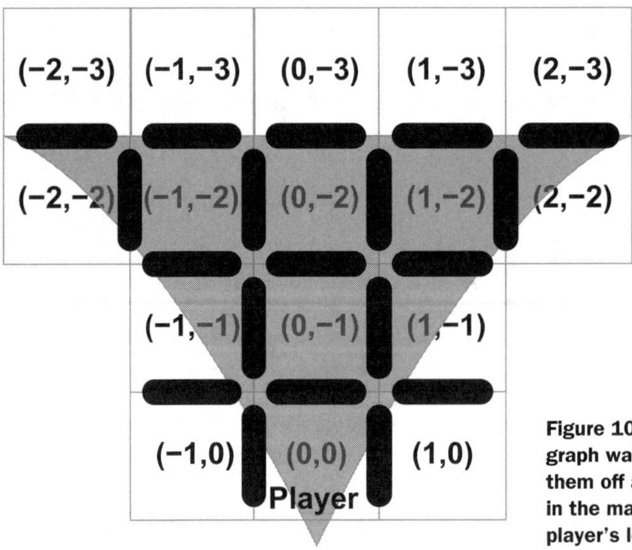

Figure 10.6 Having created our scene graph walls, we need to be able to switch them off and on depending on which cells in the map are wall blocks, relative to the player's location.

triples that control this process. Let's remind ourselves of the table, with one eye on figure 10.6, so we can see what that means:

```
def walls:Integer[] =
[   -2, 2,-3  ,
    -2,-1,-2  ,   1, 2,-2 ,
    // Snipped
]
```

The first nodes in the scene graph are the back walls, which run from coordinates (-2,-3) to (2,-3) relative to our player's position, where (0,0) is the cell the player is currently standing on. This is why our first triple is -2,2,-3 (x = -2 to x = 2, with y = -3).

Next we have four side walls, controlled by cells (-2,-2) and (-1,-2) on the left-hand side of the view and (1,-2) and (2,-2) on the right. You can see that the second line of `walls` has the corresponding triples. (We don't bother with the central cell, (0,-2), because that cell's side walls are entirely obscured by its front-facing polygon.)

The remaining lines in `walls` deal with the rest of the scene graph, row by row. All of these values are fed into a loop, translating the table into on/off settings for each wall polygon.

```
var idx:Integer = 0;
var pos:Integer = 0;
while(idx<sizeof walls) {
    var yOff:Integer = walls[idx+2];
    for(xOff in [walls[idx]..walls[idx+1]]) {
        var rot:Integer[] = map.rotateToView(xOff,yOff);
        wallVisible[pos] = not map.isEmpty
            (map.x+rot[0] , map.y+rot[1]);
        pos++;
    }
    idx+=3;
}
```

The `while` loop works its way through the `walls` table, three entries at a time; the variable `idx` stores the current offset into `walls`. Remember, the first value in the triple is the start x coordinate, the second is the end x coordinate, and the third is the y coordinate. The nested `for` loop then works through these coordinates, rotating them to match the player's direction and adding them into the current player x/y position to get the absolute cell in the map to query. We then query the cell to see if it is empty or not.

Once this code has run, each of the polygons in the scene graph will be visible or invisible, depending on its corresponding entry in the map. And voilà, our 3D display is alive!

I did warn you this was the most complex piece of scene graph code in the book, and I'm sure it didn't disappoint. You may have to scan the details a couple of times just to ensure they sink in. The purpose behind this example is to show that retained mode graphics (scene graph-based, in other words) don't have to be simple shapes. They are capable of complexity similar to immediate-mode graphics. All it takes is a little planning and imagination. You'll be glad to hear the remaining custom nodes are trivial by comparison.

10.2.2 The Map class: where are we?

Now that we've seen the MapDisplay class, it's time to introduce the *model* class that provides its data. Listing 10.5 provides the code.

Listing 10.5 Map.fx (part 1)

```
package jfxia.chapter10;

package class Map
{    def wallMap:Integer[] = [
         1,1,1,1,1,1,1,1,1,1,1,1,1,1,1,1 ,
         1,0,0,1,0,1,0,0,0,0,0,0,0,1,0,1 ,
         1,1,0,1,0,1,1,1,0,1,1,0,1,1,0,1 ,
         1,0,0,1,0,1,0,1,0,0,0,0,0,1,0,1 ,
         1,0,1,1,0,1,0,1,0,1,1,1,0,0,0,1 ,
         1,0,0,1,0,0,0,1,0,1,0,1,1,1,1,1 ,
         1,0,0,1,1,1,1,1,0,1,0,0,0,0,0,1 ,
         1,0,1,1,0,0,0,1,0,1,1,1,0,1,0,1 ,
         1,0,0,1,1,0,1,1,0,0,0,1,0,1,1,1 ,
         1,1,0,0,0,0,0,1,0,1,1,1,0,1,0,1 ,
         1,0,0,1,1,0,1,1,0,0,1,0,0,0,0,1 ,
         1,1,0,0,1,0,0,1,1,0,1,0,1,0,0,1 ,
         1,0,0,1,1,1,0,0,0,0,0,0,1,1,0,1 ,
         1,0,0,0,1,0,0,1,1,0,1,1,1,0,0,1 ,
         1,1,0,0,0,1,0,1,0,0,0,0,0,0,0,1 ,
         1,1,1,1,1,1,1,1,1,1,1,1,1,1,1,1
     ];

     package def width:Integer = 16;
     package def height:Integer = 16;

     package def startX:Integer = 1;
     package def startY:Integer = 1;
     package def endX:Integer = 14;
     package def endY:Integer = 1;

     public-read var x:Integer;
     public-read var y:Integer;
     public-read var dir:Integer;
     public-read var success:Boolean =
         bind ((x==endX) and (y==endY));
// Part 2 is in listing 10.6
```

Maze wall data; I is a wall, 0 is an empty space

Dimensions of map

Start and end cells

Current player position/direction

Reached the end yet?

In listing 10.5 have the first half of our Map class. It begins with a huge table defining which parts of the map are walls and which are passageways. Immediately following that we have the dimensions of the map, 16 x 16 cells, followed by the cells that denote the start and end locations.

The public-read variables expose the current cell (x and y) the player is standing on and which direction the player is facing. North is 0, east is 1, south is 2, and west is 3. Finally we have a convenience boolean, true when the player's location is the same as the end location (and the maze has therefore been solved).

Let's move on the listing 10.6, which is the second part of the `Map` class.

Listing 10.6 Map.fx (part 2)

```
// Part 1 is listing 10.5
    init {
        x = startX;
        y = startY;
    }

    package function isEmpty(x:Integer,y:Integer) : Boolean {
        if(x<0 or y<0 or x>=width or y>=height) { return false; }
        var idx:Integer = y*width+x;
        return( wallMap[idx]==0 );
    }

    package function moveRel(rx:Integer,ry:Integer,rt:Integer) : Boolean {
        if(rx!=0 or ry!=0)
        {   def rot:Integer[] = rotateToView(rx,ry);
            if(isEmpty(x+rot[0],y+rot[1])) {
                x+=rot[0];  y+=rot[1];
                return true;
            }
            else {
                return false;
            }
        }
        else if(rt<0) {
            dir=(dir+4-1) mod 4;
            return true;
        }
        else if(rt>0) {
            dir=(dir+1) mod 4;
            return true;
        }
        else {
            return false;
        }
    }

    package function rotateToView(x:Integer,y:Integer) : Integer[] {
        [   if(dir==1) 0-y
                else if(dir==2) 0-x
                else if(dir==3) y
                else x ,
            if(dir==1) x
                else if(dir==2) 0-y
                else if(dir==3) 0-x
                else y
        ];
    }
}
```

Annotations: Moving x/y? — Rotate coordinates — If possible, move to cell — Turn left (counterclockwise) — Turn right (clockwise) — Calculate absolute x coordinate — Calculate absolute y coordinate

In the conclusion of the `Map` class we have a set of useful functions for querying the map data and updating the player's position.

- The `init` block assigns the player's current location from the map's start location.
- `isEmpty()` returns `true` if the cell at x and y has no wall. We saw it in action during the update of the 3D maze, determining whether nodes should be visible or invisible.
- `moveRel()` accepts three parameters, controlling x movement, y movement, and rotation. It returns `true` if the move was performed. The parameters are used to move the player relative to the current position *and orientation* or rotate their view. If `rx` or `ry` is not 0, the relative positions are added to the current player location (the `rx` and `ry` coordinates are based on the direction the player is currently facing, so the `rotateToView()` orientates them the same way as the map). If the `rt` parameter is not 0, it is used to rotate the player's current orientation.
- `rotateToView()` is the function we've seen used repeatedly whenever we needed to translate relative coordinates facing in the player's current orientation to relative coordinates orientated north. If I move forward one cell, the relative movement is x = 0, y = -1 (vertically one cell up, horizontally no cells). But if I'm facing east at the time, this needs to be translated to x = 1, y = 0 (horizontally right one cell, vertically no cells) to make sense on the map data. The `rotateToView()` function translates this player-centric movement into a map-centric movement, returning a sequence of two values: x and y.

So that's our `Map` class. There are three simple custom nodes we need to look at before we pull everything together into our main application. So let's deal with them quickly.

10.2.3 The Radar class: this is where we are

The `Radar` class is a simple class for displaying the position of the player within the bounds of the maze, as show in the bottom-left corner of figure 10.7.

The radar has a kind of 8-bit retro style, in keeping with the simple, unfussy graphics of the maze. It doesn't show the walls of the maze—that would make the game too easy—just a pulsing circle representing where the player is and a yellow square for the goal.

Let's take a look at the code, courtesy of listing 10.7.

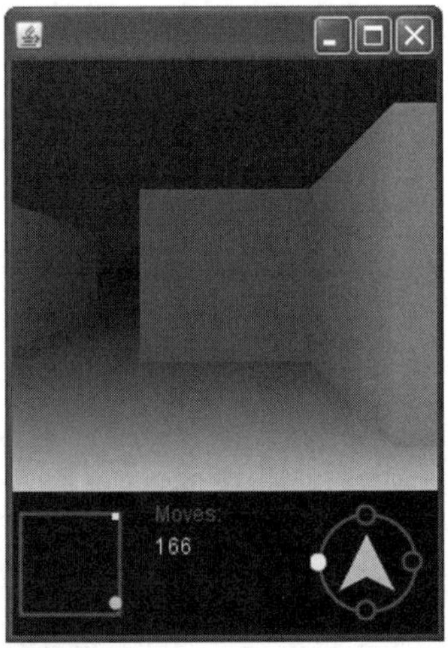

Figure 10.7 The maze game, complete with radar in the bottom left-hand corner and a compass in the bottom right

Listing 10.7 Radar.fx

```
package jfxia.chapter10;

import javafx.animation.transition.ScaleTransition;
import javafx.animation.Timeline;
import javafx.scene.CustomNode;
import javafx.scene.Group;
import javafx.scene.Node;
```

```
import javafx.scene.paint.Color;
import javafx.scene.shape.Circle;
import javafx.scene.shape.Rectangle;

package class Radar extends CustomNode
{   def cellSize:Number = 4;
    def border:Number = 8;
    public-init var map:Map;

    override function create() : Node {
        var c:Circle;
        var n:Group = Group {
            def w = map.width*cellSize;
            def h = map.height*cellSize;

            layoutX: border;
            layoutY: border;
            content: [
                Rectangle  {                    <-- Background rectangle
                    width: w;  height: h;
                    fill: null;
                    stroke: Color.GREEN;
                    strokeWidth:2;
                } ,
                c = Circle {                    <-- Circle presenting player
                    layoutX: cellSize/2;
                    layoutY: cellSize/2;
                    centerX: bind map.x * cellSize;
                    centerY: bind map.y * cellSize;
                    radius: cellSize;
                    fill: Color.LIGHTGREEN;
                } ,
                Rectangle {                     <-- End marker
                    x: map.endX * cellSize;
                    y: map.endY * cellSize;
                    width: cellSize;
                    height: cellSize;
                    fill: Color.YELLOW;
                }
            ];
            clip: Rectangle {
                width: w + border*2;
                height: h + border*2;
            }
        }

        ScaleTransition {                       <-- Infinite scale in/out
            node: c;
            duration: 0.5s;
            fromX: 0.2;  fromY: 0.2;
            toX: 1;  toY: 1;
            autoReverse: true;
            repeatCount: Timeline.INDEFINITE;
        }.play();

        n;
    }
}
```

The Radar class is a very simple scene graph coupled with a ScaleTransition. The cellSize is the pixel dimension each maze cell will be scaled to on our display. You'll recall from the Map class that the maze is 16 x 16 cells in size. At a pixel size of 4, this means the radar will be 64 x 64 pixels. And speaking of the Map class, the map variable is a local reference to the game's state and data. The border is the gap around the edge of the radar, bringing the total size to 80 x 80 pixels.

The scene graph manufactured in create() is very basic, but then it doesn't need to be fancy. Three shapes are contained within a Group, shifted by the border.

A background Rectangle, provides the boundary of the maze area, sized using the map dimensions against the cellSize constant. A Circle is used to show where the player currently is; its position is bound to the cellSize multiplied by the player's location in the map. Because a JavaFX Circle node's origin is its center point, we shift it by half a cell, to put the origin of the circle in the center of the cell. The end point in the map (the winning cell) is displayed using a yellow Rectangle.

Before we return the Group we create a ScaleTransition, continually growing and shrinking the circle from full size to just 20%. With the autoReverse flag set to true, the animation will play forward and then backward. And with repeatCount set to Timeline.INDEFINITE, it will continue to run, forward and backward, forever. (Well, at least until the program exits!)

10.2.4 The Compass class: this is where we're facing

The Compass class is another simple, retro-style class. This one spins to point in the direction the player is facing. Listing 10.8 is our compass code. It's a two-part custom node, with a static part that does not move and a mobile part that rotates to show the player's orientation. You can see what it looks like by glancing back at figure 10.7.

Listing 10.8 Compass.fx

```
package jfxia.chapter10;

import javafx.animation.transition.RotateTransition;
import javafx.scene.CustomNode;
import javafx.scene.Group;
import javafx.scene.Node;
import javafx.scene.paint.Color;
import javafx.scene.shape.Circle;
import javafx.scene.shape.Polygon;
import javafx.scene.shape.Rectangle;

package class Compass extends CustomNode {
    def size:Number = 64;
    def blobRadius:Number = 5;

    public-init var map:Map;

    var compassNode:Node;

    override function create() : Node {
        def sz2:Number = size/2;
        def sz4:Number = size/4;
```

```
        compassNode = Group {      <—— Rotating group
            content: [
                Circle {                    <—— North circle
                    centerX: sz2;               (yellow)
                    centerY: blobRadius;
                    radius: blobRadius;
                    fill: Color.YELLOW;
                } ,
                _makeCircle(blobRadius , sz2) ,                West, east, and south
                _makeCircle(size-blobRadius-1 , sz2) ,         circles (hollow)
                _makeCircle(sz2 , size-blobRadius-1)
            ]
            rotate: map.dir * 90;      <—— Initial rotation
        };

        Group {           <—— Static group
            content: [
                Circle {
                    centerX: sz2;  centerY: sz2;
                    radius: sz2-blobRadius;               Ring
                    stroke: Color.GREEN;                  circle
                    strokeWidth: 2;
                    fill: null;
                } ,

                Polygon {
                    points: [
                        sz2 , sz4 ,
                        size-sz4 , size-sz4,
                        sz2 ,  sz2+sz4/2 ,             Central
                        sz4 , size-sz4                 arrow
                    ];
                    fill: Color.LIGHTGREEN;
                } ,                                        Add in
                compassNode                         <—— rotating group
            ]
            clip: Rectangle { width:size;  height:size; }
        }
    }

    package function update() : Void {    <—— Change rotation
        RotateTransition {
            node: compassNode;
            duration: 1s;
            toAngle: map.dir * 90;      <—— Animate to
        } play();                           new direction
    }

    function _makeCircle(x:Number,y:Number) : Circle {    <—— Convenience
        Circle {                                               function:
            centerX: x;  centerY: y;                           make a circle
            radius: blobRadius;
            stroke: Color.GREEN;
            strokeWidth: 2;
        }
    }
}
```

The instance variable `size` is the diameter of the ring, while `blobRadius` helps size the circles around the ring. (Blob? Well, can *you* think of a better name?)

Inside `create()`, the `compassNode` group is the rotating part of the graph. It is nothing more than four circles (blobs) representing the points of the compass, with the northern position a solid yellow color. The other three are hollow and identical enough to be created by a convenience function, `_makeCircle()`. The `compassNode` is plugged into a static part of the scene graph, comprising a ring and an arrow polygon.

The `update()` function is called whenever the direction the player is facing changes. It kicks off a `RotateTransition` to spin the blob group, making the yellow blob face the player's direction. Because we specify only an end angle and no starting angle, the transition (conveniently) starts from the current rotate position.

10.2.5 The ScoreBoard class: are we there yet?

Only one more custom node to go; then we can write the application class itself. The scoreboard keeps track of the score and displays a winning message; its code is in listing 10.9.

Listing 10.9 ScoreBoard.fx

```
package jfxia.chapter10;

import javafx.scene.CustomNode;
import javafx.scene.Node;
import javafx.scene.layout.VBox;
import javafx.scene.paint.Color;
import javafx.scene.text.Text;
import javafx.scene.text.TextOrigin;

package class ScoreBoard extends CustomNode {
    public-init var score:Integer;
    package var success:Boolean = false;

    override function create() : Node {
        VBox {
            spacing: 5;
            content: [
                Text {
                    content: "Moves:";
                    textOrigin: TextOrigin.TOP;
                    fill: Color.GREEN;
                } ,
                Text {
                    content: bind "{score}";
                    textOrigin: TextOrigin.TOP;
                    fill: Color.YELLOW;
                } ,
                Text {
                    content: bind if(success)
                        "SUCCESS!" else "";
                    textOrigin: TextOrigin.TOP;
                    fill: Color.YELLOW;
                }
```

Static text: "Moves:"

Dynamic text: score

Success message

```
            ];
        };
    }

    package function increment() : Void
    {   if(not success)  score++;
    }
}
```

Increment score, if not success

The score panel is used in the lower-middle part of the game display. It shows the moves taken and a message if the player manages to reach the winning map cell. You can see it in action in figure 10.8.

There's not a lot to mention about this bit of scene graph; it's just three `Text` nodes stacked vertically. The `increment()` function will add to the score, but only if the `success` flag has not been set. As you'll see when we check out the application class, `success` is set to `true` once the end of the maze is reached and never unset. This prevents the score from rising once the maze has been solved.

Figure 10.8 The scoreboard sits at the bottom of the display, showing the moves used and a "SUCCESS!" message once the end of the maze is reached.

10.2.6 The MazeGame class: our application

At last we get to our application's main class, where we pull the four custom nodes previously discussed together into our game's UI. This is our application class (listing 10.10), and thanks to all the work we did with the custom nodes, it looks pretty compact and simple.

Listing 10.10 MazeGame.fx

```
package jfxia.chapter10;

import javafx.scene.Scene;
import javafx.scene.Group;
import javafx.scene.input.KeyCode;
import javafx.scene.input.KeyEvent;
import javafx.stage.Stage;

def map:Map = Map{};
var mapDisp:MapDisplay;
var scBoard:ScoreBoard;
var comp:Compass;
var gp:Group;

Stage {
    scene: Scene {
        content: gp = Group {
            content: [
```

```
                mapDisp = MapDisplay {          3D map
                    map: map;                   display
                } ,
                Radar
                {   map: map;                   Radar,
                    layoutY: 240;               lower left
                } ,
                scBoard = ScoreBoard {
                    layoutX: 88;                ScoreBoard,
                    layoutY: 248;               lower middle
                } ,
                comp = Compass {
                    map: map;                   Compass,
                    layoutX: 168;               lower right
                    layoutY: 248;
                }
            ];                                  Install keyboard
            onKeyPressed: keyHandler;           handler
        }
        width: 240;  height: 320;               Default background
        fill: javafx.scene.paint.Color.BLACK;   is white
    }
}                                               Request
gp.requestFocus();                              keyboard focus

function keyHandler(ev:KeyEvent) : Void {       Which key
    def c = ev.code;                            was pressed?
    def x:Integer =
        if(c==KeyCode.VK_LEFT) -1               Move left
        else if(c==KeyCode.VK_RIGHT) 1          or right?
        else 0;
    def y:Integer =
        if(c==KeyCode.VK_UP) -1                 Move forward
        else if(c==KeyCode.VK_DOWN) 1           or backward?
        else 0;
    def t:Integer =
        if(c==KeyCode.VK_SOFTKEY_0 or
            c==KeyCode.VK_OPEN_BRACKET) -1      Turn left
        else if(c==KeyCode.VK_SOFTKEY_1 or      or right?
            c==KeyCode.VK_CLOSE_BRACKET) 1
        else 0;

    if(x==0 and y==0 and t==0)  return;         Nothing to do? Exit!

    if( map.moveRel(x,y,t) ) {
        mapDisp.update();  comp.update();       Perform movement
        if(t==0)  scBoard.increment();          or turn
    }

    if(map.success)  scBoard.success=true;      Have we won?
}
```

After defining a few variables, we move straight into the scene graph. Since this is a top-level application class, we use a `Stage` and a `Scene` and then plug our custom nodes into it via a `Group`. The `MazeDisplay` is added first, followed by the `Radar` positioned into the bottom left-hand corner. Next to the radar is the `ScoreBoard`, and finally the `Compass` takes up the bottom right-hand corner.

The reason we used a Group, rather than plug the nodes directly into the Scene, is to give us a node we can assign a keyboard handler to. In this case it's a function by the name of keyHandler, defined outside the graph for readability sake. To make the handler work we need to request the keyboard input focus, which is the purpose of the gp.requestFocus() call.

What of the handler itself? The KeyEvent parameter contains all manner of information about the state of the keyboard when the event was generated. In this case we just want the raw code of the key that got pressed, which we copy into a handy variable. We compare this variable against the constants in the KeyCode class, to populate three more variables: x, y and t, such that x is -1 if moving left and 1 if moving right, y is -1 if moving forward and 1 if moving backward, and t is -1 if turning left (counterclockwise) and 1 if turning right (clockwise).

You'll recognize these values as the relative movements the Map class accepts to make a movement, which is precisely what we do using map.moveRel(). The function returns true if the player successfully moved or turned, which causes us to update the MazeDisplay and the Compass. If the action was a move (not a turn), we also increment the moves counter in the ScoreBoard class.

Finally we check to see if the winning cell has been reached and set the ScoreBoard's success flag if it has. Note that it never gets unset; this is so the score won't rise if the player continues to move once the maze has been solved.

And that's our complete game. Now let's try it out.

10.2.7 Running the MazeGame project

We can run the game in the usual way and navigate around in glorious 3D using the keyboard's cursor keys (the arrow keys) and the square bracket keys for turning. Without cheating by looking at the data, see if you can navigate your way to the end using only the radar and compass to aid you.

Take a look back at figures 10.7 and 10.8 to see how the game looks in action.

The game works perfectly well on the desktop, but our ultimate goal is to transfer it onto a mobile device emulator. If you're wondering how much we'll have to change to achieve that aim, then the next section might come as a pleasant surprise.

10.3 On the move: desktop to mobile in a single bound

It's time to move our application onto a cell phone or, more specifically, an emulator that simulates the limited environment of a cell phone (see figure 10.9).

In the source code for the MazeGame class (listing 10.10) you may have noticed each action of turning, either clockwise or counterclockwise, was wired to a couple of keys. The KeyCode.VK_SOFTKEY_0 and the KeyCode.VK_SOFTKEY_1 could be used in preference to KeyCode.VK_OPEN_BRACKET and KeyCode.VK_CLOSE_BRACKET. As you may have guessed, this is to accommodate the limited key input on many mobile devices.

This is really the only concession I had to make for the mobile environment. The rest of the code is mobile ready. When writing the game I was very careful to use only those classes available for the *common profile*.

The common what?

The term *profile* is used to refer to given groupings of a JavaFX class. Not every class in the JavaFX API is available across every device, because not every device has the same power or abilities. Classes that can be used only on the desktop, for example, are in the *desktop profile*. Similarly classes that may be available only on JavaFX TV are exclusive to the *TV profile* (hypothetically speaking, given that the TV platform is months from release as I write). Classes that span all environments, devices, and platforms are said to be in the *common profile*. By sticking to only the part of the JavaFX API that is in the common profile, we ensure that the maze game will work on all JavaFX platforms, including the phone emulator. But how can we find out which classes are supported by which profile?

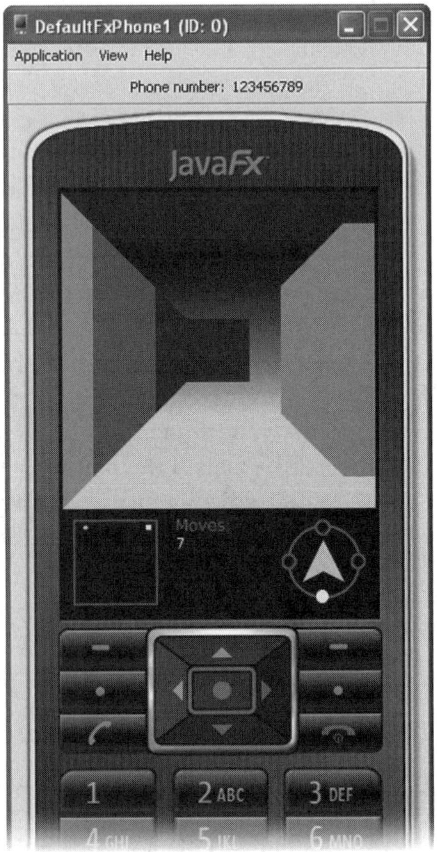

Figure 10.9 Our maze game hits the small screen. More specifically, it's running on the JavaFX 1.2 mobile emulator.

The official JavaFX web documentation features a toggle, in the form of a group of links at the head of each page, for showing only those bits of code inside a given profile. This is handy when we wish to know the devices and platforms our finished code will be able to run on. Flip the switch to "common," and all the desktop-only parts of the API will vanish from the page, leaving only those safe to use for mobile development.

So, we don't need to make any changes to the software; our game is already primed to go mobile. We just need to know how to get it there!

10.3.1 Packaging the game for the mobile profile

To get the game ready for the emulator we use the trusty `javafxpackager` tool, first encountered in the Enigma chapter, to bundle code ready for the web. In this scenario, however, we want to output a MIDlet rather than an applet (MID stands for Mobile Information Device). MIDlets are Java applications packaged for a mobile environment, and here's how we create one:

```
javafxpackager -profile MOBILE -src .\src
  -appClass jfxia.chapter10.MazeGame
  -appWidth 240 -appHeight 320
```

The example is the command line we need to call the packager with, split over several lines. If you're on a Unix-flavored machine, the directory slashes run the opposite way, like so:

```
javafxpackager -profile MOBILE -src ./src
  -appClass jfxia.chapter10.MazeGame
  -appWidth 240 -appHeight 320
```

The command assumes you are sitting in the project's directory, with `src` immediately off from your current directory (and the JavaFX command-line tools on your path). The options for the packager are quite straightforward. The application's source directory, its main class name, and its dimensions should all be familiar. The only change from when we used the packager to create an applet is the `-profile MOBILE` option. This time we're asking to output to the mobile environment instead of the desktop. (If you need to remind yourself of how the packager works, take a look back at section 9.4.2, in the previous chapter.)

A dist directory is created within our project, and inside you should find two files:

- The MazeGame.jar file is the game code, as you would expect.
- Its companion, MazeGame.jad, is a definition file full of metadata, helping mobile devices to download the code and users to know what it does before they download it.

Going mobile, with NetBeans

Once again I'm showing you how things happen under the hood, without the abstraction of any given integrated development environment (IDE). If you're running NetBeans, you should be able to build and package the mobile application without leaving your development environment. Terrence Barr has written an interesting blog entry explaining how to create and build mobile projects from NetBeans (the following web address has been broken over two lines).

http://weblogs.java.net/blog/terrencebarr/archive/2008/12/
javafx_10_is_he.html

The JAR and the JAD file are all we need to get our application onto a phone. The JAR is the code and the JAD is a property file with metadata for the application. But before our software goes anywhere near a real phone, we'd obviously want to test it in a development environment first. The next step, therefore, is to learn how to fire up the mobile emulator.

10.3.2 Running the mobile emulator

The mobile emulator is a simulation of the hardware and software environment in typical mobile phones. The emulator enables us to test and debug a new application without using an actual cell phone.

You'll find the emulator inside the emulator\bin directory of your JavaFX installation. If you're planning to run the emulator from the command line, check to make sure that this directory is on your execution search path. To run the emulator with our maze game, we merely need to point its `-Xdescriptor` option at our JAD file, like so:

```
emulator -Xdescriptor:dist\MazeGame.jad
```

When you run this command, a little service program will start up called the JavaFX SDK 1.2 Device Manager. You'll see its icon in the system tray (typically located in the southeast corner of the screen on Windows). If you are running a firewall (and I sincerely hope you are), you may get a few alerts at this point, asking you to sanction connections from this new software. Providing the details relate to Java and not some other mysterious application, you should grant the required permissions to allow the Device Manager and emulator to run. The result should look like figure 10.10.

Once the emulator has fired up, the game can be played using the navigation buttons and the two function buttons directly below the screen. The navigation buttons move around the maze, while the function buttons turn the view.

Running the mobile emulator, with NetBeans

If you want to remain within your IDE while testing mobile applications, there's a guide to working with the emulator from NetBeans under the section titled "Using the Run in Mobile Emulator Execution Model" at the following web address:

http://javafx.com/docs/tutorials/deployment/configure-for-deploy.jsp

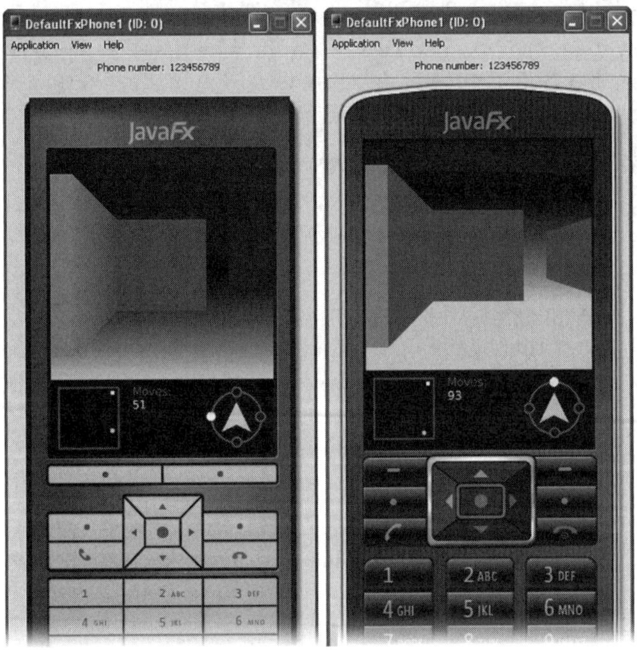

Figure 10.10 The old JavaFX 1.1 mobile emulator (left) and its 1.2 update (right) in action. Strangely, the older version seems to reproduce the gradient paints better.

And that's it; our maze has successfully gone mobile!

10.3.3 Emulator options

The emulator has a range of command-line options, outlined in table 10.1. Options have been grouped by association.

Table 10.1 Emulator options

Options	Function
`-version` `-help`	Print version or help information. Use the latter to get more information on other options.
`-Xdebug` `-Xrunjdwp`	Allow a debugger to connect to the emulator and optionally set a Java Wire Debug Protocol (JWDP) for the emulator/debugger to use when communicating.
`-Xquery` `-Xdevice`	List available devices the emulator can simulate along with their attributes, or specify which device to employ when running software on the emulator.
`-Xdescriptor` `-Xautotest`	Run a given mobile application via its JAD file, or automatically test each mobile application in a MIDlet suite (in theory it's possible to package several mobile applications into one JAR, although this feature and the associated autotest option are rarely used in practice).
`-Xjam`	Send commands to the Java Application Manager (JAM) simulator on the emulator. The JAM manages the phone's installed applications and permits OTA (over the air) installation from a URL.

Several of these options accept parameters; consult the emulator's local documentation page (it came with the rest of the documentation when you installed JFX on your computer) or use the `-help` switch to get a list of what is required for each option.

Generally you'll be using `-Xdescriptor` to test your software, perhaps with `-Xdebug` to allow a remote debugger to be used as your code runs. The `-Xquery` and `-Xdevice` options can be used to test your application on differing mobile device configurations. These configurations do not necessarily re-create specific models of a real-world phone but rather generalized approximations of devices available on the market. The `-Xjam` option allows you to re-create a true mobile application lifecycle, from over the air deployment to eventual deinstallation.

Next up is testing our application on a real phone.

10.3.4 Running the software on a real phone

We've come this far, and no doubt you're now eager to learn how to get the software onto a real phone. If so, I'm afraid this section might be a little disappointing.

As this chapter is being written, JavaFX Mobile is too new for there to be many physical devices readily available to test our application on. At JavaOne 2009 Sun made available some HTC Touch Diamond phones running JavaFX 1.2. These were intended as beta release hardware for developers to test their applications on. Consumer-focused JavaFX Mobile phones are being worked on, but right now it's not possible to walk into

More on Java ME

Judging by the emulator shipped with JavaFX SDK v1.2, the JFX mobile emulator owes a lot to recent developments in Java ME (Micro Edition). The first link (broken over two lines) points to detailed information on the new Java ME emulator and its options, while the second is a portal page to Java ME's latest developments:

http://java.sun.com/javame/reference/docs/sjwc-2.2/
pdf-html/html/tools/index.html

http://java.sun.com/javame/index.jsp

For more background on how Java ME MIDlets interact with a phone and its OS (including its lifecycle), plus details of the JAD file format, consult these links:

http://developers.sun.com/mobility/learn/midp/lifecycle/

http://en.wikipedia.org/wiki/JAD_(file_format)

a store and come out with a phone that runs JavaFX out of the box or install an upgrade to support it.

Assuming JavaFX follows the same basic deployment scheme as the current Java Micro Edition, we can make an educated guess as to how it might work once JavaFX starts to become available on actual consumer devices. By uploading both the JAR and JAD onto a web server, we can make them accessible for public download. Pointing the phone toward the JAD's URL (the file may need editing first, to provide an absolute URL to its companion JAR) should cause the phone to query the user about downloading the application. If the user accepts, the software will be transferred onto the phone and made available on its application menus.

Obviously, the process may vary slightly from phone to phone and OS to OS, but the general theory should hold true across all devices: the JAD file is the primary destination, which then references the actual application JAR file.

Who's on board?

So where is JavaFX Mobile going in terms of real-world devices? Who's on board from the handset manufacturers and other hardware providers? The following web links collect documentation and press releases detailing prominent hardware partners Sun has announced at the time of writing:

http://javafx.com/partners/

http://www.sun.com/aboutsun/pr/2009-02/sunflash.20090212.1.xml

http://developer.sonyericsson.com/site/global/newsandevents/
latestnews/newsfeb09/
p_javafxmobile_sonyericsson_announcement.jsp

It's a shame we can't currently run our applications on real-world phones, but the emulator does a good job of preparing us for the near future, when we should be able to. It allows us to see not only how the interface will work but also how the performance will rank against the desktop. Efficient performance is key to writing good mobile software, so it's worth spending our final section before the summary looking at a few simple optimization techniques.

10.4 Performance tips

When developing on the mobile platform it's important to pay particular attention to how expensive various operations are. Things a desktop computer can do without breaking a sweat may really tax smaller devices. The following are notes on how to keep your mobile applications zipping along at top speed. This list is by no means exhaustive. It's compiled from my own observations with SDK 1.2, comments from other JavaFX coders, and advice from Sun engineers.

- Binds are useful but carry an overhead. While you shouldn't avoid them altogether, you need to be sensible in their use. Too many bound variables can cause significant slowdowns in your application. Avoid binding to data that is unlikely to change during the lifetime of the application, for example, the screen resolution. When variables need to respond to changes in other variables, consider using triggers on the source to *push* updates out rather than binds on the recipients to *pull* them in.
- Image manipulation can be expensive, particularly if the images are large. Setting the `width` and `height` of an `Image` will cause it to be prescaled to the required size as it loads. Scaling images to fit a display is obviously more common on mobile applications; valuable resources can be saved by doing it up front rather than continually during live scene graph updates.
- In a mobile environment, where the UI might need to be resized to fit the device's resolution, a shapes-based approach is often better than an image-based approach. It's a lot less expensive to resize or transform shapes than images, and the results look cleaner too. However, see the next point.
- Oversized scene graphs can cause headaches. The precise problems will likely vary from device to device, depending on the graphics hardware, but in general scene graphs should be culled of unnecessary shapes, invisible nodes, or fully transparent sections when possible. Rather than hiding unused parts of a user interface, consider adding/removing them from the stage's *scene* as required. Sometimes *fixing* your UI into a bitmap image is better than forcing JavaFX Mobile to render a complex scene graph structure with every update. (Shapes versus images is something of a fine balancing act.)
- As a follow-up to the previous point, be aware that text nodes, because of their nature, are complex shapes. Devices may have efficient font rendering functions built into their OS, but these may not be so hot for drawing transformed text.

> **Credit where credit's due**
>
> You can find these tips, plus more (including examples), in an article by Michael Heinrichs titled "JavaFX Mobile Applications — Best Practices for Improving Performance." The web address has been broken over two lines:
>
> http://java.sun.com/developer/technicalArticles/
> javafx/mobile/index.html

You'll note in the maze game that I broke one of these rules. I switched the visibility of wall nodes rather than remove unwanted nodes from the scene graph. The code was tough enough, I felt, without confusing readers with more complexity. The maze game seems to work fine on the emulator, but to squeeze out maximum performance we should ditch the `wallVisible` sequence and change the `update()` function to rebuild the scene graph from scratch with each move, including only visible nodes.

10.5 Summary

In this chapter we've pushed the scene graph further than anything we've seen before, traveling beyond the flat world of two dimensions. We also got a small taste of JavaFX Mobile, although only via the emulator for now.

As always with the projects in this book, there's still plenty of room for experimentation. For example, the game works fine on 240 x 320 resolution displays but needs to be scaled and rearranged for alternative screen sizes. (Hint: the `MazeDisplay` class supports a scaling factor, which you might want to investigate.)

This chapter went through quite a journey during the writing of the book, some of which is worth mentioning from a technical point of view. It was earmarked originally as a mobile chapter, but by the fall of 2008 it looked increasingly uncertain whether mobile support would be in the initial JavaFX release. The first draft was targeted at the desktop, and featured a far more complex scene graph that applied perspective effects onto bitmap images, overlaid with translucent polygons to provide darkness. Very *Dungeon Master* (see figure 10.11). However, when JavaFX 1.0 arrived in December 2008, complete with bonus Mobile preview, the code was stripped back radically to become more suitable for a mobile device.

Originally I wanted to manufacture the 3D scene using SVG: create a vector-based wall image and replicate it for all the sizes and distortions needed to form the 19 wall pieces. Each piece would be on a different (`jfx:` labeled) layer inside a single SVG and could be switched on or off independently to show or hide the wall nodes. A little bit of extra effort up front with Inkscape (or Illustrator) would produce much cleaner source code, effectively removing the need for the `_wallFront()` and `_wallSides()` functions. Imagine my disappointment when I discovered the FXD library wasn't yet compatible with the JavaFX 1.0 Mobile profile.

Figure 10.11 A desktop version of the 3D maze, complete with bitmap walls using a perspective effect. Sadly, the bitmaps had to go when the project was adapted to fit a mobile platform.

So it's early days for the Mobile profile, clearly, but even the debut release used for this chapter shows great promise. As mobile devices jump in performance, and their multimedia prowess increases, the desktop and the handheld spaces are slowly converging. JavaFX allows us to take advantage of this trend, targeting multiple environments in a single bound through a common profile, rather than coding from scratch for every platform our application is delivered on.

So far in the book we've used JavaFX on the desktop, taken a short hop over to a web browser, then a mighty leap onto a phone, all without breaking a sweat. Is there anywhere else JavaFX can go? Well, yes! It can also run *inside* other applications, executing scripts and creating bits of UI. Although a rather esoteric skill, it can (in very particular circumstances) be incredibly useful. So that's where we'll be heading next.

11 Best of both worlds: using JavaFX from Java

This chapter covers

- Mixing JavaFX into Java programs
- Calling JavaFX Script as a scripting language
- Defining our Java app's Swing UI in JavaFX
- Adding JavaFX to the Java classpath

In previous chapters we saw plenty of examples demonstrating Java classes being used from JavaFX Script. Now it's time for an about-face; how do we call JavaFX Script from Java?

Because JavaFX Script compiles directly to JRE-compatible bytecode, it might be tempting to assume we can treat JavaFX-created classes in much the same way we might treat compiled Java classes or JARs. But this would be unwise. There are enough differences between the two languages for assumption making to be a dangerous business. For example, JavaFX Script uses a declarative syntax to create new objects; any constructors in the bytecode files are therefore a consequence of compiler implementation, not the JavaFX Script code. We can't guarantee future JavaFX Script compilers will be implemented the same way; constructors present in classes written by one JFX compiler might vanish or change in the next. So in this chapter we'll look at how to get the two languages interacting in a manner that doesn't depend on internal mechanics.

A reasonable question to ask before we get going is, "When is an application considered Java, and when is it JavaFX Script?" Suppose I write a small JavaFX Script program that relies on a huge JAR library written in Java; is my program a Java program that uses JavaFX Script or a JavaFX Script program that relies on Java? Which is the *primary* language?

Obviously, there are different ways of measuring this, but for the purposes of this chapter the primary language is the one that forms the entry point into the application. In our scenario it's JavaFX Script that runs first, placing our hypothetical application unambiguously into the category of a JavaFX application that uses Java. We've seen plenty of examples of this type of program already. In the pages to come we'll focus exclusively on the flip side of the coin: bringing JavaFX Script into an already-running Java program.

11.1 Different styles of linking the two languages

There are two core ways we might employ JavaFX Script in our Java programs.

- *As a direct alternative to Java*—We might enjoy JavaFX Script's declarative syntax so much we decide to write significant portions of our Java program's UI in it. In this scenario JavaFX Script plays no part in the final binary release (although JavaFX APIs may be used). Everything is compiled to bytecode, and JFX is merely being used as a tool to write part of the source code.
- *As a runtime scripting language*—We might want to add scripting capabilities to our Java application and decide that JavaFX Script is a suitable language to achieve this. In this scenario JavaFX Script is an active part of the final product, providing a scriptable interface to control the application as it runs.

The project we'll develop in this chapter demonstrates both uses.

11.2 Adventures in JavaFX Script

What we need now is an interesting project that demands both types of script usage, something like a simple adventure game. We can use JavaFX Script as a Java replacement to create some of the UI and as a scripting language for the game events.

The technique of breaking up an application into a *core* engine and a series of *lightweight* event scripts is well known in the video games industry, but it's also becoming increasingly common in productivity applications too. It allows programs like word processors and graphics tools to open themselves up to enhancement and customization without releasing their source code. Mostly it's the larger, more sophisticated applications that benefit from script-ability like this; thus, for the purposes of this book, it's probably best we stick to a simple game—although the techniques are exactly the same, no matter what the scale or purpose of the program.

Creating the graphics for an adventure game can take longer than writing the actual game code itself. Lucky, then, that your humble author toyed with an isometric game engine way back in the days of 16-bit consoles. Even luckier, a ready-made palette of isometric game tiles (painstakingly crafted in Deluxe Paint, I recall) survived on an old hard drive (see figure 11.1) ready to be plundered. The graphics are a little retro in appearance but will serve our needs well. Remember, kids, it's good to recycle!

The engine we'll use will be constructed in Java and just about functional enough to plug in the JavaFX Script code we want to use with it. Since this is not a Java book, I won't be reproducing the Java source code in full within these pages. Indeed, we won't even be looking at how the engine works; the game engine is a means to an end—a sample application we can use as a test bed for our JavaFX Script integration. Instead, we'll focus on the fragments binding JavaFX Script into the Java.

Download the source

The majority of the project's Java code is not reproduced in this chapter (this is a JavaFX book, after all!). You can download the full source and the associated graphics files from the book's website. The source is fully annotated; each section relating to working with JavaFX Script is clearly labeled. Try searching for the keyword *JavaFX*.

http://manning.com/JavaFXinAction/

For the sake of flexibility many video games are developed in two distinct parts. A programmer will build a *game engine*, which drives the game based on the graphics, sounds, and level/map data the designers feed into it. This data is often created with specially written tools for that particular game engine. It's a process not unlike the programmer/designer workflow we touched on with the Enigma applet project.

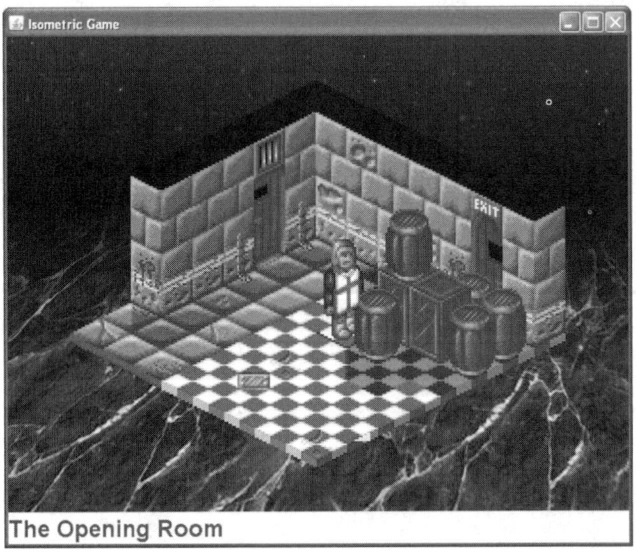

Figure 11.1 A simple Java adventure game engine, using an isometric view. The control panel at the foot of the window, as well as the in-game events, will be written using JavaFX Script.

Our simple Java isometric game engine employs a grid-based map. The game environment is broken up into rooms, and each room is a grid of stacked images, carefully placed to give an isometric 3D effect. Take a look at figure 11.2 for a visual representation of how they are arranged.

Figure 11.2 Each cell in the game environment is created from up to five images: one floor tile, two wall tiles, and two faces that modify one side of a wall tile.

Unlike the maze we developed previously, the game map isn't hardcoded into the source. A simple data file is used, which the game engine reads to build the map. Obviously, it's not enough for the game's designer to build a static map; she needs to add often quite complex interactions to model the game events. This is when the programmer reaches for a scripting engine.

11.2.1 Game engine events

Building lightweight scripting into a game engine allows the game designer the freedom she needs to program the game's *story*, without hardcoding details into the game application itself. Our game engine uses JavaFX Script as its scripting engine to support three types of game events:

- An event can run whenever the player leaves a given cell.
- An event can run whenever the player enters a given cell.
- We can define *actions*, which the player triggers by standing on a given cell and pressing the spacebar on the keyboard, for example, when the player wants to throw a wall-mounted switch.

Our game engine uses a large text file, which describes each room, including the width and height of its area (in cells), the tile images that appear in each cell, and the door locations connecting rooms. More important, it also includes the event code, written in JavaFX Script. We can see how a part of it might look in listing 11.1.

Listing 11.1 A fragment of the game data file

```
#ROOM 1 6 6
#TITLE The 2nd Room
0000010f06 000C010f06 0B00010f06 0008010f06 004C010f06 0008010f06
0000010f06 0000000006 0000002b06 0000000006 0000000006 0045000006
0000010f06 0000000006 0000002a06 0000000006 0000000003 0000000008
0000071106 0000000006 0000000005 0000000006 0000000003 0000000003
0000081006 0000001e06 0000000003 0000000003 0000000003 0000000003
000A010f06 0000000006 0000000007 0000002c06 0000002d06 0000000004
#LINK 1 5 1 1 to 0 1 2 1
#REPAINT 000000 001000 001000 000000 010000 000110
#END

#SCRIPT 1 4 1 action
def st = state as jfxia.chapter11.State;
```

Grid of tile graphics

Door link

Action event as JavaFX Script

```
if(st.getPlayerFacing()==0)
    st.setRoomCell(1,4,0 , -1,-1,-1,0x4e,-1);
    st.setRoomCell(0,6,1 , -1,0,-1,-1,-1);
}
#END
```

We have only a fragment of the data file shown here, detailing just one room. The syntax is one I made up myself to quickly test the engine; if this were a serious project, I might have used XML instead. The whole file is parsed by the game engine upon startup. We're not interested in the details, but for the record, the `#ROOM` line declares this data to be for room 1 (rooms start at 0) and 6 x 6 cells in size, the `#TITLE` line gives the room a name, and a `#LINK` line connects room 1 cell (5,1) east, with room 0 cell (1,2) east. The `#REPAINT` line is a series of flags that help optimize screen updates. Figure 11.3 shows the room in question.

The important part is the `#SCRIPT` block, attached to room 1 cell (4,1) as an *action* event type, meaning it will run when the player presses the spacebar. The script checks to see whether the player is facing north (0 means north), and if so it changes a tile at cell (4,0), flipping the switch mounted on the wall into the up position. It also changes a tile in another room, removing an obstruction.

The script does all of these things by calling functions on an object named `st`, which is a reference (cast as type `jfxia.chapter11.State`) to another object called `state`. The obvious question is, "Where does `state` come from?" I'm sure it won't come as any surprise to learn it's an object dropped into our JavaFX Script environment by the Java code that calls our script. To investigate further we need to check out that Java code, which is precisely where we'll head next.

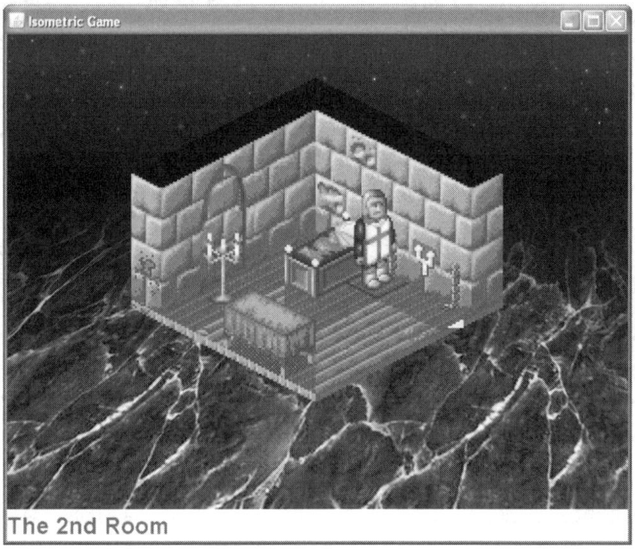

Figure 11.3 This is room 1 (room IDs start at 0), which the fragment of data file in listing 11.1 refers to. The player stands on cell (3,1), in front of him is the event cell (4,1), and beyond that the door link cell (5,1).

11.2.2 Calling the JavaFX Script event code from Java

Java SE version 6 supports JSR 223. For those who don't recognize the name, JSR 223 is the Java Specification Request for running scripting languages within Java programs. By implementing something called a *scripting engine* (not to be confused with our game engine) a language can make itself available to running Java programs. Not only can Java run scripts written in that language, but it may also be able to share objects with its scripts.

JSR 223 uses what's known as thc *service provider mechanism*. To use the scripting engine (and the language it implements) all we need do is include the engine's JAR on Java's classpath, and the engine will be found when requested. Even though we generally work with JavaFX Script as a compiled language, JavaFX comes with a scripting engine. It lives in the javafxc.jar file, inside the lib directory of your JavaFX SDK installation.

Important: Getting the classpath right

When you run a JavaFX program using the `javafx` command (directly or via an IDE), the standard JavaFX JAR files are included on the *classpath* for you. When you invoke JavaFX code from Java, however, this won't happen. You need to manually add the necessary JARs to the classpath. If you explore your JavaFX installation, you'll see subdirectories within lib for each profile. The files you need depend on which features of JavaFX you use; to get our game running I found I needed to include the following from the JavaFX 1.2 SDK:

shared/javafxc.jar (for the JavaFX Script JSR 223 scripting engine)
shared/javafxrt.jar
desktop/decora-runtime.jar
desktop/javafx-anim.jar
desktop/javafx-geom.jar
desktop/javafx-sg-common.jar
desktop/javafx-sg-swing.jar
desktop/javafx-ui-common.jar
desktop/javafx-ui-desktop.jar
desktop/javafx-ui-swing.jar

Tip: if figuring out which JARs you need is too painful for you, why not set the `java.ext.dirs` property when you run your JRE, pointing it at the necessary library directories within JavaFX? (Of course, while this solution is fine on our developer box, it doesn't easily deploy to regular users' computers, without wrapping our program in a startup script.)

```
java -Djava.ext.dirs=<search path> MyJavaClass
```

Once the javafxc.jar file is on the classpath, we need to know how to invoke its scripting engine, and that's precisely what listing 11.2 does. It shows fragments of the `Map` class, part of the Java game engine I implemented for this project. This listing shows how to set up the scripting engine; we'll deal with actually running scripts later.

Listing 11.2 Map.java: calling JavaFX Script from Java

```
import javax.script.ScriptEngineManager;
import com.sun.javafx.api.JavaFXScriptEngine;

// ...

boolean callEnterEventScript(int kx,int ky) {
    return callEventScript(currentRoom.enter , kx,ky);
}
boolean callExitEventScript(int kx,int ky) {
    return callEventScript(currentRoom.exit , kx,ky);
}
boolean callActionEventScript(int kx,int ky) {
    return callEventScript(currentRoom.action , kx,ky);
}

private boolean callEventScript(HashMap<Integer,String>hash,
int kx,int ky) {
    int x=state.playerX , y=state.playerY , f=state.playerFacing;
    Room r=currentRoom;

    int key = kx*100+ky;
    String script;
    if(hash.containsKey(key)) {
        script = hash.get(key);
        try {
            ScriptEngineManager manager =
                new ScriptEngineManager();
            JavaFXScriptEngine jfxScriptEngine =
                (JavaFXScriptEngine)manager
                .getEngineByName("javafx");

            jfxScriptEngine.put("state",state);

            jfxScriptEngine.eval(script);
        }catch(Exception e) {
            e.printStackTrace();
            System.err.println(script);
        }
    }

    return !(state.playerX==x && state.playerY==y &&
        state.playerFacing==f && currentRoom==r);
}
```

Annotations: **Import JavaFX scripting engine** (imports); **Three different event types** (the three call...EventScript methods); **Handle each game event** (callEventScript); **Event code from game data** (script = hash.get(key)); **Service provider finds JFX engine** (ScriptEngineManager / getEngineByName); **Make state available** (put("state",state)); **Run script** (eval(script)).

Remember, this is not the complete source file—just the bits relating to JSR 223.

At the head of the listing we import the classes required for Java to talk to the JavaFX Script scripting engine. The first import, `javax.script.ScriptEngineManager`, is the class we'll use to *discover* (get a reference to) the JavaFX Script engine. The second import, `com.sun.javafx.api.JavaFXScriptEngine`, is the JavaFX Script scripting engine itself.

The bulk of the code is taken from the body of the `Map` class. Each of the three event types supported has its own method. The game engine uses three hash tables to store the events. Each method defers to a central event handling method, `callEventScript()`, passing the necessary hash table for the current room, along with the cell x/y position relating to the event (typically the player's location).

The `callEventScript()` method combines the x and y positions into a single value, which it uses as a key to extract the JavaFX Script code attached to that cell. The script code is loaded into a `String` variable called, appropriately enough, `script`. This variable now holds raw JavaFX Script source code, like we saw in listing 11.1, earlier. To run this code we use a scripting engine, and that's what we see in the middle of the `callEventScript()` method.

```
ScriptEngineManager manager = new ScriptEngineManager();
JavaFXScriptEngine jfxScriptEngine =
    (JavaFXScriptEngine)manager.getEngineByName("javafx");
```

First we use Java's `ScriptEngineManager` to get a reference to JavaFX's `JavaFX-ScriptEngine`. You can see that we first create a new manager and then ask it to find (using the service provider mechanism) a scripting engine that matches the token `javafx`. Assuming the necessary JavaFX Script JAR file is on the classpath, the manager should get a positive match.

```
jfxScriptEngine.put("state",state);
```

Having acquired a reference to a JavaFX Script scripting engine, we add a Java object, `state`, into the engine's runtime environment. We encountered this variable in the event code of listing 11.1. The `state` object is where our game engine holds status data like the position of the player and references to map data. It also provides methods to modify this data, which is why it's being shared with the JavaFX Script environment. We can share as many Java objects as we please like this and choose what names they appear under in the script environment (in our code, however, we stick with `state`).

```
jfxScriptEngine.eval(script);
```

The call to `eval()`, passing the JavaFX Script code, causes the code to run. An exception handler is needed around the `eval()` call to catch any runtime errors thrown by the script. If all goes according to plan, though, we will have successfully called JavaFX Script from within a Java program, *without* relying on any compiler implementation detail to link the two.

So that's one way to hook JavaFX Script into Java, but what about the other way? This is where we'll head next.

> **Problems with JavaFX 1.2?**
>
> When I wrote this project against JavaFX 1.1, I created a single `JavaFXScriptEngine` object in the constructor, passing in the reference to `state`, and reused it for each `eval()` call. Some deep changes were made to the JSR 223 implementation for JavaFX 1.2, and I found this no longer worked; `eval()` would always rerun the first script the engine was passed, ignoring the new code passed in. The solution was to create a fresh engine for each script call. I'm not sure if this is a bug in my understanding of JavaFX's JSR 223 code, a bug in the JSR 223 implementation itself, or just a feature! Per Bothner has written a blog entry about the 1.2 changes, so if you're interested, go take a look:
>
> http://per.bothner.com/blog/2009/JavaFX-scripting-changes/

11.3 Adding FX to Java

So far we've looked at how to treat JavaFX Script as a runtime scripting language. As you'll recall, there's another way it can be used in a Java application; we can mix compiled Java and compiled JavaFX Script in the same project, developing different parts of our program in different languages.

The preview release of JavaFX (pre 1.0) featured a `Canvas` class, acting as a bridge between the JavaFX scene graph and AWT/Swing. Sadly, this class was removed from the full release, making it impossible to pass anything except Swing wrapper nodes back to a Java UI. But even without the scene graph, this technique is still useful, for the following reasons:

- It's entirely possible the JavaFX team may add a bridge between the scene graph and AWT/Swing back in at a later release.
- Depending on what you're writing, JavaFX Script's declarative syntax may be useful for building data structures other than just graphics. (Be careful: JavaFX was designed for GUI coding, and as such it likes to run its code on the UI event dispatch thread.)

> **Using a JavaFX scene graph inside Java: the hack**
>
> When JavaFX 1.0 was released, Sun engineer Josh Marinacci blogged about a quick-'n'-dirty hack from fellow Java/JFX team members Richard Bair and Jasper Potts, building a bridge between the JavaFX scene graph and Swing. Unfortunately, this code stopped working when 1.2 arrived, but the open source JFXtras project (created by Stephen Chin) took up the challenge. Their 1.2-compatible solution, however, relies on internal scene graph implementation detail and isn't guaranteed to work in future releases.
>
> http://blogs.sun.com/javafx/entry/how_to_use_javafx_in
> http://code.google.com/p/jfxtras/

As an example our project will use a very basic control panel below the main game view. The simple panel is a JavaFX Script–created `SwingLabel`. To see how it looks, see figure 11.4.

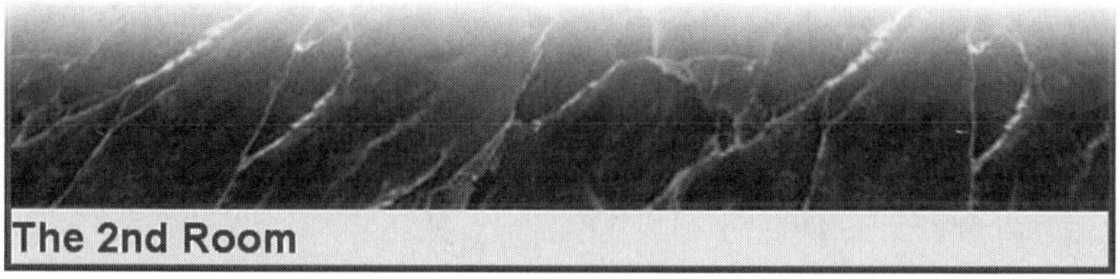

Figure 11.4 The panel at the foot of the game's window is written entirely in compiled JavaFX Script.

In the sections that follow we'll look at how to implement this panel in a way that makes it easy for the two languages to interact safely.

11.3.1 *The problem with mixing languages*

Think about what we're trying to achieve here. We have three languages in play: two high-level languages (Java and JavaFX Script) are both compiled to a common low-level language (bytecode). When we used JSR 223, the two languages were separated through the high-level abstraction of a scripting engine. Effectively the Java program was self-contained, and JavaFX Script code was treated almost as *data* (just like the map data). But in this section we're attempting to use the two languages together, creating two halves of a single program.

JavaFX Script guarantees a high degree of interoperability with Java as part of its language syntax; JavaFX programmers don't have to worry about the internals of class files created from Java code. The same is not true in the opposite direction. Although it seems likely that JavaFX Script functions will translate directly into bytecode methods, this is just an assumption. It may not be true of future (or rival) JavaFX Script compilers. How do we link the two languages in *both* directions, without making any assumptions?

Fortunately, an elegant solution emerges after a little bit of lateral thinking. If JavaFX Script's compatibility with Java classes is guaranteed, but Java's compatibility with JavaFX Script classes is undefined, can we use the former to fix the latter? Yes, we can, using Java interfaces!

11.3.2 *The problem solved: an elegant solution to link the languages*

If we encode the interactions between our two languages into a Java interface and get the JavaFX Script code to implement (or *extend*, to use the JFX parlance) this interface, we have a guaranteed Java-compatible bridge between the two languages that Java can exploit to communicate with the JavaFX Script software.

Listing 11.3 shows the Java interface created for our game engine. It has only two methods: the first is used to fetch the control panel user interface as a Java

Skinning cats

We can also form a bridge by subclassing a Java class. However, interfaces, with their lack of inherited behavior, generally provide a cleaner (sharper, less complicated) coupling. But, as the saying goes, "there's more than one way to skin a cat." Choose the way that makes sense to you and your current project.

Swing–compatible object (a `JComponent`), and the second is used to interact with the user interface.

Listing 11.3 ControlPanel.java

```
package jfxia.chapter11;

import javax.swing.JComponent;

public interface ControlPanel {
    public JComponent getUI();              // Fetch Java-compatible UI
    public void setTitle(String s);         // Interact with UI
}
```

Now that you're familiar with the interface and its methods, let's see them in action. Listing 11.4 shows fragments of the `Game` class, written in Java, displaying the first part of how to hook a JavaFX-created user interface control into Java Swing.

Listing 11.4 Game.java (part 1): adding JavaFX UIs to Java code

```
import javax.script.ScriptEngineManager;           // Imports
import com.sun.javafx.api.JavaFXScriptEngine;       // required

// ...
                                                    // Control panel reference
private ControlPanel ctrlPan;

// ...

ctrlPan = getJavaFX();                              // Create and
ctrlPan.setTitle(state.getCurrentRoomTitle());      // set up

JPanel pan = new JPanel(new BorderLayout());        // Hook into
pan.add(mapView,BorderLayout.CENTER);               // Java Swing
pan.add(ctrlPan.getUI(),BorderLayout.SOUTH);

//Part 2 is listing 11.5
```

First we create a class variable to hold our JavaFX object reference, using the `ControlPanel` interface we defined as a bridge. Then comes the meaty part: to plug the two UIs together we use the method `getJavaFX()`, which fetches the `ControlPanel` (details in listing part 2, so be patient!). We call a method on it to set the initial room name; then we use the `ControlPanel.getUI()` interface method to pull a Swing-compatible `JComponent` from the JavaFX Script code and add it into the southern position of a `BorderLayout` panel. (The other component, added to the center position, is the main game view, in case you're wondering.)

Exactly how the JavaFX object is turned into a Java object is hidden behind the mysterious `getJavaFX()` method, which will surrender its secrets next.

11.3.3 Fetching the JavaFX Script object from within Java

The code that creates the `ControlPanel` class will look very familiar. It's just a variation on the JSR 223 scripting engine code you saw earlier in listing 11.2.

Listing 11.5 is the second half of our `Game` class fragments. It shows the method `getJavaFX()` using the JavaFX Script scripting engine.

Listing 11.5 Game.java (part 2): adding JavaFX user interfaces to Java code

```
private ControlPanel getJavaFX() {
    ScriptEngineManager manager = new ScriptEngineManager();
    JavaFXScriptEngine jfxScriptEngine =
        (JavaFXScriptEngine)manager.getEngineByName ("javafx");
    try {
        return (ControlPanel)jfxScriptEngine.eval (
            "import jfxia.chapter11.jfx.ControlPanelImpl;\n"+
            "return ControlPanelImpl{};"
        );
    }
    catch(Exception e) {
        e.printStackTrace();
        return null;
    }
}
```

Since we're going to use the scripting engine only once, we lump all the code to initialize the engine and call the script into one place. The script simply returns a declaratively created JavaFX Script object of type `ControlPanelImpl`, which (you can't tell from this listing, but won't be shocked to learn) extends our `ControlPanel` interface. The object returned by the script provides the return value for the `getJavaFX()` method.

Figure 11.5 demonstrates the full relationship. Once the `ControlPanelImpl` object is created, Java and JavaFX Script communicate only via a common interface. JavaFX Script's respect for Java interfaces means this is a safe way to link the two. However, JavaFX Script's lack of support for constructors means the `ControlPanelImpl` object must still be created using JSR 223.

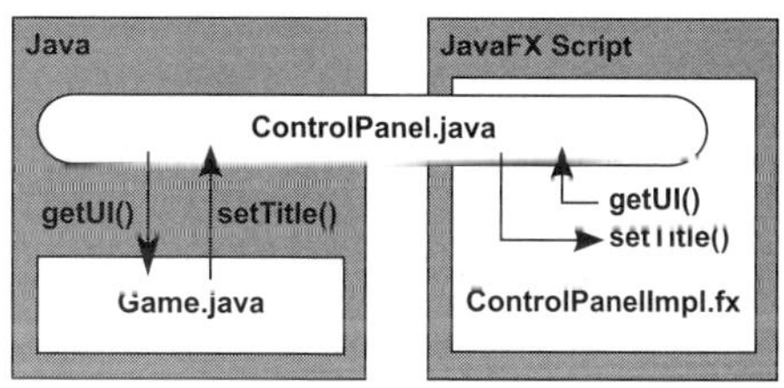

Figure 11.5 Java's `Game` class and the JavaFX Script `ControlPanelImpl.fx` class communicate via a Java interface, `ControlPanel.java`.

Let's look at `ControlPanelImpl`. Because it's written in JavaFX Script, the code is presented in its entirety (for those suffering JavaFX withdrawal symptoms) in listing 11.6.

Listing 11.6 ControlPanelImpl.fx

```
package jfxia.chapter11.jfx;

import javafx.ext.swing.SwingComponent;
import javafx.ext.swing.SwingHorizontalAlignment;
import javafx.ext.swing.SwingLabel;
import javafx.ext.swing.SwingVerticalAlignment;
import javafx.scene.CustomNode;
import javafx.scene.Node;
import javafx.scene.paint.Color;
import javafx.scene.text.Font;
import javafx.scene.text.FontWeight;

import javax.swing.JComponent;                    // Required for
import jfxia.chapter11.ControlPanel;              // Java coupling

public class ControlPanelImpl extends CustomNode, ControlPanel {   // Subclass our Java interface
    public-init var text:String;
    var myNode:SwingComponent;
    var myColor:Color = Color.BLACK;

    public override function create() : Node {    // Create and store node
        myNode = SwingLabel {
            text: bind text;
            font:
                Font.font("Helvetica",FontWeight.BOLD,24);
            horizontalTextPosition:
                SwingHorizontalAlignment.CENTER;
            verticalTextPosition:
                SwingVerticalAlignment.CENTER;
            foreground: Color.BLUE;
        }
    }

    public override function getUI() : JComponent {       // ControlPanel interface
        myNode.getJComponent();                           // methods/functions
    }

    public override function setTitle(s:String):Void {
        text = s;
    }
}
```

The script looks just like a standard Swing node. At the foot of the listing we see two functions that implement the `ControlPanel` interface. The first, `getUI()`, pulls the Swing `JComponent` from our node using the `getJComponent()` function supported by the Swing wrappers in the `javafx.ext.swing` package. The second function, `setTitle()`, allows Java to change the displayed text string of the control panel.

And that's it! We now have a successful morsel of JavaFX code running happily inside a Java Swing application. Not hard, when you know how!

Important: Compiling the code

This is a minor point but an important one: the JavaFX Script class relies on the Java interface, so whatever process or IDE we use to build the source code, we need to ensure the Java code is compiled first. The Java code doesn't need the interface implementation to be available when it builds (the whole idea of interfaces is so the implementation can be plugged in later). The JavaFX Script code needs the interface class to be available, and on the classpath, for it to build.

Using an interface has one extra advantage: providing we haven't changed the interface itself, we don't need to compile both sides of the application every time the code changes. If all our modifications are restricted to the Java side, we have to recompile only the Java, leaving the JavaFX Script classes alone. Likewise, the reverse is true if all the changes are restricted to the JavaFX Script side.

You could make use of this natural separation when designing your own projects, perhaps assigning the Java and the JavaFX Script code to different teams of developers, coding independently against interfaces that bridge their work.

11.4 Summary

In this chapter we've covered quite a simple skill, yet a sometimes useful one. Bringing JavaFX Script code into an existing Java program is something that needs to be done carefully and without assumptions about how a given JavaFX compiler works. Fortunately Java 6's scripting engine support, coupled with JavaFX Script's respect for the Java language's class hierarchy mechanism, makes it possible to link the two languages in a clean way. It may not be something we need to do every day, but it's nice to know the option is there when we need it.

Using scripting languages from within Java certainly gives us great power. (Don't forget, "With great power there must also come great responsibility!" as Stan Lee once wrote.) It allows us to develop different parts of our application in languages more suitable to the task at hand. Sooner rather than later, I hope, the JavaFX team will add a working bridge between the scene graph and AWT/Swing, so we can exploit JavaFX to the fullest within existing Java applications. JavaFX would surely give us a powerful tool in slashing development times of Java desktop apps and reducing the frequency of UI bugs.

This chapter brings the book to a close. We began in chapter 1 with excited talk about the promise of rich internet applications and the power of domain-specific languages, worked our way through the JavaFX Script language, learned how to use binds, manipulated the scene graph, took a trip to the movies, looked through our photo collection, sent some secret codes from within a web browser, got lost in a mobile maze, and ended up learning how to have the best of both worlds. What a journey! I hope it's been fun.

At the start of the book I stated that my mission was not to reproduce the API documentation blow for blow. The book was written against JavaFX SDK 1.2, and JavaFX still has plenty of room for growth in future revisions; my goal was to give you a good grounding in the concepts and ideas that surround JavaFX, so you could take future enhancements in your stride. The final chapters, as I'm sure you noticed, became more speculative, revealing what might be coming up in future revisions of the JFX platform. Any speculation was based on public material from Sun and the JavaFX team, so I hope there won't be too many surprises after the book goes to press.

Although practicality meant none of the projects in this book were as mind blowing as they could have been, I hope they gave you plenty to think about. Download the source code, play with it, add to it, and fill in the bits I didn't have the space to do. Then try building your own apps. Increasingly, modern applications are featuring sumptuous graphical effects and rich multimedia, and JavaFX gives you the power to compete with the best of them. Push your skills to the max, amaze yourself, amaze your friends, amaze the world!

Above all, have fun!

appendix A: Getting started

This section provides details on how to download, install, set up, compile, and run the JavaFX development environment. It also provides URLs to useful JavaFX web resources.

Everything you need to get started with JavaFX is free to download, for Microsoft Windows, Mac OS X, or Linux.

A.1 Downloading and installing

Before we can start writing JavaFX applications, we need the right software. Next you'll find web addresses to the downloads you need to get started. For each piece of software read the licenses (if any) and requirements carefully, and follow the download and installation instructions.

Please read over this section before downloading anything, particularly if you're new to Java. It contains information in later subsections that helps you get a solid overview of which tools you may want to download and install.

The JavaFX tools themselves fall into two categories: the JavaFX SDK for programmers and the JavaFX Production Suite for designers. Their contents are outlined in the sections that deal with each. This book primarily focuses on the programmer tools (the SDK), although for the full experience it's recommended that you download both.

A.1.1 The Java Development Kit (essential)

First, if you don't have the latest version, you need to visit the Java Standard Edition downloads page to fetch and install a copy of the Java SE JDK. Sun provides SE (Standard Edition) implementations for Microsoft Windows and Linux, including 64-bit builds. The Macintosh is covered by Apple's own JDK, which unfortunately tends to lag behind the Sun releases. If it's available for your system, you're strongly urged to get the latest update of Java 6 JDK, preferably a version after Update 10, because of radical enhancements in applet deployment and Java startup times beginning with that release. Remember, you need to download the JDK, not the JRE. The Java Runtime Environment does not contain the extra tools needed to write Java software. (The JDK comes bundled with a compatible JRE).

- Java SE Downloads (Windows and Linux)
  http://java.sun.com/javase/downloads/index.jsp
- Apple's Java Development Kit (Mac OS X)
  http://developer.apple.com/java/

At the time of writing, for JavaFX 1.2 the requirements are:

- For Windows: Windows XP (SP2) or Vista, running JDK 6 Update 13 (minimum) or JDK 6 Update 14 (recommended).
- For Mac: Mac OS X 10.4.10 or later, running JDK 5 Update 16 (aka v1.5.0_16) minimum (Java for Mac OS X 10.4 Release 7/Java for Mac OS X 10.5 Update 2)
- For Linux: Ubuntu 8.04 LTE, running JDK 6 Update 13 (minimum) or JDK 6 Update 14 (recommended). Media playback requires GStreamer 0.10.18.

Combined JDK and JavaFX SDK download

As of JDK 6 Update 13, Sun's website offered a combined download/install package for JDK 6 and the JavaFX SDK. You may choose to download this two-in-one option if you want, rather than download and install both components separately. Read the rest of these setup instructions before you decide.

A.1.2 NetBeans or other IDEs (optional)

You'll find plenty of references to NetBeans on Sun's Java pages, including options to download the NetBeans program as a bundle with the JDK. The JDK provides the raw tools for Java, such as the language compiler and runtime environment; it does not contain a source code editor or an IDE. An IDE is a seamless software environment, providing sophisticated visual tools for editing, analyzing, and debugging code. Most of these tools are available in the standard JDK, but as command-line (e.g., shell or MS-DOS) programs rather than GUI-based applications.

If you're not at home with command-line environments, you are strongly recommended to install an IDE to help you write your software. Modern IDEs are quite sophisticated; they can be extended with new technologies, like the JavaFX Script compiler used to build JavaFX code. Such extensions come in the form of *plug-ins*, installed into the IDE to teach it how to interface to new tools. NetBeans is Sun's own IDE; however, it is not the only one available (nor, indeed, is it necessarily the most popular). Rivals of note include Eclipse and IntelliJ, each with its own devoted following. You may want to investigate these alternatives before you make a choice, but it's important to check to see whether the necessary plug-ins have been crafted for your chosen IDE to integrate into the tools you want to run, especially JavaFX.

Because NetBeans is Sun's own IDE, its plug-in support for JavaFX is guaranteed and likely to be one step ahead of its rivals. By all means investigate the various options (talk to fellow programmers to see which IDE they recommend), but if you're still uncertain, download NetBeans—it's by far the safest option.

- NetBeans
  http://www.netbeans.org/
- Eclipse
  http://www.eclipse.org/
- IntelliJ
  http://www.jetbrains.com/idea/ (Warning: no JFX plug-in at time of writing)

This book does not favor one IDE over any other. Each IDE has its own tutorials and documentation, as well as a strong online fan base. Covering every IDE would place an unnecessary burden on the text, while picking only one would alienate devotees of rival platforms. Fortunately, online tutorials are available.

- Building a JavaFX Application Using NetBeans IDE
  http://java.sun.com/javafx/1/tutorials/build-javafx-nb-app/
- Developing JavaFX applications with Eclipse – Tutorial (Lars Vogel)
  http://www.vogella.de/articles/JavaFX/article.html

A.1.3 The IDE plug-ins (required, if using an IDE)

We talked about IDEs and their merits. Each IDE needs a plug-in to teach it how to use the JavaFX SDK tools. These URLs will lead you to the relevant project page.

- NetBeans JavaFX Plug-in
  http://javafx.netbeans.org/
- Eclipse JavaFX plug-in
  http://javafx.com/docs/gettingstarted/eclipse-plugin/
- IntelliJ JavaFX Plug-in
  No plug-in at the time of writing. Check for updates at
  http://plugins.intellij.net/

A.1.4 The JavaFX SDK (essential)

Having downloaded and installed the latest Java SE JDK, and perhaps a favored IDE, you now need to do the same for the JavaFX SDK. This provides the extra JFX components for creating JavaFX software to target the Java SE platform.

As well as a project website, JavaFX has a slick marketing-focused site from where you can download the latest official release. This site is the central hub for anyone who wants to download JavaFX and any *official* tools, browse an extensive list of demos, read various tutorials, or check out the JavaFX API documentation and JavaFX Script language specification. It's a one-stop shop for JavaFX downloads and information.

- The JavaFX Site
  http://www.javafx.com/
- The JavaFX Site Download page (direct link)
  http://javafx.com/downloads/all.jsp

The OpenJFX project is an open source initiative, sponsored by Sun Microsystems, to create the JavaFX Script compiler. This is where JavaFX Script, as a technology, is being engineered and experimented on; future versions of the language will spring from this project. Presumably in the future the API will be covered by an open source project too. The project site contains the latest compiler releases and their source code, although not necessarily an accompanying API release.

If you want to play an active role in shaping the future of JavaFX itself, this is a good place to start. However, if you prefer to leave the nuances of language design to more experienced compiler engineers, you can ignore this site.

- The OpenJFX Project Home Page
  https://openjfx.dev.java.net/
- The JavaFX Build Server
  http://openjfx.java.sun.com/

A.1.5 The JavaFX Production Suite (optional)

The JavaFX Production Suite, previously known under its codename of Project Nile, is a set of plug-ins for both Adobe Illustrator (CS3+) and Adobe Photoshop (CS3+), allowing export into a special JavaFX graphics format, called FXD or FXZ (FXD is the format, but files are compressed and given an .fxz extension). There's also a SVG to FXZ converter and a handy FXZ file viewer.

- Javafx Production Suite Download
  http://javafx.com/downloads/all.jsp
- Getting Started With JavaFX Production Suite
  http://javafx.com/docs/gettingstarted/production_suite/

The Production Suite is aimed at designers; you don't need it just to write software. However, if you own the CS3 version of Illustrator or Photoshop, or you fancy bringing SVG images into your JFX programs, why not give it a try? The tools output to the FXD format, which marries perfectly with the JavaFX scene graph. Image layers can be referenced and manipulated freely from inside JavaFX, meaning UI chunks can be constructed in a graphics tool and brought alive inside JavaFX programs.

Readers unfortunate enough not to own these Adobe applications might be interested in Inkscape, a highly regarded open source vector graphics program. It can save to the SVG format supported by JavaFX's FXZ conversion tool. Although it cannot currently write directly to JavaFX's own FXZ format, programmers close to the project have indicated they intend to add this feature (so check the latest release).

- Inkscape
  http://www.inkscape.org/
- Inkscape and JavaFX Working Together (Silveira Neto)
  http://silveiraneto.net/2008/11/21/inkscape-and-javafx-working-together/

Regrettably, at the time of writing, no tool appears to exist for converting PSD (Photoshop) or AI (Illustrator) files themselves into a JavaFX-compatible form. This means it is not possible to convert files from Gimp (another much-praised open source graphics tool) to FXD format. We can but keep our fingers crossed a plug-in for Gimp will be developed soon—or better still a standalone graphics-conversion tool.

A.1.6 Recap

To recap, the minimum you must have installed to begin JavaFX development is:

- The Java SE Development Kit (JDK)
- The JavaFX SDK

Optionally you may also wish to install:

- An IDE of your choice, with its associated JavaFX plug-in (if the command line isn't your thing)
- The JavaFX Production Suite
- Inkscape (as an alternative to Adobe Illustrator)

And if you're the kind of expert programmer who wants to keep your finger on the pulse of the JavaFX Script compiler project (not recommended for the faint of heart):

- The latest OpenJFX build

A.2 Compiling JavaFX

Having downloaded and installed the latest JDK and a JavaFX SDK, you'll need to know how to run the JavaFX Script compiler and execute the programs it creates. If you plan to develop all your software exclusively from within an IDE, you needn't pay too much attention to this section (although it's always handy to know what's happening under the hood).

I'm going to explain the necessary steps in a platform-agnostic way. I assume you're already familiar with the ins and outs of your computer's command-line interface, be that something like Bash on Unix-flavored platforms, Microsoft's own MS-DOS, or whatever CLI your system provides. Readers who aren't competent with a command line are strongly recommended to use an IDE.

A.2.1 Setting the path

To get access to all the tools you need to develop, you must have both the JDK and the JavaFX SDK on your path.

When you install the JavaFX SDK (on Windows, at least), the necessary directories will be added to the command path as part of the install process. To check them, right-click My Computer and choose Properties; on the Advanced tab click Environment Variables and look for Path in the list.

If they haven't been set up correctly, or you want to control them yourself (perhaps because you need to switch between versions of JavaFX), take a look at the directories where Java SDK and JavaFX SDK were installed. Inside you'll find various subdirectories, one of which should be called bin. These directories have all the Java and JavaFX command-line tools, and both need to be on your execution path.

To test that both these directories are correctly set on your path, type the following at the command line:

```
javac -version
javafxc -version
```

If the paths are correct, each command will cause the respective compiler to run, printing its version information. Next we need to check to make sure the runtime environments are set. Type the following into the command line:

```
java -version
javafx -version
```

If the compiler commands work, it's very unlikely the runtime commands will fail. However, *make sure the versions are the ones you expect!* Some operating systems come preinstalled with a JRE, sometimes woefully out of date, so it's always a good idea to double check that you have the right runtime on your path.

Because the output files (classes) created by the JavaFX Script compiler are Java compatible, the `javafx` command actually wraps `java`, adding the required JavaFX libraries so we don't have to put them on the classpath ourselves. The version information will relate to JavaFX, but options such as `-help` appear to be passed straight to the Java runtime.

A.2.2 Running the compiler

Now that you have made sure the tools are on your path, building software is merely a case of calling the compiler and pointing it at some source files. The JavaFX Script compiler takes most of the same command-line options as the Java compiler. You can get a listing of them with the command

```
javafxc -help
```

A simple compilation, on Windows or Unix, might look like this:

```
javafxc -d . src\*.fx          (Windows/MS-DOS)
javafxc -d . src/*.fx          (Unix variant)
```

The compiler will run, building all the source files inside the src directory, outputting its classes into the current directory. JavaFX Script source files typically carry the .fx extension. If the classes use packages, you'll find that the output directory will contain a directory structure mirroring the package structure.

A.2.3 Running the code

Now that you have built your code, the final step is to run it. The JavaFX runtime command wraps the Java runtime command, adding the extra JavaFX API classes onto the class path for you. A list of options can be displayed using the following command:

```
javafx -help
```

A typical invocation of the JavaFX runtime might look something like this:

```
javafx -cp . mypackage.MyClass
```

The class `mypackage.MyClass` is loaded and run, assuming it lives in the current working directory. The `-cp` option defines the class path. In the example the parameter immediately following it (the period) denotes the current directory, ensuring our classes will be found by the JRE.

A.3 Useful URLs

Learning a new platform is always hard at first. It's nice to have resources you can turn to for guidance, information, and inspiration. This section lists URLs that may be useful to you in your JavaFX work. The URLs are loosely grouped by type but are in no particular order of preference.

- Book: *JavaFX in Action*, website
  http://www.manning.com/JavaFXinAction/
- JavaFX: The JavaFX Site
  http://www.javafx.com/
- JavaFX: JavaFX Technology at a Glance
  http://java.sun.com/javafx/index.jsp
- JavaFX: JavaFX API Documentation
  http://java.sun.com/javafx/1.2/docs/api/
- JavaFX: JavaFX Script Language Reference
  http://openjfx.java.sun.com/current-build/doc/reference/JavaFXReference.html
- JavaFX: The OpenJFX Project Home Page
  https://openjfx.dev.java.net/
- Java: Sun's Java Developer Home Page
  http://java.sun.com/
- Community: Sun's Java Community website
  http://java.net/
- Community: Javalobby Developer Community
  http://java.dzone.com/
- Blog: James Weaver's JavaFX Blog
  http://learnjavafx.typepad.com/
- Blog: Chris Oliver's Blog

http://blogs.sun.com/chrisoliver/

- Blog: Joshua Marinacci's Blog
http://weblogs.java.net/blog/joshy/
- Blog: Ramblings on life, the Universe, and Java(FX)
http://weblogs.java.net/blog/javakiddy/
- Extra examples, coded during the writing of this book
http://www.jfxia.com/

appendix B: JavaFX Script: a quick reference

This appendix is an ultraterse guide to JavaFX Script, almost like flash cards for each of the topics covered in the main language tutorial chapters earlier in this book. As well as acting as a quick reference to the language syntax, it could also be used by highly confident developers (impatient to get on to the projects) as a fast track to learning the basics of the JavaFX Script language.

B.1 Comments

JavaFX Script supports comments in the same way as Java:

```
// A single line comment.
/* A multi line comment. */
```

B.2 Variables and data types—the basics

JavaFX Script variables are statically, not dynamically, typed. The language has no concept of primitives in the way Java does; everything is an object. Some types may be declared using a literal syntax. We call these the *value types*, and they are `Boolean`, `Byte`, `Character`, `Double`, `Duration`, `Float`, `Integer`, `Long`, `Number`, `Short`, and `String`. `KeyFrame`, an animation class, also has its own specific literal syntax (dealt with in the chapters dealing with animation timelines).

Aside from having their own literal syntax, value types can never be `null`, meaning unassigned value types have default values. Value types are also immutable.

Variable declaration (def, var, Boolean, Integer, Number, String)

Value types are created using the `var` or the `def` keyword, followed by the variable's name and optionally a colon and a type.

```
var valBool:Boolean = true;
var valByte:Byte = -123;
var valChar:Character = 65;
var valDouble:Double = 1.23456789;
var valFloat:Float = 1.23456789;
var valInt:Integer = 8;
var valLong:Long = 123456789;
var valNum:Number = 1.245;
var valShort:Short = 1234;
var valStr:String = "Example text";
```

If initial values are not provided, sensible defaults are used. JavaFX Script also supports type inference.

```
var assBool = true;
var assInt = 1;
var assNum = 1.1;
var assStr = "Some text";
```

The `def` keyword prevents a variable from being reassigned once its initial value is set. This aids readability, bug detection, and performance. Note: although the variable cannot be reassigned, if its body uses a one-way bind, its value can still change.

```
var canAssign:Integer = 5;
def cannotAssign:Integer = 5;
canAssign = 55;
cannotAssign = 55;// Compiler error
```

Arithmetic (+, -, etc.)

Numbers may be manipulated in mostly the same ways as Java when it comes to arithmetic. Remember, though, all variables are objects, and so are literals in the source code.

```
def n1:Number = 1.5;
def n2:Number = 2.0;
var nAdd = n1 + n2;
var nSub = n1 - n2;
var nMul = n1 * n2;
var nDiv = n1 / n2;
var iNum = n1.intValue();

var int1 = 10;
var int2 = 10;
int1 *= 2;
int2 *= 5;
var int3 = 9 mod (4+2*2);
var num:Number = 1.0/(2.5).intValue();

def dec = 16;       // 16 in decimal
def hex = 0x10;     // 16 in hexadecimal
def oct = 020;      // 16 in octal
```

Logic operators (and, or, not, <, >, =, >=, <=, !=)

Comparisons between variables are done pretty much the same way as in Java, except the `&&` and `||` symbols are replaced by the keywords `and` and `or`.

```
def testVal = 99;
var flag1 = (testVal == 99);
var flag2 = (testVal != 99);
var flag3 = (testVal <= 100);
var flag4 = (flag1 or flag2);
var flag5 = (flag1 and flag2);
var today:java.util.Date = new java.util.Date();
var flag6 = (today instanceof java.util.Date);
var flag7 = not flag6;
```

Casting (as, instanceof)

Casting is done using the as keyword, following the variable to be cast. Types can be tested using the instanceof operator.

```
var pseudoRnd:Integer =
    (java.langSystem.currentTimeMillis() as Integer) mod 1000;

var str:java.lang.Object = "A string";
var inst1 = (str instanceof String);
```

B.3 Strings

Strings largely behave as they do in Java, but there are a few interesting extra pieces of functionality specific to JavaFX Script.

String literals and embedded expressions

String literals may be written using either single or double quotes to enclose their content. Two consecutive strings in the source (with nothing but whitespace in between) are concatenated, even if separated by a new line.

```
var str1 = 'Single quotes';
var newline = "This string starts here, "
'and ends here!';
```

The same type of quote character must start and end a string. The quote not being used as a delimiter is free to be used inside the string. A backslash can be used to escape a quote.

```
println("UK authors prefer 'single quotes'");
println('US authors prefer "double quotes"');
println('I use "US" and \'UK\' quotes');
```

Embedded expressions may be run inside strings, using curly brace delimiters.

```
var rating = "cool";
var eval1 = "JavaFX is {rating}!";
var flag = true;
var eval2 =
    "JavaFX is {if(flag) "cool" else "uncool"}!";
```

String formating

Embedded string expressions may also contain formatting, using the same syntax as Java's java.util.Formatter class.

```
import java.util.Calendar;
import java.util.Date;
def magic = -889275714;
println("{magic} in hex is {%08x magic}");
def cal:Calendar = Calendar.getInstance();
cal.set(1,3,4);
def joesBirthday:Date = cal.getTime();
println("Joe was born on a {%tA joesBirthday}");
```

String localization

Strings can be localized using property files on the classpath. This permits our software to speak many different languages and allows us to add new languages easily. The property filename should follow one of two formats:

```
<SCRIPT_NAME>_<LANG_CODE>.fxproperties
<SCRIPT_NAME>_<LANG_CODE>_<REGION_CODE>.fxproperties
```

In the <SCRIPT_NAME> is the base name (no `.fx` extension) of the script to which the localization file applies, <LANG_CODE> is an ISO language code, and <REGION_CODE> is an ISO region code.

To use the localized strings in our programs, we use a double # syntax, which has two variants, as follows:

```
def str1:String = ##"Trashcan";
def str2:String = ##[TRASH_KEY]"Trashcan";
```

The first example uses `"Trashcan"` as both the property search key and the fallback value. The second example uses `"TRASH_KEY"` as the property key and `"Trashcan"` as the fallback default.

B.4 Durations

Durations are objects for storing and manipulating time. They have their own literal syntax, with a postfix `h` (hours), `m` (minutes), `s` (seconds), or `ms` (milliseconds) denoting the time units.

```
def mil = 25ms;
def sec = 30s;
def min = 15m;
def hrs = 2h;

def dur1 = 15m * 4;            // 1 hour
def dur2 = 0.5h * 2;           // 1 hour
def flag1 = (dur1 == dur2);    // True
def flag2 = (dur1 > 55m);      // True
def flag3 = (dur2 < 123ms);    // False
```

B.5 Sequences: list of objects

JavaFX has no primitive arrays as such, but what it has instead are single-dimensional lists that can be declared and manipulated in numerous ways not supported by conventional Java arrays.

Basic sequence declaration and access (sizeof)

A sequence may be declared with its initial items between square brackets. A sequence inside a sequence is expanded in place. Two sequences are equal if they contain the same quantity, type, value, and order of items. The `sizeof` operator is used to determine the length of a sequence.

```
def seq1:String[] = [ "A" , "B" , "C" ];
def seq2:String[] = [ seq1 , "D" , "E" ];
def flag1 = (seq2 == ["A","B","C","D","E"]);
def size = sizeof seq1;
```

To reference a value we use the square bracket syntax. Referencing an index outside the current range returns a default value rather than an exception.

```
def faceCards = [ "Jack" , "Queen" , "King" ];
var king = faceCards[2];
def ints = [10,11,12,13,14,15,16,17,18,19,20];
var oneInt = ints[3];
var outside = ints[-1];  // Returns zero
```

Sequence creation using ranges ([..], step)

Sequences may be populated using a range syntax. An optional step may be supplied to determine the increment between items.

```
def seq = [ 1 .. 100 ];
def range1 = [0..100 step 5];
def range2 = [100..0 step -5];
def range3 = [0..100 step -5];
def range4 = [0.0 .. 1.0 step 0.25];
```

We can also include ranges inside larger declarations. Recall that a nested sequence is expanded in place.

```
def blackjackValues = [ [1..10] , 10,10,10 ];
```

Sequence creation using slices ([..<])

We can create a sequence range using a slice of indexes from another sequence. Here the `..` syntax includes the end index in the range, while `..<` excludes the end index.

```
def source = [0 .. 100];
var slice1 = source[0 .. 10];      // 0 to 10
var slice2 = source[0 ..< 10];     // 0 to 9
var slice3 = source[95..];         // 95 to 100
var slice4 = source[95..<];        // 95 to 99 (exclude last item)
```

Sequence creation using a predicate

A predicate can be used to take a conditional slice from an existing sequence, creating a new sequence.

```
def source = [0 .. 9];
var lowVals = source[n|n<5];
def people =
```

```
    ["Alan","Andy","Bob","Colin","Dave","Eddie"];
var peopleSubset =
    people[s | s.startsWith("A")].toString();
```

Sequence manipulation (insert, delete, reverse)

Sequences can be manipulated by inserting and removing elements dynamically. We can even reverse a sequence.

```
var seq1 = [1..5];
insert 6 into seq1;
insert 0 before seq1[0];
insert 99 after seq1[2];

var seq2 = [[1..10],10];
delete seq2[0];
delete seq2[0..2];
delete 10 from seq2;  // Delete any 10s
delete seq2;  // Delete whole sequence

var seq3 = [1..10];
seq3 = reverse seq3;
```

B.6 Binds

Binds define a relationship between a data source and a data consumer. When the source changes, the bind performs a *minimal recalculation* using only those parts of the bind expression affected by any change.

Binding to variables (bind)

Bound variables are created using the bind keyword. They are read-only, so we use def instead of var.

```
var percentage:Integer;
def progress = bind "Progress: {percentage}% finished";
for(v in [0..100 step 20]) {
    percentage = v;
    println(progress);
}

var thisYear = 2008;
def lastYear = bind thisYear-1;
def nextYear = bind thisYear+1;
// lastYear=2007, thisYear=2008, nextYear=2009
thisYear = 1996;
// lastYear=1995, thisYear=1995, nextYear=1996
```

It is possible to bind to a bound variable, as follows:

```
var flagA = true;
def flagB = bind not flagA;   // Always opposite of flagA
def flagC = bind not flagB;   // Always opposite of flagB, same as flagA
```

Binding to a sequence

Binding to a sequence index is done so by way of its index.

```
var range = [1..5];
def ref = bind range[2];    // ref == 3
delete range[0];            // ref == 4
delete range;               // ref == 0
```

We can also bind against an entire sequence.

```
var seqSrc = [ 1..3 ];
def seqDst = bind for(x in seqSrc) { x*2; }    // seqDst == [2,4,6]
insert 10 into seqSrc;                         // seqDst == [2,4,6,20]
```

Binding to code

The bound expression may contain code, including function calls.

```
var mode = false;
def modeStatus = bind if(mode) "On" else "Off";

var userID = "";
def realName = bind getName(userID);
function getName(id:String) : String {
    if(id.equals("adam")) { return "Adam Booth"; }
    else if(id.equals("dan")) { return "Dan Jones"; }
    else { return "Unknown"; }
}
```

Bidirectional binds (with inverse)

For simple binds, which mirror another variable directly, it's possible to create a two-way relationship, such that changing one variable changes the other. Because this type of bind is assignable, we use `var` instead of `def`.

```
var dictionary = "US";
var thesaurus = bind dictionary with inverse;
// dictionary="US", thesaurus="US"
thesaurus = "UK";
// dictionary="UK", thesaurus="UK"
thesaurus = "FR";
// dictionary="FR", thesaurus="FR"
```

Bound functions (bound)

If a function depends on variables outside of its local scope, these are not automatically included in the bind. To change this, mark the function as `bound`, and its dependencies will trigger bind updates correctly.

```
var ratio = 5;
var posX = 5;
def coord = bind "{scale(posX)}";  // Binds posX and ratio
bound function scale(v:Integer) : Integer {
    return v*ratio;
}
```

B.7 Cooperating with Java

JavaFX Script was designed to work with existing Java libraries, and most of the time it works just fine. However, despite the best efforts of the JavaFX designers, incompatibilities between the different languages are inevitable. Fortunately, JavaFX Script provides some "get out of jail free" features, to smooth over any occasional bump.

Quoted identifiers

Quoted identifiers mark a part of the source code as an identifier, which otherwise might have confused the compiler. They are handy for referencing Java method names that clash with JavaFX Script reserved words, for example.

```
var <<var>> = "A string variable called var";
```

Java native arrays (nativearray of)

JavaFX 1.2 has a special type syntax for mapping Java native arrays (returned from Java method calls) into JavaFX Script programs, without translating them into sequences.

```
def jClass:Class = (new StringBuilder()).getClass();
def cons:nativearray of Constructor =
    jClass.getDeclaredConstructors();
println("1st: {cons[0]}");
for(i in cons) { println("{i}"); }
```

B.8 Packages (package, import)

Packages relate portions of our code together into a group. They work the same way as Java packages. Importing allows the code to avoid using cumbersome fully qualified class names. As in Java, an asterisk can be used at the end of an `import` statement instead of a class name, to include all the classes from the stated package without having to list them individually.

```
import java.util.Date;
var date1:Date = Date {};
```

Adding a class into a package is as follows:

```
package jfxia.chapter3;
public class Date
{   override function toString() : String
    {   "This is our date class";
    }
};
```

Using both Java's `Date` class and the previous one looks like this:

```
import java.lang.System;
var date1 = java.util.Date {};
var date2 = jfxia.chapter3.Date {};
```

B.9 Developing classes

JavaFX Script's support for OO is pretty rich, including mixin inheritance. Classes referenced outside of a source file must live in an individual file named after that class. Unlike with Java, not all code in JavaFX Script has to live inside a class—so called *script-level* code is bundled up and run as if it is in a Java `main()` method.

Scripts

Variables and functions can live at the script level, that is, outside of any class. When located in the script context, they behave like (and are accessed like) Java static class members.

```
// This code lives in a file called "Examples2.fx"
package jfxia.chapter3;

def scriptVar:Integer = 99;
function scriptFunc() : Integer {
    def localVar:Integer = -1;
    return localVar;
}

println(
    "Examples2.scriptVar = {Examples2.scriptVar}\n"
    "Examples2.scriptFunc() = {Examples2.scriptFunc()}\n"
    "scriptVar = {scriptVar}\n"
    "scriptFunc() = {scriptFunc()}\n"
);
```

Any loose code that lives in at the script level (code not part of a script function) can be executed as an application bootstrap.

Class definition (class, def ,var, function, this)

Variables in classes are created with the familiar `var` and `def` keywords, while behavior is implemented by way of a `function`. The keyword `this` can be used to refer to the current object, although its use is optional.

```
import javafx.lang.Duration;
class Track
{   var title:String;
    var artist:String;
    var time:Duration;
    function equals(t:Track) : Boolean
    {   return (t.title.equals(this.title) and
            t.artist.equals(this.artist));
    }
    override function toString() : String
    {   return '"{title}" by "{artist}" : '
            '{time.toMinutes() as Integer}m '
            '{time.toSeconds() mod 60 as Integer}s';
    }
}
var song:Track = Track
{   title: "Special"
    artist: "Garbage"
    time: 220s
};
```

Object declaration (init, postinit, isInitialized(), new)

JavaFX Script objects have no constructors, preferring its trademark declarative syntax instead. The `init` block of code is called once all class variables have been assigned, and once finished the object is considered initialized. The `postinit` block is then called.

The built-in function `isInitialized()` can be used to find out if a variable was assigned a value during object initialization.

```
def UNKNOWN_DRIVE:Integer = 0;
def WARP_DRIVE:Integer = 1;
class SpaceShip {
    var name:String;
    var crew:Integer;
    var canTimeTravel:Boolean;
    var drive:Integer = SpaceShip.UNKNOWN_DRIVE;
    init {
        println("Building: {name}");
        if(not isInitialized(crew))
            println("  Warning: no crew!");
    }
    postinit {
        if(drive==WARP_DRIVE)
            println("  Engaging warp drive");
    }
}

def ship1 = SpaceShip {
    name:"Starship Enterprise"
    crew:400
    drive:SpaceShip.WARP_DRIVE
    canTimeTravel:false
};
```

There may be times when we are forced to instantiate a Java object using a specific constructor to make it function the way we desire. The `new` syntax allows us to do just that. It can be used on any class, including JavaFX Script classes, although it is intended to be used only with Java classes, when the declarative syntax isn't sufficient.

```
def ship2 = new SpaceShip();
ship2.name="The Liberator";
ship2.crew=7;
ship2.canTimeTravel=false;
```

Class inheritance (abstract, extends, override)

JavaFX Script supports inheritance, using the `extends` keyword. As in Java, functions are virtual. The `abstract` keyword can be used to prevent a class from being instantiated directly. The `override` keyword is needed on any instance function or variable that overrides a parent class; overridden variables are used to change initial values.

The following code should live in a file called Animal.fx :

```
import java.util.Date;

abstract class Animal {
    var life:Integer = 0;
    var birthDate:Date;

    function born() : Void {
        this.birthDate = Date{};
    }
```

```
    function getName() : String {
        "Animal"
    }
    override function toString() : String {
        "{this.getName()}  Life: {life}  "+
            "Bday: {%te birthDate} {%tb birthDate}";
    }
}
```

The following class is a subclass of the above `Animal` class:

```
class Mammal extends Animal {
    override function getName() : String {
        "Mammal"
    }
    function giveBirth() : Mammal {
        var m  = Mammal { life:100 };
        m.born();
        return m;
    }
}
```

Mixin inheritance (mixin)

JavaFX Script supports mixin inheritance, whereby functionality from multiple *mixin* classes can be copied into a class in a single step, without the issues related to multiple inheritance. Mixin classes act like Java interfaces, except they may carry default variable values and function bodies.

```
mixin class Motor {
    public var distance:Integer = 0;
    public var battery:Integer;
    public function move(dir:Integer,dist:Integer) : Void {
        distance+=dist;
    }
}

class Robot extends Motor {
    // Motor.battery not mixed in -- already present
    override var battery = 1000;

    // Motor.distance mixed in

    // Motor.move() mixed in
}
```

Mixins are processed from first to last on the `extends` list. A regular JavaFX Script class can extend (inherit) any number of mixin classes or Java interfaces but only one other regular class. A mixin class can inherit any number of mixin classes and Java interfaces but no regular classes.

Function types

Functions in JavaFX Script are *first-class objects,* meaning we can have variables of function type and even pass a function into another function as a parameter.

```
var func : function(:String):Boolean;
func = testFunc;
function testFunc(s:String):Boolean {
    return (s.equalsIgnoreCase("true"));
}
```

The variable func in the example is of type function(:String):Boolean, which represents the signature of functions that may be assigned to it. Functions may be passed as parameters to other functions using a similar syntax.

```
function manip(s:String , f:function(:String):String) : Void {
    println("{s} = "+f(s));
}
function m1(s:String) : String {
    s.toLowerCase();
}
function m2(s:String) : String {
    s.substring(0,4);
}
manip("JavaFX" , m1);
manip("JavaFX" , m2);
```

Anonymous functions

Anonymous functions allow lightweight, single-use, nameless functions to be created within a declarative context.

```
import java.io.File;

class FileSystemWalker
{   var root:String;
    var extension:String;
    var action:function(:File):Void;

    function go() { walk(new File(root)); }
    function walk(dir:File) : Void {
        var files:File[] = dir.listFiles();
        for(f:File in files) {
            if(f.isDirectory()) {
                walk(f);
            }
            else if(f.getName().endsWith(extension)) {
                action(f);
            }
        }
    }
}

var walker = FileSystemWalker {
    root: FX.getArguments()[0];
    extension: ".png";
    action: function(f:File) {
        println("Found {f.getName()}");
    }
};
walker.go();
```

In the example an anonymous function, accepting a `File` as a parameter, is assigned to the `action` variable of a `FileSystemWalker` class instance. Anonymous functions similar to this are used extensively for event handling in JavaFX Script, instead of Java's class-heavy listener model.

Access modifiers (package, protected, public, public-read, public-init)

Using access modifiers we can restrict access to our script or instance variables and functions. Access modifiers perform the same role in JavaFX Script as they do in Java, but their implementation differs from Java. Table B.1 lists the basic access modifiers, and table B.2 lists the additive access modifiers.

Table B.1 Basic access modifiers

Modifier keyword	Visibility effect
(default)	Visible only within the enclosing script. This default mode (with no associated keyword) is the least visible of all access modes.
`package`	Visible within the enclosing script and any script or class within the same package
`protected`	Visible within the enclosing script, any script or class within the same package, and subclasses from other packages. This modifier works only with class members, not script members or the class itself.
`public`	Visible to anyone, anywhere.

Table B.2 Additive access modifiers

Modifier keyword	Visibility effect
`public-read`	Adds public read access to the basic mode.
`public-init`	Adds public read access and object literal write access to the basic mode.

The comments above each class, variable, and function in the following code explain their visibility:

```
// Instantiate: anywhere
public class AccessTest {
    // Class and script only
    var sDefault:String;
    // Class, script and package
    package var sPackage:String;
    // Class, script, package, and any subclass
    protected var sProtected:String;
    // Everywhere
    public var sPublic:String;

    // Write: class and script only / Read: anywhere
    public-read var sPublicReadDefault:String;
    // Write: class, script and package / Read: anywhere
    public-read package var sPublicReadPackage:String;
```

```
    // Write: class, script, package and subclass - plus anywhere
    //   when creating object literals / Read: anywhere
    public-init protected var sPublicInitProtected:String;
}
```

B.10 Conditions

JavaFX Script's conditions look and behave in a not-too-dissimilar fashion to the conditions of other languages, Java included. However, JavaFX Script's expression-based syntax affords some interesting twists.

Basic conditions (if, else)

The `if/else` syntax is the same as Java's. JavaFX Script has no keyword for `else/if`; instead we should use an `if` construct directly after an `else`.

```
ivar someValue = 99;

if(someValue==99) {
    println("Equals 99");
}

if(someValue >= 100) {
    println("100 or over");
}
else {
    println("Less than 100");
}

if(someValue < 0) {
    println("Negative");
}
else if(someValue > 0) {
    println("Positive");
}
else {
    println("Zero");
}
```

Because JavaFX's conditions are expressions, they give out a result and as such can be used on the right-hand side of an assignment, or as part of a bind, or in any other situation in which a result is expected.

```
var negValue = -1;
var sign = if(negValue < 0) { "Negative"; }
    else if(negValue > 0) { "Positive"; }
    else { "Zero"; }
```

Ternary expressions and beyond

Because all conditions are also expressions, JavaFX Script requires no explicit syntax for ternary expressions.

```
var asHex = true;
java.lang.System.out.printf(
    if(asHex) "Hex:%04x%n" else "Dec:%d%n" ,
    12345
);
```

Using the expression language syntax, it is possible to go beyond the standard true/false embedded condition.

```
var mode = 2;
println(
    if(mode==0) "Yellow alert"
    else if(mode==1) "Orange alert"
    else if(mode==2) "Mauve alert"
    else "Red alert"
);
```

B.11 Loops

Loops allow us to repeatedly execute a given section of code until a given condition is met. In JavaFX Script `for` loops are tied firmly to sequences and work as expressions just like conditions. A more traditional type of loop is the `while` loop, which runs a block of code until a condition is met.

Basic sequence loops (for)

`for` loops work like the `for/each` loop of other languages.

```
for(a in [1..3]) {
    for(b in [1..3]) {
        println("{a} x {b} = {a*b}");
    }
}
```

`for` loops are expressions, returning a sequence.

```
var cards =
    for(str in ["A",[2..10],"J","Q","K"])
        str.toString();
```

In each pass through the loop in the example, an element is plucked from the source sequence, converted into a string, and added to the destination sequence, `cards`.

Rolling nested loops into one expression

The loop syntax gives us an easy way to create loops within loops, allowing us to drill down to access further sequences held within the objects inside a sequence.

```
import java.lang.System;
class SoccerTeam {
    var name: String;
    var players: String[];
}
var fiveAsideLeague:SoccerTeam[] = [
    SoccerTeam {
        name: "Java United"
        players: [ "Smith","Jones","Brown",
            "Johnson","Schwartz" ]
    } ,
    SoccerTeam {
        name: ".Net Rovers"
```

```
        players: [ "Davis","Taylor","Booth",
            "May","Ballmer" ]
    }
];
for(t in fiveAsideLeague, p in t.players) {
    println("{t.name}: {p}");
}
```

Controlling flow within for loops (break, continue)

JavaFX Script supports both the `continue` and `break` functionality in its `for` loops, to skip to the next iteration or terminate the loop immediately. Loop labels are not supported.

```
var total=0;
for(i in [0..50]) {
    if(i<5) { continue; }
    else if (i>10) { break; }
    total+=i;
}
```

Filtering for expressions (where)

Filters selectively pull out only the elements of the source sequence we want.

```
var divisibleBy7 =
    for(i in [0..50] where (i mod 7)==0) i;
```

The result of the example code is a sequence whose contents are only those numbers from the source evenly divisible by 7.

While loops (while, break, continue)

JavaFX Script supports `while` loops in a similar fashion to other languages. As with `for` loops, the `break` keyword can be used to exit a loop prematurely (labels are not supported), and `continue` can be used to skip to the next iteration.

```
var i=0;
var total=0;
while(i<10) {
    total+=i;
    i++;
}
i=0;
total=0;
while(i<50) {
    if(i<5) { i++; continue; }
    else if (i>10) { break; }
    total+=i;
    i++;
}
```

B.12 Triggers

Triggers allow us to assign code to run when a given variable is modified. Triggers can be used with either regular variables or sequences.

Single-value triggers (on replace)

The trigger syntax is used at the end of a variable declaration with the keywords `on replace` and two variables, one for the current value and one for the incoming value. In the following example, `previous` always holds the last value of its companion, `current`.

```
class TestTrigger
{   var current = 99 on replace oldVal = newVal {
        previous = oldVal;
    };
    var previous = 0;
}
```

It is permissible to leave off the new value and use the variable name itself or to leave off both values.

```
var a = 99 on replace oldVal {
    println("Old={oldVal}  New={a}");
}
var b = 99 on replace {
    println("New={b}");
}
```

Sequence triggers (on replace [..])

We can assign a trigger to a sequence. To do this we need to also tap into not only the existing and replacement values but also the range of the sequence that is being affected. The old and new values refer to sequences, and a range-like syntax is used to give the index span of the elements affected.

```
var seq1 = [1..3]
    on replace oldVal[lo..hi] = newVal {
        println(
            "Changing [{lo}..{hi}] from "+
            "{oldVal.toString()} to "+
            "{newVal.toString()}"
        );
    };
```

For an insert the *low index* is the insert point, the *high index* is the low index minus 1, the *old sequence* is empty, and the *new sequence* contains the values being added. For a delete the *low index* and the *high index* define the range being removed, the *old sequence* is the sequence as it currently is, and the *new sequence* is empty. For a change (including a reverse) the *low index* and *high index* define the range, the *old sequence* is the content as it currently is, and the *new sequence* is the content after the change is applied.

B.13 Exceptions (try, catch, any, finally)

Exceptions give us a way to assign a block of code to be run when a problem occurs or to signal a problem within our own code to outside code that may be using our API. `catch` blocks can trap exceptions of a particular type, or `any` can be used to create a catch-all default exception handler. `finally` blocks are always run when the `try` block exits, whether cleanly or as the result of an exception. As in Java, the `try/finally` construct may be used on its own, without any exception-handling blocks.

```
import java.lang.NullPointerException;
import java.io.IOException;

var key = 0;
try {
    println(doSomething());
}
catch(ex:IOException) {
    println("ERROR reading data {ex}")
}
catch(any) {
    println("ERROR unknown fault");
}
finally {
    println("This always runs");
}

function doSomething() : String {
    if(key==1) {
        throw new IOException("Data corrupt");
    }
    else if(key==2) {
        throw new NullPointerException();
    }
    "No problems!";
}
```

B.14 Keywords

Table B.3 lists JavaFX Script keywords and reserved words. Implemented keywords are shown in fixed width font; reserved (but unused) words are shown in regular text.

Table B.3 Keywords and reserved words

`abstract`	`after`	`and`	`as`	assert
`at`	attribute			
`before`	`bind`	`bound`	`break`	
`catch`	`class`	`continue`		
`def`	`delete`			
`else`	exclusive	`extends`		
`false`	`finally`	first	`for`	from
`function`				
`if`	`import`	`indexof`	`in`	`init`
`insert`	`instanceof`	`into`	`inverse`	
last	lazy			

Table B.3 Keywords and reserved words *(continued)*

mixin	mod			
new	not	null		
on	or	override		
package	postinit	private	protected	public-init
public	public-read			
replace	return	reverse		
sizeof	static	step	super	
then	this	throw	trigger	true
try	tween	typeof		
var				
where	while	with		

B.15 Operator precedence

Table B.4 lists operators, grouped by precedence (the priority order in which they take effect).

Table B.4 Operators

Priority	Operator	Evaluation mode	Description
1	function()	Class	Function call
1	()		Bracketed expression
1	new	Class	Object instantiation
1	*Object literal*	Class	Object instantiation and initialization
2	++ (suffixed)	Right to left	Post-increment assign
2	-- (suffixed)	Right to left	Post-decrement assign
3	++ (prefixed)	Right to left	Pre-increment assign
3	-- (prefixed)	Right to left	Pre-decrement assign
3	not	Boolean	Logical negation
3	sizeof	Sequence	Sequence length
3	reverse	Sequence	Sequence reverse
3	indexof	Sequence	Element index in sequence
3	=>		Tween
4	*	Left to right	Multiplication

Table B.4 Operators *(continued)*

Priority	Operator	Evaluation mode	Description
4	/	Left to right	Division
4	`mod`	Left to right	Remainder
5	+	Left to right	Addition
5	-	Left to right	Subtraction
6	==	Left to right	Equality
6	!=	Left to right	Inequality
6	<	Left to right	Less than
6	<=	Left to right	Less than or equal to
6	>	Left to right	Greater than
6	>=	Left to right	Greater than or equal to
7	`instanceof`	Class	Type check
7	`as`	Class	Type cast
8	`or`	Right to left	Logical OR
9	`and`	Right to left	Logical AND
10	+=		Add with assign
10	-=		Subtract with assign
10	*=		Multiple with assign
10	/=		Divide with assign
10	%-		Remainder with assign
11	=		Assign

B.16 Pseudo variables

JavaFX Script is host to a handful of handy predefined global variables, for accessing environment and script/class details, as shown in table B.5.

Table B.5 Pseudo variables

Variable	Purpose
`__DIR__`	Returns the location of the current class file as a URL, as a directory if the class is a regular bytecode file, or as a JAR file if the class is inside a Java archive.
`__FILE__`	Returns the full filename and path of the current class file as a URL.
`__PROFILE__`	Returns `browser`, `desktop`, or `mobile`, depending on the runtime environment.

appendix C: Not familiar with Java?

This appendix is a collection of brief introductory texts that back up the material in the language tutorial chapters and elsewhere. Many of this book's readers will have arrived at JavaFX from Java, but not all of you. JavaFX is deliberately designed to have a broad appeal beyond just the regular Java desktop programmers. The problem was this: how to supply the necessary background knowledge about the Java platform to the latter, without boring the former. This appendix is the solution.

Each section in this appendix deals in detail with those nuanced workings of the Java platform that apply to JavaFX, as well as other associated background material.

C.1 Static types versus dynamic types

Although JavaFX Script started life as a scripting language, it does not adopt the loose laissez-faire attitude toward variable types found in other scripting languages. If you came here from a design background (perhaps with some basic scripting experience thanks to early versions of JavaScript or ActionScript), you may not be familiar with how a statically typed language differs from a dynamically typed one.

```
someVariable = "123"
someVariable = someVariable+1
```

This code fragment (in no particular language) demonstrates the difference between JFX's static typing and the dynamic typing of other scripting languages. The variable `someVariable` is being loaded with the string `"123"`, then an arithmetic operation is being performed on its contents—what should the result of this operation be?

One answer might be to throw a runtime error, because arithmetic cannot be performed on text. Another answer might be to silently normalize the two operands, either by converting the string to a number (resulting in the value 124) or the value to a character string (resulting in the string "1231"). Or the operation could simply be flagged as invalid before the code runs; a string is a string, a value is a value, and never the twain shall meet (except under strict predefined conditions, where run-time consequences can always be anticipated).

JavaFX Script, following Java's lead, uses the static typed solution. Variables are clearly delineated as to their content type and, by inference, what operations are valid on them. This approach can sometimes add coding overhead—for example, explicit operations are needed to convert user input (typically character data) into value types—but the plus side is it might spare us a few embarrassing crashes when the company CEO stupidly types "Forty Nine" into our application's age field during a live demo.

C.2 Casts

In statically typed languages (see section C.1) the type of a variable is important, but there are times when data doesn't arrive in the form we want it to. Casting is a way of asking JavaFX Script to translate one data type into another compatible type. Most programming languages insist on casts when there's risk of a potential loss of information, for example, if a 64-bit value is stored in a 32-bit variable. Casting generally isn't required to go the other way, because the operation is guaranteed to be safe from data loss.

```
import java.lang.System;
var pseudoRnd:Integer =
    (System.currentTimeMillis() as Integer) mod 1000;
```

In this example we want to take the milliseconds part of the current time to use as a very rough pseudo random number between 0 and 999. The Java API method `System.currentTimeMillis()` returns the current time as the total number of milliseconds since the Unix/POSIX epoch (midnight on 1 January 1970), which returns a 64-bit number. Since it takes only a regular 32-bit integer to store a value between 0 and 999, we cast the result to an JFX `Integer`, before taking only the lower three decimal digits.

As demonstrated, JavaFX uses the keyword `as` to perform casts, with the destination type immediately following. This contrasts with the syntax of Java, C, C++, and others, where the type prefixes the data and is surrounded by parentheses.

The most common usages of casts are:

- When there's risk of data loss (the aforementioned 64- to 32-bit example)
- When an object is being handled by a super type and needs to be converted into its true type (see section C4)
- When the parameters of a function call are ambiguous, matching more than one possible overloaded function

Fortunately, if we miss a cast when one is necessary, the compiler will inform us, which is handy given that even experienced programmers are prone to forget them from time to time.

C.3 Packages

Packages allow us to relate portions of our code together into a group. There are several reasons why this might be handy, including:

- *Convenience*—Just as grouping files into directories imposes order on our data, so grouping code into packages can impose order within our software. Anything that allows us to organize our code so we can better manage it is useful when writing nontrivial applications.
- *Integrity*—It's possible to allow functions and variables to be visible to other members of a package yet deny access to nonmembers (see section C.5). This permits creation of functionality that spans several classes without exposing implementation details to third-party developers who may be using our API. It means we can write sophisticated software yet still lock other programmers out of parts we wish to control ourselves.
- *Flexibility*—We can have two classes that share the same name, providing they live in different packages. This means we can mix APIs without fear of class-naming clashes.

C.3.1 Importing classes from a package

Throughout the source in this book you'll see lines such as

```
import javafx.stage.Stage;
```

crop up frequently near the start of many listings. This line is necessary to refer to the `Stage` object of the `javafx.stage` package without using its *fully qualified class name*. (In case you're reading this before chapter 4, `Stage` is a top-level user interface container.)

Importing classes means we can avoid getting repetitive motion injuries from typing those long (and frankly quite ugly) package prefixes each time we wish to refer to a given class. Once imported, the package prefix can be omitted; the `import` statement is a heads-up to the compiler as to which classes may appear in the current source code file. The compiler will silently add the missing package prefix to any class reference that does not have one. (Importing just makes our source readable; it doesn't change what our source code does.)

Let's take a look at a more complete example:

```
import java.util.Date;

var date1:Date = Date {};
var date2:java.util.Date = java.util.Date {};
```

Date lives in the package java.util

We see two different ways of creating a `Date` object in the example—the first makes use of the `import` statement at the start of the code (and would fail without it), while the second does not.

As in Java, an asterisk can be used at the end of an `import` statement instead of a class name. The asterisk acts as a wild card to include all the classes from the stated package without having to list them individually.

C.3.2 Packages and physical files

Obviously the class files written by the JavaFX Script compiler have to be arranged in a manner that allows them to be identified as belonging to a given package.

Typically Java has used directories to arrange its classes into packages, so `game.ui.Menu` would be represented by a file called Menu.class (plus any support class files the compiler creates) living inside a directory called ui, which in turn is inside a directory called game.

Both the Java and JavaFX compilers support an option, `-d`, allowing us to specify where to write this directory structure when compiling. When running the compiled code, this directory should be placed on the classpath for the classes to be found. So, if we compile our classes to the CoolGame directory, then `game.ui.Menu` would end up in a file called CoolGame/game/ui/Menu.class (using Unix directory slashes), and CoolGame would need to be on the classpath for `game.ui.Menu` to be found.

C.3.3 Creating packaged classes and dealing with name clashes

You've seen how to import a class from a package, but how do we create our own packages? And what happens if we need to work with two classes that have identical names but live in different packages? The next example will deal with both these issues. But first we need to create a demonstration class.

```
package jfxia.chapter3;
class Date {
    function toString() : String {
        "This is our date class";
    }
}
```

Should go in the file Date.fx

In the example, we have the definition for a class called `Date` (in the file Date.fx, so the compiler can find it), which does nothing more than return a message when its `toString()` function is called. The `package` statement at the head of a source file places the code into `jfxia.chapter3`, which is the package we want it to live in. Now we need some more code to test it:

```
var date1 = java.util.Date {};
var date2 = jfxia.chapter3.Date {};
println(date1.toString());
println(date2.toString());
```

```
Mon Aug 04 18:33:03 BST 2008
This is our date class
```

We didn't bother to import our package! Why? In this example we're using both our own `Date` class and the one in the Java API package `java.util`. This is a naming conflict: we now have two classes with the same name. If we neglect to provide their *fully qualified name* (the class name including its package prefix), how can the compiler tell which class we are referring to?

The answer is, it can't! Unfortunately, in this instance we need to provide the fully qualified name of each class to avoid ambiguity. This makes importing either class rather academic. Imports wouldn't throw a compilation error, but we couldn't use abbreviated names for either `Date` class, not so long as we have a name clash in our source code file.

NOTE *Packages are not a heirarchy* Despite the misleading impression their names often suggest, Java and JavaFX packages are not arranged in a hierarchy. The package `java.awt.event` is actually a sibling of `java.awt`, not a child. If you import all the classes from the latter, you do not automatically get the former. This is a common newbie mistake.

Once we've compiled our code, we can bundle the package into a JAR file to make it easy to distribute. A JAR file is a zip archive with a standardized/recognized layout and content. By convention all of the classes in a given package are bundled inside a single JAR. It's possible to split a package over multiple JARs, but the practice is rarely used. However, JAR archives frequently contains multiple related packages.

C.4 Object orientation

Classes are an integral part of object orientation, encapsulating state and behavior for each component in a larger system, thereby allowing us to express our software in terms of the structures and relationships that link its autonomous component parts. Object orientation has become an incredibly popular way of constructing software in recent years: both Java and its underlying JVM environment are heavily object-centric. But what is object orientation?

The following sections describe object orientation from a JVM point of view, although I've stuck with JavaFX Script terminology (*functions*, not *methods*). This is only a whistle-stop tour through OO; consult a book on the topic if you want to know more.

C.4.1 Modeling the world with classes

At the sharp end of object-oriented software everything tends to boil down to types. What *type* is an object? For example, is it a plane, a train, or an automobile? Of course, all three are types of vehicle and share common properties and functionality. They all move and therefore have a speedometer and an odometer (mileage) and consume power. They all carry passengers as well. They all need some form of engine to drive them forward and a braking system to slow them down. But, of course, they also have a lot of differences. Trains cannot arbitrarily turn left or right because they are bound by the constraints of a track (or at least they shouldn't be able to under normal operating conditions). Cars cannot fly through the air like a plane (again, under normal operating conditions!), but they can move in reverse, which is something a plane in flight cannot do. (Unless it's a Harrier Jump Jet!)

We build up object-oriented software by modeling these relationships. Classes are the nodes we link together to create such models. If we were building a transport simulator, we might start with a `Vehicle` class that contains all the data and functionality we know is common to all vehicles in our system. The `odometer`, for example, could be included in this top-level class, because all vehicles have a mileage. We could also define a few functions, perhaps `speedUp()` and `slowDown()`, because increasing and decreasing speed is common to all vehicles.

C.4.2 Classes from classes: subclassing and overriding

Once we have a generic `Vehicle` class, we can define more specific vehicles based on it. We might define a `Plane` class, which adds an altitude attribute. We might also define an `Automobile` class, which adds turn-left and turn-right functions, and so on. The process of creating a more specific class in terms of a more general one is known as *subclassing*. Java and JavaFX Script also use the synonym *extending*.

When a class subclasses another, it can replace the implementations of variables and functions in its parent (*super*) class with its own. This is known as *overriding*. It cannot change their type—an integer variable must remain an integer—but it can change their default value or (in the case of a function) their code body. Each `Vehicle` subclass, for example, could define its own implementation of `speedUp()` and `slowDown()`, simulating the specific mechanics of the given type of vehicle they represent.

C.4.3 An object can be referenced in different ways: polymorphism

An object on our simulation may be created as a type of the `HarrierJumpJet` class, which in turn is a type of `Plane`, which in turn is a type of `Vehicle`. Because we know the `HarrierJumpJet` inherited all the functionality of `Plane` (even if it did override some of it with its own implementation), and by proxy inherited all the functionality of `Vehicle` (again, even if it replaced some of it), the `HarrierJumpJet` object can be treated as being of type `HarrierJumpJet`, `Plane`, or `Vehicle`.

This ability to treat objects by way of their superclass types (parents in the class hierarchy) is known as *polymorphism*. It means we can create a variable of `Vehicle` type and store any subclass from `Vehicle` in it, including `SteamTrain`, `FordModelT`, and `ApolloSpaceCapsule`. Likewise, a variable of type `Plane` can hold any object that is of type `Plane` or a subclass of `Plane` (`HarrierJumpJet`, `Boeing747`, `Spitfire`, etc.)

A variable of type `Plane` could not hold a `BatMobile`, however, because `BatMobile` is a subclass of `Automobile`, not `Plane`.

C.4.4 Partial implementation: abstract functions and interfaces

Sometimes we want to create classes that are intended only for subclassing. For example, we probably do not want to create objects of type `Plane` directly, because the class is too generic; instead we want to create objects of specific plane types (`HarrierJumpJet`, `Boeing747`, etc.) that subclass `Plane`. By marking a class as *abstract* we can prevent it from being used to create objects directly. An *abstract class* must be subclassed before it can be used.

Abstract classes can contain *abstract functions*. These are functions that have no functionality (no code body) and must be overridden before being used. For example, the `speedUp()` and `slowDown()` functions in `Vehicle` would likely be abstract, with each subclass overriding them to simulate precisely how its given type of vehicle accelerates or decelerates. If a class contains abstract functions, the class itself must be abstract.

C.5 Access modifiers

Access modifiers allow us to control the visibility of parts of our class.

Consider the following scenario: as part of a larger system we constructed a class that dealt with dates, but for some reason we bothered to record only the last two digits of the year. So 2005 is stored as only 05. This isn't a problem, because the class supports a `getYear()` function that adds on 2000 before it returns a result. Then our boss comes to see us and explains that the system is being expanded to deal with data from as far back as 1995—time to change our class to store dates as four digits. But as soon as we publish the change a fellow programmer, from another part of the team, complains that we're making his code break! Extensively throughout his code he was reading the year directly, not bothering with our `getYear()` function, and so what we assumed would be a localized change is now a major global headache.

What we need is some way to lock other programmers out of the implementation detail of our code, to effectively mark parts of the code as "no go" areas and force everyone to use a class the way we intended it to be used. Access modifiers provide just such a mechanism, by getting the compiler to enforce rules we describe for each class, variable, or function. There are different levels of access that can be granted: the most closed limits visibility to just the immediate class or script, while the most open allows total access to anyone.

If we'd used access modifiers correctly in the scenario we began with, our fellow programmer would not have had direct access to the data in our class; he would need to work through the *public interface* functions we provided for him. This would leave us free to fix bugs and upgrade the class internals, because we would know for sure which parts of our code others are dependent on and which parts are under our total control.

appendix D: JavaFX and the Java platform

JavaFX is not Java, but it rests within a sea of tools and technologies designed to support Java. Thus it shares the unusual dualistic characteristic of being *of* Java (the platform) but not Java (the language)!

Given JavaFX's intentions it's reasonable to assume a minority of readers may have been drawn to it (and thereby to this book) without first having come through Java; they would no doubt benefit from a little background, whereas Java-savvy readers will surely be keen to hear how the new platform and the old cooperate. So for young pups and old dogs alike, this appendix provides some background material, introducing Java and exploring how JavaFX fits into the existing Java environment.

D.1 How not to go native

Java is a software platform that seeks to fulfill the mantra "write once, run anywhere." Software is compiled to bytecode files in the form of machine code instructions runnable on a virtual machine called a JVM.) The virtual machine provides a layer of abstraction, allowing the program to be run on many devices without needing to be specifically compiled to the machine code of the underlying hardware. Figure D.1 shows the lifecycle of a typical Java application.

Once the source code files are compiled into bytecode class files, they can be bundled into a single archive known as a JAR for easy distribution. JARs can contain runnable applications or support libraries. There are numerous ways of getting the software onto the end-user computer, from the traditional (ship it on a CD-ROM) to the modern (embed it in a web page).

JavaFX Script compiles to bytecode files, just like Java, although because of the way the language works, each pure JavaFX Script class is translated into both a class

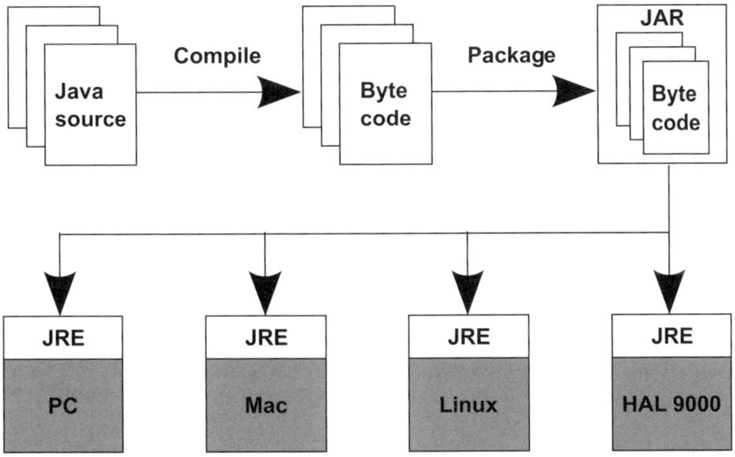

Figure D.1 From compile time to runtime: the lifecycle of a typical Java application

and an interface. JavaFX Script can also access classes in a Java package, both the standard API packages and any third party packages that are on the classpath when the JavaFX software is run.

D.2 Java SE/ME/EE and JDK/JRE: three editions, two audiences

For programmers unfamiliar with Java it should be noted that there are three main Java markets: *Standard Edition* targets regular desktop users, *Micro Edition* is an extension to the Standard Edition adding tools and libraries for small devices like cell phones, and *Enterprise Edition* enhances the Standard Edition for writing web applications and web services. (Note: although applets are used on the web, they are part of Java SE, not Java EE).

There exist two basic audiences for Java: the regular user who merely wants to run the software and the programmer who wants to create the software. On the desktop (Java SE) these are personified by the *Java Runtime Environment* and the *Java Development Kit.* The JRE has the tools necessary to run a Java program and is often shipped preinstalled on desktop computers, while the JDK bolsters the JRE with extra tools to create and debug Java software.

Obviously, for cell phones the various handset manufacturers take care of providing a runtime environment on their phones (so there's no JRE download for Java ME), but to actually develop mobile applications one needs the Java ME SDK (formerly known as the Java ME Wireless Toolkit) as well as the standard JDK.

If all this seems like a jumble of names and acronyms, don't worry—the introduction of JavaFX greatly simplified things! To develop JavaFX programs (capable of running on the desktop, on the web as applets, and on mobile devices) one only needs to install the Java SE JDK and the JavaFX SDK. These two downloads are sufficient to target all the various JFX platforms.

D.3 Release versions: a rose by any other name

One source of confusion for novice Java programmers is release names and versions. Since 1995 Java has been through many revisions. In the beginning it was simple; the first commonly used version of Java was 1.02, which was succeeded by 1.1 shortly thereafter. Someone then apparently decided 1.2 didn't sound important enough, so Java acquired the nom de plume *Java2*. Thus we got *Java2 Standard Edition version 1.2*, more commonly written as *J2SE v1.2*. This schizophrenic naming convention continued until version 1.5, when it was replaced by a new schizophrenic naming convention; *Java2* reverted to *Java* once more, and 1.5 became 5.0; however, due to technical issues the 1.5 label continued to be used as a kind of internal version number in some places.

(It is left as an exercise for the reader to guess what medication the people who came up with the above may have been on.)

Java SE 6 Update 14 (or later) is the version of the Java platform currently recommended for writing and running JavaFX software on Windows. On the Mac, later revisions of Java 5 may work, with minor issues and inefficiencies. Support for older versions enables a wider potential user base on the Mac, where JVM/JRE releases have sometimes trailed Sun's own release schedule.

Since JavaFX really tries to push what's possible in the realms of graphics and media, it's recommended that you install as recent a version of Java as you can get your hands on. Not only do later revisions have bug fixes, but they often feature even better graphics performance and so are always preferred over older versions. If you're running an old JVM/JRE, why not make JavaFX your excuse for upgrading?

index

K

L

M

N

O

MORE TITLES FROM MANNING

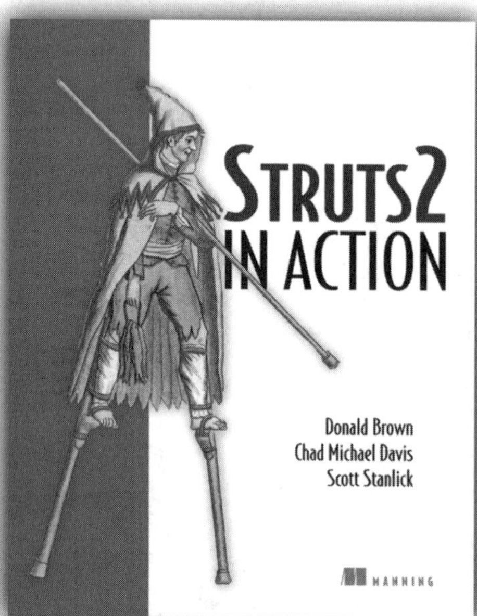

Struts 2 in Action
by Donald Brown, Chad Michael Davis, and Scott Stanlick

ISBN: 1-933988-07-X
424 pages
$44.99
May 2008

Hibernate Search in Action
by Emmanuel Bernard and John Griffin

ISBN: 1-933988-64-9
488 pages
$49.99
December 2008

For ordering information go to www.manning.com